"A seminal work and on   lassical
Reformed doctrine of Gᴜ   ᵢngages
with both the Thomistic and Barthian theological legacies simultaneously while
also navigating core challenges from Kantian and analytic philosophical traditions. God, analogy, the immanent Trinity, and the incarnation are all discussed
with sophistication and judicious discernment. This book can serve as a touch-
stone and exemplar for future projects in Reformed Thomistic thought."

Thomas Joseph White, Thomistic Institute, Angelicum, Rome

"Steven Duby has written a lovely book! He writes with a pastor's heart, showing
with great insight the importance of God in himself in the life of the disciple
and for a pilgrim theology. We have much to learn, following Duby's lead, from
this neglected but altogether crucial teaching."

Christopher Holmes, associate professor of systematic theology and head of the theology
program, University of Otago

"This is a magisterial book; every Christian theologian should read it. With
clarity and charity, Steven Duby cuts through the misunderstandings that have
grown up around the doctrine of God. By the end of his book, the treasure of
the God who reveals himself in Jesus Christ is shining forth with renewed bril-
liance, and our speech about him has been purified so as to be fully capable of
praise. Duby accomplishes all this by drawing on the patristic and medieval
traditions as received and engaged by Reformed thinkers, in conjunction with
a broad mastery of modern philosophy, biblical exegesis, and theology. An
amazing accomplishment!"

Matthew Levering, James N. and Mary D. Perry Jr. Chair of Theology, Mundelein Seminary

"Showing his characteristic depth, Duby articulates an insightful and profound
recovery of classical Christian theism for constructive theology today. Keeping
an eye on contemporary instincts, Duby mines the tradition to clarify misunderstanding, critique overreactions, and suggest ways to appropriate the
wisdom of our tradition. I highly recommend it!"

Kyle Strobel, associate professor at Biola University, author of *Formed for the Glory of God*

"This rich and rewarding study demonstrates how the contemplation of God himself, theologia, is not some idle speculation—a distraction from the Christian life or descent into abstraction—but is in fact a spiritual exercise that fuels our communion with God and affirms the shocking nearness of God to us in Jesus Christ. *God in Himself* is a courageously scriptural work of theology, for Steve Duby dares to let Scripture lead where some have supposed that only metaphysics will take us: to gaze upon the resplendently complete life of the triune God."

Kent Eilers, professor of theology, Huntington University

"To know the only true God through Jesus Christ by the Spirit is eternal life (John 17:3). With the combination of deep and reverent scholarship that we have come to expect from him, Steve Duby seeks to retrieve the supreme object of Christian theology—God in himself—by rehabilitating topics like natural theology, metaphysics, and analogy for the practice of Christian theology. In doing so, Duby demonstrates how the proper coordination of these topics contributes to the supreme end of Christian theology, communion with the Holy Trinity. This is a masterful work of biblical, historical, philosophical, and dogmatic theology by a master theologian that deserves a wide readership."

Scott R. Swain, president and James Woodrow Hassell Professor of Systematic Theology, Reformed Theological Seminary, Orlando

STUDIES IN
CHRISTIAN
DOCTRINE
AND
SCRIPTURE

GOD IN HIMSELF

Scripture, Metaphysics, and the
Task of Christian Theology

◆◆◆◆◆◆◆◆◆◆◆◆◆◆◆◆◆◆◆◆◆◆◆◆

Steven J. Duby

ivp
Academic
An imprint of InterVarsity Press
Downers Grove, Illinois

InterVarsity Press
P.O. Box 1400, Downers Grove, IL 60515-1426
ivpress.com
email@ivpress.com

InterVarsity Press® is the book-publishing division of InterVarsity Christian Fellowship/USA®, a movement of students and faculty active on campus at hundreds of universities, colleges, and schools of nursing in the United States of America, and a member movement of the International Fellowship of Evangelical Students. For information about local and regional activities, visit intervarsity.org.

Scripture quotations, unless otherwise noted, are the author's translation.

Cover design: David Fassett
Interior design: Beth McGill
Images: © Apexphotos / Moment Collection / Getty Images

ISBN 978-0-8308-4884-3 (print)
ISBN 978-0-8308-4374-0 (digital)

Printed in the United States of America ♾

InterVarsity Press is committed to ecological stewardship and to the conservation of natural resources in all our operations. This book was printed using sustainably sourced paper.

Library of Congress Cataloging-in-Publication Data
A catalog record for this book is available from the Library of Congress.

P	25	24	23	22	21	20	19	18	17	16	15	14	13	12	11	10	9	8	7	6	5	4	3	2	1
Y	38	37	36	35	34	33	32	31	30	29	28	27	26	25	24	23	22	21	20	19					

For Ivor Davidson, theologian and mentor
of the highest order

Contents

Acknowledgments

THIS BOOK HAS BEEN HELPED ALONG in different ways by a number of people. I am grateful to Dan Treier and Kevin Vanhoozer for granting me the opportunity to contribute to this series and for their patience, encouragement, and insight throughout the process. I am grateful to John Webster for his feedback and encouragement on the idea shortly before his death. Matthew Levering's wisdom and incessant kindness also have been tremendously valuable to me. David McNutt's work as an editor has been a great help in the publication process.

In the summer of 2018, I completed a research fellowship at Calvin College's H. Henry Meeter Center for Calvin Studies, where I spent many enjoyable hours reading and writing. I am grateful to Professor Karin Maag and those working with her at the Meeter Center for access to the library and for their hospitality.

My wife, Jodi, and our children (Charlie, Evangeline, Wyatt, George) provide constant reminders of the goodness of God. I am thankful for the ways in which they prod me to relate academic theology to the Christian life.

Finally, Ivor Davidson's rare combination of erudition and genuine humility, scholarly rigor and Christian faithfulness, continue to inspire not only me but also many others in their theological work. This book is dedicated to him.

Series Introduction

Studies in Christian Doctrine and Scripture (SCDS)

DANIEL J. TREIER AND KEVIN J. VANHOOZER

THE STUDIES IN CHRISTIAN DOCTRINE and Scripture (SCDS) series attempts to reconcile two disciplines that should never have been divided: the study of Christian Scripture and the study of Christian doctrine. Old walls of disciplinary hostility are beginning to come down, a development that we hope will better serve the church. To that end, books in this series affirm the supreme authority of Scripture, seeking to read it faithfully and creatively as they develop fresh articulations of Christian doctrine. This agenda can be spelled out further in five claims.

1. We aim to publish constructive **contributions to systematic theology** rather than merely descriptive rehearsals of biblical theology, historical retrievals of classic or contemporary theologians, or hermeneutical reflections on theological method—volumes that are plentifully and expertly published elsewhere.

The initial impetus for the SCDS series came from supervising evangelical graduate students and seeking to encourage their pursuit of constructive theological projects shaped by the supremacy of Scripture. Existing publication venues demonstrate how rarely biblical scholars and systematic theologians trespass into each other's fields. Synthetic treatments of biblical theology garner publication in monograph series for biblical studies or evangelical biblical theology. A notable example is a companion series from IVP Academic, New Studies in Biblical Theology. Many of its volumes have theological significance, yet most are written by biblical scholars. Meanwhile, historical retrievals of theological figures garner publication in monograph series for historical and systematic theology. For instance, there have been entire series devoted to figures such as Karl Barth or the patristic era, and even series named for systematic theology tend to contain figure-oriented monographs.

The reason for providing an alternative publication venue is not to denigrate these valuable enterprises. Instead, the rationale for encouraging constructively evangelical projects is twofold and practical: The church needs such projects, and they form the theologians undertaking them. The church needs such projects, both addressing new challenges for her life in the world (such as contemporary political theology) and retrieving neglected concepts (such as the classic doctrine of God) in fresh ways. The church also needs her theologians not merely to develop detailed intellectual skills but also ultimately to wrestle with the whole counsel of God in the Scriptures.

2. We aim to promote **evangelical** contributions, neither retreating from broader dialogue into a narrow version of this identity on the one hand, nor running away from the biblical preoccupation of our heritage on the other hand.

In our initial volume, *Theology and the Mirror of Scripture*, we articulate this pursuit of evangelical renewal. We take up the well-known metaphor of mere Christianity as a hallway, with particular church traditions as the rooms in a house. Many people believe that the evangelical hallway is crumbling, an impression that current events only exacerbate. Our inspection highlights a few fragmenting factors such as more robust academic engagement, increased awareness of the Great Christian Tradition and the variety of evangelical subtraditions, interest in global Christianity, and interfaces with emergent Christianity and culture. Looking more deeply, we find historical-theological debates about the very definition of *evangelical* and whether it reflects—still, or ever—a shared gospel, a shared doctrine of God, and a theological method that can operationalize our shared commitment to Scripture's authority.

In response, prompted by James 1:22-25, our proposal develops the metaphor of a mirror for clarifying evangelical theology's relation to

Scripture. The reality behind the mirror is the gospel of God and the God of the gospel: what is revealed in Christ. In disputes about whether to focus on a center or boundaries, it may seem as if evangelicalism has no doctrinal core. But we propose treating what is revealed in Christ—the triune God and the cross of Christ, viewed in the mirror of Scripture—as an evangelical anchor, a center with a certain range of motion. Still, it may seem as if evangelicalism has no hermeneutical coherence, as if interpretive anarchy nullifies biblical authority. But we propose treating Scripture as *canonical testimony*, a God-given mirror of truth that enables the church to reflect the wisdom that is in Christ. The holistic and contextual character of such wisdom gives theology a dialogic character, which requires an evangelical account of the church's catholicity. We need the wisdom to know the difference between church-destroying heresy, church-dividing disagreements that still permit evangelical fellowship, and intrachurch differences that require mutual admonition as well as forbearance.

Volumes in the SCDS series will not necessarily reflect the views of any particular editor, advisory board member, or the publisher—not even concerning "evangelical" boundaries. Volumes may approach perceived boundaries if their excellent engagement with Scripture deserves a hearing. But we are not seeking reform for reform's sake; we are more likely to publish volumes containing new explorations or presentations of traditional positions than radically revisionist proposals. Valuing the historic evangelical commitment to a deeply scriptural theology, we often find that perceived boundaries are appropriate—reflecting positions' biblical plausibility or lack thereof.

3. We seek fresh understanding of Christian doctrine **through creatively faithful engagement with Scripture**. To some fellow evangelicals and interested others today, we commend the classic evangelical commitment of *engaging Scripture*. To other fellow evangelicals today, we commend a contemporary aim to engage Scripture with *creative fidelity*. The church is to be always reforming—but always reforming according to the Word of God.

It is possible to acknowledge *sola Scriptura* in principle—Scripture as the final authority, the norming norm—without treating Scripture as theology's primary source. It is also possible to approach Scripture as theology's primary source in practice without doing that well.

The classic evangelical aspiration has been to mirror the form, not just the content, of Scripture as closely as possible in our theology. That aspiration has potential drawbacks: It can foster naive prooftexting, flatten biblical diversity, and stifle creative cultural engagement with a biblicist idiom. But we should not overreact to these drawbacks, falling prey to the temptation of paying mere lip service to *sola Scriptura* and replacing the Bible's primacy with the secondary idiom of the theologians' guild.

Thus in *Theology and the Mirror of Scripture* we propose a rubric for applying biblical theology to doctrinal judgments in a way that preserves evangelical freedom yet promotes the primacy of Scripture. At the ends of the spectrum, biblical theology can (1) rule out theological proposals that contradict scriptural judgments or cohere poorly with other concepts, and it can (5) require proposals that appeal to what is clear and central in Scripture. In between, it can (2) permit proposals that do not contradict Scripture, (3) support proposals that appeal creatively although indirectly or implicitly to Scripture, and (4) relate theological teaching to church life by using familiar scriptural language as much as possible. This spectrum offers considerable freedom for evangelical theology to mirror the biblical wisdom found in Christ with contextual creativity. Yet it simultaneously encourages evangelical theologians to reflect biblical wisdom not just in their judgments but also in the very idioms of their teaching.

4. We seek **fresh understanding of Christian doctrine**. We do not promote a singular method; we welcome proposals appealing to biblical theology, the history of interpretation, theological interpretation of Scripture, or still other approaches. We welcome projects that engage in detailed exegesis as well as those that appropriate broader biblical themes and patterns. Ultimately, we hope to promote relating Scripture to doctrinal understanding in material, not just formal, ways.

As noted above, the fresh understanding we seek may not involve altogether novel claims—which might well land in heresy! Again, in *Theology and the Mirror of Scripture* we offer an illustrative, nonexhaustive rubric for encouraging various forms of evangelical theological scholarship:

projects shaped primarily by (1) hermeneutics, (2) integrative biblical theology, (3) stewardship of the Great Tradition, (4) church dogmatics, (5) intellectual history, (6) analytic theism, (7) living witness, and (8) healing resistance. While some of these scholarly shapes probably fit the present series better than others, all of them reflect practices that can help evangelical theologians to make more faithfully biblical judgments and to generate more creatively constructive scholarship.

The volumes in the SCDS series will therefore reflect quite varied approaches. They will be similar in engaging one or more biblical texts as a key aspect of their contributions while going beyond exegetical recital or descriptive biblical theology, yet those biblical contributions themselves will be manifold.

5. We promote scriptural engagement **in dialogue with catholic tradition(s)**. A periodic evangelical weakness is relative lack of interest in the church's shared creedal heritage, in churches' particular confessions, and more generally in the history of dogmatic reflection. Beyond existing efforts to enhance understanding of themes and corpora in biblical theology, then, we hope to foster engagement with Scripture that bears on and learns from loci, themes, or crucial questions in classic dogmatics and contemporary systematic theology.

Series authors and editors will reflect several church affiliations and doctrinal backgrounds. Our goal is that such commitments would play a productive but not decisive hermeneutical role. Series volumes may focus on more generically evangelical approaches, or they may operate from within a particular tradition while engaging internal challenges or external objections.

We hope that both the diversity of our contributor list and the catholic engagement of our projects will continually expand. As important as those contextual factors are, though, these are most fundamentally studies in Christian *doctrine* and *Scripture*. Our goal is to promote and to publish constructive evangelical projects that study Scripture with creative fidelity and thereby offer fresh understanding of Christian doctrine. Various contexts and perspectives can help us to study Scripture in that lively way, but they must remain secondary to theology's primary source and soul.

We do not study the mirror of Scripture for its own sake. Finding all the treasures of wisdom in Christ to be reflected there with the help of Christian doctrine, we come to know God and ourselves more truly. Thus encountering God's perfect instruction, we find the true freedom that is ours in the gospel, and we joyfully commend it to others through our own ministry of Scripture's teaching.

Abbreviations

BDAG	Danker, Frederick W., Walter Bauer, William F. Arndt, and F. Wilbur Gingrich. *Greek-English Lexicon of the New Testament and Other Early Christian Literature*. 3rd ed. Chicago: University of Chicago Press, 2000 (Danker-Bauer-Arndt-Gingrich).
BECNT	Baker Exegetical Commentary on the New Testament
CCSL	Corpus Christianorum: Series Latina
CD	Barth, Karl. *Church Dogmatics*. Edited by Geoffrey W. Bromiley and Thomas F. Torrance. Translated by Geoffrey W. Bromiley et al. London: T&T Clark, 2009.
De Trin.	Thomas Aquinas. *Super Boetium De Trinitate*. In *Opera omnia*, 50:1-230. Leonine ed. Rome: Commissio Leonina; Paris: Éditions du Cerf, 1992.
Exp. fid.	John of Damascus. *Die Schriften des Johannes von Damaskos*. Vol. 2, *Expositio fidei*. Edited by Bonifatius Kotter. Berlin: de Gruyter, 1973.
IJST	*International Journal of Systematic Theology*
Inst.	Turretin, Francis. *Institutio theologiae elencticae*. 3 vols. 2nd ed. Geneva, 1688.
JRT	*Journal of Reformed Theology*
JTI	*Journal of Theological Interpretation*
LCC	Library of Christian Classics
LCL	Loeb Classical Library

MT	*Modern Theology*
NICNT	New International Commentary on the New Testament
PG	Patrologia Graeca. Edited by Jacques-Paul Migne. Paris, 1857–1865.
PL	Patrologia Latina. Edited by Jacques-Paul Migne. Paris, 1844–1855.
RD	Bavinck, Herman. *Reformed Dogmatics.* 4 vols. Edited by John Bolt. Translated by John Vriend. Grand Rapids: Baker Academic, 2003–2008.
SCG	Thomas Aquinas. *Opera omnia.* Vols. 13-15, *Summa contra Gentiles.* Leonine ed. Rome: Typis Riccardi Garroni, 1918–1930.
SJT	*Scottish Journal of Theology*
ST	Thomas Aquinas. *Opera omnia.* Vols. 4-12, *Summa theologiae.* Leonine ed. Rome: ex Typographia Polyglotta, 1888–1906.
Syntagma	Polanus, Amandus. *Syntagma theologiae Christianae.* Hanoviae, 1615.
TPT	Mastricht, Peter van. *Theoretico-practica theologia.* 2nd ed. Utrecht, 1724.
WBC	Word Biblical Commentary

Introduction

CHRISTIAN THEOLOGY AT THE BEGINNING of the twenty-first century exhibits an encouraging interest in discussing who God is and how he is known by us. While questions directly concerned with the human condition and its restoration in Christ are certainly vital, inquiring about the triune God himself remains paramount if he is the one from whom and for whom all things exist (Rom 11:36; 1 Cor 8:6; Col 1:16). Happily, there is evidence that the significance of the doctrine of God is being recognized on a number of fronts. In biblical studies, scholars have written on the attributes, triunity, and acts of God in the Old and New Testaments,[1] some reflecting particularly on Jesus' place in the identity of the God of Israel and the links between biblical theology and later formulation of the doctrine of the Trinity.[2] Discussions in systematic theology also persist, with some authors seeking to modify claims and patterns of thought inherited from

---

[1]E.g., Marianne Meye Thompson, *The God of the Gospel of John* (Grand Rapids: Eerdmans, 2001); Andreas Köstenberger and Scott R. Swain, *Father, Son and Spirit: The Trinity and John's Gospel*, New Studies in Biblical Theology 24 (Downers Grove, IL: InterVarsity Press, 2008); Larry W. Hurtado, *God in New Testament Theology* (Nashville: Abingdon, 2010); Reinhard Feldmeier and Hermann Spieckermann, *God of the Living: A Biblical Theology* (Waco, TX: Baylor University Press, 2011); Wesley Hill, *Paul and the Trinity: Persons, Relations, and the Pauline Letters* (Grand Rapids: Eerdmans, 2015); Matthew W. Bates, *The Birth of the Trinity: Jesus, God, and Spirit in New Testament and Early Christian Interpretations of the Old Testament* (Oxford: Oxford University Press, 2015).

[2]E.g., C. Kavin Rowe, "Biblical Pressure and Trinitarian Hermeneutics," *Pro Ecclesia* 11 (2002): 295-312; Larry W. Hurtado, *Lord Jesus Christ: Devotion to Jesus in Earliest Christianity* (Grand Rapids: Eerdmans, 2003); Richard Bauckham, *Jesus and the God of Israel: God Crucified and Other Studies in the New Testament's Christology of Divine Identity* (Grand Rapids: Eerdmans, 2008); Chris Tilling, *Paul's Divine Christology* (Grand Rapids: Eerdmans, 2015); Michael F. Bird, *Jesus the Eternal Son: Answering Adoptionist Christology* (Grand Rapids: Eerdmans, 2017).

patristic and scholastic accounts of God and others seeking to retrieve and revitalize such claims and methods of reasoning about God.[3] In the field of analytic theology, theologians and philosophers are expending remarkable energy in revisiting the doctrines of the divine attributes, the Trinity, and the person of Christ, advancing new proposals for describing God in a logically rigorous manner[4] and generating conversation about how the tools of philosophy relate to theological epistemology.[5]

---

[3]E.g., Robert W. Jenson, *Systematic Theology*, vol. 1, *The Triune God* (Oxford: Oxford University Press, 1997); Thomas G. Weinandy, *Does God Suffer?* (Notre Dame, IN: University of Notre Dame Press, 2000); Wolf Krötke, *Gottes Klarheiten: Eine Neuinterpretation der Lehre von Gottes Eigenschaften* (Tübingen: Mohr Siebeck, 2001); Colin E. Gunton, *Act and Being: Towards a Theology of the Divine Attributes* (Grand Rapids: Eerdmans, 2002); Paul L. Gavrilyuk, *The Suffering of the Impassible God: Dialectics of Patristic Thought*, Oxford Early Christian Studies (Oxford: Oxford University Press, 2004); Matthew Levering, *Scripture and Metaphysics: Aquinas and the Renewal of Trinitarian Theology*, Challenges in Contemporary Theology (Oxford: Blackwell, 2004); Gilles Emery, *The Trinitarian Theology of St Thomas Aquinas*, trans. Francesca Aran Murphy (Oxford: Oxford University Press, 2007); Bruce L. McCormack, *Orthodox and Modern: Studies in the Theology of Karl Barth* (Grand Rapids: Baker Academic, 2008); James F. Keating and Thomas Joseph White, eds., *Divine Impassibility and the Mystery of Human Suffering* (Grand Rapids: Eerdmans, 2009); James E. Dolezal, *God Without Parts: Divine Simplicity and the Metaphysics of God's Absoluteness* (Eugene, OR: Pickwick, 2011); Stephen R. Holmes, *The Quest for the Trinity: The Doctrine of God in Scripture, History and Modernity* (Downers Grove, IL: IVP Academic, 2012); John Webster, *God Without Measure: Working Papers in Christian Theology*, vol. 1, *God and the Works of God* (London: Bloomsbury, 2015); Paul R. Hinlicky, *Divine Simplicity: Christ the Crisis of Metaphysics* (Grand Rapids: Baker Academic, 2016); Steven J. Duby, *Divine Simplicity: A Dogmatic Account* (London: Bloomsbury, 2016); D. Stephen Long, *The Perfectly Simple Triune God: Aquinas and His Legacy* (Minneapolis: Fortress, 2016); Christopher R. J. Holmes, *The Lord Is Good: Seeking the God of the Psalter*, Studies in Christian Doctrine and Scripture (Downers Grove, IL: IVP Academic, 2018); Tyler R. Wittman, *God and Creation in the Theology of Thomas Aquinas and Karl Barth* (Cambridge: Cambridge University Press, 2018).

[4]E.g., Jay Wesley Richards, *The Untamed God: A Philosophical Exploration of Divine Perfection, Simplicity and Immutability* (Downers Grove, IL: InterVarsity Press, 2003); Thomas H. McCall and Michael C. Rea, eds. *Philosophical and Theological Essays on the Trinity* (Oxford: Oxford University Press, 2009); Thomas H. McCall, *Which Trinity? Whose Monotheism? Philosophical and Systematic Theologians on the Metaphysics of Trinitarian Theology* (Grand Rapids: Eerdmans, 2010); William Hasker, *Metaphysics and the Tri-personal God*, Oxford Studies in Analytic Theology (Oxford: Oxford University Press, 2013); Eleonore Stump, *The God of the Bible and the God of the Philosophers* (Marquette: Marquette University Press, 2016); Timothy Pawl, *In Defense of Conciliar Christology: A Philosophical Essay* (Oxford: Oxford University Press, 2016); R. T. Mullins, *The End of the Timeless God* (Oxford: Oxford University Press, 2016); Oliver D. Crisp, *The Word Enfleshed: Exploring the Person and Work of Christ* (Grand Rapids: Baker Academic, 2016).

[5]See, e.g., Alvin Plantinga, *Warranted Christian Belief* (Oxford: Oxford University Press, 2000); Nicholas Wolterstorff, *Inquiring About God: Selected Essays*, vol. 1, ed. Terence Cuneo (Cambridge: Cambridge University Press, 2010); Oliver D. Crisp and Michael C. Rea, *Analytic Theology: New Essays in the Philosophy of Theology* (Oxford: Oxford University Press, 2011); Kevin Diller, *Theology's Epistemological Dilemma: How Karl Barth and Alvin Plantinga Provide a Unified Response*, Strategic Initiatives in Evangelical Theology (Downers Grove, IL: IVP Academic, 2014); Thomas H. McCall, *An Invitation to Analytic Theology* (Downers Grove, IL: IVP Academic, 2015).

While a number of studies have indicated by now that a strict bifurcation of biblical and "Greek" or "metaphysical" accounts of God is too simplistic,[6] tensions among different camps in contemporary theology still exist and sometimes give the impression that there is a straightforward choice to be made between a speculative doctrine of God driven by natural theology or "metaphysics" and a Christ-centered doctrine of God driven by the economy of salvation. It could be tempting to epitomize the two conflicting sensibilities in the figures of Thomas Aquinas and Karl Barth, but recent scholarship has reminded us that Thomas's thinking was rooted in and shaped by biblical exegesis.[7] For his part, though Barth was firm in his rejection of natural theology, he could certainly acknowledge the universal implications of God's self-revelation and its reception beyond its original Jewish context.[8] However, while various works have initiated conversations between the perspectives represented by these figures,[9] there are still disagreements about the place of natural theology and metaphysics in theology proper and about the decisiveness of the incarnation for our knowledge of God.

In relevant discussions of theology and "metaphysics," the latter is often presented as a matter of wrongly speaking of God by inferring from created, limited being what God must be like instead of starting with God's revelation in the incarnate Son. Sometimes "metaphysics" is shorthand for any talk of

---

[6]See, e.g., Weinandy, *Does God Suffer?*; Gavrilyuk, *Suffering of the Impassible God*; Janet Martin Soskice, "Athens and Jerusalem, Alexandria and Edessa: Is There a Metaphysics of Scripture?," *IJST* 8 (2006): 149-62; Christoph Markschies, "Does It Make Sense to Speak About a 'Hellenization of Christianity' in Antiquity?," *Church History and Religious Culture* 92 (2012): 5-34.

[7]Levering, *Scripture and Metaphysics*; Michael Dauphinais and Matthew Levering, eds., *Reading John with St. Thomas Aquinas: Theological Exegesis and Speculative Theology* (Washington, DC: Catholic University of America Press, 2010); Michael Dauphinais and Matthew Levering, eds., *Reading Romans with St. Thomas Aquinas* (Washington, DC: Catholic University of America Press, 2012).

[8]Barth speaks of a "Christian universalism," but with a "particularist character" focused on Jesus as a "man of Israel" (*CD* IV/1, 167).

[9]E.g., Eugene F. Rogers, *Thomas Aquinas and Karl Barth: Sacred Doctrine and the Natural Knowledge of God* (Notre Dame, IN: University of Notre Dame Press, 1996); Christopher A. Franks, "The Simplicity of the Living God: Aquinas, Barth, and Some Philosophers," *MT* 21 (2005): 275-300; Keith L. Johnson, *Karl Barth and the Analogia Entis* (London: Bloomsbury, 2011); Matthew Levering, "Christ, the Trinity, and Predestination: McCormack and Aquinas," in *Trinity and Election in Contemporary Theology*, ed. Michael T. Dempsey (Grand Rapids: Eerdmans, 2011), 244-73; Bruce L. McCormack and Thomas Joseph White, eds., *Thomas Aquinas and Karl Barth: An Unofficial Catholic-Protestant Dialogue* (Grand Rapids: Eerdmans, 2013); Archie J. Spencer, *The Analogy of Faith: The Quest for God's Speakability*, Strategic Initiatives in Evangelical Theology (Downers Grove, IL: IVP Academic, 2015).

God that affirms that God is complete in himself without reference to the economy. Of particular relevance here is post-Barthian reservation about knowledge of God predicated on the God-world relation or the Creator-creature distinction and outside the ambit of the doctrine of the person and work of Christ. Barth himself warned against "fatal speculation about the being and work of the λόγος ἄσαρκος, or a God whom we think we can know elsewhere, and whose divine being we can define from elsewhere than in and from contemplation of His presence and activity as the Word made flesh." He was therefore wary of affirming the so-called *extra Calvinisticum* in an un-qualified manner.[10] T. F. Torrance distinguished between "a metaphysical conception of the inertial Nature or Being of God" and a "powerful soterio-logical approach to the doctrine of God."[11] Likewise, Colin Gunton worried that the divine attributes had often been construed "largely cosmologically," prioritizing "timeless relations between the eternal and the temporal" at the expense of concentrating on God's activity and revelation in time. Gunton himself aimed to overcome what he regarded as a penchant for a priori the-ologizing by focusing on the economy and granting God's historical action a constitutive role in the knowledge of God's being.[12]

Similar concerns can be seen on both sides of the recent debates about election and the Trinity in Barth's theology, even if the resultant material conclusions may differ from one writer to another. Bruce McCormack, for example, rejects the claim of classical theism "to know what God is before a consideration of Christology." For McCormack, theology should avoid such "metaphysical" tendencies and resolve "never to speak about God on any other basis than that of the incarnation."[13] Any "metaphysical gap" between God's being and God's eternal act of deciding for the incarnation must be closed down. For there is no "abstract" divine essence behind the act of

---

[10]Barth, *CD* IV/1, 181.

[11]T. F. Torrance, *The Christian Doctrine of God: One Being, Three Persons* (Edinburgh: T&T Clark, 1996), 248.

[12]Colin E. Gunton, *Act and Being: Towards a Theology of the Divine Attributes* (Grand Rapids: Eerdmans, 2002), 17-18, 96, et passim.

[13]Bruce L. McCormack, "The Actuality of God: Karl Barth in Conversation with Open Theism," in *Engaging the Doctrine of God: Contemporary Protestant Perspectives*, ed. Bruce L. McCormack (Grand Rapids: Baker Academic, 2008), 188, 211-12. Compare his "Why Should Theology Be Christocentric? Christology and Metaphysics in Paul Tillich and Karl Barth," *Wesley Theological Journal* 45 (2010): 63-65, 77, 79.

election and no *Logos asarkos* who is not also in his very deity the *Logos incarnandus* (predestined to be incarnate).[14] According to McCormack, those who want to maintain an "analogical interval" between the "immanent" and "economic" Trinity will likely end up (mistakenly) advocating "natural theology" and an *analogia entis* between God and the creature.[15] Paul Molnar has argued against McCormack that God's triune being is not constituted by God's decision for the incarnation, aligning his position on divine aseity and divine freedom with more traditional accounts of God. Yet Molnar still takes up Barth's criticism of the "error of Protestant orthodoxy which began its doctrine of God elsewhere than with the revelation of God in Jesus Christ."[16] In clarifying his own position and his reading of Barth, Molnar distances himself from "classical theology" or "classical metaphysics," with its particular understanding of divine impassibility.[17]

The landscape of contemporary theology proper thus evokes a number of important questions. What do we mean by *natural theology*? Can natural theology indicate who and what God actually is, not merely our own (fallible) assumptions about who and what he must be? In what sense is God's revelation in the incarnation decisive for our knowledge of God? Does that revelation preclude knowledge of God that has no obvious reference to the incarnation? What might that imply about the ontological relationship between God and his economic works? How should we understand the term *metaphysics* in this conversation? Is it still viable to engage in metaphysical reasoning in Christian theology?

In light of such questions, the present study will argue that instead of generating conflicting agendas for a Christian account of God, natural

---

[14]Bruce L. McCormack, "Grace and Being," in *The Cambridge Companion to Karl Barth*, ed. John Webster (Cambridge: Cambridge University Press, 2000), 93-101; McCormack, "Seek God Where He May Be Found: A Response to Edwin Chr. van Driel," *SJT* 60 (2007): 68; McCormack, "Election and the Trinity: Theses in Response to George Hunsinger," *SJT* 63 (2010): 210, 214, 222; McCormack, "The Lord and Giver of Life: A 'Barthian' Defense of the Filioque," in *Rethinking Trinitarian Theology: Disputed Questions and Contemporary Issues in Trinitarian Theology*, ed. Robert J. Wozniak and Giulio Maspero (London: T&T Clark, 2012), 231, 246-47.

[15]Bruce L. McCormack, "Processions and Missions: A Point of Convergence Between Thomas Aquinas and Karl Barth," in McCormack and White, *Thomas Aquinas and Karl Barth*, 117-19, 125-26.

[16]Paul D. Molnar, "Can the Electing God Be God Without Us? Some Implications of Bruce McCormack's Understanding of Barth's Doctrine of Election for the Doctrine of the Trinity," *Neue Zeitschrift für Theologie und Religionsphilosophie* 49 (2007): 210.

[17]Molnar, "Can the Electing God," 217-20.

theology, metaphysics, and the incarnation should be brought together and rightly ordered in a constructive account of the Christian practice of *theologia* taken in the strict sense of the word (discourse about the triune God in himself without primary reference to the economy).[18] The purpose of the book is thus to offer, on the basis of the Bible's account of human knowledge of God in the arc of redemptive history, a sketch of the rationale and practice of Christian reflection on God himself in his transcendence of the economy, which will enable us to reframe the roles of natural theology, metaphysics, and the incarnation in the doctrine of God. This will involve making a case that, rather than being a capitulation to "metaphysics," a theology proper in which God's aseity and completeness are underscored in fact emerges from God's own self-revelation and makes use of metaphysics—the study of (created) being as such—as a subordinate disciplinary resource. The line of argument will also give occasion along the way to address several subsidiary issues in contemporary theology, including the *extra Calvinisticum* and the *analogia entis*.

At this point, I should acknowledge that a number of recent authors working to appropriate classical accounts of God have treated various aspects of the relationship between the economy and God's being and have begun to advocate what I have called here the Christian practice of *theologia*. Among other things, this has involved tracing out the manner in which the economy reveals something of God's own eternal life, the manner in which God's eternal life grounds and structures his triune activity in the economy, and the manner in which we might still today present our claims about God's being in "metaphysical" terms.[19] Some theologians who are committed to developing a genuinely Christian understanding of God have begun to speak about the need to rethink the influence of Christology over the doctrine of God. In the first volume of her *Systematic Theology*, Katherine Sonderegger, for example, begins with God in his oneness and writes,

---

[18]For patristic and later examples of the distinction between θεολογία and οἰκονομία, see chap. 1.

[19]E.g., Levering, *Scripture and Metaphysics*; and Levering, "Does the Paschal Mystery Reveal the Trinity?," in Dauphinais and Levering, *Reading John with St. Thomas Aquinas*, 78-91; Kevin J. Vanhoozer, *Remythologizing Theology: Divine Action, Passion, and Authorship*, Cambridge Studies in Christian Doctrine (Cambridge: Cambridge University Press, 2010); Scott R. Swain, *God of the Gospel: Robert Jenson's Trinitarian Theology*, Strategic Initiatives in Evangelical Theology (Downers Grove, IL: IVP Academic, 2013); Christopher R. J. Holmes, "The Aseity of God as a Material Theological Concern," *JRT* 8 (2014): 61-78.

"A repeated refrain in this work must be that not all is Christology!" Again, "It will be the aim of this dogmatics to honor Christ throughout a doctrine of God that is nevertheless not grounded nor derived from his incarnate life."[20] John Webster's approach to the person of Christ and the doctrine of God moves in a similar direction.[21] A tireless proponent of allowing a right view of God's perfection to shape every other topic in Christian theology, Webster sounds a hopeful note for theology and, indeed, for the Christian life: "The burden of the Christian doctrines of the Trinity, creation, and incarnation is that, because God is from and in himself, he is God for us in ways we can scarcely imagine."[22] With Webster, I intend to indicate at different points in this study how a strong understanding of God's aseity can shape our understanding of God's economic works (not least the incarnation) and our own sense of identity as creatures of God.

Throughout this volume I will seek to add to the efforts of authors like Sonderegger and Webster to enrich Christian discourse about God *in se* by providing a scriptural account of the knowledge of God and by facing the challenge of integrating natural theology, Christology, and the proper use of metaphysics in the doctrine of God. It is worth noting that the engagement with Scripture in this volume will be primarily material, which is to say that it will be concerned with setting forth the meaning of Scripture's teaching and reasoning toward theological conclusions regarding our knowledge of God. Insofar as the book deals with the relationship between Scripture and Christian theology, it will do so chiefly by the actual practice of theological exegesis, though there will be some formal points made about the role of Scripture in dogmatics. Indeed, in this study the topic of the knowledge of God is not taken to be a strictly prolegomenal matter to be settled somehow before coming to the content of the Bible. Instead, it is viewed as a doctrinal issue that must be informed by God's revelation in the biblical canon. In addition to reasoning from Holy Scripture, the volume will incorporate insights from the catholic theological tradition. This will include patristic and

---

[20]Katherine Sonderegger, *Systematic Theology*, vol. 1, *The Doctrine of God* (Minneapolis: Fortress, 2015), xvii.

[21]See esp. Webster, *God Without Measure*, chap. 4.

[22]John Webster, "*Non ex aequo*: God's Relation to Creatures," in *Within the Love of God: Essays on the Doctrine of God in Honour of Paul S. Fiddes*, ed. Anthony Clarke and Andre Moore (Oxford: Oxford University Press, 2014), 107.

medieval authors but also the Reformed orthodox, who are gradually gaining recognition as valuable conversation partners in contemporary theology proper.[23] As we will see, the Reformed orthodox firmly position themselves in the catholic tradition and develop that tradition in a number of helpful ways, offering a Protestant approach to the doctrine of God that is significantly different from that of Barth.[24] This study will suggest how theologians today can appropriate Reformed orthodox insights on matters like the nature of theological knowledge, the viability of natural theology, and the theological use of metaphysics.

Chapter one will examine the purpose of human knowledge of God in the biblical narrative, following the outworking of God's plan to grant us knowledge of God himself (not just his outward relationship to creatures) and sketching the object, nature, and limitations of that knowledge. Given that chapter one will address the serious limitations of human knowledge of God, it might be helpful here to pause and allay some potential concerns about whether this study will overestimate our ability to know God this side of eschatological glory. Let me be clear, then, from the outset: we can know God only by his self-revelation. We can never comprehend him. We cannot know his essence as such and in its entirety. Yet, according to God's own good purposes, we can know God himself (not just his relationship to us or his works *ad extra*). We must approach him through the mediator Jesus Christ and in reverent faith, but he still grants us knowledge that pertains to his own being. Thus, when we affirm a Christian knowledge of God *in se*

---

[23]See, e.g., Richard A. Muller, *Post-Reformation Reformed Dogmatics: The Rise and Development of Reformed Orthodoxy ca. 1520 to 1725*, vol. 3, *Divine Essence and Attributes* (Grand Rapids: Baker Academic, 2003); Muller, *Post-Reformation Reformed Dogmatics: The Rise and Development of Reformed Orthodoxy ca. 1520 to 1725*, vol. 4, *The Triunity of God* (Grand Rapids: Baker Academic, 2003); J. Martin Bac, *Perfect Will Theology: Divine Agency in Reformed Scholasticism as Against Suárez, Episcopius, Descartes, and Spinoza* (Leiden: Brill, 2010); Dolf te Velde, *Paths Beyond Tracing Out: The Connection of Method and Content in the Doctrine of God, Examined in Reformed Orthodoxy, Karl Barth, and the Utrecht School* (Delft: Eburon, 2010); Duby, *Divine Simplicity*; and Duby, "Election, Actuality and Divine Freedom: Thomas Aquinas, Bruce McCormack and Reformed Orthodoxy in Dialogue," *MT* 32 (2016): 325-40.

[24]In his introduction to *Thomas Aquinas and Karl Barth*, Thomas Joseph White offers an incisive presentation of major challenges in modern theology and gives an excellent apology for bringing Thomas and Barth into dialogue with one another ("Introduction: Thomas Aquinas and Karl Barth—An Unofficial Catholic-Protestant Dialogue," in McCormack and White, *Thomas Aquinas and Karl Barth*, 1-39). I aim to add the contributions of the Protestant orthodox here and hope to indicate at various points how they may be placed in fruitful dialogue with Thomas and Barth.

here, the *in se* does not indicate that we overcome our dependence on his revelation or come to comprehend God. But it does indicate that we can know something of the triune God as he is in his self-referential completeness and transcendence of the economy.

In light of chapter one, the second chapter will focus on one particular kind or mode of theological knowledge granted by God in redemptive history: natural knowledge of God, particularly its role in the Christian work of *theologia* and its connection to the supernatural revelation that culminates in the incarnation. Chapter three will then treat the role of supernatural revelation—especially the incarnation—in communicating knowledge of God in his transcendence of the economy. Given the use of metaphysical terminology in the Christian doctrine of God and the tendency of some to characterize *theologia* as "metaphysics" in a negative sense, chapter four will explicate how the Christian practice of *theologia* transcends but still utilizes the science of metaphysics as the study of (created) being. Finally, chapter five will consider how human beings can speak of God in creaturely terms without either denying the limitations of our theological understanding or denying the reality of knowledge of God in himself, which will involve a reappraisal of the doctrine of analogy.

Before proceeding to the first chapter, it may be good to comment briefly on the practical relevance of the subject in view. I believe there are at least three ways in which the issues under consideration bear on the life of the church. First, exploring our knowledge of God in his transcendence of the economy reinforces for Christian believers that while God does indeed care for his creatures, he is already complete in himself without any need of us. By his redeeming work, God draws us into a love and glory already perfect in God's triune existence, which engenders a humility and gratitude in the Christian life that contrasts with the narcissistic ways of our culture. This also encourages restful confidence in God, for he is not served by human hands as though needing anything. He will never be inclined to use us in order to become something greater than he already is. Instead, it pleases him generously to share his life and give good gifts to his creatures (Acts 17:24-25; Rom 8:17; Heb 12:10; Jas 1:17; 2 Pet 1:4).

> With God alone, I am dealing with what does not need to construct or negotiate an identity, what is free to be itself without the process of struggle.

Properly understood, this is the most liberating affirmation we could ever hear. God does not and cannot lay claim upon me so as to "become" God; what I am cannot be made functional for God's being; I can never be defined by the job of meeting God's needs.[25]

So too Webster: the "non-reciprocity of the creator-creature relation . . . is the ground of the creatures' worth. The dignity of creatures does not consist in furnishing God with an object without which his love would be undirected; it consists simply in creatures being themselves, having proper creaturely integrity, order and movement in prospect of an end."[26]

Second, if knowing the triune God is the essence of eternal life (Jn 17:3), then to undertake the Christian practice of pondering and speaking about God in himself is to have a foretaste of the eschatological joy into which Christ invites his people. One might wonder whether an "academic" exercise such as this can truly involve the kind of personal knowledge Christ has in mind in John 17:3. This question will come up in chapter one, but for now it can be said that the question may reflect both the undercurrent of anti-intellectualism in contemporary culture, which often detaches the heart from the mind, and also an inattentiveness to the real character of Christian theology as a profoundly spiritual, moral, and doxological undertaking.

Finally, because the missionary task of the church involves bringing the gospel to those who do not yet have access to God's revelation in Christ, it is beneficial for us to consider afresh the relationship between the natural theological knowledge that God makes available to all and the supernatural theology that the church conveys in its proclamation of the gospel. If we can expect to encounter genuine traces of the knowledge of God among those who do not know Christ or the Bible, if we can expect, even from within a thoroughly Christian view of God, some cognitive commensurability in the work of Christian witness, this can help to inform and encourage evangelism and missions. Of course, there is demanding exegetical and dogmatic work to do before one can attempt to draw out all the practical implications.

---

[25]Rowan Williams, *On Christian Theology*, Challenges in Contemporary Theology (Oxford: Blackwell, 2000), 72-3.
[26]John Webster, "Trinity and Creation," *IJST* 12 (2010): 14.

ONE

Theologia Within the Divine Economy

T HE BURDEN OF THIS CHAPTER is to situate human knowledge of
God within the context of the scriptural narrative of redemptive
history. This will press us to take into account the divine purpose of theological understanding (principally, facilitating and shaping communion
with God) and to take seriously the fact that the triune God is complete in
himself without reference to the economy and wills to grant us knowledge
of himself in his transcendence of his economic works. To ensure that the
scriptural purpose of our knowledge of God determines the discursive
practice of theology proper, I will then explore the object and nature (or
"genus") of theological knowledge (e.g., science or wisdom). After this I will
take into account the limitations of our theological knowledge and the development of it in redemptive history on the way to the state of glory. In view
of the limitations and the developmental aspect of Christian *theologia* in this
life, I will present some theological considerations needed to address the
potential problem of what Martin Luther famously called a *Deus absconditus*
(hidden God).

THE PURPOSE OF THEOLOGICAL KNOWLEDGE

The chief end of human existence and the greatest good bestowed on human
beings is communion with God, the author of life. The covenants that God
establishes with his people in the Old Testament consistently underscore that
he will be their God and they will be his people. Even as YHWH promises
to bless Abraham with earthly riches and a great many descendants, he

emphasizes that he will be God forever to Abraham and to his offspring (Gen 17:1-21). Similarly, as YHWH promises to deliver the Israelites from slavery and into the land of Canaan, he announces that he will be God to the people of Israel, and they will know that he is their God and that it was he who brought them out of Egypt (Ex 6:2-8). When YHWH offers Israel a "covenant invitation" anticipating all that will take place at Sinai,[1] he tells them that if they obey him, they will be his "treasured possession" from among all the peoples of the earth. They will be a "kingdom of priests" and a "holy nation"—"the beginning of the outworking of [YHWH's] intention to bring close to himself a people that will join him for all eternity as adopted members of his family" (Ex 19:1-6).[2] The psalmists make clear that true beatitude consists in fellowship with the living God. David proclaims that he has no good apart from YHWH. He certainly values YHWH's preservation of his life, but ultimately YHWH himself is his portion, in whose presence there is fullness of joy (Ps 16:2, 5, 11). YHWH's love is better than life itself (Ps 63:3). To be in YHWH's dwelling place for one day is better than a thousand days elsewhere (Ps 84:1, 10). When the prophet Jeremiah speaks of the new covenant, YHWH once more promises to be God to the people of the covenant and to grant all of them, from the least to the greatest, knowledge of himself (Jer 31:31-34).

Many New Testament passages bear mentioning here, but Jesus' prayer in John 17 stands out as he says to the Father regarding his followers, "This is eternal life, that they know you, the only true God, and Jesus Christ, whom you sent" (Jn 17:3). Augustine comments that "if knowledge of God is eternal life, we tend toward living inasmuch as we advance in this knowledge."[3] Of course, Jesus prays that the disciples would accomplish the mission of taking the gospel to the world (Jn 17:14-19), but the ultimate aim is that all who believe in Jesus would be united in love to the triune God, living in his presence and beholding his glory (Jn 17:20-26). John

---

[1]Brevard S. Childs, *The Book of Exodus: A Critical, Theological Commentary*, Old Testament Library (Philadelphia: Westminster, 1974), 367.

[2]Douglas K. Stuart, *Exodus*, New American Commentary (Nashville: B&H, 2006), 422.

[3]Augustine, *In Evangelium Ioannis, tractatus CXXIV*, CCSL 36 (Turnhout: Brepols, 1954), 105.3 (605). Throughout the book, references to primary sources by book, chapter, paragraph number, etc. are followed with parentheses containing the page numbers of the editions in which they are found.

Chrysostom comments that "this is rest: the act of looking upon the Son of God."[4] The end of the Apocalypse gives us a striking picture of this as God dwells with humanity in unprecedented nearness in the new creation: "*God himself* [αὐτὸς ὁ θεὸς] will be with them" (Rev 21:3). There is no need for a temple or sun or moon, for God himself is the temple and the light by which the nations walk (Rev 21:22-25).

Given that talk of communion with God is readily characterized as a matter of knowing God, the point may seem almost too obvious to state, but if humanity's chief end is communion with God, then all the capacities and activities of the human person are ordered to that end, including the human intellect and the practice of theology in both church and academy. Growth in the knowledge of God is meant to facilitate and shape communion with God. For in his good jealousy God has called us to worship him in truth. Accordingly, he has imbued his self-revelation with intelligible content to instill discernment and to keep us from false gods (Jn 4:24; 1 Jn 2:20-27). We are often tempted to treat the knowledge of God or the practice of theology as a means by which we can arrive at some good other than the triune God himself, be it social transformation, fulfillment of the Great Commission, or fresh insights into the subject matter of other academic disciplines. Of course, we would be disobedient to God and show that we did not truly know him if we neglected our earthly vocations and the advancement of the gospel in this age (Lk 19:11-27; 1 Jn 3:9-10). However, the need for social transformation and for missions will one day cease. We will reign over the earth in the new creation, but at the center of our eschatological happiness will be the sight of the Lord (Rev 22:4-5).[5] Indeed, as Martha learned, the activities of even the present age must be framed and guided by a prioritization of knowing Christ (Lk 10:38-42; cf. Phil 3:8).

According to Holy Scripture, the God with whom we have communion and to whom our knowing is ordered is not constituted by his relationship to us or by his works in the economy of salvation. Rather, he has life in and of himself and is complete in his eternal, triune existence without reference to the economy. According to many authors in the Christian tradition, this

---

[4]John Chrysostom, *Homiliae CXXXVIII in Johannem*, PG 59 (Paris, 1862), 82.3 (445).
[5]On this, see Michael Allen, *Grounded in Heaven: Recentering Christian Hope and Life on God* (Grand Rapids: Eerdmans, 2018).

note is sounded in the giving of the divine name in Exodus 3:13-16, where God identifies himself as "I AM WHO I AM" (אֶהְיֶה אֲשֶׁר אֶהְיֶה) or just "I AM" (אֶהְיֶה).[6] Though the notion that this passage signals the plenitude of God's being is now often dismissed as unduly "metaphysical,"[7] various biblical scholars still affirm that the name in the context of Exodus conveys something of the underived and free character of God's gracious presence and activity (cf. Ex 33:19).[8] This aspect of the name is brought out in the book of Isaiah, where God announces multiple times "I am he" in texts that accentuate his underived identity, self-sufficiency, and sovereign power (Is 41:4; 43:13; 43:25; 46:4; 48:12; 51:12).[9] In the Septuagint, the name is translated ἐγώ εἰμι ὁ ὤν (I am he who is), which then influences relevant New Testament material. Jesus invokes the divine name to express his eternal existence: "Before Abraham was born, I am" (Jn 8:58). God calls himself "the Alpha and the Omega, the one who is and who was and who is coming" (ὁ ὤν καὶ ὁ ἦν καὶ ὁ ἐρχόμενος) (Rev 1:8; cf. Rev 1:4; 4:8; 11:17; 16:5).[10] If the divine name in canonical perspective conveys not only that the God of Israel is faithful to his people but also that he is the one, underived, abundant, and eternal God, then it is rightly included in a biblical rationale for commending the doctrine of divine aseity.

---

[6]E.g., Hilary of Poitiers, *La Trinité*, ed. G. M. de Durand et al., 3 vols., Sources Chrétiennes 443, 448, 462 (Paris: Éditions du Cerf, 1999–2001), 1.5 (1:211-12); Augustine, *De Trinitate, libri XV*, ed. W. J. Mountain, 2 vols., CCSL 50-50A (Turnhout: Brepols, 1968), 5.3 (1:207-8); John of Damascus, *Exp. fid.* 1.9 (31).

[7]E.g., Gerhard von Rad, *Old Testament Theology*, vol. 1, *The Theology of Israel's Historical Traditions*, trans. D. M. G. Stalker (New York: Harper & Row, 1962), 180; Roland de Vaux, "The Revelation of the Divine Name YHWH," in *Proclamation and Presence: Old Testament Essays in Honour of Gwynne Henton Davies*, ed. John I. Durham and J. R. Porter (Richmond: John Knox, 1970), 70; Christopher R. Seitz, *Figured Out: Typology and Providence in Christian Scripture* (Louisville: Westminster John Knox, 2001), 140.

[8]E.g., Childs, *Book of Exodus*, 596; J. A. Motyer, *The Message of Exodus*, The Bible Speaks Today (Downers Grove, IL: InterVarsity Press, 2005), 70; Reinhard Feldmeier and Hermann Spieckermann, *God of the Living: A Biblical Theology*, trans. Mark E. Biddle (Waco, TX: Baylor University Press, 2011), 30. For more positive reappraisals of traditional readings of the divine name, see R. Michael Allen, "Exodus 3 After the Hellenization Thesis," *JTI* 3 (2009): 179-96; Andrea D. Saner, *"Too Much to Grasp": Exodus 3:13-15 and the Reality of God* (Winona Lake, IN: Eisenbrauns, 2015); Grant Macaskill, "Name Christology, Divine Aseity, and the I Am Sayings in the Fourth Gospel," *JTI* 12 (2018): 217-41.

[9]On the connection between Ex 3 and these statements in Isaiah, see John Goldingay and David Payne, *Isaiah 40–55*, International Critical Commentary (London: T&T Clark, 2006), 1:149-51.

[10]See Richard Bauckham, *The Theology of the Book of Revelation*, New Testament Theology (Cambridge: Cambridge University Press, 1993), 28-30.

John's Gospel expounds God's aseity in trinitarian terms. The Father has "life in himself" and communicates that "life in himself" to the Son (Jn 5:26). God gives life to believers in the Son, but that life is distinct from the life that the Father gives to the Son, for the latter is a prevenient life by which the Father originally made the world through the Son and by which the Son raises those who are physically and spiritually dead (Jn 1:3-4; 5:25; 11:25-26). Accordingly, the life the Father gives to the Son is a divine life, a life that pertains to the divine being of the Son (not merely to his human nature or economic office).[11] The Father and Son thus dwell together in an eternal fellowship of love "before the foundation of the world" (Jn 17:24). God's life and love are fulfilled eternally in the processions in God, so that he has no need of actualizing himself or producing an external counterpart.[12] As Hilary of Poitiers repeatedly phrases it, God is not a "solitary" or "lonely" God (*Deus solitarius*).[13]

The meaning of God's triune aseity for his relationship to creatures is exhibited in various texts. In Psalm 50 God chastises his people for presuming that he needs their worship:

> If I were hungry, I would not tell you,
>> for the world and all that is in it is mine. (Ps 50:12 NRSV)

Similarly, in Acts 17:24-25, Paul explains to the Greeks that the true God does not dwell in temples built by human hands and does not need the service of human hands. God stands indebted to no one, for from him and through him and to him are all things (Rom 11:35-36). But God's aseity does not mean that he is aloof or capricious. For by virtue of it he is the one who does not faint or grow weary in leading his people (Is 40:27-31; Phil 4:19). He cannot be thwarted or corrupted in his determination to give good gifts to his creatures (Jas 1:13-17).

It follows from this line of scriptural teaching that God is complete in himself without reference to the economy. What God is and what he does

---

[11]Compare Paul A. Rainbow, *Johannine Theology: The Gospel, the Epistles and the Apocalypse* (Downers Grove, IL: IVP Academic, 2014), 101-2; D. A. Carson, "John 5:26: *Crux Interpretum* for Eternal Generation," in *Retrieving Eternal Generation*, ed. Fred Sanders and Scott R. Swain (Grand Rapids: Zondervan, 2017), 79-97.

[12]Space does not allow for offering a full exegetical defense of the doctrine of the processions of the Son and Spirit, but it is a catholic doctrine that emerges from reading a mosaic of scriptural texts (e.g., Jn 5:26; 6:45-46; 7:29; 15:26; Rom 8:9; Gal 4:6; Heb 9:14).

[13]Hilary of Poitiers, *La Trinité* 5.39 (2:168); 7.3 (2:282).

ad intra in the eternal processions is distinct from what God does *ad extra* or economically, even if the nature of that distinction must be handled carefully to avoid giving the impression that there are two different versions of God. Furthermore, God intends to grant us knowledge of himself in his completeness and transcendence of the economy. It is difficult to avoid affirming this when one considers the simple fact that he reveals truth about himself that does not immediately pertain to his relationship to us or to his economic works. The revelation of that truth takes place in the economy and gives shape to our worship and discipleship, but its content is not reducible to the economy. The psalmists, for example, speak of what God is, even if they do so with a view to how God acts. Because YHWH *is* righteous (כִּי־צַדִּיק יְהוָה) and loves righteousness, he tests human hearts and opposes the wicked and the violent (Ps 11:4-7).[14] YHWH's justice is the basis of his outward rule and judgment ("the foundation of his throne") (Ps 97:2). In Psalm 119, the writer says to YHWH, "You are good and do good" (טוֹב־אַתָּה וּמֵטִיב) (Ps 119:68 NRSV, ESV), calling our attention to a divine perfection that describes what God is (goodness) in addition to the outward enactment of that perfection (beneficence).[15] In several places the Gospels inform us that the efficacy of God's power is greater than its outward manifestation in the economy. To the chagrin of the Pharisees and Sadducees, God could raise up children for Abraham from mere stones (Mt 3:9). God could have commanded legions of angels to defend his Son in Gethsemane (Mt 26:53).[16] To put it rather crudely, there is more to God than what takes place in the economy.

John writes, "In the beginning was the Word, and the Word was with God, and the Word was God" (Jn 1:1). In the context of the prologue of the Gospel,

---

[14]For an overview of Hebrew nominal (verbless) clauses serving to identify who the subject is or describe what it is or what it is like, see Bill T. Arnold and John H. Choi, *A Guide to Biblical Hebrew Syntax* (Cambridge: Cambridge University Press, 2003), 5.1.1 (165).

[15]For an excellent treatment of this, see Christopher R. J. Holmes, *The Lord Is Good: Seeking the God of the Psalter*, Studies in Christian Doctrine and Scripture (Downers Grove, IL: IVP Academic, 2018), 31-54.

[16]In traditional treatments of the divine attributes, these texts are routinely invoked to ground the distinction between God's *potentia absoluta* (his power to do all that is absolutely possible) and his *potentia ordinata* (that same power taken with respect to God's ability to do what he in fact plans to do) (e.g., Bartholomäus Keckermann, *Systema s.s. theologiae*, in *Operum omnium quae extant* [Geneva, 1612], 1.5 [2:103-6]; Stephen Charnock, *The Existence and Attributes of God*, 2 vols. in 1 [Grand Rapids: Baker, 1996], 2:12-13).

this statement prepares the way for the incarnation, but the content of the statement itself transcends the incarnation. The incarnate work of the Logos has its origin in the eternal triune life of God. And he evidently wants us to understand that it is so. Likewise, in applying the divine name to himself in John 8:58, Christ clearly intends that his hearers understand something of his transcendence of his own human nature and historical existence. In 1 Peter 1 the apostle gives us what might be called a Christ-centered view of the knowledge of God, but at the same time he directs our attention beyond the incarnate work of Christ. He writes that we have been redeemed by the precious blood of the Lamb, "who was, on the one hand, foreknown before the foundation of the world, but, on the other hand, revealed in the last times on account of you, who through him believe in God [τοὺς δι' αὐτοῦ πιστοὺς εἰς θεὸν], who raised him from the dead and gave glory to him, so that your faith and hope are in God" (1 Pet 1:19-21). One could claim from this text that we believe in God through Christ in that what Christ does in the economy constitutes the being of God or exhausts the content of our knowledge of God. But this conflicts with the Old Testament and early Christian alertness to God's prevenient fullness and independence seen in texts already canvassed here. I will say more about the role of Christology in the knowledge of God in chapter three, but for now, in relation to 1 Peter 1, it is fitting to say that we believe in God through Christ in that what God does in Christ is the culminating revelation of God in the economy and is the greatest assurance that we can trust in the benevolence and power of God, whose own life nevertheless does exceed what takes place in the economy. John Owen's comment on the text is helpful:

> What we believe with divine faith, we believe upon this account—that God hath revealed and spoken it. And the ultimate object of faith is God's all-sufficiency. . . . [Faith] will not rest and be satisfied till it comes, as it were, to be immersed in the all-sufficiency of God, like the stream of a river that runs with great swiftness, and presses on till it comes to the ocean, where it is swallowed up. . . . Christ is the immediate object of faith, but God in his all-sufficiency is the ultimate object of faith.[17]

---

[17]John Owen, "God the Saints' Rock," in *The Works of John Owen*, vol. 9, *Sermons to the Church*, ed. William H. Goold (Edinburgh: Banner of Truth, 1965), 250. Cf. William Ames, *Medulla theologica*, 2nd ed. (Amsterdam, 1634), 1.3.7-8 (6).

That the biblical God wills to be known in his triune completeness and transcendence of the economy is expressed in a number of ways in the Christian theological tradition. Various church fathers utilize the distinction between *theologia* and *oikonomia*. Basil of Caesarea, for example, warns against confusing the apostles' teaching about the divine essence of the Logos ("the way of theology," τρόπος θεολογίας) with the "logic of the economy" (οἱ λόγοι οἰκονομίας) described in a text like Acts 2:36 ("God made this Jesus both Lord and Messiah").[18] John of Damascus speaks of the Son as perfect and unchanging God and then speaks of the οἰκονομία in which the Son became flesh.[19] Drawing from Augustine, Peter Lombard's *Sentences* and the body of medieval literature that grew up around it clarifies that some names are attributed to God without respect to creatures, while others like "Creator" and "Lord" are attributed to God "relatively" (in relation to the creature) and "temporally" on account of the creature's temporal mode of existence.[20] Thomas Aquinas picks up these ways of speaking and uses others too, like the distinction between God in himself (*Deus secundum quod in se*) and God as principle and end of created being (*Deus secundum quod est principium rerum et finis earum*). His discussion of the distinction between the processions and missions of the divine persons is particularly rich, asserting that the mission of the Son or Spirit does not signal a new actuality in God but does involve the addition of an outward, temporal *terminus* (e.g., the Son's human nature) to the already actualized procession.[21]

The Reformed orthodox carry forward these traditional patterns of Christian teaching, showing an awareness of the distinction between *theologia* and *oikonomia* but also incorporating other ways of speaking.[22] Girolamo Zanchi, for example, offers a taxonomy of divine names and writes that some names signify the divine essence or essential attributes common to the persons while others directly signify the persons or that which is proper to the persons. Even if God had chosen not to create the world, these

---

[18]Basil of Caesarea, *Contre Eunome*, trans. B. Sesboüé, G. M. de Durand, and L. Doutreleau, Sources Chrétiennes 305 (Paris: Éditions du Cerf, 1983), 2.3 (2:16).

[19]John of Damascus, *Exp. fid.* 3.2 (109-10).

[20]Peter Lombard, *Sententiae in IV libris distinctae*, 3rd ed., Spicilegium Bonaventurianum 4B (Rome: Collegii S. Bonaventurae ad Claras Aquas, 1971), 1.30.1 (220-22).

[21]Thomas Aquinas, *ST* Ia.2, prol. (27); 13.7 (152-54); 43.1-2 (445-46); IIIa.2.6 ad 1 (37).

[22]On *theologia* as distinct from *oikonomia*, see, e.g., Polanus, *Syntagma* 2.25 (192); Turretin, *Inst.* 1.1.8 (1:3); 3.28.5 (1:311); 13.19.8 (2:403).

would still apply to God: "for even if God would have created nothing, he was nevertheless God." Other names (e.g., Creator, king), however, cannot be said of God apart from a relation to creatures.[23] Amandus Polanus provides an incisive and succinct account of the *opera Dei*, distinguishing the "essential" and "personal" works of God and ramifying the latter into "simply" or *ab intra* personal works (the processions) and qualified (*certo modo*) or *ab extra* personal works (economic acts peculiarly attributed to one person).[24] For Polanus, the "internal actions of God pertain to consideration of God in himself [*in se*]."[25] Thus "God is considered in a twofold way: *in se* and *extra se. In se* again in a twofold way, in respect of essence and in respect of internal works. *Extra se,* in respect of external works."[26]

William Ames states that "God as he is in himself [*in se*] can be apprehended by no one except himself" (so 1 Tim 6:16). "As he has revealed himself to us, he is conceived, from the back, as it were, not the face" (see Ex 33:23). Yet Ames then in some sense affirms that God can be known as he is in himself, for he says that "what can be known of God is his sufficiency and efficiency," calling God's sufficiency his having "enough in himself [*in se*], for himself and for us," while God's "efficiency" concerns his turning toward creatures in the divine decree and in creation and providence. Ames includes in the divine sufficiency both "essence" (what is common to the persons) and "subsistence" (what pertains distinctly to the persons). He clarifies that "because the essence cannot be sufficiently comprehended by us through one act, it is explicated by us multiply, as it were: by many attributes."[27]

Francis Turretin is similar in his use of the *in se* language. On the one hand, he is adamant that "God is not to be considered simply and as God in himself [*in se*], for thus he is incomprehensible to us, but as revealed and as he has seen fit to disclose himself to us in his word."[28] On the other hand, Turretin is still prepared to make claims about God *in se* in a certain sense.

---

[23]Girolamo Zanchi, *De natura Dei, seu de divinis attributis, libri V* (Neostadii Palatinorum, 1598), 1.4 (7-8).

[24]Polanus, *Syntagma* 4.1-5 (236-38).

[25]Polanus, *Syntagma* 2.1 (132).

[26]Polanus, *Syntagma* 5.1 (255).

[27]Ames, *Medulla* 1.4.2-3, 8, 10, 12, 18 (9-11); 7.1 (25); 8.1 (34).

[28]Turretin, *Inst.* 1.5.4 (1:18).

The justice of God, for example, may be considered either as "the universal comprehension of all virtues . . . by which God is most just and most holy *in se*" or as, for example, the "distributive justice" by which God outwardly "is occupied in the distribution of punishments and rewards."[29] Likewise, the goodness of God can be considered that by which he is "absolutely and *in se* supremely good and perfect . . . and the only good (Mk 10:18), because he is such originally, perfectly and immutably." It can also be considered "relatively" and "extrinsically" as God's beneficence toward creatures.[30] Furthermore, in the doctrine of the Trinity, Turretin distinguishes between the persons' "subsisting," on the one hand, and their "working," on the other, treating both that which concerns the persons "inwardly" and that which concerns the persons "outwardly."[31]

The use of the *in se* language in the present study is thus not a departure from catholic or Reformed ways of speaking. It is simply a way of communicating that, even though we always depend on God's gracious revelation and cannot comprehend God, we do still receive truth about God himself, truth whose content would obtain even if God had never created the world. Karl Barth makes some similar comments in *CD* II/1. He criticizes Philip Melanchthon for failing to include a doctrine of God in the first edition of his *Loci communes*. According to Barth, because God is who he is even without respect to his outward works, an adequate body of Christian teaching requires some treatment of God prior to treating the benefits of Christ.[32] Elsewhere Barth insists that it is problematic to collapse God's omnipotence into his "omnicausality" or economic activity.[33]

In preparation for the next section of this chapter, it is vital to note that Holy Scripture instructs us to grow in the knowledge of God. Paul, for example, prays that God would grant the Ephesians the "Spirit of wisdom and revelation" so that by the Spirit's illumination they may know the richness of their hope and inheritance and the surpassing power of the God who raised Jesus from the dead (Eph 1:17-19). Later Paul prays that the Ephesians would have the ability to grasp with all the saints the greatness of

---

[29]Turretin, *Inst.* 3.19.2 (1:259-60).
[30]Turretin, *Inst.* 3.20.2 (1:266).
[31]Turretin, *Inst.* 3.27.16 (1:308-9).
[32]Barth, *CD* II/1, 259-60.
[33]Barth, *CD* II/1, 526-32; III/3, 100-107.

Christ's love, a love that ultimately surpasses knowledge (Eph 3:18-19). Peter exhorts his readers not to distort the teaching of the Scriptures but rather to "grow in the grace and knowledge of our Lord and Savior Jesus Christ" (2 Pet 3:14-18). Insofar as we believe "through Christ in God," growth in the knowledge of Christ will include growth in the knowledge of "God in his all-sufficiency," as Owen put it. This does not involve bare repetition and affirmation of the words of the gospel. It includes the enlargement and expansion of knowledge that is gained through reasoning about competing claims and refuting arguments leveled against Christian doctrine (2 Cor 10:5; 1 Tim 1:3; 1 Jn 4:1-6). Accordingly, the elders and teachers of the church are responsible to uphold and expound Christian doctrine for the edification of Christ's body (Eph 4:11-16; 1 Tim 3:2; 4:11, 13; 6:2-3; 2 Tim 4:2-4). It is the urgency of these texts—not idle curiosity or professional ambition—that provides the impetus for theology as a discursive or academic discipline. In view of this scriptural impetus for discourse about God, we turn next to the object and nature (or "genus") of theology.

THE OBJECT AND NATURE OF THEOLOGICAL KNOWLEDGE

The previous section discussed the scriptural teaching that God wills believers to apprehend truth about himself, and in this section I am allowing that reality to inform the conception of theology as a discursive discipline. It is important to bear in mind that the character of theology taken in the sense of knowledge given by God and received in faith by all Christian believers precedes and determines the character of theology taken in the sense of a discursive reasoning about God or a developed system of teaching about divine things explored in an academic environment. The former has often been called "infused theology" because it is a knowledge of God built into the reception of the gospel: "the salvific knowledge of God and our Savior Christ and other divine things necessary for salvation."[34] This knowledge can be taken with respect to either the objective content of Christian teaching that is believed (*fides quae*) (see Acts 6:7; Gal 1:23) or with respect to the subjective *habitus* (disposition) or act of understanding and trusting by which one believes (*fides qua*).[35] Theology in the sense of a

---

[34]Polanus, *Syntagma* 1.13 (15).
[35]Polanus, *Syntagma* 2.1 (130); Turretin, *Inst.* 1.6.1 (1:20).

developed system of teaching about divine things has often been called "acquired theology": a knowledge of the necessary consequences and conclusions following from the principles of infused theology that is obtained by study and discursive effort.[36] This too can be taken objectively with respect to its content or subjectively with respect to its *habitus*.[37] To add to this analysis of the word *theology*, it may be said that contemporary use of the term often signifies "acquired" or scientific theology with regard to the activity or practice itself of reasoning about God (as distinct from both the objective content of that scientific theology and the eventual subjective understanding of that content). If infused theology ultimately includes knowledge of God himself in his aseity, then it will be necessary to discuss the fact that theology as a scientific undertaking develops such knowledge of God *in se*.

Taking the time to consider the object and the genus of the discipline of theology in a technical manner and in dialogue with the Christian dogmatic tradition will promote a conception of the practice of theological reasoning that corresponds to its ground and charter (i.e., the Bible's description of theological knowledge). Careful consideration of the object will promote a framing of the discipline of theology that answers to infused theology's distinction and relation between God himself and God's outward works, with a number of implications for the organization of a system of divinity.[38] Careful consideration of the genus will promote a conception of theological

---

[36]Polanus, *Syntagma* 1.13 (15). Peter van Mastricht comments that this theology is taught "partly by God" in "outward revelation" and "inward illumination," "partly by human beings, who are designated 'doctors'" (Eph 4:11) (*TPT* 1.1.38 [13]).

[37]In a relatively rare commendation of Scotus, Polanus judges that theology is thus a "mixed or composite habit," including both infused and acquired understanding of revealed truth (*Syntagma* 1.13 [15]).

[38]In various works toward the end of his life, John Webster was particularly attentive to this distinction and relation and its structural implications for Christian dogmatics. For example: "Theology's first object is the divine essence and properties, and the persons of the godhead. . . . The nature of God's works *ad extra* cannot be grasped without immediate reference to God's intrinsic self-satisfaction which is their principle or ground. . . . Outward communication is for God not natural or necessary but gratuitous. Yet, because God has so acted—because from his inner personal acts there flow his transitive operations—theological attention to God in his absolute being must be accompanied by attention to those acts in which of his charity God sets himself in relation to other beings as their first cause and final end" ("What Makes Theology Theological?," *Journal of Analytic Theology* 3 [2015]: 18). On Webster's movement toward this view, see Kenneth Oakes, "Theology, Economy and Christology in John Webster's *God Without Measure* and Some Earlier Works," *IJST* 19 (2017): 491-504.

work that comports with the biblical telos of theological knowledge (i.e., communion with God).

The object of theological knowledge. Various representations of the object of theology and its attendant topical organization are worth exploring, but only a few can be taken into account here. In the thirteenth century, Bonaventure, for example, gave the church a methodical presentation of Christian doctrine in his *Breviloquium.* According to the Seraphic Doctor, *sacra doctrina* "principally treats the first principle, namely, the God who is three and one" and contains seven major topics: the triune God, the creation of the world, the corruption of sin, the incarnation of the Word, the grace of the Holy Spirit, the "sacramental medicine," and the state of final judgment. Holy Scripture, or theology, "gives us sufficient knowledge of the first principle according to our pilgrim state [*secundum statum viae*]," but then God remains central even throughout all the topics that deal with economic matters, for he is the "effective and exemplar principle" in creation, the "restorative principle" in redemption, and the "perfective principle" in judgment.[39] Thomas writes that the object of any science is that of which it principally treats, so the object of theology is God. For in theology all things are treated *sub ratione Dei* ("under the reason of God," or as they stand in relation to him), because they either are God himself or have an order toward God as their principle and end. Those things that are not God himself can be treated in other sciences, but here they are treated "according to their order toward God."[40] For Thomas, then, the "principal intention of *sacra doctrina* is to pass down the knowledge of God," both as he is *in se* and as "principle and end of things, especially the rational creature." This requires treating God himself, the movement of the rational creature toward God, and the person of Christ, who is the way to God.[41]

The Reformed orthodox exhibit some diversity of thought regarding the object of theology, but it is not a stretch to say that in general they attempt to conceive of the discipline of theology (with respect to its content, *habitus,* praxis) by reference back to the Bible's account of the infused theology from

---

[39]Bonaventure, *Opera omnia,* vol. 5, *Breviloquium* (Florence: ex Typographia Collegii S. Bonaventurae, 1891), 1.1 (210).

[40]Thomas Aquinas, *ST* Ia.1.7 corp. (19).

[41]Thomas, *ST* Ia.2, prol. (27).

which theological science arises. Polanus, for example, asserts that Christian
dogmatic theology is simply the gathering, ordering, and exposition of the
things taught in Scripture and must therefore adopt a structure in accordance with the material content (if not the formal layout) of Scripture.[42] It
is not uncommon for the Reformed orthodox to point out, in view of texts
like Ecclesiastes 12:13 or 2 Timothy 1:13, that the content of Christian
teaching and therefore the content of a developed body of divinity incorporates two major "parts" or divisions: matters of faith and matters of "works"
or "observance."[43] Theology needs these two parts because its end is to
"inform true religion," which centers on reverent faith expressed in good
works to the glory of God (so Gal 5:6).[44] This is why Ames and Peter van
Mastricht, for example, can say that theology is "the teaching of living to
God [through Christ]."[45]

The component concerning matters of faith more directly treats things to
be known and believed, though addressing "things to be done" presupposes
knowledge of God and his commands: "Right judgment of things to be done
depends on the knowledge of God."[46] With respect to the things that must
be known and believed, Polanus identifies theology's object or subject ("that
about which it is turned") as God's essence (including the three modes in
which it subsists) and God's works, or "divine things, that is, God and
whatever is of God as much as it is ordered and referred to God, as pertaining to the knowledge and worship of him." Theology treats "not merely
of God but truly also of angels, human beings, and other creatures, but not
equally. For it treats of God principally, as of its subject, but of creatures as
they conduce to the manifestation of the subject, that is, as they are ordered
and referred toward rightly knowing and worshiping God."[47]

However, a number of the Reformed orthodox qualify this representation
of theology's object. According to Ames, God is the object of faith and
theology "considered not as he is in himself, but as much as it is by him that

---

[42]Polanus, *Syntagma* 2.1 (130).

[43]So Polanus, *Syntagma* 2.1 (130); Ames, *Medulla* 1.2.1, 5 (3-4); 3.1-9 (5-6); cf. Mastricht,
TPT 1.1.47-48 (14-15).

[44]Polanus, *Syntagma* 2.1 (130-31).

[45]Ames, *Medulla* 1.1 (1); Mastricht, *TPT* 1.1.36 (12).

[46]Polanus, *Syntagma* 2.2 (132); 5 (135).

[47]Polanus, *Syntagma* 1.2 (2); 13 (13); 14 (16).

we live well to him."[48] In Turretin's view, the object of theology is "God and divine things" or "God directly and indirectly, namely, God and the things of God as his works, the things under God as his creatures and the things tending to him as the duties of humanity." However, Turretin insists, God is the object of theology "not simply as God in himself . . . but as revealed." Thus divine revelation is the "formal reason" under which God is considered. In other words, Scripture is theology's "external principle of knowing."[49] Nor is God considered "absolutely under the aspect of deity [*praecise . . . sub ratione Deitatis*], as Thomas and many scholastics after him will." For such knowledge is not salutary but "deadly" for sinners. He is to be considered as "our God . . . covenanted in Christ, as he has revealed himself to us not only to be known but also to be worshiped."[50]

In light of scriptural teaching and these historical examples, how might we speak about the object of theology? In view of the Bible's teaching about God's aseity and transcendence of the economy, it seems fitting to say with authors like Bonaventure, Thomas, and Polanus that the object of theology is principally God himself and then, derivatively, other things as they stand in relation to God, which, as an author like Turretin usefully summarizes, will include God's economic acts, God's creatures, and the responsibilities and offices borne by God's creatures (especially the people of God). Given that God is not just *a se* but also, as the one who is *a se*, the principal actor in the economy, it is fitting to emphasize with Bonaventure, Thomas, and others that the triune God comes into view and is the orienting factor in all the various loci of dogmatic theology. On the one hand, this indissoluble relation between *theologia* and *oikonomia* does not erase the distinction between them. The organizational distinction remains important precisely because of God's aseity and the consequent the Creator-creature distinction. Because he does not have to establish his own identity via the economy, God is free to let creatures be creatures and history be history. Thus, although theological anthropology, soteriology, ecclesiology, and so on will be framed in relation to God, their subject matter will have its own integrity and

---

[48] Ames, *Medulla* 1.3.7 (6).
[49] To clarify, in this way of speaking about objects of knowledge, the means by which the object is known is called its formal *ratio*, or formal "aspect" (so, e.g., Thomas, *ST* IaIIae.1.1 corp. [7]).
[50] Turretin, *Inst.* 1.5.2-3 (1:18); 7.6 (1:24).

features that will add something distinct to a system of Christian theology.[51] *Theologia* is not the whole.[52] On the other hand, because the triune God is the author and end of creation and because he wills to grant us knowledge of himself (not just his outward effects), *theologia* is the principal and orienting part of a system of Christian theology. In the present study, then, the goal is to encourage discourse in one particular domain of dogmatic theology (i.e., theology proper), but doing well in this domain will enrich all that happens in the others.

Figures like Ames and Turretin press us to take into consideration the covenantal and salvific context in which infused theology is given and acquired theology is developed. If they make an important point—and I think they do—then we should bear in mind that dogmatic exposition of the doctrine of God can take place at all only in dependence on God's initiative in revelation, the purpose of which is not the bare transmission of information but the glory of God and good of the creature in fellowship with him. Furthermore, it can take place in a salutary and edifying manner only in union with Christ the mediator, who alone reconciles us to God and stands before us as the one "in whom are hidden all the storehouses of wisdom and knowledge" (Col 2:3). Yet, as Turretin's own positive use of the *in se* language attests (see above), while discursive development of the doctrine of God is governed by these realities, the covenant people do, in union with Christ, apprehend and delight in the covenant God as the one whose rich life exceeds what takes place in the economy and the covenant.[53]

The nature (or "genus") of theological knowledge. Turning to the question of the "genus" of theology, we should recall that consideration of the genus is crucial to aligning the discipline of theology with the scriptural purpose of the knowledge of God (i.e., communion with God). Discussion

---

[51]Allowing these topics their own space entails that not everything about their subject matter will be directly inferred from the doctrine of God. The importance of this is illustrated well in the clumsiness with which some evangelical theologians have attempted to deduce particular views of relationships between men and women from the relationship between God the Father and God the Son.

[52]As Polanus comments, it is a "part" of theology and therefore cannot be its "adequate object" (i.e., all that it treats) (*Syntagma* 2.1 [131]).

[53]Given what I will have to say in the next chapter about Thomas's view of the relationship between natural and supernatural theology, I do not think Thomas would ultimately disagree with this line of thinking.

of theology's genus concerns what sort of *habitus* theology is. Discussion of that *habitus* is informed by an understanding of what sort of *habitus* faith itself is. To facilitate clarity on this issue, Christian authors have borrowed and critically used language from Aristotle's *Ethics* and some of his other works where he identifies diverse virtues or habits of the mind with which one knows what is true and can speak what is true. These habits are distinguished not on the basis of psychological conjecture but on the basis of the various kinds of objects that human persons know. They include (1) knowledge of how to produce things (*ars*), (2) knowledge of actions that are good and beneficial in various circumstances (*prudentia*), (3) demonstrative, certain knowledge that is obtained by grasping the necessary consequences and conclusions of known principles (*scientia*), (4) basic knowledge of common things or universals that can function as principles from which scientific knowledge may be derived (*intellectus*), and (5) knowledge of the first principles of things (*sapientia*).[54]

Significantly, many theologians have pointed out the difficulty in straightforwardly applying any one of these habits to faith's apprehension of divine things or, by extension, to the discipline of theology.[55] Faith (and acquired theology) cannot, strictly speaking, be called *ars* or *prudentia* because faith's knowledge encompasses more than how to produce things or how to act well. It cannot be called *scientia* without qualification because it is not a demonstrative knowledge proceeding directly from self-evident principles, and it is emphatically concerned with singulars, especially the triune God himself. It cannot be called *intellectus* without qualification because its object is not clearly seen like ordinary (creaturely) objects of the intellect. It apprehends its object by the testimony of another.[56] Moreover, faith is not merely an intellectual habit but a "composite habit" present in both the

---

[54]See, e.g., Thomas's explanation in *Opera omnia*, vol. 47/2, *Sententia libri Ethicorum*, Leonine ed. (Rome: ad Sanctae Sabinae, 1969), 6.3-5 (339-50). The first two habits concern contingent things, while the latter three concern necessary things (so *ST* IaIIae.57.5 ad 3 [369]).

[55]In what follows, I am attempting to collate and distill lines of thought found in Thomas, *De Trin.* 3.1 (107-9); *ST* Ia.1.2 (8-9); 1.6 (17-18); IIaIIae.1.2 corp. (11); 1.4 (13-14), 2.1-2 (26-27); 2.9 (37-78); 4.1-2 (43-45); Polanus, *Syntagma* 1.13 (13-15); Ames, *Medulla* 3.1-22 (5-9); Turretin, *Inst.* 1.6.1-8 (1:20-22); Mastricht, *TPT* 1.1.46 (14).

[56]Thomas notes that the object of sense or the intuitive, direct cognition of the intellect (intellectual "seeing") by itself generates the mind's assent to it, while the object of faith generates assent with the involvement of the will (*ST* IIaIIae.1.4 [13-14]). In keeping with this, Ames points out that theology is fundamentally *doctrina* (rather than any inward mental habit), for it

intellect and the will.[57] That is, it apprehends its object under the aspect of both the true and the good, a goodness to be sought and obtained by the prospective believer. The intellect apprehends the grace of God in Christ. The will, rightly disposed and reformed by the Spirit, desires that grace and reposes in it, directing the intellect to assent and cling to this object.[58] In the more colloquial expression of Stephen Charnock, faith's knowledge or apprehension is not a merely speculative knowledge "floating in the head" but an "experimental" knowledge "sinking into the heart," which is accompanied by pleasure and "renders us happy."[59] Further, faith is a *habitus* that is not developed naturally like the others but given by God in his supernatural grace.

---

arises by "divine revelation and instruction" and not by things resident in or automatically available to the human mind (*Medulla* 1.2-3 [1-2]).

[57]The phrase "composite habit" is taken from Turretin, *Inst.* 15.8.13 (2:616). Though not all earlier theologians agree that one habit can be present in two "powers" (i.e., intellect and will), Thomas, for example, argues that one habit can be in one power principally and then "extend itself" toward another by exerting a certain influence on it (*ST* IaIIae.56.2 [356]).

[58]Thomas and Turretin represent two different ways of expressing the relation of the intellect and will here. In their shared repertoire of anthropological and epistemological resources are the concepts of the "speculative" and "practical" intellect, which are not separate faculties but one faculty taken according to two distinct ends toward which the intellect's object may be ordered (i.e., consideration of truth or operation) (so Thomas, *ST* Ia.79.11 [278-79]; IIaIIae.4.2 ad 3 [45]). For Thomas, the speculative intellect apprehends an object as true and good, and the "good understood" (*bonum intellectum*) is the object of the will's desire. Moved by a desire for its object, the will directs the intellect to firm assent to that object (see *ST* Ia.82.3-4 [298-99, 303-4]; IIaIIae.2.1-2 [26-27]; 4.2 [44-45]). Turretin explicitly commends Thomas's readiness to locate faith partly in the will (*Inst.* 15.8.14 [2:616]), but he does speak somewhat differently about the relation between the intellect and will. Turretin states that there is a "theoretical assent" of faith and also a "fiducial and practical assent" or "persuasion of the practical intellect" that judges the gospel to be not only true but good as well. This persuasion of the practical intellect apprehends the gospel setting forth God as the highest good and salvation in Christ as the way to that good and "determines and leads [the will] after itself" (*Inst.* 15.8.7 [2:613-14]). Thus, whereas Thomas holds (1) that the desire of the rightly disposed will for the good of a certain end leads the practical intellect to form a knowledge of how to pursue that end (*prudentia*) and (2) that faith is a practical *habitus* only with respect to its object ultimately eliciting love (so *ST* IIaIIae.4.2 ad 3 [45]), Turretin holds (1) that the practical intellect apprehends a given object as good and determines the will to form a desire for that object (cf. *Inst.* 10.2.4, 7 [1:729-31]) and (2) that faith is by definition a *habitus* of not just the speculative but also the practical intellect, in which case it might be described as a *prudentia* (knowledge of right action) as in Keckermann, *Systema s.s. theologiae* 1.1 (2:68). But the difference ought not to be exaggerated. Turretin is not denying a "speculative" apprehension of the truth of the gospel; he is simply locating the intellect's apprehension of its object as good in what he calls the practical intellect. And he clearly affirms that the practical intellect as the faculty apprehending the good needs a new moral habit given by the Spirit to judge rightly about the good and lead the will to adhere to it (*Inst.* 15.4.13, 23, 30-31, 49 [2:569-70, 573-74, 578-79, 589]).

[59]*The Works of Stephen Charnock*, vol. 4, *A Discourse on the Knowledge of God* (Edinburgh: Banner of Truth, 1985), 16-22. Like Owen (e.g., *Pneumatologia*, in *The Works of John Owen*, vol. 4, *The*

Nevertheless, though faith is a habit of believing founded on testimony rather than a strictly scientific habit, it is still a habit of knowing resident in the intellect in that it apprehends what is real. Faith is a cognitive habit, *cognitio* being a Latin term applicable to many kinds of knowing.[60] It includes and begins with *notitia*: basic apprehension and understanding of its object that is not obtained ratiocinatively by inference from other known truths.[61] In addition, though it does not proceed from ordinary self-evident principles like *scientia*, faith is a firm habit of knowing that, unlike mere opinion, does not stand in fear of an opposing position that might have stronger support in its favor. Indeed, Christian faith is even firmer than *scientia* because it rests not on fallible human reasoning but on the testimony of God himself given in Holy Scripture.[62] Furthermore, with its

---

Work of the Holy Spirit, ed. William H. Goold [Edinburgh: Banner of Truth, 1967], 6.2.8 [225]), Charnock concedes that someone without saving faith can "notionally" apprehend the propositions of Scripture, but he denies that an unbeliever has a "real" apprehension of or union with the spiritual things (*res*) signified by them.

[60]It is, according to Polanus, *cognitio obscura* (*Syntagma* 2.9 [144]). In older epistemological accounts, knowledge is sometimes discussed as *scientia* in particular, with *scientia* broadly encompassing both *intellectus* (νοῦς) and *scientia* in the proper sense of demonstrative knowledge of conclusions (ἐπιστήμη) (e.g., Thomas Aquinas, *In libros Posteriorum Analyticorum expositio*, in *Opera Omnia*, vol. 1, Leonine ed. [Rome: ex Typographia Polyglotta, 1882] 1.3.7.6 [165]; Polanus, *Syntagma* 2.18 [156]). When knowledge is taken in the particular sense of a *habitus sciendi* (not merely a *habitus cognoscendi*), it involves firsthand apprehension or discursive reasoning, rendering it distinct from faith as a *habitus credendi*. Even so, faith too is still a mental, cognitive habit. This is the approach of Turretin (*Inst.* 1.6.2-3 [1:20-21]), where he says that there are three kinds of mental habits (*sciendi, credendi, opinandi*) and takes *scientia* to encompass the five Aristotelian intellectual habits. Turretin comments that the three kinds of mental habits have three respective kinds of assent (the *actus sciendi, credendi*, and *opinandi*), which have three respective bases: "certain and firm reason," "testimony," and "merely probable reason."

[61]In making use of some traditional epistemological language here, it may be worth pointing out that the meaning of some terms varies depending on context and will sometimes overlap with the range of meaning of other terms. *Intellectus* can be taken as a power or "part" of the soul that properly apprehends common natures, universals, and necessary things and moves by ratiocination from premises to conclusions, or it can be taken as a particular habit in this power of the soul by which one knows such things. There is some overlap here with the semantic domain of *notitia*, which is basic apprehension that may involve (1) intuitive awareness of things that are currently present to the knowing subject and not apprehended via another object or (2) abstract awareness of an object that is not currently present to the knowing subject (see Polanus, *Syntagma* 1.8 [11]). Under the first meaning of *notitia* there is a distinction between *notitia sensualis* (awareness by sense perception) and *notitia intellectualis* (mental awareness as distinct from sense perception) (Polanus, *Syntagma* 2.18 [156]).

[62]Compare Thomas, *ST* IIaIIae.4.8 (52-53), where he argues that faith is more certain than the five intellectual habits with respect to its cause (i.e., divine truth) if not with respect to the constitution of the knowing subject (since, unlike the objects of the ordinary habits, the objects of faith exceed our intellect and are not evident or visible to our intellect). Similarly, Polanus states that

principles in place (the basic articles of Christian doctrine revealed by God and apprehended by faith), the believing intellect reasons from these principles to their necessary implications, which means that in this respect acquired theology is *scientia*.[63]

Yet faith's knowledge and the enlargement of it in acquired theology is wisdom as well, for it pertains to the first and highest principle (the triune God), in light of whom all other things can be rightly estimated and all the activities of life can be directed toward their proper end (i.e., the glory of God). There is an important resonance between theology as *sapientia* and the vision of the wise person in Proverbs, who is able by wisdom to judge rightly and order their affairs toward good and godly ends.[64] The discipline of acquired theology is thus not merely theoretical but practical also.[65] In its theoretical or speculative aspect it certainly does apprehend its object under

---

faith is *notitia* made certain by reference to another, while *scientia* is *notitia* "evidently perceived by the natural light of the intellect" (*Syntagma* 2.18 [156]).

[63]See Thomas, *De Trin.* 2.2 esp. ad 7 (95-97), where the first principle of theological science is God's own intellect and the "proximate" principle is the faith present in the believer's intellect. Cf. also *ST* Ia.1.2 (8-9); Turretin, *Inst.* 1.8.3, 6, 7, 11-14 (1:27-30); 9.4, 13, (1:34-35); 10.1-2, 4, 6, 8, 16 (1:36-39). In Thomas's discussion of this, the principles from which reasoning begins are known by the habit of *intellectus* (or in *sacra doctrina*, by faith). The reasoning itself is a movement of the intellect from principles to conclusions. The conclusions are then known by the habit of *scientia* (*ST* Ia.79.8-9 [274-76]). For theology, it is significant that even that which is contingent will have in it "something of necessity" according to which reason may move toward scientific conclusions (*ST* Ia.86.3 [351]).

[64]On the nature of wisdom as a habit of the intellect by which it knows the highest principles, compare Augustine, *De Trinitate* 12.21-25 (1:375-80); Thomas, *ST* Ia.79.9 (275-76). Thomas maintains that there is a "judgment" that is wrought by mere knowledge (*cognitio*) and of which an unspiritual person is capable, while there is a "judgment" wrought by the wisdom that is given to the spiritual person by God and includes an inclination to follow right judgments (*ST* Ia.1.6 ad 3 [18]).

[65]A number of the Reformed orthodox affirm that Christian theology is both theoretical and practical (e.g., Polanus, *Syntagma* 1.13 [15]; Turretin, *Inst.* 1.7 [1:22-26]; Mastricht, *TPT* 1.1.48 [15]). Such authors consciously seek to integrate a theoretical approach associated with Thomism and a practical approach associated with Scotism. In *ST* Thomas argues that *sacra doctrina* is more theoretical or ("speculative") than practical because it is primarily about God rather than human actions and because human actions are ultimately ordered to our coming to a beatific knowledge of God (Ia.1.4 [14]). Denying that faith is a "speculative habit," Scotus identifies theology as a practical science (*Opera omnia*, vols. 1-4, *Ordinatio*, ed. P. Carolo Balić [Vatican City: Typis Polyglottis Vaticanis, 1950–1956], prol., pars 5, q. 1, esp. nn. 314-55 [1:207-31]). Among the Reformed, the practical emphasis is particularly strong in Keckermann, *Systema s.s. theologiae* 1.1 (2:67-69) and Ames, *Medulla* 1.9-13 (2-3), for example. But authors like Polanus, Turretin, and Mastricht (rightly, I think) take it to be the case that (1) a number of the articles of faith are not about human action; (2) even the articles that are not about human action incite contemplation, enjoyment, and worship; and (3) contemplation, enjoyment, and worship in a certain way count as actions (even if they are somewhat different

the aspect of truth, which is primarily God and not things to be done by humanity. Yet faith apprehends God as the end and beatitude of the human race, which incites operation: reverent, loving contemplation and worship of God and moral action within the horizon of human relationships. In a sense, joyful contemplation of God is itself an action. Furthermore, as it hastens our transformation into the image of Christ (so 2 Cor 3:18), it gives rise to all sorts of other actions in the Christian life.

With the transformative influence of theological contemplation in mind, we are in a position to affirm the theoretical or "speculative" dimension of theology and explore in earnest the properly theological part of Christian doctrine (*theologia*), without worrying that we are indulging in idle curiosity. At the same time, we are in a position to recognize the ultimately practical nature of the doctrine of God since theology proper draws us into the love of God, reforms our desires, and drives us to orient all things to God. For the present work on Christian *theologia*, this means that careful and even technical study of God in his aseity and transcendence of the economy can and should be a spiritual exercise, informing communion with God and, derivatively, all the other elements of discipleship. To continue setting the stage for subsequent description of the practice of *theologia*, it is important next to take into account the serious limitations that mark our knowledge of God in himself and the development of that knowledge in redemptive history.

THE LIMITATIONS AND DEVELOPMENT OF THEOLOGICAL KNOWLEDGE

The limitations of theological knowledge. If our pursuit of knowledge of God *in se* is to correspond to God's own account of theological knowledge given to us in Scripture, we will have to consider Scripture's teaching on the limitations and historical development of such knowledge. Though the Bible conveys that God is *a se* and reveals truth that pertains to God in his transcendence of the economy, it also stresses God's incomprehensibility to human creatures. In so doing, it takes away any foothold that the practice of *theologia* (mistakenly conceived) might appear to grant to a triumphalist epistemology. The book of Job makes clear that God exceeds even our

---

from other human actions treated in theology). This enables them to identify theology as both theoretical and practical.

profoundest thoughts of him. Job speaks of God's creating the world, marking out the proper boundaries for the heavens and the waters, and so forth. Yet,

> These are indeed but the outskirts of his ways;
>> and how small a whisper do we hear of him!
>> But the thunder of his power who can understand? (Job 26:14 NRSV)

At the end of Job, after God's staggering inquiry about the work of creation and the unfathomable movements of the universe, Job simply acknowledges,

> I am of small account; what shall I answer you?
>> I lay my hand on my mouth. (Job 40:4 NRSV)

As the psalmist says, YHWH is "unsearchable" in his greatness (Ps 145:3). He is immeasurable and incomparable, everlasting and full of inexhaustible knowledge and power (Is 40:12-31).

To be sure, the prologue of John's Gospel announces that God has decisively revealed himself in the incarnation: "And the Word became flesh and dwelt among us, and we have seen his glory, glory as of the only Son of the Father, full of grace and truth" (Jn 1:14). No one has ever seen God, but God the Son, being "in the bosom of the Father," has made him known (Jn 1:18). Later in the Gospel when Philip asks to see the Father, Jesus responds that whoever has seen him has seen the Father. For he is in the Father, and the Father is in him (Jn 14:6-11). Indeed, following the ascension of Jesus, the Holy Spirit, who knows the very mind and "deep things" of God, has come to reveal the divine mind to us (1 Cor 2:10-11). Nevertheless, even after the incarnation and Pentecost it remains the case that we do not comprehend God or know God as God knows himself. For these epochal events do not constitute the being of God or reduce the infinite plenitude of God. Nor do they render the created intellect adequate to that plenitude. After unfolding the plan of salvation for Jews and Gentiles in Christ, Paul exalts the unfathomable wisdom of God (Rom 11:33-36). It is not that God is duplicitously holding back some features of his plan that will be accomplished apart from the summing up of all things in Christ (Eph 1:10). Rather, the divine wisdom taken as an essential perfection of God by which he has ordained and will accomplish these things remains beyond human comprehension. The same is true of the "surpassing greatness" of God's power that exceeds human imagination (Eph 1:19; 3:20) and of the love of God, which "surpasses knowledge" (Eph 3:19). In fact, although he had seen the risen Christ on the way to Damascus, Paul can still write that God dwells in "unapproachable light" and in a sense neither has been nor can be seen by human beings (1 Tim 6:16).

The finitude of our theology is ineradicable and marks all our discourse about God. In this regard, John of Damascus confesses that human creatures do not know what the essence of God is or exactly how one divine person is begotten or proceeds from another. According to John, we cannot speak of God "beyond the things divinely explained . . . and revealed to us by the divine words of the old and new covenant."[66] Thomas notes that to comprehend something is to know it perfectly, to know it in the "perfect mode in which it is knowable." The created, finite intellect thus cannot comprehend God's infinite essence. Even in receiving the "light of glory" (a capacity for knowing God that is given by God himself) in greater degrees, our intellect remains finite and does not comprehend God's essence.[67] John Duns Scotus writes that the knowledge of God under the aspect of his essence pertains in the strictest sense to what he calls *theologia in se* (the knowledge of God that God alone possesses) rather than *theologia nostra*, which is the knowledge of God accommodated to the capacity of our intellect.[68]

To explicate the distinction and relationship between God's infinite knowledge and our finite knowledge, the Reformed orthodox use the language of "archetypal" and "ecyptal" theology. Archetypal theology is a designation of God's own knowledge of himself, which is uncreated, essential (not existing in God as a mere habit added to his essence), absolute, infinite, and present all at once (not in successive stages). Though it is incommunicable in its infinite fullness, it is the exemplar and prototype of the ectypal theology that finite human beings can have. Ecyptal theology is a designation of the limited copy of God's self-knowledge that human beings can have by God's gracious communication of theological knowledge to us. This knowledge is created, habitual (given as a habit inhering in the creature's essential constitution), finite,

---

[66]John of Damascus, *Exp. fid.* 1.2 (9-10).

[67]Thomas, *ST* Ia.12.7 (127-28).

[68]Scotus, *Ordinatio*, prol., pars 3, q. 3, nn. 141, 168 (1:95-96, 110-12). Scotus takes the object of *theologia nostra* to be God as infinite being, which he believes is the most perfect concept of God possible for us in this life (cf. *Ordinatio* 1.3.1, nn. 58-60 [3:40-42], where he applies this to natural knowledge of God in particular).

and developed over time. The Reformed orthodox often distinguish further between *theologia ectypa in se* (the fullness of theological understanding communicable to creatures from the storehouse of God's own knowledge) and *theologia ectypa in subjecto* (the theological understanding actually communicated to and present in diverse human subjects in varying degrees). To clarify that our knowledge of God is entirely dependent on and inadequate to God's knowledge, the Reformed point out that ecyptal theology and archetypal theology are not equals within a genus of knowledge. Ectypal theology is derived from archetypal theology and only analogically one with it.[69]

The development of theological knowledge. The biblical narrative also locates our finite knowledge of God within a developing history of revelation. Our theological understanding in this age is situated between the greater limitations experienced by Old Testament saints and the culmination of knowledge shared by the blessed in heaven, who see God face-to-face. According to the Old Testament, creation from its very beginning has communicated knowledge of its Creator to humankind (e.g., Ps 8:1; 19:1-6), but this natural mode of divine revelation was never intended to be sufficient for humanity apart from God's verbal, supernatural revelation. Though it is not discussed in detail in Genesis, prior to the fall Adam and Eve enjoyed a communion with God in which God spoke to them and "walked" among them in the garden (Gen 2:15-25; cf. Gen 3:8). After the fall, God still spoke intermittently to various biblical figures like Cain and Noah regarding his will for human life, but it is in his interaction with the family of Abraham that God begins a much more focused and expansive revelation of himself and his will for humanity. When God works through Moses to deliver Israel from Egypt and lead them to Mount Sinai, he gives the people his name, YHWH, and makes clear its significance in a fresh and fuller sense (Ex 6:2-8). Yet he keeps the people from approaching him on the holy mountain (Ex 19:1-25). He speaks directly to Moses, but his revelation takes written form for the people (Ex 33:7-11; 34:1-3). In Jeremiah, God promises a "new covenant" in which "all of them will know me, from the least of them to the greatest" (Jer 31:34).

The earthly ministry of the Son, who establishes that new covenant, becomes the climax of God's self-revelation (Mt 11:25-27; Jn 1:18; 14:7-11). But

---

[69]See Franciscus Junius, *De vera theologia* (Leiden, 1594), 3-5 (28-45); 17 (139-58); Polanus, *Syntagma* 1.3-4 (2-3).

together with the Father the Son sends his Spirit to expound and apply this revelation over time through the apostolic ministry (Jn 14:26; 15:26; 16:12-14; 1 Cor 2:10-16). As the apostles labor to fulfill the Great Commission, they sometimes draw on God's natural revelation to proclaim the gospel as the word of the true God and Creator of the world, already in some limited sense known to the Gentiles (Acts 14:15-17; 17:24-31; Rom 1:18-32). However, it is evident from the apostolic writings that God's revelation in the new covenant far surpasses both natural revelation and the supernatural revelation of the Old Testament. Paul conceives of this in terms of the veil that Moses wore after speaking with God so that the Israelites could not see the radiance of his face in Exodus 34:33-35. For Paul, under the ministry of the new covenant, believers no longer look at or through a veil but "with unveiled faces behold the glory of the Lord" (2 Cor 3:7-18). Paul also writes of the "mystery" of God's manifold purpose for redemptive history being revealed at last in the gospel of Christ (Rom 16:25; Eph 1:9; 3:1-13; Col 1:26-27; 2:2; 4:3). Yet this sort of mystery is revealed rather than "solved." Its transcendent and inexhaustible character remains even after it is made known.[70] Similarly, Peter writes that the prophets of old and the angels too longed to look into the great salvation wrought by Christ (1 Pet 1:10-12). But there is more to come. In a sense God's salvation is still yet to be revealed (1 Pet 1:5). The church believes and hopes without yet "seeing" Christ (1 Pet 1:8).

The language of "seeing" is prominent in scriptural characterizations of the saints' eschatological blessedness. The object of the saints' vision is ultimately not just the benefits of Christ or the beauty of the new creation but, above all, the triune God himself. In 1 Corinthians 13 Paul reminds us of the partial nature of our current theological knowledge (1 Cor 13:9). We now know in part and "see through a mirror dimly," but in the eschaton we will see "face-to-face" and know just as we are known (1 Cor 13:12). According to John, when Christ returns, we will be made like him, for then "we will see him as he is" (1 Jn 3:2). According to the book of Revelation, the throne of God and of the Lamb will be in the midst of the heavenly city with God's servants: "They will see his face and his name will be on their foreheads" (Rev 22:3-4). The Bible presents this vision of God as the outcome of a holy

---

[70]Steven D. Boyer and Christopher A. Hall, *The Mystery of God: Theology for Knowing the Unknowable* (Grand Rapids: Baker Academic, 2012), 5-7.

life. "Blessed are the pure in heart, for they shall see God" (Mt 5:8). "Pursue . . .
the holiness without which no one will see the Lord" (Heb 12:14). While our
own works of holiness are never the basis on which we are accepted by God,
a life of increasing holiness—usually slow, always affected by sin, and
marked by repentance—is the necessary pathway along which we proceed
to the sight and city of God (cf. Ps 11:7; Rom 8:13-14; 2 Pet 1:10-11).[71] For it
would be incongruous for anyone to come into the presence of the holy God
and his holy city without a trajectory of life tending, however feebly, toward
holiness (Ps 5:5-6; 24:3-4; Rev 21:27). Owen pointedly comments, "No man
shall ever behold the glory of Christ by sight hereafter, who doth not in some
measure behold it by faith here in this world. Grace is a necessary preparation for glory, and faith for sight. Where the subject (the soul) is not previously seasoned with grace and faith, it is not capable of glory or vision."[72]
Without a pursuit of such holiness, one may know truths about God, but
one will not know God in the full scriptural sense either now or in the
coming age. For in the scriptural sense the knowledge of God involves what
Thomas calls an "affective knowledge" in which human persons delight in
God.[73] Owen makes a similar point in stating that "evangelical" knowledge
includes a fear of God marked by a holiness that gives rise to obedience.[74]

In light of this biblical teaching, we have to commend the practice of
theologia without flattening out the soteriology and eschatology of the Bible.
I would suggest it will be helpful to take into account the way Thomas and
some of the Reformed orthodox handle this matter, not least because
mapping out some of their work here will help prepare for the tasks in
chapters two and three. Cast in terms of an "assimilation" of the created
intellect to God, Thomas's alertness to the epistemological turning points of
the economy is exemplary. As Thomas phrases it, if human persons are to
attain to their ultimate end and happiness (knowing the triune God), they

---

[71]See Owen's helpful exegesis of Rom 8:13-14 in *Of the Mortification of Sin in Believers*, in *The Works of John Owen*, vol. 6, *Temptation and Sin*, ed. William H. Goold (Edinburgh: Banner of Truth, 1967), 6.

[72]John Owen, *Meditations and Discourses on the Glory of Christ*, in *The Works of John Owen*, vol. 1, *The Glory of Christ*, ed. William H. Goold (Edinburgh: Banner of Truth, 1965), 288.

[73]Thomas Aquinas, *Super Evangelium S. Ioannis lectura*, ed. P. Raphael Cai, 5th ed. (Turin-Rome: Marietti, 1952), 17.6.2.2265 (426).

[74]John Owen, *The Works of John Owen*, vol. 17, *Theologoumena pantodapa*, ed. William H. Goold (Edinburgh: T&T Clark, 1862), 6.6.6-7, 15 (441, 445).

must undergo a "participation" and "assimilation" or union of the human intellect to God.[75] According to the biblical story line, the conformity of the intellect to God takes place in different ways in the different states of human existence. We know God by his works or effects in both nature and grace. Our intellect is informed by a "similitude" or likeness of God present in his outward effects, whether those effects are from creation and providence or from salvific grace.[76] Those effects are "inadequate" to their divine cause in that they do not formally share or reflect the infinite fullness that God is. Nevertheless, they do teach us that God exists and tell us something of the perfection that God has in himself (wisdom, love, power, and so forth).[77] In seeking natural knowledge of God, humanity ascends from created effects to a very limited knowledge of God as their principle (as in Rom 1:20). The intellect identifies common perfections, discerns causal connections among its objects, and can ultimately arrive at an incomplete knowledge of God the Creator.[78] This natural knowledge includes some apprehension of what belongs to God himself, but in an important sense it is not a knowledge of God *in se* since it apprehends God indirectly as the principle of other things. Apprehending God *in se* (without the practice of thinking from effect to cause) belongs more properly to the study of Scripture and sacred doctrine, which offers more direct description of God and enables us to view created things in light of God.[79]

In grace, Thomas notes, humanity believes the supernatural revelation of Scripture that descends from God and exceeds our natural knowledge. We

---

[75]Thomas, *De Trin.* 3.1 corp. (107-8); *SCG* 4.1 (3); *ST* Ia.12.1 corp. and ad 4 (114-15); 12.2 corp. (117); 12.9 ad 1 (132); 12.11 ad 4 (135).

[76]Thomas notes that the human soul with its intellective power is united to the body and maintains that the intellect depends on the body's sense perception of outward objects in order to gain knowledge. Thus, in Thomas's anthropology, of which his epistemology is a subtopic, the proper object of the human intellect is that which is common or universal in corporeal things, not incorporeal things (*ST* Ia.85.1 [330-32]).

[77]Thomas Aquinas, *Scriptum super libros Sententiarum*, ed. R. P. Mandonnet (Paris: Lethielleux, 1929), 1.2.1.2-3 (1:63-72); *De Trin.* 1.2 corp. and ad 3 and 4 (84-85); 2.2 corp. and ad 2 (95, 96); *ST* Ia.1.7 ad 1 (19); 4.2 (51-52); 12.2 (116-17); 12.3 corp. and ad 3 (119-20); 12.11 (134-35); 12.12 corp. and ad 1 and 2 (136); 88.2 ad 4 (367). It is not that God and his effects occupy a common genus or are distinct only by quantity or degrees. Rather, God is the principle of those effects and communicates to them an analogical likeness of himself (*De Trin.* 1.2 ad 3 and 4 [85]).

[78]Thomas, *De Trin.* 2.2 corp. (95); 6.3 corp. (167); 6.4 ad 1 and 2 (171); *ST* Ia.12.4 (120-21); 12.13 corp. (137); 88.2-3 (367-68); 84.7 ad 3 (326).

[79]Thomas, *De Trin.* 5.4 corp. (154).

receive the "light of faith." Instead of proactively reasoning toward the truth of God we receive God's own testimony about himself. Though faith is not a matter of seeing God firsthand or demonstrating what is true about him, it is a kind of knowledge (*cognitio*). Furthermore, while the description of God in supernatural revelation draws from created effects and similitudes of God, the faith that receives such revelation imperfectly partakes of and anticipates *in via* the immediate knowledge of the beatific vision. For even if it is not entirely independent of the pedagogy of created similitudes, Christian faith does apprehend God without requiring discursive reasoning. Indeed, Christian theological knowledge is wisdom, a habit of understanding higher things and then lower things in light of those higher things. It follows what Thomas calls the "way of judgment" (*via iudicii*) that evaluates temporal things by eternal things, rather than the "way of discovery" (*via inventionis*) that proceeds from temporal things to limited understanding of eternal things.[80]

In glory, Thomas writes, humanity knows God by God's essence. The fact that we will see God "face-to-face" entails that it is characteristic of the knowledge of the blessed in heaven (*in patria*) that they see God without the mediation of created effects. Insofar as God remains incorporeal and invisible, this knowing or seeing is not a corporeal vision. It is an intellectual vision wrought by a "light of glory," a divine gift elevating our intellect and enabling us to know God intuitively. The intellectual vision or intuitive knowledge of God requires an assimilation or union of the human intellect with God's essence, but our natural intellect does not have the capacity to apprehend God without created media. For this reason, God grants a new power of understanding above our natural powers to strengthen and perfect the intellect, enabling us to see God in his essence. The gift of this capacity of understanding is described in terms of the biblical metaphor of light that appears, for example, in Revelation 21:23, where the heavenly city is illumined not by sun or moon but by the glory of God. The augmenting of the natural intellect with a "supernatural" or "superadded" disposition is designated "illumination,"

---

[80]Thomas, *De Trin.* 1.2 corp. (85); 2.2 corp. (95); 3.1 (107-8); 6.3 corp. (167); 6.4 ad 3 (171); *SCG* 4.1 (3-4); *ST* Ia.1.6 (17-18); 1.7 ad 1 (19); 12.13 ad 3 (138); 79.8 corp. (274); 86.2 ad 1 (349-50). The *via iudicii* is a way of knowing that in fact corresponds to the order of being, a point that will come up in the reflection on the incarnation in chap. 3.

and the disposition itself is called "light." By this new light the intellect can apprehend and receive God's essence. In apprehending and receiving God's essence, the intellect is actuated by and assimilated to God's essence. In this way, for Thomas, the human person becomes "deiform."[81] Nevertheless, even *in patria* we do not comprehend all that God is.[82] The light of glory is a supernatural gift in that it exceeds the capacities of our original constitution, but it does not remove human finitude or lead to a conflation of our knowledge with God's infinite knowledge.

Recipients and developers of the resources of Thomas and other medieval lights, the early Reformed authors can help to stimulate and order our thinking about the eschatological development of the knowledge of God. The Reformed often expand the archetypal-ectypal distinction by identifying different kinds of ectypal theology that play a role in the unfolding of redemptive history. In so doing, they direct us toward the hope of glory and at the same time remind us of our limits in this life. First, there is the "theology of union," which Christ possesses according to his human nature. The name of this theology is taken from the fact that Christ has his human knowledge in the unity of his person and thus in union with the divine nature and knowledge that he has from eternity. Christ's human knowledge is created and finite in accord with its genuinely human character (Mk 13:32; Lk 2:40, 52), but since Christ has the Spirit in a unique way he has a fullness of human knowledge that surpasses all other creatures. From the well of his own knowledge of God Christ gives us knowledge of God.[83]

---

[81]Thomas, *De Trin.* 1.2 ad 4 (85); 2.2 corp. (95); 6.4 ad 3 (171); *SCG* 3.37-40 (92-99); 4.1 (4); *ST* Ia.12.2 corp. and ad 3 (116-17); 12.4 corp. (121); 12.5 corp. and ad 2 (123); 12.6 corp. (126); 12.11 ad 4 (135). Whereas the knowledge of God *in via* involves the intellect engaging an image ("phantasm") in a sense organ (or in the imagination) generated by encountering a (corporeal) created effect that is itself but an image of God, the intuitive knowledge of the blessed bypasses this and apprehends God directly.

[82]Thomas, *ST* Ia.12.1 ad 1 and 3 (115); 86.2 ad 1 (350).

[83]See Junius, *De vera theologia* 6 (45-52); Polanus, *Syntagma* 1.7 (11); Turretin, *Inst.* 1.2.6 (1:5); 13.12-13 (2:377-83). Within the early Reformed tradition Girolamo Zanchi argued that Christ's human soul would be ignorant of some things in itself but not in union with his divinity. For Zanchi, Christ's human soul knows all that is decreed by God (if not all that is possible) and enjoys the blessed vision of God in his earthly ministry (*De Incarnatione Filii Dei* [Heidelberg, 1593], 2.2 [119-20]; 11 [362-78]). Zanchi's position aligns with that of Thomas, which is defended by several contemporary Roman Catholic authors (see Simon Francis Gaine, *Did the Savior See the Father? Christ, Salvation and the Vision of God* [London: Bloomsbury, 2015]; Thomas Joseph White, "The Voluntary Action of the Earthly Christ and the Necessity of the Beatific Vision," *The Thomist* 69 [2005]: 497-53).

Second, there is the "theology of revelation," which we possess now in varying degrees while we walk by faith and not yet by sight (2 Cor 5:7). The Reformed also call this a "theology of pilgrims" (*theologia viatorum*) or "our theology" (*theologia nostra*). As the name suggests, this theological knowledge is communicated to us by the media of God's revelation, not by a direct sight of God. If it is called a "seeing," it is but an obscure and imperfect seeing that can grow to some degree in this life but awaits completion in the life to come.[84] Sometimes biblical figures are said to see God on earth, but this is a matter of seeing symbolically under a visible sign commandeered by God, like Jacob when he wrestled with God under the appearance of a man (Gen 32:30).[85] This theology *in via* glimpses God "from the back" (*ex dorso*) (Ex 33:23) rather than beholding God's face directly.[86] It requires the senses, for faith comes by hearing (Rom 10:14).[87] The theology of pilgrims can be considered as it is offered in its fullness in God's revelation (*theologia viatorum absolute dicta*) or as it is present in varying degrees in particular human persons (*theologia viatorum secundum quid*).[88] Various Reformed authors add that the theology of pilgrims includes both natural theology and supernatural theology (or "revealed" theology in the stricter sense). These are not two different species of pilgrim theology but two distinct modes of it,[89] whose distinction and relation will be discussed in chapter two. Furthermore, to distill the historical development that takes place in Scripture within the supernatural mode of pilgrim theology, there is a distinction between "old pilgrim theology" (*theologia viatorum vetus*), before the incarnation, and "new pilgrim theology" (*theologia viatorum nova*), after it.[90] Some Reformed works also trace out the unfolding of revelation and theological understanding in detail through the covenants and epochs of biblical history, anticipating at least some modern conceptions of the discipline of "biblical theology."[91]

Third, in light of Scripture's promise that we will see God face-to-face in the age to come, there is the theology of the blessed (*theologia beatorum*),

---

[84]Junius, *De vera theologia* 8 (62).

[85]Turretin, *Inst.* 20.8.11 (3:683); Mastricht, *TPT* 2.3.5 (77).

[86]Mastricht, *TPT* 2.2.18 (70).

[87]Turretin, *Inst.* 20.8.4 (3:681).

[88]Polanus, *Syntagma* 1.12-13 (12-13).

[89]Turretin, *Inst.* 1.2.8 (1:5); Mastricht, *TPT* 2.2.18 (70).

[90]So Polanus, *Syntagma* 1.12 (12).

[91]E.g., Owen, *Theologoumena pantodapa*; Mastricht, *TPT* 8.1-3 (963-1190).

which glorified saints possess in heaven and in the new creation. It is procured and given to God's elect by Christ the Savior, the one who died and was raised to lead many sons and daughters to glory (Heb 2:9-10).[92] The description of this knowledge of God underscores the limits of our pilgrim theology. The theology of the blessed is communicated to the human person by (intellectual) vision, not revelation. Franciscus Junius speaks quite strongly about the relative perfection of this mode of theology: the supernatural grace that transfers the human person to the blessed condition will not only "vindicate" or "absorb" our present partial knowledge but also "abolish" it. The theology of the blessed is an abiding knowledge of just spirits perfected in heaven (Heb 12:23) and free of the need for scientific movement from principles to conclusions.[93] Polanus designates this theology a *notitia intuitiva*, a direct apprehension of God as present and not merely perceived by some other object or by ratiocination.[94]

Turretin expresses the theological progression of redemptive history in terms of a "threefold school of God, of nature, grace, and glory."[95] Given God's spirituality and invisibility, the beatific vision in the "school of glory" is a decidedly intellectual (rather than "sensitive" or corporeal) seeing, though, according to Turretin, the glory of the soul's happiness will "redound to the body."[96] At the same time, Turretin does note that we will behold God with our eyes in that we will see God the Son according to his visible human nature (so Job 19:25-27).[97] Furthermore, the blessedness of the saints is not merely intellectual but involves the will too and integrates vision, love, and joy (Mt 25:21; Jn 17:26; 1 Cor 13:13; 1 Jn 4:16).[98] To establish the intellective dimension of our beatitude, God provides a supernatural

---

[92]Junius, *De vera theologia* 7 (53-58); Polanus, *Syntagma* 1.8 (11).

[93]Junius, *De vera theologia* 7 (54, 56); 10 (77).

[94]Polanus, *Syntagma* 1.8 (11).

[95]Turretin, *Inst.* 1.2.10 (1:6).

[96]Turretin, *Inst.* 20.8.3-4 (3:681). Turretin comments that the beatific vision involves the senses only "consequently."

[97]Turretin, *Inst.* 20.8.11 (3:683). Cf. Mastricht, *TPT* 2.2.18 (70); 3.5 (77). Note also that Thomas affirms an involvement of the body in the beatific state (*ST* Ia.12.3 ad 1-2 [119-20]).

[98]Turretin, *Inst.* 20.8.5-7 (3:681-82). Here Turretin is consciously drawing together the intellectual emphasis associated with Thomas and the volitional emphasis associated with Scotus. In his anthropology Turretin makes clear that he believes the practical judgment of the intellect leads the activity of the will (10.2.4, 7 [1:729-31]), but he refuses to separate them in his account of the beatific state. Compare Mastricht, *TPT* 8.4.10 (1197).

light or elevation of the faculty of knowing. This is not a removal of the intellect's finitude but a heightening of its power by degree. The beatific vision is thus intuitive and apprehensive without being comprehensive. It is a creaturely knowing that remains "inadequate" to God's being and knowing.[99]

Turretin also acknowledges that there is debate about whether the blessed will see God's essence immediately or see some effulgence of God. He concludes that it is more probable that we will not see God's essence immediately since God dwells in unapproachable light (1 Tim 6:16) and since there is no *proportio* or traversable distance between the finite (the human intellect) and the infinite (the divine essence).[100] Though I find Turretin's description of the beatific vision to be helpful on the whole, there may be a tension between his acknowledgment of the intuitive and direct nature of this knowledge and his claim that we will likely see God by a shining forth of his glory.[101] In addition, it may be that while there is no *proportio* between the finite and the infinite, the affirmation of the merely apprehensive mode of this knowledge will already secure this point without our having to reject the notion that we will behold God's essence.[102] Exploring Reformed teaching on the beatific vision also brings us to the question of whether or to what extent the content of the vision centers on Christ the God-man. As noted above, Turretin and Mastricht affirm that we will see Christ with our glorified physical sight in the age to come. Owen, however, takes this further. He argues in light of the principle that the finite cannot comprehend the infinite that "the blessed and blessing sight which we shall have of God will be always 'in the face of Jesus Christ.' Therein will that manifestation of the glory of God, in his infinite perfections, and all their blessed operations, so shine into our souls, as shall immediately fill us with peace, rest, and glory."[103]

---

[99]Turretin, *Inst.* 20.8.8, 12-14 (3:682-84). Thus the language of sight is employed not to indicate comprehension but the intuitive and clearer mode of knowing (*Inst.* 20.8.14 [3:684]). Cf. Mastricht, *TPT* 2.2.18 (70).

[100]Turretin, *Inst.* 20.8.14 (3:684). Compare Mastricht, *TPT* 2.3.5-7 (77-78), whose reticence to affirm a direct and positive knowledge of God's essence is shaped by his aversion to the Cartesian claim that "infinite thought" is a formally adequate representation of God's essence.

[101]Cf. Polanus, *Syntagma* 1.5 (3).

[102]Cf. Thomas, *ST* Ia.12.1 ad 4 (115).

[103]Owen, *Meditations*, 292-93. Owen in fact denies that there will be any intuitive knowledge of God in heaven (*Christologia*, in *Glory of Christ*, 65-67). Suzanne McDonald has emphasized that this sets Owen apart from authors like Thomas and Turretin ("Beholding the Glory of God in the Face of Jesus Christ: John Owen and the 'Reforming' of the Beatific Vision," in *The Ashgate*

This issue will come up in chapter three, in discussion of the role of Christology in the knowledge of God.

In this section I have sought to take seriously the Bible's description of the limitations and incompleteness of our knowledge of God. If we fail to take this seriously, we risk overestimating the prospects of Christian *theologia* in this life. Having thereby risked disillusionment, we may then miss out on the real benefits of the practice of *theologia* rightly framed by the biblical narrative. But once we have acknowledged our limitations we open ourselves up to questions about whether discourse about God in himself may lead to doubts or even despair in this life. If there is a God whom we should know "in himself" but cannot comprehend or see directly *in via*, do we truly know God? What if this incomprehensible God sometimes "hides himself" (Is 45:15)? What if he turns out to be fundamentally other than the God we presently think we know? Such questions should prompt us to consider what sort of theological resources will be required for a spiritually sound and edifying practice of pilgrim *theologia*.

PILGRIM *THEOLOGIA* AND THE HIDDENNESS OF GOD[104]

Luther and Barth. Though it is not possible to cover all the intricacies of his doctrine of God here, Martin Luther speaks about such matters in striking ways.[105] For Luther, God's "bare essence" (*nuda essentia, nuda*

Research Companion to John Owen's Theology, ed. Kelly M. Kapic and Mark Jones [New York: Routledge, 2012], 142-58). See also the response of Simon Francis Gaine arguing that Thomas's doctrine of the beatific vision remains stronger than Owen's ("Thomas Aquinas and John Owen on the Beatific Vision: A Reply to Suzanne McDonald," *New Blackfriars* 97 [2016]: 432-46). For a recent study of the beatific vision incorporating a variety of Christian thinkers, see Hans Boersma, *Seeing God: The Beatific Vision in the Christian Tradition* (Grand Rapids: Eerdmans, 2018).

[104]The theme of the hiddenness of God has received significant attention in recent times. It is a multifaceted topic with both intellectual and existential difficulties. Though my discussion here will focus on Luther and Barth, see Adam Green and Eleonore Stump, eds., *Hidden Divinity and Religious Belief* (Cambridge: Cambridge University Press, 2016), and Michael C. Rea, *The Hiddenness of God* (Oxford: Oxford University Press, 2018) on the various ways in which God's hiddenness is being discussed today.

[105]For reflection on Luther's notion of the *Deus absconditus*, see, e.g., Paul Althaus, *The Theology of Martin Luther*, trans. Robert C. Schultz (Philadelphia: Fortress, 1966), 20-24; B. A. Gerrish, "'To the Unknown God': Luther and Calvin on the Hiddenness of God," *Journal of Religion* 53 (1973): 263-92; Steven D. Paulsen, "Luther on the Hidden God," *Word and World* 19 (1999): 363-71; Robert Kolb, *Martin Luther: Confessor of the Faith* (Oxford: Oxford University Press, 2009), 56-58; and Kolb, *Bound Choice, Election, and Wittenberg Theological Method: From Martin Luther to the Formula of Concord* (Minneapolis: Fortress, 2017), 32-38. See also John

divinitas) is incomprehensible to us. To seek to understand God's "bare majesty" is like trying to ascend to heaven "without ladders" and leads to death. Indeed, seeking to understand it characterizes and fosters heretical thinking like that of Arius.[106] "God must be left in his majesty and in his own nature, for we have nothing to do with him in this way, nor has he willed that we should have to do with him in this way."[107] God in his majesty is the "hidden God" (*Deus absconditus*), especially with regard to his secret will to predestine some to salvation and others to damnation. For example, the statement in Ezekiel that God does not desire the death of a sinner applies not to the hidden will of God that ordains all things but to the "preached and offered mercy of God" revealed in the gospel. The *Deus absconditus* in his majesty "works life, death and all things in all." He has not "defined himself by his word but has kept himself free over all things." By contrast, the "pious God" (*Deus pius*) or "preached God" (*Deus praedicatus*) does not will the death of sinners.[108]

In the *Heidelberg Disputation*, Luther expresses the importance of avoiding speculation about the majestic and hidden God by distinguishing between a *theologia gloriae* and *theologia crucis*.[109] Luther stresses that those who seek the "invisible things of God" apart from the cross and suffering are blinded by a love of power and glory. In their pursuit of wisdom, they become fools (Rom 1:20-23). They become averse to God's gracious way of leading us out of our sin and hubris, namely, by God's "hiding" himself in the lowliness of the cross. Although the wisdom that perceives the majesty of God may not be evil per se, arrogant sinners abuse this wisdom and do not benefit from it apart from the cross. Though the law of God is good in

---

Dillenberger, *God Hidden and Revealed: The Interpretation of Luther's* Deus Absconditus *and Its Significance for Religious Thought* (Philadelphia: Muhlenberg, 1953); Wolf Krötke, *Gottes Klarheiten: Eine Neuinterpretation der Lehre von Gottes "Eigenschaften"* (Tübingen: Mohr Siebeck, 2001), 42-59.

[106]Martin Luther, *Genesisvorlesung (cap. 1-17)*, in *Martin Luthers Werke: Kritische Gesamtausgabe* (Weimar: Böhlau, 1911), 42:10-12.

[107]Martin Luther, *De servo arbitrio*, in *D. Martin Luthers Werke: Kritische Gesamtausgabe* (Weimar: Böhlau, 1908), 18:685.

[108]Luther, *De servo arbitrio*, 18:631-32, 684-85.

[109]For commonly cited studies, see, e.g., Althaus, *Theology of Martin Luther*, 25-34; Walther von Loewenich, *Luther's Theology of the Cross*, trans. Herbert J. A. Bouman (Minneapolis: Augsburg, 1976); Alister E. McGrath, *Luther's Theology of the Cross: Martin Luther's Theological Breakthrough* (Oxford: Blackwell, 1985). See also Barth, *CD* I/1, 169-79.

itself, sinners approaching God apart from the grace and knowledge given by the cross will not obtain righteousness and life by that law. The true theologian will therefore seek to know God in the crucified Christ.[110] For Luther, then, seeking to know the "bare essence" or "bare majesty" of the *Deus absconditus* is tied to a presumptuous neglect of our sin and an attempt to approach God on the basis of law and good works rather than the gospel of Christ. Pursuit of the *Deus absconditus* in a *theologia gloriae* thus appears to be an ethical and soteriological problem.

Accordingly, Luther insists that we are to seek and know not the *Deus absconditus* in his bare majesty but rather the *Deus revelatus* made known under various "wrappings" (*involuera*), "faces" (*facies*) or "masks" (*larva*) that he takes up in redemptive history, like the pillar of cloud and fire in the wilderness or the mercy seat in the tabernacle.[111] We are to seek God as he is "clothed and set forth in his own word, in which he offers himself to us."[112] But meeting God under these "masks" does not eliminate the believer's awareness of the *Deus absconditus*. In addressing this problem, Luther advises us not to pry into the mysteries of God's hiddenness. We can assign no cause or reason (*ratio*) to the divine will, though Luther does say that God himself is not evil. Indeed, if God's will had a cause or reason, it would no longer be the *divine* will. Instead, we must revere and adore the mystery of God's hiddenness and secret will. In Luther's reasoning, this approach is rooted in scriptural texts like Romans 9:19-20 that underscore the sovereign freedom and inscrutability of God (cf. Rom 11:33; 1 Tim 6:16). God has granted us an awareness of his hiddenness and inscrutability in order to elicit faith on our part. Luther states that it is the "highest degree of faith" to believe God is merciful when he saves so few and damns so many and to believe God is just when "he makes us necessarily damnable by his own will." "If I could comprehend by any reason how this God is merciful and just who shows so much wrath and iniquity, there would be no work in faith."[113]

---

[110]Martin Luther, *Disputatio Heidelbergae habita*, in *D. Martin Luthers Werke: Kritische Gesamtausgabe* (Weimar: Böhlau, 1883), 1:353-54, 356-57, 362-63.

[111]Luther, *Genesisvorlesung*, 9-11; *D. Martin Luthers Werke: Kritische Gesamtausgabe, In epistolam S. Pauli ad Galatas commentarius* (Weimar: Böhlau, 1911), 40/1:173-74.

[112]Luther, *De servo arbitrio*, 18:685.

[113]Luther, *De servo arbitrio*, 18:632, 633, 684, 686, 709, 711, 712.

It is not difficult to anticipate pastoral problems that might arise from this conception of the "hidden God." In his assessment of Luther, Michael Gillespie remarks that Luther calls us to "avert our eyes from the truth" and

> accept and live the scriptural story, even though we know that there is a deeper and more all-encompassing story that calls into question the story we live by. There is thus good reason to doubt that this path can satisfy human beings, for it cannot eliminate the uncertainty and anxiety evoked by the monstrously incomprehensible God who stands behind the stage and is responsible for everything that occurs on it.[114]

Even a sympathetic interpreter of Luther like Carl Trueman calls Luther's discussion of God's hidden will "brutal." Trueman asks, "If God's revelation can itself be contradicted and is thus not the final word, then where is assurance to be found?"[115]

Barth's treatment of God's hiddenness also can alert us to questions that may arise for pilgrim practitioners of Christian *theologia*. On the one hand, the concept of divine hiddenness has a positive role in Barth's understanding of our knowledge of God. Barth uses this concept to contend that we do not have an innate power by which we can know God. Rather, we depend on God graciously to reveal himself and put to flight "idolatrous pictures" of God. God's hiddenness is shorthand for God's incomprehensibility and for our need of God in his prevenience to grant us knowledge of himself. Revelation is itself a "veiling" of God in that it underscores God's hiddenness and our noetic dependence on God. But revelation is also an "unveiling" in that it enables us to become active in having authentically human knowledge of God.[116] Thus, on the other hand, Barth will ultimately reject any notion of a *Deus absconditus* that might conflict with the *Deus revelatus*. He is concerned that Luther posited a God of "arbitrary power" that would correspond "only accidentally to God's real work" and undermine the believer's confidence in God.[117]

Barth's desire to secure the agreement between God *in se* and God *pro nobis* appears at various points in the *Church Dogmatics*. He has this goal

---

[114]Michael Allen Gillespie, *The Theological Origins of Modernity* (Chicago: University of Chicago Press, 2008), 157.
[115]Carl R. Trueman, *Grace Alone: Salvation as a Gift of God* (Grand Rapids: Zondervan, 2017), 107-8.
[116]Barth, *CD* II/1, 181-204.
[117]Barth, *CD* II/1, 541-42.

in mind when he chastises authors like Thomas and the Reformed orthodox for their accounts of divine simplicity. According to Barth, their articulation of God's simplicity implies that the attributes by which we know God pertain to the economy only and not to the being of God himself. The attributes of holiness, power, and so on are "rooted, not in the *essentia* as such, but . . . only in its relation to us and our relations to it." They "lose their reality" before God's *nuda essentia* and "can have no further value than that of a concession, a purely secondary truth." But if this is the case,

> faith in Him can never free itself from ultimate suspicion in face of a Lord whom it pleases to yield Himself to us in this or that form in a kind of sport, without disclosing Himself in reality, without giving us any pledge that in Himself He is not perhaps quite other, and so radically different from the forms of glory in the game played with us that it is not worth while perhaps to take part in this game or this economy.[118]

The issue appears again in Barth's treatment of election and the divine decree. He criticizes the Lutheran and Reformed orthodox for positing a *decretum absolutum* in which God's "absolute freedom" and "good pleasure" determine the content of God's plan, prior to any "christological reference." For Barth, the "christological reference" (election "in Christ" as in Eph 1:4) is left "standing in the air," with no ontological basis. This opens up an "abyss of uncertainty." For, though the early Protestants insisted that believers should not focus on the *decretum absolutum* for pastoral purposes, there is no real reason to discourage speculation about it: "the decisive word for salvation is spoken at that hidden and secret place." Barth's solution is to assert that the "electing God" is none other than Jesus Christ himself.[119] This carries over into his statements about the *Logos asarkos*, where he argues that there is a liability in the doctrine of the *extra Calvinisticum* in that it can lead us to "fatal speculation" about a God whom "we think we can know elsewhere, and whose divine being we think we can define from elsewhere than in and from the contemplation of His presence and activity as the Word made flesh."[120]

---

[118]Barth, *CD* II/1, 324-25, 329.
[119]Barth, *CD* II/2, 63-67.
[120]Barth, *CD* IV/1, 181.

After Barth, a number of authors have taken these lines of thinking further.[121] Robert Jenson, for example, has sought to eliminate the possibility of
speculation about God in himself by asserting that God is identified *with*
and not just *by* historical events like the exodus or the resurrection.
Otherwise "the revealing events would be our clues *to* God, but would not
be God," leaving a "space . . . between revelation and deity itself . . . across
which we make our idolatrous projections."[122] Alternatively, Bruce
McCormack has sought to close down any "metaphysical gap" between God
in se and God *pro nobis* by arguing that there is no God *in se* that is not in
his very deity also God *pro nobis*. For, according to McCormack, God
constitutes his very being by his eternal decision for the incarnation.[123]

Response. How should we respond to these concerns and seek to clarify
that pilgrim discourse about God in his transcendence of the economy does
not lead us into a theological or existential crisis before a *Deus absconditus*?
I offer nine points in response in support of the claim that the practice of
theologia actually circumvents rather than induces such a crisis.

1. It will be wise to untangle certain things that could be mistakenly
lumped together in light of Luther's statements about the *Deus absconditus*
and *theologia gloriae*. In this volume, I am not identifying God *in se* with a
Deus absconditus. In fact, we are actually emphasizing that God *in se* is
known to us, albeit in a limited manner that presently stands under the
"not-yet" of biblical eschatology. Nor are we identifying knowledge of God
in se with a knowledge of God pursued by metaphysics and natural theology
over against the incarnation. One of the claims of this book is that human
knowledge of God *in se* arises from natural and supernatural revelation

---

[121]A survey of relevant figures can be found in George Hunsinger, *Evangelical, Catholic, and Reformed: Doctrinal Essays on Barth and Related Themes* (Grand Rapids: Eerdmans, 2015), 21-31.

[122]Robert Jenson, *Systematic Theology*, vol. 1, *The Triune God* (Oxford: Oxford University Press,
1997), 59.

[123]See, e.g., Bruce L. McCormack, "Grace and Being," in *The Cambridge Companion to Karl Barth*,
ed. John Webster (Cambridge: Cambridge University Press, 2000), 92-110; McCormack, "Elec-
tion and the Trinity: Theses in Response to George Hunsinger," *SJT* 63 (2010): 203-24;
McCormack, "The Lord and Giver of Life: A 'Barthian' Defense of the Filioque," in *Rethinking
Trinitarian Theology: Disputed Questions and Contemporary Issues in Trinitarian Theology*, ed.
Robert J. Wozniak and Giulio Maspero (London: T&T Clark, 2012), 230-53; McCormack,
"Processions and Missions: A Point of Convergence Between Thomas Aquinas and Karl Barth,"
in *Thomas Aquinas and Karl Barth: An Unofficial Catholic-Protestant Dialogue*, ed. Bruce L.
McCormack and Thomas Joseph White (Grand Rapids: Eerdmans, 2013), 99-126.

working together to lead us into communion with the triune God. Moreover, the practice of *theologia* is not a Pelagian approach to God conducted on the basis of our law-keeping rather than the work of Christ. As noted above in the discussion of the object of theology, I am advocating a contemplation of God *in se* from within the covenant of grace where sinners are cleansed by the blood of Christ. What I am advocating in this study is therefore not encumbered by the moral and soteriological problems that Luther associates with the *theologia gloriae*.[124]

2. Given that God is already complete *in se* without reference to creatures and their history, God *in se* and God *pro nobis* are the same God. There is no *Deus absconditus* ontologically distinct from the *Deus revelatus*. Such might be the case if God had to endeavor to actualize himself through his dealings with creatures, but Scripture's teaching on God's aseity eliminates precisely this problem. God just is the God that he is, without having to become something or obtain something from us. This means that the God active in the economy is not an enlarged or attenuated version of an original and unknown deity. He is the same triune God he eternally was. He can be no other. Of course, God remains incomprehensible to finite creatures. Much of his providential activity is unknown to us in this life, but the fact that we do not comprehend God or all the details of God's plan will hardly entail that we have to do with a *Deus revelatus* and a *Deus absconditus* as two distinct Gods. It follows that we should not fear that behind what Luther calls the "pious" God there is a God of caprice and iniquity. To borrow language from John of Damascus, the only true God is αὐτοαγαθότης, goodness itself beyond which there is no other fount of goodness.[125]

3. The identity of God *in se* and God *pro nobis* may be fleshed out with the help of the doctrine of divine simplicity. If God is complete *a se*, then his attributes are not "parts" or qualities that must be added to his essence. They are nothing other than his eternal essence itself considered under diverse aspects. To be God is to be good, omnipotent, and so forth.[126] In light of this, when God

---

[124]This is an important point in view of contemporary tendencies to conflate the claim about God being complete in himself with the notion of a *Deus absconditus* who might be in conflict with the God revealed in Christ (see, e.g., Krötke, *Gottes Klarheiten*, 58).

[125]John of Damascus, *Exp. fid.* 1.8 (18).

[126]So Augustine, *De Trinitate* 7.4 (1:260); Thomas, *ST* Ia.3.6 (45-46). See also Polanus: "God is immense and great without quantity, good, true and just without quality, act without motion,

reveals his many attributes to us in the economy, he is genuinely revealing *himself*. He is not giving us arbitrary constructs that keep us from knowing him as he truly is. Thomas points out that the *ratio* of each divine attribute (what the intellect apprehends about God as signified by the attribute of wisdom, goodness, and so on) is present in God himself and would be present even if God had never created the world. The descriptive content of the attributes corresponds to, is rendered true by, the "full and multifaceted [*omnimoda*] perfection of God."[127] In other words, divine attributes like wisdom and goodness signify God's substance or essence itself, albeit incompletely according to the mode of our limited understanding that always begins from knowledge of created, composite things.[128] Although Thomas contends that we do not know God's quiddity or the fullness of God's essence, he aptly affirms that our knowledge of whether God is (*an est*) must involve at least some imperfect or "indistinct" (*confusa*) knowledge of what God is (*quid est*). According to Thomas, this knowledge is obtained by "negation, causality, and excess": denying of God imperfections that do not apply to him, discerning that the perfections of created effects are present in God, predicating those perfections of him in a manner that reflects his plenitude and preeminence.[129]

The Reformed author Johann Alsted makes the point in an alternative way by clarifying that even if we do not have a comprehensive "quidditative knowledge" (*cognitio quidditativa*) we do have an apprehensive "knowledge of quiddity" (*cognitio quidditatis*) in which "some quidditative predicate is known, although the whole quiddity is not known."[130] We know what

---

merciful without passion, everywhere present without position, first and newest without time and outside time, Lord of all things without habit or accession" (*Syntagma* 2.7 [141]).

[127]Thomas, *Sententiarum* 1.2.1.2-3 (63-72).

[128]E.g., Thomas Aquinas, *Opera omnia*, vol. 22/1.2, *Quaestiones disputatae de veritate*, Leonine ed. (Rome: ad Sanctae Sabinae, 1970), 2.1 (37-42); Thomas, *De potentia*, in *Quaestiones disputatae*, ed. P. Bazzi et al., 10th ed. (Rome-Turin: Marietti, 1965), 7.5 (2:198-200); *ST* Ia.13.2 (141-42); 13.4 (144-45); 13.6 (150); 13.12 (164-65).

[129]Thomas, *De Trin.* 6.3 (167-68). Cf. *ST* Ia.13.1 corp. (139). On Thomas's discussion of "quidditative knowledge," see John Wippel, *The Metaphysical Thought of Thomas Aquinas: From Finite Being to Uncreated Being* (Washington, DC: Catholic University of America Press, 2000), 501-43. See also the qualifications attending the negation of quidditative knowledge in later Thomism discussed in Igor Agostini, "The Knowledge of God's *Quid Sit* in Dominican Theology: From Saint Thomas to Ferrariensis," *American Catholic Philosophical Quarterly* 93 (2019): 191-210.

[130]Johann Alsted, *Theologia naturalis* (Frankfurt, 1615), 1.9 (80-81). Compare the similar statement of Mastricht: "By the attributes we think not so much the essence of God itself as something about the essence [*de essentia*]" (*TPT* 2.3.3 [77]).

pertains to God's own being, though we do not know God's being in its entirety and without mentally prescinding one aspect of God's perfection at a time under the representation of our inadequate creaturely terms.[131] Put differently, the attributes are the divine essence in the "identical sense" (i.e., the thing signified by each is really identical with the essence) if not the "formal sense" (i.e., the definition or formal content of each attribute used by us does not capture all that God is).[132] In view of this, Barth did not need to fear that a doctrine of divine simplicity like that of Thomas and the Reformed orthodox would create a rift between God *in se* and God *pro nobis*, the former being an unknown God whose revelation is but a "game" or "sport." Instead, the doctrine of divine simplicity helps us at this point by illuminating how the God who meets us in the economy is the eternal God who transcends the economy. The attributes given to us in the economy are descriptions of God's own essence and, indeed, really are God's own essence. We therefore apprehend God *in se* truly, if not completely. We can therefore be confident that in the Christian practice of *theologia* we are contemplating God himself, not a façade that must eventually give way before a more ultimate *Deus absconditus*.

4. Our knowledge of God in himself is not merely a negative knowledge, a knowing what God is not. It certainly does include an understanding of what ought not to be predicated of God, but it includes positive knowledge as well. In other words, we are not merely denying a few things and then

---

[131]So Turretin, *Inst.* 3.5.3-4 (1:205-6). We thus speak of God's attributes as if they were "properties" or qualities added to God's essence when in fact they are just the essence itself diversely represented (Turretin, *Inst.* 3.5.2 [1:205]).

[132]Mastricht, *TPT* 2.3.19, 21 (81, 82). See also 2.5.5 (93) on the inadequacy of our concepts. The Reformed sometimes (though not always) state that the attributes concern *qualis* (of what sort) God is and that by which he is distinguished from false gods, rather than *quid* (what) God is (for diverse approaches, see Girolamo Zanchi, *De natura Dei* 1.1 [1-3]; 7 [14-17]; Ames, *Medulla* 1.4.31-38, 50-51 [12-14]; Turretin, *Inst.* 3.1.2 [1:85]; 24.8 [1:289]; Mastricht, *TPT* 2.3.7 [78]). But see Zanchi, for example, for an explanation that the attributes do not signify *qualitates* added to the essence but merely the essence itself. The denial that the attributes express God's quiddity is just intended to clarify that they do not represent the essence in its infinite fullness. The Reformed also sometimes ramify the attributes into various taxa, with some concerning the essence itself (e.g., "spiritual," "simple," "eternal") without respect to what would be, in creatures, particular faculties, virtues, or operations (e.g., knowledge, wisdom, will, justice, mercy) (see Polanus, *Syntagma* 2.7 [141]; Ames, *Medulla* 1.4.27, 32-66 [11-15]; Mastricht, *TPT* 2.3.3 [77]; 3.16 [80-81]; 5.7, 9 [94-95]). But such ramifications arise from heuristic patterns in our mode of understanding, not because attributes like justice and goodness have an accidental or secondary status in God.

seeking to put out of mind whatever it is that God might be in himself. Rather, we are considering what God positively is in himself, even if this knowledge is marked by significant creaturely limitations. Indeed, negative knowledge itself implies having some positive knowledge. Thomas puts this quite strongly in his criticism of Maimonides's reticence to say that the divine attributes positively signify God's substance: "The understanding of negation is always founded in some affirmation." Thomas can make a strong statement about the negative knowledge of God: for example, "It is the height of human knowledge of God that it knows itself not to know God." But this is not because we lack positive knowledge of God altogether. It is simply because "God exceeds everything that we understand about him."[133] Similarly, Mastricht rightly notes that it is easier for us to understand what God is not than what he is, but he goes on to identify a variety of positive essential attributes and observes that even negative attributes like independence and infinity imply something positive about God: "While in their own formal signification they remove imperfections from God, nevertheless in the material concept they involve positive perfections."[134] If we refuse a needless separation of the apophatic and the kataphatic in the practice of *theologia*, we position ourselves to honor both the infinite, ineffable plenitude of God and also the knowability of God that keeps us from having to worry about the prospect of a capricious *Deus absconditus*.

5. In an important sense, the action of God in the economy is nothing other than the divine essence itself, which is a point that will require some explanation and will be developed more in chapter five. If God is complete *a se* and already fully active in triune fellowship, then his outward action does not require a transition from passive potency to actuality. His outward action does not necessitate an augmenting of his prevenient actuality.

---

[133]Thomas, *De potentia* 7.5 corp. and ad 14 (198, 200). Against the interpretation of someone like Krötke, *Gottesklarheiten*, 5, I take Thomas's strongly apophatic statements like this (and in *SCG* 1.14 [40]; *ST* Ia.3 prol. [35]) to be balanced out by such considerations (cf. *ST* Ia.13.12 [164-65]). On the kataphatic element in Thomas's doctrine of God, see Gregory P. Rocca, *Speaking the Incomprehensible God: Thomas Aquinas on the Interplay of Positive and Negative Theology* (Washington, DC: Catholic University of America Press, 2004), 27-48, 297-313; Rudi te Velde, *Aquinas on God: The "Divine Science" of the "Summa Theologiae"* (repr., New York: Routledge, 2016), 72-77; Thomas Joseph White, *Wisdom in the Face of Modernity: A Study in Thomistic Natural Theology*, Faith and Reason: Studies in Catholic Theology and Philosophy, 2nd ed. (Ave Maria, FL: Sapientia, 2016), 255-74.

[134]Mastricht, *TPT* 2.3.3 (77); 5.7-8 (94).

Positively, the actuality of God's outward action just is that of God's own essence. Thomas, for example, affirms this in discussing the act of creation: "Creation actively signified signifies divine action, which is [God's] essence with a relation to the creature."[135] The divine power is thus not a "principle of operating" (as if there were unfulfilled potential in God awaiting actualization) but only a "principle of effect" (since the term "power" designates that by which one can effect something).[136]

The Reformed pick up on this approach to divine action. Though he clarifies that a transient divine act (one whose object is external to God) is not identical to God insofar as it is not so much "in" but "from" God, Turretin affirms that "to be," "to be able," and "to operate" (*esse, posse, operari*) are identical in God. For "God does not act as creatures by something superadded to his own nature, but by his own essence determining itself in the manner of a vital principle to this or that." No free action of God is God "absolutely," but it can be called "God observed relatively, in the manner of a vital act determining itself spontaneously." The act of the divine decree in particular is "nothing other than God himself decreeing."[137]

Mastricht likewise states that in creatures one can distinguish between the agent operating, the faculty or power of operating, the operation itself, and the thing operated (i.e., the resultant work). For "in the operations of creatures, both the one operating and the work pass over from potency to act, insofar as the one operating, which before was merely able to operate, now operates in act, and the work, which before was merely able to be produced, now is produced in act." But since God is simple and wholly active already, God's operation is nothing but "the essence operating." Put differently, "Divine operation encompasses two things: the active essence of God and the relation of it to the work."[138] In this connection, Alsted points out that God's action is called "motion" in only an analogical sense, for though God does produce outward effects, he does not undergo a transition from idleness to activity.[139] The real identity of operation and essence—or, more precisely, the real identity of the actuality of God's operation and the

---

[135]Thomas, *ST* Ia.45.3 ad 1 (467).

[136]Thomas, *De potentia* 1.1 ad 1 (9).

[137]Turretin, *Inst.* 4.1.15 (1:344).

[138]Mastricht, *TPT* 3.1.4 (273).

[139]Alsted, *Theologia naturalis* 1.16 (140-42, 147-51); 17 (171, 174).

actuality of God's essence—reinforces the sameness of God *in se* and God *pro nobis*. God meets us in the economy without having to transition from a state of idleness to a state of activity. In coming to us he does not change himself but only applies his essential actuality to accomplish his works *ad extra*. In this way, the completeness and pure actuality of God allay concerns one might have about a *Deus absconditus* that could have (or might still) become contrary to the good God revealed in Christ.

6. In accordance with God's essential completeness and simplicity, Scripture alerts us to God's ethical simplicity and his simplicity in his outward action.[140] Paul teaches us that when God fulfills his promises in Christ he does not deliver a "Yes" to us and then withdraw that "Yes" with a "No." All God's promises are "Yes" in Christ (2 Cor 1:19-20). For that reason, the apostle himself did not vacillate in his commitment to those to whom he ministered (2 Cor 1:17-18). He and his companions conducted themselves in the "simplicity [ἁπλότητι] and sincerity of God" (2 Cor 1:12). Elsewhere Paul writes that God "cannot deny himself" and therefore remains faithful to us even when we are faithless (2 Tim 2:13). James urges us to appeal to God for wisdom in the face of trials because God "gives to all simply [ἁπλῶς] and without reproaching" (Jas 1:5). The one seeking wisdom from God must imitate God's simplicity by not being "double-souled and unstable in all his [or her] ways" (Jas 1:8). God is never the author of sin because he "cannot be tempted by evil" (Jas 1:13). Rather, he is the immutably good giver of all gifts (Jas 1:17). First John makes a similar point: "God is light, and in him there is no darkness at all" (1 Jn 1:5). In sum, God cannot contradict himself or act with evil motives. He is constant in justice, goodness, and mercy and acts accordingly in relation to us. Thus, as we contemplate and speak of God *in se* with the recognition that we do not see him directly in this life, we may rest assured that God is greater than but never contrary to the content of his revelation.[141]

7. Although this is not a book about predestination, it is worth addressing it briefly given Luther's and Barth's statements about predestination in

---

[140]In speaking of an "ethical simplicity," I am not seeking to drive a wedge between God's goodness and faithfulness, on the one hand, and God's essence, on the other. That would in fact be an implicit denial of simplicity. The use of the phrase "ethical simplicity" here arises merely from the fact that in our finitude we conceive of justice, goodness, and faithfulness as moral attributes that must be predicated of God's essence.

[141]Cf. Polanus, *Syntagma* 2.8 (143); Mastricht, *TPT* 2.6.27 (106).

relation to the *Deus absconditus*. In light of God's aseity and self-sufficiency, predestination is not a divine act undertaken in order for God to complete himself. This ought to be a point of agreement for "Calvinists" and "Arminians." God does not need to save some and damn others in order to satisfy himself. He does not have to actualize himself by setting up evil as a counterpart and then striving to overcome it. The reprobate are therefore not a means of divine self-enhancement. As Charnock observes, God's "essential glory" can "suffer no detriment" or be "interrupted." Of course, Charnock points out, the outward "manifestation" of God's glory may be "obscured."[142] Thus God does glorify himself in that he outwardly manifests and vindicates his perfection before creatures. Nevertheless, it is creatures who gain something by God securing justice and mercy in the world. Further, while God will manifest his justice in reprobation, he would never condemn the innocent (e.g., Gen 18:25; Jas 1:13). The object of divine predestination (whether election or reprobation) is, I would contend, humanity as fallen and sinful.[143] In addition, though God does allow some to persist in sin, he does not pass over those who trust in Christ. The way to know whether one is engaging in the practice of *theologia* under the saving grace of God is simply to trust in God's Son. Over against the tenor of some of Luther's statements, those who will believe are called "many" and an innumerable multitude (Rom 5:15-21; Heb 2:10; Rev 7:9-10). The reputedly austere Canons of Dort express this by declaring that "the Reformed churches detest with their whole heart" the suggestion that God has "created and predestined the greatest part of the world to damnation by a bare and pure choice of will, without any respect or knowledge of sin."[144]

8. With such theological considerations in place, one can heed calls to avoid theological speculation (in the negative sense of that term) without having to wonder whether there might be a capricious *Deus absconditus* lurking behind the *Deus revelatus*. Convinced that God's aseity and transcendence are good news for us creatures, a spiritually sound approach to discourse about God *in se* can focus on what God has

---

[142]Charnock, *Discourse on the Knowledge of God*, 5.

[143]See the infralapsarian position advanced by Turretin, *Inst.* 4.9 (1:376-86). See also Duby, "Election, Actuality and Divine Freedom," 332-36.

[144]Conclusion, translated from Philip Schaff, *The Creeds of Christendom*, vol. 3, *The Evangelical Protestant Creeds with Translations*, 4th ed. (New York: Harper and Brothers, 1877), 576.

revealed about himself and cheerfully obey the biblical command to mortify excessive curiosity. "The secret things belong to the LORD our God, but the things that are revealed belong to us and to our children forever" (Deut 29:29 ESV). Perhaps Psalm 131 is the theologian's best medicine when he or she needs to rest in what we do know and avoid despair over what we do not:

> O LORD, my heart is not lifted up;
>   my eyes are not raised too high;
> I do not occupy myself with things
>   too great and too marvelous for me.
> But I have calmed and quieted my soul,
>   like a weaned child with its mother;
>   like a weaned child is my soul within me.
> O Israel, hope in the LORD
>   from this time forth and forevermore. (Ps 131:1-3 ESV)

Believers pondering the fullness and transcendence of God may find themselves susceptible to what the seventeenth-century Reformed minister Wilhelmus à Brakel calls a "spiritual darkness" that arises from "exerting our spiritual vision too much to comprehend the perfections and incomprehensible mysteries of God" in an attempt to have an "immediate beholding" of him like that of the blessed. According to Brakel, when we "depart from the light of God's Word and cannot attain to an immediate beholding, our corrupt intellect and irrational reason will come to the foreground, deceiving the soul with false contemplations whereby true light is increasingly obscured." In such circumstances, Brakel wisely counsels his readers to "keep a low profile":

> Refrain from exerting yourself to have views of lofty matters, but cling humbly to the Word of God. Whenever you read it and whenever a passage of Scripture occurs to you, then think: "This is the truth." If it is a promise, esteem it as such, and do not lift your heart above that Word. At the same time, reflect upon God Himself, but do not go beyond what His Word describes him to be. . . . Thus, by keeping a low profile, you will come to the light in the most prudent manner.[145]

---

[145]Wilhelmus à Brakel, *The Christian's Reasonable Service*, ed. Joel Beeke, trans. Bartel Elshout (Grand Rapids: Reformation Heritage, 1992), 4:261-62.

The drift of this sort of approach is quite different from Luther's (at least in the way it appears in Luther's response to Erasmus on predestination). Whereas Luther, in his characteristic bluntness, exhorts us to believe that God is merciful despite there being a *Deus absconditus* who may in some sense falsify the revealed goodness of God, Brakel issues a needed call to believe that what Scripture teaches about God himself is true and then to be content with that.

9. Finally, pilgrim *theologia* should not be undertaken without partici-pation in the worship of the church. Public worship is vital to the spiritual and intellectual health of the theologian because it calls us out of our own mental strivings. In it God addresses us from without through his ordained servants and alerts us afresh to his rich goodness. The elements of the liturgy reorient us to revealed truths that we may be apt to neglect by native dispo-sition or by circumstance. The singing of psalms, hymns, and spiritual songs may remind us that God's incomprehensibility is an occasion for reverence, wonder, and joy. The confession of sin may remind us of our truly unde-serving state and of the humbling fact that we live and have communion with God at all only by his free grace. The pastoral prayers and supplications about the needs of the congregation and the world may remind us that suf-fering is a dire problem to be eradicated by the self-sufficient God who transcends the economy, not something to be glamorized by our locating God within the broken system of the world and implying that God had to become God by overcoming it.

Conclusion

The first main section of this chapter considered scriptural teaching on the knowledge of God, particularly its purpose of facilitating communion with God and its inclusion of knowledge of God in himself, not just God's outward works. In light of this and the scriptural command to grow in such knowledge, the next section discussed God as the primary object of theology as a discursive discipline. In an attempt to ensure that the biblical purpose of the knowledge of God would determine the character of theology proper as a discursive undertaking, that section also examined the nature or "genus" of theological knowledge, noting its points of commonality with various mental habits and suggesting that discourse about God *in se* is theoretical and practical. In order to offer a biblically faithful and realistic portrayal of human discourse about God in himself, the following section took into account the serious limitations that we face in contemplating the incomprehensible God, especially in our present state en route to the beatific vision. To address potential concerns that might arise from the acknowledgment that we do not comprehend or see God directly, the last section discussed the problem of the "hidden God" found in authors like Luther and Barth and made a case that the practice of pilgrim *theologia* can be a source of assurance *in via* and can be carried out in a spiritually healthy manner. In the next chapter we will turn to the question of whether there is a natural knowledge of God that still has a positive role to play in our anticipation of the blessed vision.

TWO

"Preparation for the School of Grace"
The Role of Natural Theology

IN LIGHT OF THE PURPOSE of human knowledge of God laid out in the previous chapter, we come now to a closer consideration of the role of natural theology in grounding the Christian practice of *theologia*. In contemporary discussion the mention of natural theology inevitably calls to mind a number of pressing questions. Is natural theology bound up with an overly optimistic or naive view of the mind of sinful humanity? Can reflection on the created order actually yield knowledge of God himself, or will it tell us only about what creatures assume God must be? Is natural theology a decidedly Roman Catholic endeavor, or can one be a consistent Protestant and embrace some positive role for natural theology?

This chapter will present a case for seeing natural theology or natural knowledge of God as a positive element in the divine economy in which God leads us rational creatures to our appointed end: the blessedness of loving fellowship with himself.[1] In order to make this case, I will look more closely at scriptural teaching regarding the origin, content, purpose, and limitations of natural knowledge of God. After this, I will describe and assess some ways in which major figures in the Christian tradition have built

---

[1]Throughout this volume I have favored the phrase "natural revelation" over "general revelation." The former focuses more on the manner in which knowledge of God is communicated, while the latter focuses more on the extent of its availability. The two phrases typically signify the same thing and can be viewed as complementary. I have favored the former not out of any disdain for the latter but only because it seems to me that the manner of communication is basic to the extent of availability and because the Reformed orthodox treatments appropriated below often express the distinction in terms of natural versus supernatural theology.

on this scriptural foundation and conceived of the nature and purpose of the natural knowledge of God. Next I will take into account some challenges to be addressed in articulating the positive place of that knowledge in grounding Christian *theologia*. After giving a response to these challenges, the conclusion of the chapter will draw together the scriptural teaching and the insights gleaned from engagement with historical figures in an effort to express in an integrative manner the role of natural theology in the pursuit of knowledge of God *in se*.

SCRIPTURE AND THE NATURAL KNOWLEDGE OF GOD

That God is not a God of confusion but a God of order and peace (1 Cor 14:33) is displayed well in the creation account of Genesis 1. Though the earth was initially "without form," the Spirit of God hovers over the deep to make it ready for life and order. As the narrative develops, God makes and separates, assigning to each creature its proper role in the universe and observing that it is "good." He creates things "according to their kind," providing order and structure for both animate and inanimate parts of his world. The various features of creation obey his command and take up their designated places at his word ("And it was so"), which entails at least that creation exhibits a "conformity to the divine will."[2] Indeed, the canon of Scripture teaches that the created order expresses not only the divine will but also the divine wisdom and goodness. In creating the world, God exercises his wisdom, which is like a "craftsman" producing his work according to plan (Prov 8:30; cf. Ps 104:24; Jer 10:12).[3] God exercises his communicative goodness in creation and in his ongoing providential activity. Instead of creating human beings to escape the burden of laboring for sustenance like the pagan gods, the God of Holy Scripture generously provides for the needs of humanity, even as he calls on them to participate in the work of cultivating the potential of the natural world (Gen 1:28-29).[4] As the psalmist says, God gives water and provides dwelling places for his creatures, satisfying the earth's needs (Ps 104:10-13, 16-18, 27-30). He

---

[2]Gordon J. Wenham, *Genesis 1–15* (Waco, TX: Word, 1987), 38.

[3]On which, see Tremper Longman III, *Proverbs*, Baker Commentary on the Old Testament Wisdom and Psalms (Grand Rapids: Baker Academic, 2006), 196.

[4]John H. Walton, *Ancient Near Eastern Thought and the Old Testament: Introducing the Conceptual World of the Hebrew Bible* (Grand Rapids: Baker Academic, 2006), 215.

provides grass and plants, wine to gladden us, and bread to strengthen us (Ps 104:14-15). He governs the seasons and ensures each day that the sun knows its time to set (Ps 104:19-20). "YHWH is good to all. His mercy is on all he has made" (Ps 145:9). All his works give thanks to him. All look to him to provide their food in season. He opens his hand to satisfy the desire of all living things (Ps 145:10, 15-16).

Jesus confirms this in Matthew's Gospel where he teaches that the Father causes the sun to rise and the rain to fall on both the just and the unjust, which is the reason believers must show kindness even to enemies and thereby imitate the Father's perfection (Mt 5:43-48). Paul appeals to this divine generosity in his preaching at Lystra in Acts. After being wrongly exalted for the healing of a disabled man, Paul emphasizes that he and Barnabas are simply messengers of good news from God, according to which the people should turn to the living God who made heaven and earth and the sea and all that is in them. Though this God in previous generations largely allowed the Gentiles to go their own way, he did not leave himself "without witness," for he "does good," giving rain and crops and satisfying the hearts of the nations with food and joy (Acts 14:15-17). Although Paul's appeal to God's oversight of the natural order does not initially dispel the crowd's desire to exalt him and Barnabas, it is clear that the gospel ultimately took root in Lystra (Acts 14:18, 21; 16:1-2).

A few Old and New Testament texts warrant more attention in this section. Certain psalms are among the classic texts dealing with the natural knowledge of God. In Psalm 8, David stands in awe of the majesty of God: "YHWH, our Lord, how majestic is your name in all the earth" (Ps 8:1a). This exclamation of praise identifies the covenant God of the Old Testament as the ruler of all creation.[5] The "name" of God here arguably signifies God himself, or God's presence and power as well as God's self-revelation to human observers of the world.[6] In what way is God's name majestic in all the earth? David says that God has set his glory on or over the heavens (Ps 8:1b). Indeed, God's good plan for his creation is not thwarted by his enemies, which is evidenced in God's showing his strength even in the life

---

[5] So, e.g., Willem A. VanGemeren, "Psalms," in *The Expositor's Bible Commentary*, ed. Tremper Longman III and David E. Garland, rev. ed. (Grand Rapids: Zondervan, 2008), 5:138.
[6] Cf. Peter C. Craigie, *Psalms 1–50*, WBC 19 (Waco, TX: Word, 1983), 107.

of the smallest of human beings (Ps 8:2). Returning to God's glory in the heavens, David illumines the meaning of his statement in Psalm 8:1b by calling the heavens God's "handiwork," all their features being put in place by his determination (Ps 8:3). The glory of God—the outward manifestation of God's greatness, knowledge, and power—is visible in the heavens. They bear the marks of his wisdom and might. All of this causes David to ask YHWH why he should concern himself with the affairs of seemingly insignificant human beings, but David recognizes that we are crowned with honor and given dominion over God's works (Ps 8:4-9). It is worth noting, as one commentator puts it, that while the "vast expanse of the firmament impresses the psalmist deeply," "it does not overawe to the point where the personal dimension of faith is squelched."[7] In other words, David's apprehension of the divine revelation in nature does not preclude his drawing near to nature's majestic author. Throughout the psalm he addresses YHWH, the king of creation, in the second person. On the one hand, David's engagement with natural revelation takes place within the sphere of covenant relationship with YHWH. On the other hand, though, it seems that the covenant context is not absolutely requisite for some apprehension of natural revelation. YHWH's wisdom and power truly are discernible from the grandeur and order of nature, even if one does not know that the Creator has instituted the Abrahamic and Mosaic covenants and revealed himself more particularly as the God of Israel.

In Psalm 19 David announces that the heavens declare the glory of God and the sky or "firmament" above proclaims the work of his hands (Ps 19:1). Day to day it pours forth speech, and night to night it gives knowledge (Ps 19:2). Of course, "there is no speech, no noise, from a literal, acoustic perspective." Yet from a metaphorical perspective "there is a voice that penetrates to the furthest corners of the earth" in that the heavens, not least the rising and setting sun, point the observer back to the wisdom and power of their maker (Ps 19:3-5).[8] Instead of portraying the phenomena of the heavens as deities worthy of praise, the psalm provides a "tacit polemic against Israel's neighbors" in teaching that these phenomena simply attest the glory

---

[7]Nancy deClaissé-Walford, Rolf A. Jacobson, and Beth LaNeel Tanner, *The Book of Psalms*, New International Commentary on the Old Testament (Grand Rapids: Eerdmans, 2014), 123.
[8]Craigie, *Psalms 1–50*, 181.

of the true God.[9] Quite abruptly David then shifts to extolling the law of YHWH: "The law of YHWH is perfect, restoring the soul" (Ps 19:6). The psalm contains no overt directives for relating Psalm 19:1-5 and Psalm 19:6-14, though it can be said that it identifies the God of Israel as the Creator and neatly juxtaposes the knowledge of God in nature and the knowledge of God in the Torah.[10] Peter Craigie intimates that the nonverbal character of natural revelation coupled with the presence of the material on the law in this psalm signals that the natural knowledge of God is gained only by those who have already been made "sensitive" to YHWH's purposes (presumably by supernatural revelation).[11] It is true that David speaks more effusively about the knowledge of YHWH accessible in the law and says that the law engenders a greater wisdom, but the psalm nowhere indicates that possessing the deliverances of YHWH's law is necessary for obtaining some understanding of God from the created order. In this connection, James Barr cheekily comments, "No Barthian Psalmist would have written the 19th as it is."[12] As in Psalm 8, David's own apprehension of natural revelation takes place within the context of the knowledge of God's revelation to Israel, but this does not entail that only those who have supernatural revelation have the capacity for a natural knowledge of God.

In the New Testament, Paul's speech at the Areopagus in Acts 17 includes several apparently positive references to pagan knowledge of God. While in Athens Paul is distressed to see the multitude of idols there, which leads him to speak to both Jews and Greeks in the synagogue and the marketplace. A group of Epicurean and Stoic philosophers begin debating with Paul and characterize him as an amateurish "babbler" (σπερμολόγος) incapable of handling serious philosophical matters with due competence and subtlety. They want to hear more from him and therefore take him to the Areopagus for further inquiry (Acts 17:16-21). The content of his speech progresses "from 'the unknown god' to the Creator to the one whom God has appointed

---

[9]deClaissé-Walford, Jacobson, and Tanner, *Book of Psalms*, 207.

[10]For discussion of linguistic connections between the two parts of the psalm, see, e.g., John Goldingay, *Psalms*, vol. 1, *Psalms 1–41*, Baker Commentary on the Old Testament Wisdom and Psalms (Grand Rapids: Baker Academic, 2006), 284-86.

[11]Craigie, *Psalms 1–50*, 181.

[12]James Barr, *Biblical Faith and Natural Theology* (Oxford: Clarendon, 1993), 89. Barr speaks of Ps 104 also as "part of that dominant tendency of Hebrew natural theology" that "focus[es] on the existing cosmos as evidence and manifestation of the divine beneficence" (84).

to judge the world."[13] "The language used builds as much as possible on contacts with the wider philosophies of the time (particularly Stoicism) but is basically Jewish monotheism and creation theology presented in its universal implications."[14]

Paul begins his address by affirming that the Athenians are in all things "very religious" (Acts 17:22), using an adjective (δεισιδαίμων) that could be employed to signal reverence or superstition.[15] Since Paul is clearly disturbed by the presence of idolatry in Athens and will even connect idol worship to demonic activity in 1 Corinthians 10:14-22, the religion of the Greeks should be seen as seriously corrupted. Yet, insofar as he utilizes it as a positive evangelistic starting point it seems that Paul finds something in that religion—perhaps its recognition that human beings are meant to revere something or someone that exercises a dominion over them[16]—which still contains a certain (limited and warped) knowledge of God. Paul calls attention to the fact that nearby is an altar for an "unknown god." He frames his account of the biblical God as a description of who this "unknown god" really is (Acts 17:23). This God is the maker of all things and the self-sufficient Lord who has given life, place, and time not just to the Jewish people but to all human beings, with the goal that they may perhaps seek and find him (Acts 17:24-27a). The verb and the grammatical construction that Paul uses to speak of the Gentiles seeking God (εἰ ἄρα γε ψηλαφήσειαν, rendered "and perhaps grope for him and find him" in the NRSV) leaves open the possibility that they may arrive at some knowledge of him but also cautions against a naively optimistic view of the specificity and purity of that knowledge.[17] However, Paul adds, the Creator is not far from us, for, as one pagan author puts it, "in him we live and move and exist" (Acts 17:27b-28a). Indeed, according to the Stoic poet Aratus, "we are his offspring" (Acts 17:28b). Even as he takes up the language of Gentile authors, Paul immediately challenges the Gentiles' idolatrous practices. Because God has created us, he cannot be an image we have created. Because he has made us living beings in his image,

---

[13]Darrell L. Bock, *Acts*, BECNT (Grand Rapids: Baker Academic, 2007), 558.

[14]James D. G. Dunn, *The Acts of the Apostles* (Grand Rapids: Eerdmans, 2016), 230.

[15]So, e.g., H. Bietenhard, "Δαιμόνιον," in *New International Dictionary of New Testament Theology*, ed. Colin E. Brown (Grand Rapids: Zondervan, 1975), 1:453.

[16]Cf. Dunn, *Acts of the Apostles*, 234.

[17]Dunn calls such knowledge "unformed" and "indistinct" (*Acts of the Apostle*, 235).

he, the archetype, cannot be a lifeless statue (Acts 17:29).[18] Pressing further into the "radical particularity of the Christian message," Paul then proclaims that God has tolerated the Gentiles' ignorance but now is calling all to repentance and will judge the entire world through one man whom he has appointed (Acts 17:30-31).[19] Though interrupted and mocked at the mention of the resurrection, Paul's speech does yield converts, two of whom are named by Luke (Acts 17:32-34).[20]

There is some debate over the extent to which Paul's speech involves a transformation of the meaning of pagan theological concepts for use in Christian proclamation. C. Kavin Rowe, for example, has stressed the "deep and critical transformation of pagan philosophy wrought by its incorporation into a different comprehensive story." In Rowe's judgment, by contextualizing the conversation with pagan philosophy within the biblical narrative of creation and resurrection, "Luke renders hermeneutically ineffective the original intellectual structures that determined philosophically the meaning of the pagan phrases." Paul's speech is not a Christian transposition of pagan thought but rather offers a "rival conceptual scheme." It bears witness to "gentile ignorance *in toto*" and to a "profound incommensurability" between the Christian story and Greco-Roman thought.[21] There is "no general category of 'deity'" under discussion in Christian and pagan theology. Rather, the meaning of the words employed in theological description is always particularized and informed by the broader narrative in which they are located. Hence the word θεός in a pantheistic Stoic text refers to something that would, in the Christian milieu, be regarded as part of the created order.[22]

In response, Matthew Levering has emphasized that while "Greek philosophers do not get God's identity right," their philosophies do not always purport to offer a definitive account of God's identity in the first place. If they allow room for additional specification, Levering asks, "Why suppose

---

[18]See Bock, *Acts*, 568-69; C. Kavin Rowe, *World Upside Down: Reading Acts in the Graeco-Roman Age* (Oxford: Oxford University Press, 2009), 38.

[19]Rowe, *World Upside Down*, 39.

[20]On Paul's success at Athens, see Eckhard J. Schnabel, *Paul the Missionary: Realities, Strategies and Methods* (Downers Grove, IL: IVP Academic, 2010), 104.

[21]Rowe, *World Upside Down*, 40, 50.

[22]C. Kavin Rowe, "God, Greek Philosophy, and the Bible: A Response to Matthew Levering," *JTI* 5 (2011): 72-74. See also Rowe's *One True Life: The Stoics and Early Christians as Rival Traditions* (New Haven, CT: Yale University Press, 2016), 205, 224-28.

that Greek philosophy is at war with the Christian story, which must 'subvert' it and reject any 'rapprochement' with it?" In Levering's view, at least some of the philosophers' statements express not merely an intellectual framework that they have inherited but rather truthful conclusions drawn from an encounter with the structure of reality itself. They contain true insights about God that have a veracity and integrity even prior to being resituated within the biblical narrative, though they must be explicated more fully within the Christian account of God and creation. Such insights are thus "appropriated critically but not necessarily conflictually."[23]

In my view, Rowe and Levering both make important points. There is a certain sense in which the meaning of the philosophical concepts and statements that Paul appropriates in Athens is transformed in the Christian framework in that their erroneous and idolatrous elements (i.e., that there are many gods, that the gods are to be identified with features of the world and represented by images) are purged and their truthful aspects (i.e., that human beings owe reverence to a deity that governs and sustains our existence, that our existence is derived from a deity) are brought to a greater specificity and coherence via the biblical Creator-creature distinction and the Christian gospel. This is not to posit an "abstract" or neutral theological ground where the Gentiles in their concrete thinking supposedly possess a kernel of truth about God that is already insulated from the potentially negative effects of other (false) theological commitments. It is rather to suggest that Paul discerns within the Greeks' flawed philosophical theology elements of truth that can be isolated by a Christian believer and then affirmed and appropriated in Christian preaching.[24] As Levering puts it, "The error does not negate the insight."[25] Indeed, if there were an *absolute* incommensurability between Paul's view of God and that of the Athenians, if intellectual subversion were the only strategy in play at the Areopagus, then Paul's positive references to pagan religious notions would be nonsensical and counterproductive.[26]

---

[23]Matthew Levering, "God and Greek Philosophy in Contemporary Biblical Scholarship," *JTI* 4 (2010): 180-85.

[24]Thomas's discussion of the analogical (not univocal or equivocal) way in which the term "God" is used by pagans and Christians is helpful here (*ST* Ia.13.10 [160-61]).

[25]Levering, "God and Greek Philosophy," 183.

[26]It seems to me that the phrase "subversive fulfillment" (or "fulfilling subversion") used by Daniel Strange may be a nicely balanced expression of the way in which Christian thought addresses

In Romans 1 Paul teaches that Gentiles living outside the community of God's revelation through Moses and the prophets still have some natural knowledge of God. In Romans 1:18-32 there are echoes of the apocryphal book of Wisdom 13:1-9, where humanity is chided for perceiving the beauty of created things and even deifying the elements and heavenly lights while failing to discover the one who is in fact Lord of those things. Paul declares that the wrath of God is being revealed against the unrighteousness of human beings who suppress the truth about him, explaining that there is a knowledge of God available to all in creation (Rom 1:18-20). Significantly, Paul does not detach this natural knowledge of God from God's will or action: "the thing known of God" (τὸ γνωστὸν τοῦ θεοῦ) is revealed, "for God revealed it to them" (Rom 1:19).[27] Natural knowledge of God, then, from a scriptural perspective is not something that humanity obtains of its own initiative or by following a pathway never opened or authorized by God. Instead, it is made available by God's own purposeful self-revelation in order to render all persons aware of and accountable to their Creator. From the creation of the world, Paul writes, the "invisible attributes" of God have been understood by the things he has made. The content of the knowledge Paul has in mind is God's "eternal power and divinity," the latter implying not a knowledge of all that God is, which is incomprehensible for human beings, but rather a knowledge of God as the immortal and transcendent one who stands in contrast to corruptible creatures that ought not to be worshiped (cf. Rom 1:23, 25). The understanding of God's eternal power and divinity is given in order that all may be "without excuse" (Rom 1:20).

The Gentiles also know that their idolatry, malice, and sexual immorality elicit the judgment of God. They know that the "righteous requirement" (δικαίωμα) of God stipulates that those who engage in the evil practices included in Romans 1:21-31 are "worthy of death" (Rom 1:32). Each person has an awareness of their obligation to "[live] in recognition of and in harmony with the reality of creation's God-given order and of one's place

---

pagan theology (*Their Rock Is Not Like Our Rock: A Theology of Religions* [Grand Rapids: Zondervan, 2014]).

[27] Cf. C. E. B. Cranfield, *A Critical and Exegetical Commentary on the Epistle to the Romans*, International Critical Commentary (London: T&T Clark, 1975), 1:114.

within it."[28] Even if the Gentiles in Romans 2:14-15, who have "the work of the law written on their hearts" and whose consciences accuse or excuse them, are in fact Gentile Christians,[29] it remains clear in Romans 1:32 that those who lack the revelation given to God's chosen people are cognizant of God's righteousness and their own moral responsibility and guilt before God. In light of Romans 1, it is not just reason but faith itself (or apprehension of God's supernatural revelation given in Scripture) that compels us to affirm the reality of a natural knowledge of God.[30]

Already I have touched on the limitations of the natural knowledge of God in humanity's current state, and these limitations must be taken just as seriously as the biblical testimony to the reality and positive function of that knowledge. After all, Christ instructs us that the world does not know the Father (Jn 17:25). The limitations of the natural knowledge of God pertain both objectively to its content and subjectively to the manner in which it is treated by human agents. In the passages covered here, the content of this knowledge includes God's wisdom, power, transcendence, beneficence, and righteousness, but it tells us nothing of God's trinitarian life or his compassion for sinners enacted in the incarnation. The subjective aspect of the limitations of the natural knowledge of God consists in that the content it does include is wickedly "suppressed" by human persons (Rom 1:18). It is there in the human mind, for suppressing presupposes possessing. Indeed, as C. E. B. Cranfield points out, the suppressing here is "conative": "Sin is always an assault upon the truth . . . but it is of the essence of sin that it can never be more than an *attempt* to suppress the truth, an attempt which is always bound in the end to prove futile."[31] It is with and in spite of the knowledge that they do possess ("although they knew God . . .") that human beings refuse to glorify God. Instead, in rejecting the true God, their thoughts become futile and their hearts darkened, exchanging the worship of the true God for the worship of mortal creatures (Rom 1:21-23).

---

[28]Stephen Westerholm, *Perspectives Old and New on Paul: The "Lutheran" Paul and His Critics* (Grand Rapids: Eerdmans, 2004), 266.

[29]On the debate, see, e.g., Douglas J. Moo, *The Epistle to the Romans*, NICNT (Grand Rapids: Eerdmans, 1996), 148-53; Simon J. Gathercole, "A Law unto Themselves: The Gentiles in Rom 2:14-15 Revisited," *Journal for the Study of the New Testament* 85 (2002): 27-49.

[30]Cf. Denys Turner, *Faith, Reason and the Existence of God* (Cambridge: Cambridge University Press, 2004), x-xi.

[31]Cranfield, *Romans*, 1:112.

In this passage Paul states repeatedly that because of the Gentiles' suppression of the knowledge of God that is available to them, God "hands them over" to further depravity of mind and conduct (Rom 1:24, 26, 28). Paul reasserts this in Ephesians, where he urges believers to turn from the futility of the Gentiles' thinking (Eph 4:17). The Gentiles who do not know Christ suffer a darkness of reason and an alienation from the life of God following on an ignorance that stems from the hardness of their hearts (Eph 4:18). Thus Paul elsewhere warns believers not to be drawn into "philosophy and vain deception" (or "vain and deceptive philosophy") "according to human traditions, according to the principles of the world and not according to Christ" (Col 2:8).

In view of the fallen intellect's hostility toward the truth of God, Paul teaches that a right apprehension of the supernatural revelation of the gospel requires a work of the Holy Spirit. It is not just that reason or natural theology by itself cannot discover the truth of the gospel (though that is true). Rather, fallen reason in its hubris and darkness is actively set against the gospel. For Paul, the wisdom of the world takes the wisdom of God displayed on the cross to be foolishness. The rulers of this age do not understand God's wisdom (1 Cor 2:6-8). God therefore makes known his wisdom by his Spirit. For no one knows the things of God except the Spirit of God, who knows the mind of God and helps us to understand the things God has given to us (1 Cor 2:9-12). Consequently, ministers of the gospel impart the wisdom and truth of God not by promulgating human wisdom but "by words taught by the Spirit," interpreting "spiritual things" for those who are "spiritual." The "natural" person does not "receive" the things of God's Spirit, for he or she thinks they are folly. Such a person is "unable to know," for such things are "spiritually discerned." Those who are "spiritual" and have the "mind of Christ" receive and discern these things "under the influence of God's renewing and enlightening Spirit" (1 Cor 2:13-16).[32]

Paul also speaks of the gospel's being "veiled" among those who are perishing, for "the god of this age has blinded the minds of unbelievers" so that they do not see the "light of the gospel of the glory of Christ, who is the

---

[32]Joseph A. Fitzmyer, *First Corinthians: A New Translation with Introduction and Commentary*, Anchor Yale Bible (New Haven, CT: Yale University Press, 2008), 184.

image of God" (2 Cor 4:3-4).[33] By contrast the gospel has been received by
those in whose hearts God has shone "the light of the knowledge of the glory
of God in the face of Jesus Christ" (2 Cor 4:6). On the one hand, the objective "light," the content of the gospel, is proclaimed clearly. On the other
hand, it appears that a subjective "light," an inward dispelling of the darkness
of the human heart, also is needed for the reception of the gospel.[34] In
keeping with the necessity of the Spirit's illuminating and reviving work in
the believer's initial reception of Christ, Christian believers undergo a
continual renewal and reorientation of the mind by the word and Spirit of
God (Rom 12:2; Eph 1:17-18; 4:23; Col 3:10).

We could certainly examine more biblical passages in this section, but we
have covered enough ground to ask how we might begin to draw together
and distill the Bible's teaching on the subject of the natural knowledge of
God. I will thus conclude this section with a brief summary of the scriptural
teaching. After considering the contributions and challenges of various
theologians on this topic, I will later elaborate more on the role of the natural
knowledge of God in the Christian practice of *theologia* at the end of
the chapter.

First, the origin of the natural knowledge of God is God the Creator in
his self-revelation. This has to be emphasized so that we do not slip into
thinking that any talk of natural knowledge of God or "natural theology" is
automatically a circumventing of God's itinerary for the pilgrim intellect.
The author and giver of this knowledge is God: "What is known of God is
revealed, for God revealed it to them" (Rom 1:19). This is one reason why I
have often employed the phrase "natural knowledge of God" instead of
"natural theology," for the latter often conjures up for the contemporary
reader thoughts about looking away from God's revelation in an arrogant
attempt to claim knowledge of God on our own.[35] The knowledge in view

---

[33]Presumably those who are blind and perishing include both Jews and Gentiles (cf. 2 Cor 2:15;
3:13-16).

[34]Cf. the "outward" and "inward" dimensions of God's illuminating work noted in Paul Barnett,
The Second Epistle to the Corinthians, NICNT (Grand Rapids: Eerdmans, 1997), 224. Barnett
(with others) notes also that Paul appears to be recalling his own experience of the light of Christ
on the way to Damascus but presents it as akin to the common experience of all believers.

[35]One example of the separation of natural knowledge from divine action appears in Hermann
Cremer, *Die christliche Lehre von den Eigenschaften Gottes*, 2nd ed. (Gütersloh: C. Bertelsmann,
1917), 23.

in this chapter is the knowledge of God the Creator given by the Creator himself in the marks of his wisdom and power in the grandeur and order of creation. In the light of Scripture, this is the first and most fundamental sense of the phrase "natural theology." Any discursive or formal presentation of this knowledge—"natural theology" in the sense of a systematic development of the knowledge of God in creation—must be grounded in and transparent to "natural theology" in that first sense. Second, the content or object of the natural knowledge of God is God the Creator in his eternal transcendence, wisdom, power, beneficence, and righteousness. God is both subject and object of natural revelation and the ultimate efficient cause of the resultant natural knowledge of God.

Third, the purpose of the natural knowledge of God in the biblical narrative is humanity's awareness of the majesty of the Creator and the Creator's rightful claim to worship and obedience. In the biblical text, the knowledge of God available in the created order inspires wonder and praise (Ps 8:1; 19:1). It also renders sinners without the Mosaic law accountable and culpable before their righteous Creator. The natural knowledge of God is thus designed to maintain for those outside (and even inside) the community of supernatural revelation an epistemic and ethical connection to God the Creator, a connection on which Christian proclamation may draw as it speaks of a transcendent, righteous God to whom human beings must be reconciled through the work of Jesus Christ. Finally, the limitations of the natural knowledge of God are both objective and subjective. Objectively, it is a knowledge whose content does not include the mysteries of the Trinity and the incarnation, which lie at the heart of the Christian faith and life. Subjectively, it is a knowledge that is suppressed and distorted. In the concrete circumstances of humanity's fallen state, it is no longer pure and free from error. Given the depictions of pagan idolatry in the biblical text, the elements of the natural knowledge of God that turn on the Creator-creature distinction appear to be particularly susceptible to distortion. Instead of honoring the knowledge that the Creator of the world is distinct from the world's many features, fallen humanity has identified the Creator with corruptible created beings. Nevertheless, the suppression of this knowledge assumes that it is still present after the fall. Accordingly, the natural knowledge of God in its positive function and in its failure to facilitate true communion with God both prepares humanity for the super-natural revelation that culminates in the incarnation and elicits the renewing effects of that revelation.

For a fuller understanding of the implications and problems associated with the knowledge of God given in nature, and for the sake of offering a responsible account of its place in Christian *theologia* today, I will consider how the matter is handled by major authors in the Christian tradition. Among other things, this will involve reflecting more on how the content of natural revelation is actually apprehended and developed by human persons and how it is related to supernatural revelation.

HISTORICAL CONCEPTIONS
OF THE NATURAL KNOWLEDGE OF GOD (I)

It is possible here to cover only a few significant Christian authors on the natural knowledge of God and its relationship to supernatural revelation and the illuminating work of the Spirit. Because discussion of the continuity or discontinuity between the theological epistemologies of Augustine and Thomas Aquinas can stimulate helpful reflection on the nature of the natural knowledge of God and the connection between nature and grace in God's economy, the former will appear first in this section, followed by a few me-dieval authors (chiefly Thomas) and some early Reformed authors.[36]

Augustine and Thomas. In *The City of God*, Augustine takes into account the ancient Roman author Varro's threefold division of theology: the mythical theology of the poets, the natural theology of the philosophers, and the civil theology of a given citizenry.[37] In Augustine's judgment, the greatest natural theology to be found among the non-Christian philosophers be-longs to the Platonists since they recognize that there is only one unchanging deity who created all things and transcends the world. In discussing Pla-tonist philosophical theology, Augustine follows Paul in Acts 17:24-28, Romans 1:18-32, and Colossians 2:8, observing that there is a knowledge of God among the philosophers and that it is, however, a knowledge very often

---

[36]It would be particularly beneficial to include the distinct contributions of Anselm and Bonaven-ture, for example, but space does not permit me to do so here.

[37]Augustine, *De civitâte Dei*, ed. Bernard Dombart and Alphonse Kalb, 2 vols., CCSL 47-48 (Turn-hout: Brepols, 1955), 6.5 (1:170-72).

mixed with error. Augustine speculates about whether the level of agreement between Plato and Christian theology may have arisen by Plato's having some contact with the Old Testament Scriptures, but he concludes that it is more likely due to the knowledge of God conveyed by the created order. The bishop of Hippo is thus willing both to affirm points of common ground with the Platonists and to recognize that they have become vain in their thoughts, especially where they grant the service of λατρεία to beings other than the one true God and where they deny the incarnation.[38] To dispel this spiritual and intellectual vanity, in which the mind is hindered by vices and intolerant of God's "immutable light," the mind must be "imbued" and "purged" by faith in Christ so that it can be "renewed and healed" (*renovata atque sanata*) and rendered "capable of felicity."[39]

Taken from a different angle, true philosophy, true knowledge of God, is wisdom. Knowledge (*scientia*) is "rational cognition of temporal things" (*temporalium rerum cognitio rationalis*). It can include some truth about God obtained through reasoning about the created order, but in sinful humanity it also engenders conceit and alienation from the true God. By contrast, wisdom (*sapientia*) is "intellectual cognition of eternal things" (*aeternarum rerum cognitio intellectualis*). It apprehends God in God's own light and Logos and includes the love of God characterized by piety and worship. In our fallen condition we lack this sapiential cognition of God, so God restores it (and its guiding of our *scientia*) through the incarnation and through the cleansing of the mind by faith and participation in Christ, the repository of all knowledge and wisdom (Col 2:3).[40]

As one might suspect from Augustine's use of the language of "light," the question of human knowledge of God in his thought is related to his epistemological concept of illumination.[41] For Augustine, God's activity of

---

[38]Augustine, *De civitate Dei* 8.1, 5-6, 10-12 (1:216-17, 221-24, 226-29); 10.3, 29 (1:274-76, 304-7).

[39]Augustine, *De civitate Dei* 11.2 (2:322).

[40]Augustine, *De Trinitate, libri XV*, ed. W. J. Mountain, 2 vols., CCSL 50-50A (Turnhout: Brepols, 1968), 4.4, 21, 24 (1:163-64); 12.21-25 (1:375-80); 13.2, 24 (2:381-82, 415-17); 14.1, 21 (2:421-22, 449-51). Cf. Luigi Gioia, *The Theological Epistemology of Augustine's "De Trinitate,"* Oxford Theology and Religion Monographs (Oxford: Oxford University Press, 2008), 43-47, 219-31.

[41]Augustine's doctrine of illumination is a debated topic in contemporary theology. For description of its place in his epistemology, see, e.g., R. A. Markus, "Augustine: Reason and Illumination," in *The Cambridge History of Later Greek and Early Medieval Philosophy*, ed. A. H. Armstrong (Cambridge: Cambridge University Press, 1967), 362-73; Ronald H. Nash, *The Light of the Mind: St. Augustine's Theory of Knowledge* (Lexington: University of Kentucky Press, 1969); Gareth B.

enlightening the human mind is crucial for human discovery of (theological) truth, particularly truth that is not grasped by sense experience. There is no single place in Augustine's works where he comprehensively deals with the nature of divine illumination, but various texts touch on different aspects of it. For example, in the *Confessions* he comments that the mind must be "enlightened" in order to become a "partaker of truth." For the mind "is not itself the nature of truth." Augustine prays to God, "You will illumine my lamp, Lord. My God, you will illumine my darkness. . . . For you are the true light that illumines every man coming into the world."[42] Later he writes that two persons who both see that something is true see its truthfulness not in themselves but "in the immutable truth itself which is above our minds."[43] In his *De magistro* Augustine acknowledges that a human speaker's words may occasion understanding in the hearer, but he identifies Christ as the one who dwells in the "inner man" (*interiore homine*), teaching and providing necessary counsel so that the hearer obtains understanding.[44] It is not the human speaker who teaches what the intellect apprehends or conceives; rather, the things themselves teach the mind with God inwardly working to make them "manifest" even prior to the speaker's discussing them.[45]

Questions about the nature of God's involvement in human knowing continued to occupy theologians well into the medieval period. How does God enable the human mind to understand truth about himself? Is the human mind in its own right furnished with the capacity to arrive at a knowledge of God, or does it require special divine intervention to arrive at such knowledge? What is the relationship between the natural endowments

---

Mathews, "Knowledge and Illumination," in *The Cambridge Companion to Augustine*, ed. Eleonore Stump and Norman Kretzmann, 1st ed. (Cambridge: Cambridge University Press, 2001), 171-85. For a succinct orientation to the interpretive issues, see Lydia Schumacher, *Divine Illumination: The History and Future of Augustine's Theory of Knowledge* (Oxford: Wiley-Blackwell, 2011), 1-13.

[42] Augustine, *Confessionum libri XIII*, ed. Lucas Verheijen, CCSL 27 (Turnhout: Brepols, 1981), 4.15.25 (53).

[43] Augustine, *Confessionum* 12.25.35 (235).

[44] Augustine, *De magistro*, ed. K. D. Daur, CCSL 29 (Turnhout: Brepols, 1970), 11.38 (195-96).

[45] Augustine, *De magistro* 12.40 (197-99). Augustine does clarify that he does not hold the Platonic doctrine of the preexistent soul furnished with prior memories. Rather, he maintains that the mind is constituted by the Creator so that by a natural order it can understand things (*De Trinitate* 12.24 [378]).

and operations of the human mind and the redemptive, renewing grace given in Christ?[46]

Because Thomas is a figure of significant constructive influence in the present study, he will receive some extra attention here. He maintains that there are multiple legitimate ways of obtaining knowledge of God. In his commentary on Boethius's *De Trinitate*, Thomas writes that through philosophical study of created beings we can come to know God as their principle or cause. Though God in himself and as first principle is supremely knowable, the "natural light of reason" can attain to knowledge of God only by beginning with created effects and tracing them back to their divine cause. Thomas anchors this in Romans 1:20: the *invisibilia Dei* are "perceived by the intellect by the things which have been made." But there is another "mode of knowing" the things of God, namely, by God himself revealing them (1 Cor 2:10-12). In this way of knowing, "divine things are treated as they subsist in themselves and not only as they are principles of things." The former is the way of "metaphysics" or "philosophical theology," which deals with God not directly as its subject but rather only as the principle of its proper subject (created being), while the latter is the way of the "theology handed down in sacred Scripture."[47]

Thomas discusses this further at the beginning of book four of the *Summa contra Gentiles*, where he notes that the human intellect in this life always relies on sense perception as a starting point for knowledge. God exceeds sensible things and indeed all beings. He has no "proportion" to them (no quantifiable number of degrees by which God is greater than them and no mutually constitutive relation to them). Nevertheless, God has still provided

---

[46]On the concept of illumination in particular in connection with medieval scholastic epistemologies, see Steven P. Marrone, *The Light of Thy Countenance: Science and the Knowledge of God in the Thirteenth Century*, 2 vols. (Leiden: Brill, 2001). More recently, Schumacher in *Divine Illumination* has critiqued a common understanding of Augustine's influence on his medieval interpreters. Often it has been thought that Augustine's view of illumination was carried forward by Bonaventure, criticized by Thomas, and abandoned by Scotus and later Franciscans. Schumacher maintains that Bonaventure in fact advanced a different account of illumination after engaging the work of the Muslim philosopher Avicenna (leading to the later Franciscan abandonment of it) and that Thomas actually reaffirmed Augustine's doctrine of illumination. I do not take a position here regarding this larger historical narrative and will only point out ways in which Thomas and others treat God's work of facilitating human knowledge of God and incorporate the concept of illumination along the way.

[47]Thomas, *De Trin.* 5.4 (154).

a way for us to know him from creatures and thus to begin to attain our end (i.e., knowing God). Consideration of the perfections that have "descended" from God the Creator to creatures allows us to "ascend" back to God the first principle, in whom all the perfections of diverse created effects must be present in a preeminent and unified manner. However, Thomas immediately comments on the serious limitations and difficulties in the "way of ascent." When our intellect is occupied with sensible things, it struggles to move from outwardly observable accidents to the natures of sensible things. The difficulty is greater when there are fewer sensible accidents to observe and even greater still when there are no sensible accidents at all, and one must rely on moving backward from deficient effects to some knowledge of the object of inquiry as the cause of those effects. Indeed, even when one does know the natures of things, we only "slightly" know their mutual order toward one another and their appointed end in God's providence. For we do not know the inner logic or way (*ratio*) of God's providence. In this sense we know the "way" or the causal relations in the way of ascent only imperfectly, so how should we arrive at complete knowledge of the principle of this way (i.e., God)? And even if we did have perfect knowledge of the "way" in the way of ascent, its principle (God) exceeds created effects "without proportion." After profoundly qualifying the prospects of the way of ascent, Thomas then comments that God in his "superabundant goodness" has opened up a way of "descent" by revealing divine truths that exceed the intellect in order to provide a "firmer" knowledge of himself. Unlike the way of ascent, the knowledge of God in the way of descent is not a matter of vision or the demonstration of truth by reason but a matter of hearing and trusting revealed mysteries (Jn 17:17; Rom 10:17; 1 Cor 13:12).[48]

According to Thomas, God's being (*esse*) is not self-evident (*per se notum*) to us, and God is not the first thing known by the human mind. God's being in itself (*secundum se*) is self-evident since God himself or God's own essence and God's *esse* are one and the same, but it is not self-evident to us like the basic laws of logic. Nor is God's *esse* the first thing known with respect

---

[48]Thomas, *SCG* 4.1 (3-4). Though willing to speak of a *duplex veritatis modus* (double mode of truth) or even *duplex veritas* (double truth)—truth about God demonstrable by natural reason and truth about God accessible only by supernatural revelation (*SCG* 1.3 [7]; 9 [22])—Thomas is clear that he is not speaking of two bodies of conflicting truths but of two ways in which the human person can arrive at (coherent) knowledge of God.

to us (*quoad nos*) since our intellect begins to acquire knowledge from sense perception and since we do not know God's essence or (at least not initially) the identity of God's essence and existence.[49] To be sure, there is a human knowledge of God that arises "immediately" (*statim*) in the sense that we see in the order and movement of the world that there must be one who orders and causes it.[50] Further, there is implanted in us by nature a "confused" or indistinct knowledge of God as the beatitude we naturally desire, but this knowledge lacks particularity: it is like knowing someone is coming toward us without knowing who it is. Moreover, someone may understand the word *God* to signify "something than which nothing greater can be conceived," but this does not grant that person knowledge of whether that being actually exists.[51] Ultimately, it is possible to speak of an "innate knowledge" of God (*cognitio innata*) just in the sense that upon encountering sensible created effects we can, through the use of native cognitive principles (basic principles of demonstration and their various terms like being and nonbeing, whole and part, and so on), arrive at a knowledge of God's existence.[52] Accordingly, for Thomas, the natural knowledge of God must be drawn out in a causal analysis of creatures that points back to God as the actual first cause.[53]

---

[49]Thomas can affirm that we understand and judge all things "by the light of the first truth" in that the "light" that is our intellect understands by having an impression or participation of the "light" that is God in his own understanding. However, the light of our intellect is not that which we understand but that *by which* we understand. Accordingly, neither is the light of God of which our intellect partakes that which we first understand but that *by which* we understand (*ST* Ia.88.3 ad 1 [368]).

[50]Thomas, *De Trin.* 1.3 esp. ad 2 and 6 (86-8); *SCG* 3.38 (94); *ST* Ia.2.1 corp. (27-28).

[51]Thomas, *ST* Ia.2.1 ad 1 and 2 (28).

[52]Thomas, *De Trin.* 1.3 ad 6 (88).

[53]So Thomas, *ST* Ia.12.12 (136-37).

EXCURSUS

Thomas on the Discovery of God Through Causal Analysis

It is common knowledge that Thomas offers several different ways of demonstrating the existence of God,[54] but in this excursus I will attempt to summarize his reasoning that leads him to the conclusion that there is a first cause whose essence is identical to his existence. Though some elements of Thomas's epistemology may seem strange to the contemporary reader, I take this to be worthwhile for three reasons: (1) it will illustrate some premodern reasoning about the mind's ascent to God; (2) it will help us respond to some of the objections to natural theology later on; and (3) the identity of God's essence and existence will come up later when we talk about the application of metaphysical concepts to God.[55]

Before delving into the specifics of Thomas's line of reasoning, it is worth acknowledging that some interpreters of Thomas argue that his analogical approach to the question of being and theological language (discussed in detail in chapter five) ultimately prevents him from offering a strict scientific demonstration of God's existence by the exercise of natural reason.[56] This interpretation of Thomas actually resonates with John Duns Scotus's insistence that the exactness of univocal concepts is required to ensure valid scientific demonstration.[57] Thomas, however, contends quite straightforwardly

---

[54]E.g., Thomas, *ST* Ia.2.3 (31-32). Some Thomists (e.g., Ralph McInerny, *Praeambula Fidei: Thomism and the God of the Philosophers* [Washington, DC: Catholic University of America Press, 2006], esp. part 3) have argued that in Thomas's thought demonstrations of God's existence must begin in natural science and can only afterward proceed to distinctly metaphysical lines of reasoning about immaterial beings and, ultimately, God. Without wanting to minimize the role of natural science at this point, I do not assume here that it must precede metaphysical reasoning in Thomas's thought in order for the latter to arrive at a knowledge of God (see Thomas Joseph White, *Wisdom in the Face of Modernity: A Study in Thomistic Natural Theology*, 2nd ed., Faith and Reason: Studies in Catholic Theology and Philosophy [Ave Maria, FL: Sapientia, 2016], 204-16).

[55]For helpful accounts that have influenced the presentation of Thomas's thought here, see John Wippel, *The Metaphysical Thought of Thomas Aquinas: From Finite Being to Uncreated Being* (Washington, DC: Catholic University of America Press, 2000), esp. chaps. 2 and 5; White, *Wisdom in the Face of Modernity*, 120-32. With Wippel, White, and others, I affirm that natural reason is, at least in principle, capable of arriving at Thomas's real distinction between essence and existence in creatures (without having to presuppose scriptural teaching on God's aseity).

[56]See, e.g., John Milbank, "Intensities," *MT* 15 (1999): 454-56.

[57]See John Duns Scotus, *Opera omnia*, vols. 1-4, *Ordinatio*, ed. P. Carolo Balić (Vatican City: Typis Polyglottis Vaticanis, 1950–1956), 1.3.1.1, nn. 39-40 (3:26-27).

that even if an effect is not "proportionate" to its cause and cannot supply a complete knowledge of its cause, knowledge of the effect can still yield at least some knowledge of the existence of its cause.[58] Furthermore, following Aristotle's *Posterior Analytics* 1.13, Thomas, Scotus, and other medievals recognize two kinds of rational demonstration. One kind is a *propter quid* (διότι) demonstration, in which things are proved to be as they are from a knowledge of their underlying, immediate causes that sufficiently account for their being. Another kind is a *quia* (ὅτι) demonstration, in which certain things are demonstrated to be from a knowledge of effects that signal their existence, without disclosing their underlying rationale.[59] In the latter kind of demonstration, under which the demonstration of God's existence falls, there is no need to begin with an exact knowledge of what the cause is that features in the demonstration. Instead, a knowledge of the character of an effect (with a readiness to purge the content of that knowledge of any limitations associated with the effect) functions as a placeholder for a knowledge of the quiddity of the cause to be demonstrated.[60] Furthermore, it should be noted that a self-consciously analogical application of certain terms to God (including existence) is not strictly speaking the means by which the existence of God initially must be demonstrated, an attribution that would itself (in circular fashion) presuppose a knowledge of God's existence and causal relation to creatures on which analogical description is based. Rather, upon inferring from created effects the existence of a divine cause, reason can then return to the terms and logic in play and clarify the analogical nature of the discourse in light of the acquired knowledge of a transcendent cause.[61]

---

[58]Thomas, *ST* Ia.2.2 ad 3 (30).

[59]See Thomas Aquinas, *In libros Posteriorum Analyticorum expositio*, in *Opera Omnia*, vol. 1, Leonine ed. (Rome: ex Typographia Polyglotta, 1882), 13.23.2-4, 9 (229-30, 232).

[60]Thomas, *De Trin.* 2.2 ad 2 (96); *SCG* 1.12 (29); *ST* Ia.1.7 ad 1 (19); 2.2 ad 2 (30); 12.12 corp. and ad 1-2 (136); 13.1 corp. (139). Compare Wippel, *Metaphysical Thought of Thomas Aquinas*, 443. Gregory Rocca comments that when the demonstration of God's existence is set within a philosophical (rather than theological) context, "the meaning of *God* in this case is not a necessary presupposition to the demonstration of God's existence but is what comes to light as philosophical reason searches out and attempts to understand the world's intelligibility" (*Speaking the Incomprehensible God: Thomas Aquinas on the Interplay of Positive and Negative Theology* [Washington, DC: Catholic University of America Press, 2004], 185). As the scholastics often put it, one begins with a "nominal definition" of the word *God* in this case (compare Lawrence Dewan, "The Existence of God: Can It Be Demonstrated?," *Nova et Vetera* 10 [2012]: 749-51).

[61]Cf. Rocca, *Speaking the Incomprehensible God*, 183-84; Turner, *Faith, Reason and the Existence of God*, 202-11.

To understand Thomas's thinking on the demonstration of God's existence, it is helpful to have some familiarity with the epistemological framework he develops in the context of his anthropology. He holds that the
human person is composed of body and soul (*anima*) and that in view of
the Christian doctrine of creation, the union of body and soul is natural and
(*pace* Plato) not an unfortunate obstacle to human cognition.[62] The human
person as a body-soul composite, with corporeal sense organs as well as a
rational mind, is the knowing subject in Thomas's epistemology.[63] The human being does not have multiple souls but rather one intellectual, rational soul that includes "virtually" (as to its powers or capacities) things that,
in nonrational animals and plants, would belong to a "sensitive" and "veg-
etative," or "nutritive," soul.[64] In human cognition, the sensitive "power" or
"part" of the soul apprehends its objects through the body's corporeal
organs. The intellectual power apprehends its objects immaterially through
engagement with the sensitive power's "storehouse" (*quasi thesaurus*) of
impressions or images of external objects (i.e., the imagination).[65]

Within this epistemological framework, the intellect operates in
conjunction with sensitive apprehension of real existents outside the mind.
Indeed, according to Thomas, all our knowledge begins with sense perception of concrete external objects.[66] We encounter a sensible object that
makes an impression on a corporeal organ, producing an image or likeness
of itself (called a "phantasm") in the sense, which is a "passive power" acted
on from without by the external object.[67] Reception of the "phantasm" provides (sensitive) apprehensive knowledge, but this knowledge is comple-
mented by a properly intellectual knowledge of what the object is, grasped
as indivisible (simpler than the composite individual itself) and as a universal. At first a "blank slate" (*tabula rasa*), the intellect is a "passive power": to
understand is in some way to "suffer" or "undergo" (*pati*). Yet the intellect
has an active power (*intellectus agens*) with which it abstracts from a

---

[62]Thomas, *ST* Ia.76.1 (208-10); 84.3 corp. (318); 84.5 corp. (322).
[63]Thomas, *ST* Ia.77.5 (244-45). Cf. *ST* Ia.12.4 corp. (121), where the sense organ and the intellect
are both "cognitive powers."
[64]Thomas, *ST* Ia.76.3, 220-21.
[65]Thomas, *ST* Ia.78.4 corp. (256); 84.6-7 (323-26); 85.1 (330-32); 86.1 (347).
[66]E.g., Thomas, *De Trin.* 6.2 resp. (164); *ST* Ia.84.6 (323-24).
[67]Thomas, *ST* Ia.78.3 corp. (253-54).

phantasm the "intelligible species" of an external object (its essence or quiddity viewed by the mind as a universal applicable to many individuals). The "agent" or "active" power of the intellect presents or impresses the intelligible species of the object to the "passive" power of the intellect (the *intellectus possibilis*), which may possess the species habitually or consider it actively. It is important to recognize, however, that, like the phantasm in the sense, the intelligible species in the intellect is not what is understood but rather that *by which* the intellect understands its objects (*non est quod . . . sed id quo*).[68] This first operation of the intellect in which it grasps the quiddity of something is often called "simple apprehension." Yet the intellect also undertakes a second operation (often called "judgment"), in which it "composes" and "divides." To "compose" in this context is to affirm various things about the object (that it exists, that it has certain accidents and relations, and so on). To "divide" is to negate or deny that various things pertain to the object.[69] Though the intellect's proper object is the species of a thing, it still knows the individual indirectly in its connection with the sense's apprehension and recollection of the individual, by a return to and reflection on the phantasm.[70]

In its first operation, the intellect grasps the essence of a thing; in its second, it grasps the existence (*esse*) of a thing, consistently maintaining contact with real beings in their extramental actuality.[71] The human knower then has an awareness that external objects are of certain kinds and that they exist or are actual in distinction from others, which enables a primitive understanding of the universal of "being" (*ens*) taken as "that which is" or "that which has existence."[72] It is significant that an

---

[68]Thomas Aquinas, *Opera omnia*, vol. 45/1, *Sentencia De anima*, Leonine ed. (Rome: Commissio Leonina; Paris: J. Vrin, 1984), 3.4 (218-23); *De Trin.* 1.1 corp. (81-82); *SCG* 2.77 (488-89); *ST* Ia.79.2-4, 6-7, 10 (259-60, 264-65, 267-68, 270-71, 272-73, 277-78); 84.3, 7 ad 1 (317-18, 325); 85.2 (333-35).

[69]Thomas, *ST* Ia.85.5, 341.

[70]Thomas, *ST* Ia.84.7 (325-26); 85.1 (330-32); 86.1 (347). Robert Pasnau comments, "Given that the intellect's role is to understand universal natures *as existing in a particular*, it is only to be expected that the intellect is *constantly* casting its attention on those particulars" (*Thomas Aquinas on Human Nature: A Philosophical Study of "Summa Theologiae" Ia 75-89* [Cambridge: Cambridge University Press, 2002], 287).

[71]E.g., Thomas, *De Trin.* 5.3 corp. (147). Language of "first" and "second" is not meant to imply that there must be a temporal gap between these operations.

[72]See, e.g., Thomas Aquinas, *De ente et essentia*, in *Opera omnia*, vol. 43, Leonine ed. (Rome: Editori Di San Tommaso, 1976), prol. (369); Thomas, *Opera omnia*, vol. 22/1.2, *Quaestiones*

awareness of individuals and their particular modes of existing leads to
(and is not derived from) the complex concept of being. The concept of
ens in the mind is thus not anterior to human encounter with real existents, nor is *esse* or *ens* another essence into conformity with which the
mind must wrestle real existents. This point distinguishes Thomas's
epistemology from an "essentialist" approach in which the mind's
concepts must be used proactively to determine what and how things
are.[73] There are places where Thomas says that *ens* is first in the intellect's conception,[74] but this is not because *ens* is conceived prior in time

---

disputatae de veritate, Leonine ed. (Rome: ad Sanctae Sabinae, 1970), 1.1 (5); Thomas, *Expositio
libri De hebdomadibus*, in *Opera omnia*, vol. 50, Leonine ed. (Rome: Commissio Leonina; Paris:
Éditions du Cerf, 1992), 2 (270-71). The (analogical) way in which, according to Thomas, *ens*
may be applied to the many will be discussed in chap. 5, but here it may be worth noting that
even at the precritical level the human knower may begin to grasp that what something is (its
essence) pertains to what it has in common with others while *that* it is (its existence) pertains
to what distinguishes it as an individual.

[73]The point is underscored where Thomas clearly situates *esse* not on the side of that which pertains
a thing's nature but on the side of that which pertains to the individual *suppositum* (*Opera omnia*,
vol. 25/2, *Quaestiones de quolibet*, Leonine ed. [Rome: Commissio Leonina; Paris: Éditions du Cerf,
1996], 2.2.2 [4] ad 1 [218]). For those interested in the details of the interpretation of Thomas on
these points, it may be worth pointing out that my reading and appropriation of Thomas differs
in some ways from both an "essentialist" reading of him and an "existentialist" reading of him of
the sort often associated with Etienne Gilson among others (see, e.g., his *Being and Some Philosophers*, 2nd ed. [Toronto: Pontifical Institute of Mediaeval Studies, 1952]). In contrast to some
interpretations of Thomas that are charged with "essentialism," I do not think his approach encourages us to begin with the principles of reason in order to establish a framework for understanding extramental being. The order is in fact the reverse: extramental reality presses in on the
mind and generates its (responsive) patterns of understanding and reasoning. In addition, for
Thomas, *esse* is not one more quiddity in the mind's register of intelligible species. It is, instead,
simply a thing's act of existing. At the same time, in contrast to at least some "existentialist" approaches, I take it that in Thomas's view *esse* is not independent from concrete beings and natures
but rather applies only to concrete beings with their given natures. See, e.g., *In libros Peri Hermeneias expositio*, in *Opera omnia*, vol. 1, Leonine ed. (Rome: ex Typographia Polyglotta, 1882), 3.5.19
(27); and *De Trin.* 5.3 corp. (147), where Thomas says, respectively, that the "font and origin" of
esse is *ens* and that *esse* "results" from a thing's essential principles. Furthermore, it is not utterly
beyond the mind's conception but rather, given the intellect's acts of judgment, can be conceived
by the mind and included in the complex concept of *ens* (so, e.g., *In Peri Hermeneias* 3.5.20-22
[28]; *De hebdomadibus* 2 [272-73]; *Opera omnia*, vol. 22/3.1, *Quaestiones disputatae de veritate*,
Leonine ed. [Rome: ad Sanctae Sabinae, 1973], 21.1 corp. [593]). Finally, in the intellect's second
operation of judgment, *esse* is grasped in the sense of the basic fact that a thing exists but not yet
in the sense of a thing's intrinsic act of being distinct from its essence as such. That discovery of
a thing's *actus essendi* as distinct from its essence lies within philosophical investigation of being
as being (metaphysics) and, indeed, is attainable by natural reason even as natural reason is helped
along by supernatural revelation and its description of the Creator-creature distinction.

[74]Thomas, *De ente et essentia*, prol. (369); *Quaestiones disputatae de veritate* 21.1 corp. (593); *In
duodecim libros Metaphysicorum Aristotelis expositio*, ed. M.-R. Cathala and R. M. Spiazzi (Turin-
Rome: Marietti, 1950), 1.2.46 (13).

to sense perception or the intellect's judgment of existence. Rather, it is because all our knowledge of things includes a knowledge of those things as beings. To state it in a rather banal and, indeed, tautological manner: everything that is and that we know is a being. The mind thus "resolves" all things into being, not by negating their distinct modes of existing and individuating principles (which would be a *separatio in re* conducted by the intellect's negative judgment) but by considering the one (*ens*, which is not by nature ordered to any one kind or individual without which it would be unintelligible) without reference to the other (here, a thing's specific and individuating principles) in what Thomas calls a "simple and absolute consideration."[75] "Being" in this sense is supremely indivisible and universal and thus becomes the subject of the "most intellectual science" of metaphysics.[76]

More will be said about the relationship between Christian *theologia* and metaphysics in chapter five, but for now it may be noted that in the discipline of metaphysics one studies the causes and proper features of being, the principal category of which is substance (that which subsists *per se* and in its own right) since beings in the other categories (the various sorts of accidents) cannot exist except in substances.[77] Yet any given substance in the world is contingent and caused. Thomas accounts for this by observing a distinction between a thing's essence and its *esse* (not just the observable fact that it exists but its intrinsic act of existing).[78] If a thing is

---

[75]Thomas Aquinas, *De ver.* 1.1 (5); *De Trin.* 5.3 corp. (147-48); *ST* Ia.5.2 corp. (58); 85.1 ad 1 (331). Cf. Wippel, *Metaphysical Thought of Thomas Aquinas*, 41-44; Rocca, *Speaking the Incomprehensible God*, 172-73; Robert Sokolowski, "The Science of Being as Being in Aristotle, Aquinas, and Wippel," in *The Science of Being as Being: Metaphysical Investigations*, ed. Gregory T. Doolan (Washington, DC: Catholic University of America Press, 2011), 12-15.

[76]Thomas, *In Metaphysicorum*, prooemium (1).

[77]E.g., *In Metaphysicorum* 4.1.539-47 (152-53). The study of being (metaphysics) is not only the most intellectual but also the first science in the sense that certain principles in metaphysics are in a precritical fashion already operative in sciences that might precede metaphysics in a formal order of education (so *De Trin.* 3.1 corp. [107]).

[78]Gilson (e.g., *Being and Some Philosophers*, chap. 5) and others have emphasized that Thomas's real distinction between essence and *esse* constitutes a major advancement or break from Aristotle's metaphysics. For his part, Thomas does attribute to Aristotle a doctrine of creation in which God causes the *esse* of creatures (e.g., *De potentia*, in *Quaestiones disputatae*, vol. 2, ed. P. M. Pession, 10th ed. [Rome-Turin: Marietti, 1965], 3.5 corp. [49]; *De substantiis separatis*, in *Opera omnia*, vol. 40/D-E, Leonine ed. [Rome: ad Sanctae Sabinae, 1968], 9 [57]; cf. White, *Wisdom in the Face of Modernity*, 124-28). Note also earlier adumbrations of such a distinction in the Christian tradition in, e.g., John of Damascus, *Dialectica*, in *Die Schriften des Johannes von Damaskos*, vol. 1, ed.

brought into existence, then what it is (its essence or quiddity) does not automatically entail that it actually exists. There is thus a "real" distinction between a thing's essence and *esse*—not a distinction between two "things" (*res*) but an extramental distinction between the essence and the intrinsic act of being. Thomas explains this as a distinction between potency and act: essence is that by which something is what it is or may be what it may be, while *esse* is that by which something actually is what it is (i.e., the actuality of the substance).[79] But there must be one whose essence and existence are identical, lest there be an infinite regression of contingent, caused beings with no first efficient cause.[80] Moreover, there can be only

---

P. Bonifatius Kotter (Berlin: de Gruyter, 1969), fus. μ′ (108), with the talk of a substance (οὐσία) "having" existence or subsistence (εἶναι, ὕπαρξις). For an account of early Christian engagement with Aristotle, see, e.g., Mark Edwards, *Aristotle and Early Christian Thought* (London: Routledge, 2019). However, Aristotle did not develop the distinction between the essence and existence of created beings and, given his doctrine of the eternal existence of the world, did not have the impetus to do so quite like Christian authors who are bound to the doctrine of *creatio ex nihilo* and have a strong awareness of the radical contingency of creation (compare Rocca, *Speaking the Incomprehensible God*, 218-20, 224-31). As Thomas himself recognizes, the temporal finitude of the universe drives home to us the contingency of created being (*SCG* 2.38 [356]). Thus it might be said that, in an Aristotelian metaphysic that is not leavened by the insights of scriptural revelation, it is easier to take the question of being to be a question about what kinds of beings there are, without fully confronting the surprising fact that there are beings at all when there did not have to be (compare Rudi te Velde, *Aquinas on God: The "Divine Science" of the "Summa Theologiae"* [repr., New York: Routledge, 2016], 88-89; John M. Rist, "Augustine, Aristotelianism, and Aquinas: Three Varieties of Philosophical Adaptation," in *Aquinas the Augustinian*, ed. Michael Dauphinais, Barry David, and Matthew Levering [Washington, DC: Catholic University of America Press, 2012], 81-88). Thomas (and other Christian theologians) had to express the Creator-creature distinction in a more thoroughgoing manner. He did so by developing the distinction between a thing's quiddity and its act of being, deploying the Aristotelian notions of potency and act to do so.

[79]Thomas, *De quolibet* 2.2.1(3) ad 2 (215); *ST* Ia.3.4 corp. (42). In the quodlibetal question cited, Thomas is careful to indicate that if *esse* is described as "accidental" to a thing, this is because it is the actuality of the thing and not ingredient in its creaturely essence as such, not as though it were a thing extrinsic and added to its essence like an accident, which is a point that distinguishes his position from that of Avicenna. For a brief history of the essence-*esse* distinction in the medieval period, see John F. Wippel, "Essence and Existence," in *The Cambridge History of Later Medieval Philosophy: From the Rediscovery of Aristotle to the Disintegration of Scholasticism 1100-1600*, ed. Norman Kretzmann, Anthony Kenny, and Jan Pinborg (Cambridge: Cambridge University Press, 1982), 385-410.

[80]Another way of arriving at the essence-*esse* distinction in creatures in Thomas's thought is by considering the intrinsically limited nature of the being of creatures and identifying essence as that which renders a thing what it is and, by implication, what it is not relative to others. In this connection, one essence contains the negation of other essences (see *De Trin.* 4.1 corp. [120-21]). Put differently, essence is a limiting or determining principle of *esse*, while *esse*, if taken absolutely (as in God's case), is the fullness of all perfection (*De ente et essentia* 5 [378-79]; *De hebdomadibus* 2 [273]; *ST* Ia.4.2 corp. [52]; cf. Wippel, *Metaphysical Thought of Thomas Aquinas*, 170-75). In this line of thinking, *esse* is limited or "contracted" by the various "modes" or

one whose essence and existence are identical, who is subsisting *esse* itself, that is, a being who does not "have" or receive *esse* by participation in a source of *esse* but rather is the absolute fullness of *esse* subsisting. For if subsisting *esse* itself were to be individuated, then that would require non-being to serve as an individuating factor, which is impossible. It would also entail that one instance of subsisting being would lack what another has and therefore that neither would in the end be full and pure subsisting *esse*. Thomas therefore concludes that there is one—and only one—who is subsisting *esse* itself and identifies this one as the God of the Bible.[81]

In Thomas's view, natural reason, even without God's saving grace and revelation in Scripture, can proceed through causal analysis of created being and its perfections to arrive at a knowledge of God.[82] Like Augustine, Thomas does affirm the need for God to illumine the mind, but he emphasizes that the naturally endowed light of the active power of the intellect (*intellectus agens*)—under God's providence and participating in the divine intellect that contains the eternal types of created things—suffices for understanding those things to which natural reason "extends itself," though a "superadded" light is needed to understand things known only by faith.[83]

"degrees" of being identified in the Aristotelian categories of being (substance, quantity, quality, and so on) (so *De ver.* 21.1 corp. [593]; *Opera omnia*, vol. 2, *In octo libro Physicorum Aristotelis*, Leonine ed. [Rome: ex Typographia Polyglotta, 1884], 3.5.15 [114]; *In Metaphysicorum* 4.1.540-43 [152]; 5.9.889-92 [238-39]). It is also, as just noted, limited by the essential principles of things in those categories. At the same time, essence is individuated not only by matter and various accidents but also by the individual subject's particular act of existing (e.g., *De ente et essentia* 5 [378]; *De hebdomadibus* 2 [270]; *De quolibet* 2.2.2 [4] ad 2 [218]; *ST* Ia.3.5 corp. [44]. On the interdependence of essence and *esse* as limiting factors, see Wippel, *Metaphysical Thought of Thomas Aquinas*, 124-31). Influenced by Thomas (and other medieval authors), the Reformed orthodox philosopher and theologian Johann Alsted thus calls existence the *forma individuifica* of created beings (*Metaphysica* [Herbornae Nassoviorum, 1613], 1.4 [47]).

[81]E.g., Thomas, *De ente et essentia* 5 (378); *De hebdomadibus* 2 (273); *ST* Ia.3.4 corp. (42); 11.3 corp. (111). In the *De hebdomadibus* commentary, for example, Thomas can still call God an *ens* in a certain sense (one who exists or subsists in distinction from others), but the word applies to him only analogically since he does not "have" *esse* or participate in a source of *esse* but rather is the absolute *esse* that is the source of all other beings (cf. *ST* Ia.13.1 ad 2-3 [139-40]).

[82]See *De Trin.* 5.4 corp. (154); *SCG* 1.3 (7); 4.1 (3-4); *ST* Ia.1.8. ad 2 (2)2.

[83]Thomas, *De Trin.* 1.1 (81-83); *ST* Ia.84.5 (321-22). On the notion of illumination in Thomas's thought in relation to Augustine, see, e.g., Pasnau, *Thomas Aquinas on Human Nature*, 302-10; Turner, *Faith, Reason and the Existence of God*, 84-88. Thomas's position is worked out in opposition to the claim of some of the Muslim Aristotelians that the light of the active intellect, instead of being a power of the individual human being's soul, is a separate substance by which all persons gain understanding.

While many persons "perceive" from the order of the world that there must be someone who has so ordered it, the discursive analysis that leads to more complete knowledge of the matter is undertaken by relatively few human beings. And, given the weakness of the human mind, it is mixed with error.[84] Indeed, in accord with Romans 1, it is not merely that the Gentiles sin because they are ignorant. Rather, they are ignorant because they have sinned and refused to use the natural knowledge of God to glorify him. The fault is not from the ignorance but the ignorance from the fault.[85] In keeping with Jesus' prayer in John 17, the world lacks knowledge of God not only because it lacks certain truths of "speculative" knowledge given by super-natural revelation (e.g., God is triune) but also because "it does not know [God] with affective knowledge, because it does not love him."[86]

In Thomas's thinking, while it is important that all persons have an awareness of God by the light of nature, which is a "preamble to grace,"[87] it is not necessary to work through an elaborate system of natural theology prior to dogmatic exposition of the articles of faith in order to justify the claims of the theology based on Holy Scripture.[88] For Thomas, when we consider the use of rational argumentation in the study of divine things, it is clearly an

---

[84]Thomas, *De Trin.* 3.1 corp. (108); *SCG* 1.4 (11); 3.38 (94); *ST* Ia.1.1 corp. (6); IaIIae.2.4 corp. (30). In presenting the logic of a Thomistic progression from knowledge of creatures to natural knowledge of God, White acknowledges that, though this progression is natural in its character, "it might never have come into being concretely" in a culture lacking "the workings of grace" (*Wisdom in the Face of Modernity*, 283n103).

[85]Thomas Aquinas, *Super epistolas S. Pauli lectura*, vol. 1, *Super epistolam ad Romanos lectura*, ed. P. Raphaelis Cai, 8th ed. (Turin-Rome: Marietti, 1953), 1.7.124-31 (24).

[86]Thomas Aquinas, *Super Evangelium S. Ioannis lectura*, ed. P. Raphael Cai, 5th ed. (Turin-Rome: Marietti, 1952), 17.6.2.2265 (426).

[87]Thomas, *De Trin.* 2.3 corp. (99).

[88]Thomas therefore ought not to be labeled a "foundationalist" in this sense. On whether Thomas was a "foundationalist," compare Ralph McInerny, "Analogy and Foundationalism in Thomas Aquinas," in *Rationality, Religious Belief, and Moral Commitment*, ed. Robert Audi and William J. Wainwright (Ithaca, NY: Cornell University Press, 1986), 280-88. At the same time, Thomas does affirm that there is a natural, common knowledge of God granted to all human persons prior to the reception of supernatural revelation. This knowledge is open to elaboration and demonstration by natural reason. It seems to me that Bruce Marshall's "postliberal" or "coher-entist" Thomas risks neglecting this important fact ("Aquinas as Postliberal Theologian," *The Thomist* 53 [1989]: 353-402; Marshall, "*Quod Scit Una Uetula*: Aquinas on the Nature of Theology," in *The Theology of Thomas Aquinas*, ed. Rik Van Nieuwenhove and Joseph Wawrykow [Notre Dame, IN: University of Notre Dame Press, 2005], 1-35). See Gilles Emery's related critique of the "postliberal" Thomas in *Trinity, Church, and the Human Person: Thomistic Essays*, Faith and Reason: Studies in Catholic Theology and Philosophy (Naples, FL: Sapientia, 2007), 263-90.

error to hold that reason precedes faith in the things that must be known by faith. For though good arguments will follow and reinforce the things known by faith, the arguments do not precede faith. Thomas invokes Hilary of Poitiers: "By believing, begin."[89] *Sacra doctrina* is scientific not because reason produces its subject matter but because it takes the articles of faith as principles and from these makes various inferences and draws various conclusions about reality.[90] Because it has higher principles, *sacra doctrina* is a higher science than that of the philosophers. Indeed, because it regulates and orders other sciences, dogmatic theology is not only science but wisdom as well.[91] Accordingly, as it operates from higher principles proceeding from God's own unerring self-knowledge and bearing the authority of God, it provides a surer foundation for theological knowledge even in treating those things already knowable by reason.[92] As grace does not destroy but perfects nature, so *sacra doctrina* perfects the true insights of philosophy and makes threefold use of philosophical reasoning: (1) demonstrating things that are included in the *praeambulum fidei* of the light of nature (e.g., God's existence and unity); (2) illumining by created similitudes certain features of the articles of faith; and (3) defusing arguments advanced by opponents of the faith. Thomas also identifies a twofold misuse of philosophy in *sacra doctrina*: (1) taking up false notions that belong not to philosophy per se but to its corruption or abuse and (2) assuming that the things of faith must be included under and justified by philosophical reasoning if they are to be believed.[93]

---

[89]Thomas, *De Trin.* 2.1 corp. and ad 3 (93-94). Like other disciplines, theological science does not attempt rationally to prove its principles (the articles of faith). Its polemical strategy against those who deny the things known by faith alone is a matter of exhibiting how the articles of faith do not violate basic logic and of responding to various arguments put forth against faith (*De Trin.* 2.1 ad 5 [94]; *ST* Ia.1.8 corp. [22]; IIa.IIae.1.5 ad 2 [17]).

[90]*Scientia* is properly speaking a kind of knowing in which, from something known, one understands its necessary consequents also to be true.

[91]Thomas, *De Trin.* 2.2 corp. and ad 1, 4-6 (95-96); *ST* Ia.1.2 corp. (9); 1.6 (17-18).

[92]*De Trin.* 3.1 (106-9); *SCG* 1.4 (11); *ST* Ia.1.1 (6-7); 1.6 ad 1 (18); 1.8 ad 2 (22). John Jenkins explores Thomas's representation of *sacra doctrina* as a "subaltern" *scientia* dependent for its principles on God's own knowledge in *Knowledge and Faith in Thomas Aquinas* (Cambridge: Cambridge University Press, 1997).

[93]Thomas, *De Trin.* 2.3 corp. and ad 2 and 6 (98-100). In one sense, Thomas does not describe natural reason as such as something that is essentially altered by supernatural grace. Rather, natural reason (and the truth it discovers) is authored by the God who both creates and saves. Philosophical reasoning retains its range of objects and argumentative structures even when used in the context of *sacra doctrina* to refute objections to Christian teaching (cf. *SCG* 1.2 [6]; 4.1 [5]; Turner, *Faith, Reason and the Existence of God*, 16-17; White, *Wisdom in the Face of*

All of these considerations shape how Thomas presents *sacra doctrina*
in the *Summa theologiae*. *Sacra doctrina* proceeds not from the principles
of other sciences but from principles "immediately from God by revelation." It does not depend on other sciences but where expedient makes
use of them as "handmaidens" (*ancillae*) in order to expound the articles
of faith to the weak human intellect.[94] Thus *sacra doctrina* judges other
sciences and will reject their conclusions whenever they conflict with it
(2 Cor 10:4-5).[95] Unlike philosophical theology, which arrives at knowledge
of God only indirectly as principle of created effects, *sacra doctrina* treats
God directly and all things in reference to or under the aspect of God,
even as God's essence is incomprehensible to us and God's revelation of
himself must draw on our knowledge of created effects.[96] In so doing, this
science proves its conclusions not by appeals to the philosophers or even
the doctors of the church, whose arguments are taken to be at best
"probable," but by the authority of Holy Scripture.[97] In light of this, Thomas
includes the proofs of God's existence in Ia.2.2-3 not because God's existence must be accepted by rational demonstration in order to justify
faith's speech about God but because some natural knowledge of God's
existence, expounded discursively in the proofs, is presupposed in faith
and because Thomas simply wants to exhibit the coherence of faith and
reason on this point.[98]

Modernity, passim). In another sense, though, philosophical reasoning is changed—"converted"
like water to wine—in that it is brought into the service of the higher and more trustworthy
science of *sacra doctrina* (see *De Trin.* 2.3 ad 5 [100]). For additional critique of "postliberal"
readings of Thomas that deny the viability of genuinely *natural* knowledge of God in Thomas's
thought, see Anna Bonta Moreland, *Known by Nature: Thomas Aquinas on Natural Knowledge of
God* (New York: Crossroad, 2010), esp. 143-56.

[94] Thomas, *ST* Ia.1.5 ad 2 (16); 1.8 ad 2 (22).

[95] Thomas, *ST* Ia.1.6 ad 2 (18).

[96] Thomas, *ST* Ia.1.7 corp. and ad 1 (19); 84.7 ad 3 (326); 86.2 ad 1 (349-50).

[97] Thomas, *ST* Ia.1.8 ad 2 (22).

[98] See esp. *ST* Ia.2.2 ad 1 (30). On this point, compare Rocca, *Speaking the Incomprehensible God*,
184; Turner, *Faith, Reason and the Existence of God*, 36-38, 45-46, 240-41; Thomas Joseph White,
introduction to *The Analogy of Being: Invention of the Antichrist or the Wisdom of God?*, ed.Thomas
Joseph White (Grand Rapids: Eerdmans, 2011), 20; Richard A. Muller, "The Dogmatic Function
of St. Thomas' Proofs: A Protestant Appreciation," *Fides et Historia* 24 (1992): 15-29. To integrate
this with other claims made in this section, it remains that the proofs are natural in that their
premises are open to and logically structured according to natural reason (without having to be
taken up within the sphere of faith), even as the proofs are not necessary to justify the work of
dogmatic description of God.

HISTORICAL CONCEPTIONS
OF THE NATURAL KNOWLEDGE OF GOD (II)

Scotus and Ockham. Though Thomas receives the majority of the attention in this description of medieval figures, the positions of Scotus and William of Ockham also should be noted in order at least to gesture toward some other relevant historical and theological issues pertaining to the natural knowledge of God. Shortly after Thomas died in 1274, the bishop of Paris, Stephen Tempier, published a list of philosophical and theological articles that were formally rejected in 1277. The Condemnations of 1277 addressed the work of Siger of Brabant and others who were deemed to have advocated certain philosophical principles that conflicted with Christian teaching. Among other things, the Condemnations called into question the viability of philosophical investigation as an endeavor distinct or independent from Christian theology. They emphasize God's infinite power and ability to do what is by nature impossible, arguably stipulating a lower view of reason's capacity to learn of God from natural principles without reference to supernatural revelation and divine illumination.[99]

Writing in the wake of this, Scotus upheld the legitimacy of natural theology but presumably did so with an awareness of the problems to be faced by those who would affirm the reliability of natural or philosophical study of God. On the one hand, Scotus clearly insists that human beings can know God through the use of reason and seeks to show how God's existence and infinite perfection are rationally demonstrable.[100] In fact, one of Scotus's

---

[99]For summaries, see John F. Wippel, "Thomas Aquinas and the Condemnation of 1277," *The Modern Schoolman* 72 (1995): 233-71; Wippel, "The Parisian Condemnations of 1270 and 1277," in *A Companion to Philosophy in the Middle Ages*, ed. Jorge J. E. Garcia and Timothy B. Noone (Oxford: Blackwell, 2002), 65-73; Jan A. Aertsen et al., eds., *Nach der Verurteilung von 1277: Philosophie und Theologie an der Universität von Paris im letzten Viertel des 13. Jahrhunderts. Studie und Texte/After the Condemnation of 1277: Philosophy and Theology at the University of Paris in the Last Quarter of the Thirteenth Century. Studies and Texts*, Miscellanea Mediaevalia 28 (Berlin: de Gruyter, 2001). Alexander W. Hall, *Thomas Aquinas and John Duns Scotus: Natural Theology in the High Middle Ages* (London: Continuum. 2000), 3-6. Among other things, this chastening of philosophy's role pushed back against the problem of a *duplex veritas* (on which, see, e.g., the Reformed author Bartholomäus Keckermann, *Brevis et simplex consideratio controversiae hoc tempore a nonnullis motae, de pugna philosophiae et theologiae*, in *Praecognitorum philosophicorum, libri duo* [Hanau, 1612], 2 [181-200]).

[100]Scotus, *Ordinatio* 1.2.1, nn. 39-190 (2.148-243), Scotus, *A Treatise on God as First Principle: A Latin Text and English Translation of "De Primo Principio,"* ed. and trans. Allan B. Wolter (Chicago: Franciscan Herald Press, 1966). On Scotus's use of causation to arrive at knowledge of God, see, e.g., Rega Wood, "Scotus's Argument for the Existence of God," *Franciscan Studies* 47

stated aims in developing a doctrine of the univocity of being is to ensure that there is a basis for natural theology.[101] Moreover, he interprets Augustine's teaching on illumination in a way that affirms the natural, intrinsic capacity of human beings to understand reality.[102] On the other hand, Scotus holds that natural reason cannot attain to a knowledge of God's essence as such and in itself (*sub ratione huius essentiae ut haec et in se*). It obtains only a *per accidens* or indirect knowledge of God.[103] While it is possible to exaggerate the difference between Scotus and Thomas on natural theology, Alexander Hall, for example, argues that Scotus is "more circumspect than Aquinas as regards the reliability of knowledge derived through experience."[104] Scotus recognizes different degrees of certainty that one might gain from scientific demonstration, showing more reservation about demonstrations that utilize sense perception of frequent connections between effects and their presumed causes.[105] From this, Hall infers that Scotus's "devaluation of experiential knowledge may . . . impact his estimation of Aristotelian natural theology." The "traits" that we perceive in nature would be only "apt" to apply to God (rather than predicable of God with certainty). More specifically, "Experiential scientific knowledge depends on the principle that like causes generate like effects, and is therefore less certain than unqualified scientific knowledge, which is of propositions true by definition." According to Hall, the emphasis on divine omnipotence in the Condemnations undercuts "Aristotelian naturalism and thus cast[s] lasting suspicion on proofs from the natural order."[106]

(1987): 257-77; Timothy O'Connor, "Scotus on the Existence of a First Efficient Cause," *International Journal for Philosophy of Religion* 33 (1993): 17-32; Richard Cross, *Duns Scotus on God* (Aldershot: Ashgate, 2005), 17-48. For a broader summary of Scotus on proving God's existence, see Allan B. Wolter, *The Philosophical Theology of John Duns Scotus*, ed. Marilyn McCord Adams (Ithaca, NY: Cornell University Press, 1990), 254-77.

[101]Scotus, *Ordinatio* 1.3.1.1, nn. 39-40 (3:26-27); 1.8.1.3, nn. 70-9 (4:184-89). I will explore Scotus on univocity in chap. 5.

[102]Scotus, *Ordinatio* 1.3.1.4, nn. 261-80 (3:160-72).

[103]John Duns Scotus, *Opera philosophica*, vols. 3-4, *Quaestiones super libros Metaphysicorum Aristotelis libri I-V*, ed. R. Andrews et al. (St. Bonaventure: St. Bonaventure University, 1997), 1.1, n. 163 (3:71-72); *Ordinatio* 1.3.1, nn. 56-57 (3:38-39).

[104]Hall, *Thomas Aquinas and John Duns Scotus*, 76.

[105]Scotus, *Ordinatio* 1.3.1.4, nn. 234-37 (3:140-44).

[106]Hall, *Thomas Aquinas and Duns Scotus*, 83-85; Hall, "Natural Theology in the Middle Ages," in *The Oxford Handbook of Natural Theology*, ed. Russell Re Manning (Oxford: Oxford University Press, 2013), 67.

Ockham is more pessimistic than both Thomas and Scotus about the theological competency of natural reason. To be sure, Alfred Freddoso points out, Ockham would affirm philosophy's role in promoting "logical skills and intellectual habits that are required for the articulation of true wisdom within Christian theology; it can even provide Christian thinkers with new and useful conceptual resources. But it cannot on its own make any noteworthy progress toward providing us with the substance of absolute wisdom."[107] On the one hand, Ockham cites the authority of Augustine to assert that some theological truths are "naturally known or knowable," like "God is, God is wise, God is good, etc.," while others are known only supernaturally (e.g., God is triune, God is incarnate).[108] On the other hand, Ockham expresses serious doubts about whether observation of the natural world and causal analysis can generate knowledge of God's existence or attributes, often finding weaknesses in traditional arguments.[109] For example, Ockham maintains that it is "difficult" to uphold Scotus's argument that there cannot be an infinite procession of productive causes and that there must therefore be a first cause distinct from all effects, though Ockham does acknowledge that the presence of a "conserving cause" would imply that there cannot be an infinite series of causes since a conserving cause and the effects conserved are contemporaneous (assuming the presence of a contemporaneously infinite series would problematically entail there being an actual infinite).[110] In addition, if the term "God" is taken to signify "that than which nothing is better or more perfect," it can be shown that "God" exists (lest there be an infinite regression of things with nothing prior to all of them), but it cannot be shown that there is just *one* God.[111] Ockham also

---

[107] Alfred J. Freddoso, "Ockham on Faith and Reason," in *The Cambridge Companion to Ockham,* ed. Paul Vincent Spade (Cambridge: Cambridge University Press, 1999), 346. Freddoso calls Ockham's separation of faith and reason an "irenic separatism." Compare Armand Maurer, *The Philosophy of William of Ockham: In the Light of Its Principles* (Toronto: Pontifical Institute of Mediaeval Studies, 1999), 106-7, 132-35.

[108] William of Ockham, *Opera theologica,* vols. 1-4, *Scriptum in librum primum Sententiarum (Ordinatio),* ed. Gedeon Gál et al. (St. Bonaventure: St. Bonaventure University, 1967-2000), 1, prol., q. 1 (1:7).

[109] See, e.g., Maurer, *Philosophy of William of Ockham,* 167-83.

[110] William of Ockham, *Ordinatio* 1.2.10 (2:354-57). For a summary of Ockham's criticism of Scotus's approach to causality and the knowledge of God, see Gordon Leff, *William of Ockham: The Metamorphosis of Scholastic Discourse* (Manchester: Manchester University Press, 1975), 388-98.

[111] William of Ockham, *Opera theologica,* vol. 9, *Quodlibeta septem,* ed. Joseph C. Wey (St. Bonaventure: St. Bonaventure University, 1980), 1.1 (1-3).

takes aim at Scotus's attempts to prove by the use of natural reason that God is "intensively infinite," claiming that various lines of reasoning given by Scotus do not fully establish Scotus's claim.[112] God's intensively infinite power is certain as a matter of faith but only probable if taken as a conclusion of philosophical argument.[113]

An underlying factor in Ockham's reservations about natural theology is his approach to causality. He cautions against assuming that God must be the cause of something when it is possible that another being (like an angel) is responsible for it.[114] In fact, God can cause something and (even if he never actually does this) delegate the conservation of it to another being.[115] In general, while knowledge of an effect will yield knowledge that there is some cause behind it, the effect cannot afford "particular" or "proper" cognition of the cause as an individual (*illud quod est causa*).[116] Such a claim perhaps resonates with something Thomas or Scotus could say about our not knowing all that is proper to God by natural reason alone. However, Ockham goes further in saying that knowledge of an effect (which some presume would be similar to its cause) does not produce knowledge "of that of which it is the similitude," unless one already possesses "habitual knowledge of that of which it is the similitude." For example, if someone views a statue of Hercules with no prior knowledge of Hercules, one would not learn from it more about Hercules than Achilles.[117] To be sure, Ockham was a realist rather than a staunch skeptic: "What makes belief cognition is the right causal relation between the knower and what is known."[118] But he prioritizes intuitive cognition of singular existents present to the human knower and states that nothing should be posited unless it is "self-evident [*per se notum*],

---

[112]See William of Ockham, *Quodlibeta septem* 7.11-17 (738-74); cf. 3.1 (200-208). In this sense, if something is "intensively" infinite, it has some perfection in an infinite degree, while if something is "extensively" infinite, it has the full range of perfections in whatever degree it may have them.

[113]Ockham, *Quodlibeta septem* 7.18 (774-79).

[114]Ockham, *Quodlibeta septem* 2.1-2 (107-17).

[115]William of Ockham, *Ordinatio* 1.48 (4:669).

[116]Ockham, *Ordinatio* 1.1.4 (1:436).

[117]Ockham, *Ordinatio* 1, prol., q. 9 (1:254). Thomas would of course assert that the perfections of an effect are necessarily present in an eminent way in the cause (e.g., *ST* Ia.4.2 [51-52]).

[118]John Lee Longeway, introduction to *Demonstration and Scientific Knowledge in William of Ockham: A Translation of "Summa Logicae III-II: De Syllogismo Demonstrativo," and Selections from the Prologue to the "Ordinatio"* (Notre Dame, IN: University of Notre Dame Press, 2007), 1.

known by experience or proved by the authority of sacred Scripture."[119] Further, Ockham advocates what might be called a minimalist ontology in which certain things (like relations) are thought to be reducible to other things (especially substance and quality). He cautions against taking observed correlations between objects to establish demonstrative, necessary knowledge of causal relations. It is not surprising that some have taken these points in Ockham's philosophical program to undermine our confidence in traditional proofs of God's existence, but close interpreters of Ockham have also pointed out that he is not a forerunner to a thoroughgoing Humean skepticism about knowledge of causality.[120] In sum, Ockham calls into question how much or how confidently God's causal activity may be known apart from supernatural revelation, without denying the reality of God's causal activity or our ability to have some knowledge of causation.

Preliminary comments on Thomas, Scotus, and Ockham. In the conclusion of this chapter I will attempt to draw together some of the insights that can be gathered from authors like Augustine and Thomas, from the Reformed authors to be discussed below, and from the engagement with more recent concerns about natural theology. It may be worth pausing here, however, to indicate how our conclusions about the natural knowledge of God will be affected (or not affected) by the general drift of the Condemnations of Paris or the more cautious approaches of thinkers like Scotus and Ockham. Doing this will involve anticipating some of the useful material in Reformed orthodoxy and will then lead us naturally into the next part of this section.

First, while there are obvious dangers in taking philosophy as an authority that is above the correction of scriptural theology, this does not mean

---

[119]Ockham, *Ordinatio*, 1.30.1 (4:290). Ockham does argue, however, that God by his "absolute power" (as distinct from his "ordained power") can cause intuitive knowledge of himself in the intellect of the Christian pilgrim (*Ordinatio* 1, prol., q. 1, 5 [1:48-49, 72]). For pertinent treatments of Ockham on cognition, see Elizabeth Karger, "Ockham's Misunderstood Theory of Intuitive and Abstractive Cognition," in Spade, *Cambridge Companion to Ockham*, 205-11; Claude Pannacio, *Ockham on Concepts* (Aldershot: Ashgate, 2004).

[120]Relevant texts include Ockham, *Ordinatio* 1, prol., q. 2 (1:75-129); *Quodlibeta septem* 6.8-12 (611-33). See Leff, *William of Ockham*, 580-84; Marilyn McCord Adams, *William Ockham* (Notre Dame, IN: University of Notre Dame Press, 1987), 2:741-98; Paul Vincent Spade, "Ockham's Nominalist Metaphysics: Some Main Themes," in Spade, *Cambridge Companion to Ockham*, 100-117; Gyula Klima, "Ockham's Semantics and Ontology of the Categories," in Spade, *Cambridge Companion to Ockham*, 118-42; Jenny E. Pelletier, *William Ockham on Metaphysics: The Science of Being and God* (Leiden: Brill, 2013), 206-70.

that the natural intellect must forfeit its proper observation of natural objects or its basic patterns of logical inference. Sin has not altogether destroyed nature or the natural knowledge of God. In keeping with a figure
like Thomas, then, the natural mind continues to have some capacity of
arriving at a knowledge of God as the first cause, though the practice of
reasoning about God from creation is best undertaken within the sphere of
Christian faith seeking understanding, which is a point made quite well by
the Reformed orthodox. In line with Thomas and Scotus, it also seems that
the genuinely natural character of natural theological knowledge implies
that the light or power of apprehension whereby the human mind arrives at
truth about God is not given only intermittently or in radical disjunction
from the regular operations of the mind. It is better to understand illumination (as it applies to natural theology, not salvific apprehension of the
gospel) as a matter of God's giving a capacity of knowing that is permanently
resident in individual human subjects and exercised under the providence
of God in the ordinary course of human life.

Second, with Scotus, it seems fitting to affirm that the natural knowledge
of God is indirect in an important sense. For it does not lead us *immediately*
to a knowledge of God in himself but along a path of inferring from natural
things certain truths about God the Creator. Thomas would agree here, as
shown above in the way he distinguishes between the way of philosophical
knowledge of God and the way of *sacra doctrina* in the *De Trinitate*
commentary. Third, with Scotus and Ockham, it is wise to note that the
natural knowledge of God, in a certain sense, does not touch on what is
proper to God. It arguably can attain to some understanding of things that
would pertain to God alone (perhaps, e.g., pure actuality or omnipotence),
but, in discerning that there is a God to whom such would apply, it does not
fully identify who this God is in all his distinguishing marks or economic
acts. The Reformed orthodox will help on this point too in discussing how
the natural knowledge of God is "common" rather than "proper."

Fourth, turning to the question of the rational demonstration of God's
existence or perfections, I would refer back to a statement made in the previous section on scriptural exegesis: such demonstration is secondary to the
primary meaning of "natural theology," namely, a spontaneous (rather than
ratiocinative) awareness of God's eternal power, righteousness, and so on

from human encounter with the created order. Quibbles about the success or deficiencies of any one of the traditional proofs are ultimately relativized by a prioritization of what the Reformed orthodox call an "implanted" or "infused" (versus an "acquired") natural theological knowledge. Nevertheless, it is worth commenting on Ockham's desire—I do not know that Scotus is so skeptical—to limit what can be known of God from causal analysis. For example, he contends that an effect need not have a similarity to its cause that is discernible without prior knowledge of the cause itself. But if God is uniquely *a se* and absolute, he cannot (and need not) initially draw on something beyond himself to serve as an archetype of his effects. His attributes will therefore be displayed in his effects in some finite degree, even if some created effects have causal powers themselves and will be directly responsible for effecting various things in the world. Moreover, Ockham's analogy involving the statue of Hercules seems to be poorly framed, for even if there might be a scenario in which one would not learn more about Hercules than Achilles from the statue, one would still have to say that the statue as it stands does reveal something about the one who made it (at least that he or she has some degree of intelligence and artistic skill). Finally, broadly speaking, Ockham is arguably right to prioritize perception of singular existents in his epistemology, but this need not entail an empiricist rejection of the inborn human tendency to perceive causation in certain relations between things. This matter will come up again below in our consideration of Immanuel Kant.

Early Reformed reflections. Through the influence of twentieth-century authors like Karl Barth and Cornelius Van Til, the contemporary student of Reformed theology may not readily associate it with a strong natural theology tradition, but the early Reformed do in fact emphasize that the human race possesses a natural knowledge of God, even if that knowledge has been tragically corrupted by sin.[121] Many of the early Reformed in fact exhibit a broadly Thomistic conception of natural and supernatural theology and of faith and

---

[121]Barth's thoughts on natural theology will appear below and in chap. 5. For relevant material in Van Til, see, e.g., his *The Defense of the Faith*, ed. K. Scott Oliphint, 4th ed. (Phillipsburg, NJ: P&R, 2008). For recent work emphasizing the positive role of natural theology and natural law in the Reformed tradition, see, e.g., Michael Sudduth, *The Reformed Objection to Natural Theology* (Farnham, UK: Ashgate, 2009); David VanDrunen, *Natural Law and the Two Kingdoms: A Study in the Development of Reformed Social Thought* (Grand Rapids: Eerdmans, 2010); J. V. Fesko, *Reforming Apologetics: Retrieving the Classical Reformed Approach to Defending the Faith* (Grand Rapids: Baker Academic, 2019).

reason (without necessarily excluding the insights of other medieval authors). John Calvin affirms that it is "beyond controversy" that there is "in the human mind, by natural instinct, a sense of divinity [*sensus divinitatis*]." To prevent our claiming to be ignorant about him, God has "endowed" us with an understanding of his own majesty and, indeed, continually "renews" that understanding.[122] Because the blessed life involves the knowledge of God (see Jn 17:3), God has not only endowed our minds with a "seed of religion" (*religionis semen*) but has also revealed himself in the whole "handiwork" of the world, engraving on his works "certain marks of his own glory" so that all (including the unlearned) "cannot open their eyes except that they are constrained to see him."[123] Nevertheless, sinful humanity has corrupted that knowledge of God so that we now require the "spectacles" of Scripture to direct us back to a right understanding of the Creator.[124]

In the development of the early Reformed tradition, theologians take up a number of scholastic distinctions to locate natural theology (and supernatural theology) within the broader field of divine and human knowledge of God. Though their accounts of natural theology are not entirely uniform, enough cohesion exists to permit a composite sketch drawn from representative treatments. The early Reformed often accentuate the limitations and corruption of natural theology after the fall, but the positive function of natural theology before and after the fall is not overlooked. Natural theology in one sense may be identified as a kind of "false theology" (*theologia falsa*) that bears the name of "theology" only by equivocation. *Theologia falsa* is a false view of God that emerges either from the "incomplete principles of our nature" without the development of philosophical reasoning (*theologia falsa vulgaris*) or from those principles with the development of (erroneous) philosophical reasoning (*theologia falsa philosophica* or *acquisita*, under which heading, in keeping with Augustine in *City of God*, *theologia naturalis* appears).[125]

However, natural theology in another sense can be treated more positively under the rubric of "true theology" (*theologia vera*) as one mode of

---

[122]John Calvin, *Ioannis Calvini opera quae supersunt omnia*, vol. 2, *Institutio Christianae religionis* (1559), ed. Guilielmus Baum et al. (Brunswick: Schwetschke, 1864), 1.3.1 (36).

[123]Calvin, *Institutio Christianae religionis* 1.5.1 (41).

[124]Calvin, *Institutio Christianae religionis* 1.4.1-3 (38-40); 5.4-5, 11-15 (43-45, 49-52); 6.1 (53).

[125]Franciscus Junius, *De vera theologia* (Leiden, 1594), 1 (22-24); Polanus, *Syntagma* 1.1 (1). Cf. Turretin, *Inst.* 1.2.5 (1:4-5).

the "theology of revelation," more particularly the revealed theology of pilgrims, or "our theology."[126] For God communicates knowledge of himself to creatures by nature as well as grace, which is to say by principles intrinsic to the created order as well as principles extrinsic to it. In fact, God himself is the common underlying principle of both nature and grace, for he is the author of all that is good "according to nature" and all that is good "above nature." Since God "graciously" gives knowledge of himself by principles native to the human intellect, natural theology may even be called a "natural grace," even if as a *natural* grace it is distinct from the "grace of revelation" strictly so called due to supernatural revelation's externality to the created order. Before the fall, this "natural grace" and the "supernatural grace" of revelation from beyond the created order stood together in coherence, but after the fall nature and natural theology are corrupted so that there is now a *duplex theologia* in fallen human experience, one natural (and corrupted) and the other supernatural.[127]

For the Reformed orthodox, natural theology may be defined as a knowledge about God that "proceeds from principles known . . . by the natural light of the human intellect, in the mode of human reason." By contrast, supernatural theology is a knowledge of or discourse about God that "proceeds from principles known . . . by the light of a superior knowledge" (i.e., "by divine revelation, illumination, and persuasion above the mode of human reason"). The two do not share a common genus or univocal agreement, for the principles of each (respectively, nature and the transcendent grace of God) are not in a common genus. For some Reformed theologians, natural theology, unlike supernatural theology, is not to be called "wisdom," though it is often called such among the philosophers by equivocation. The distinction between natural and supernatural theology may be fleshed out by observing the object and etiology of each. The object or subject of natural theology is "divine things" "partly properly" (i.e., as they truly are) and "partly improperly" (i.e., taken according to false human opinion), while the object of supernatural theology is "divine things properly

---

[126]Not all the Reformed speak in this way. Polanus, for example, is more negative on the whole about natural theology and does not explicitly include natural theology as a mode of "our theology," though see his more positive reflections in *Syntagma* 5.5 (265-66).

[127]Junius, *De vera theologia* 9 (63-66); Turretin, *Inst.* 1.2.7 (1:5).

and simply so called" (as they truly are). The efficient cause of natural theology is "nature and the natural light of our intellect," while the efficient
cause of supernatural theology is the grace of God and the supernatural light
of Spirit-wrought revelation and illumination. Though natural theology is
revealed theology in a broad sense, supernatural theology (called such because of its supernatural origin) is more strictly called revealed theology
because it is graciously given to us from beyond any principles intrinsic to
the created order. The material cause of natural theology is "the principles
or precepts implanted [*insita*] in humanity by nature" (e.g., God exists, God
is one, God is to be worshiped), while the material cause of supernatural
theology is "principles or precepts unknown by nature and graciously revealed" or "truths . . . had by inspiration or revelation from God in the Holy
Scriptures" (i.e., God is triune, the Father generates the Son, the gospel of
Jesus Christ). The formal cause of natural theology consists in that it proceeds from natural, self-evident (*secundum se nota*) principles set forth by
human reason, while the formal cause of supernatural theology consists in
that it proceeds from principles of a superior light, by divine revelation.[128]

The natural knowledge of God is commonly distinguished as either "implanted" (*insita*) or "acquired" (*acquisita*). The former is an awareness of God
the Creator spontaneously generated by human encounter with the created
order, including conscience. The latter is a discursive knowledge of God
obtained by inferring true conclusions about God from the existence and
characteristics of the created order. That the former is "implanted" does not
signal that there are fully formed propositions or acts of knowing in the
mind prior to any experience of the world.[129] As Francis Turretin puts it, it
is not a knowledge "immediately in act" like the "act of life" of a living thing
is present even in the womb. There is no inborn "actual cognition" in that
sense; indeed, the human mind is a *tabula rasa* with respect to such cognition. Rather, the *cognitio Dei insita* is *insita* in that the human person is
created by God with a "potency" or "natural faculty" that possesses a "power
of understanding" (*potentia intelligendi*) and "natural principles of knowledge

---

[128]Junius, *De vera theologia* 9 (66); 10 (66-68); 11 (84-86); Polanus, *Syntagma* 1.9-10 (12).

[129]Interestingly, Polanus faults Thomas and "other scholastics" for denying that God's existence is
per se notum (self-evident), but it is clear that he, like Thomas and other Reformed orthodox
writers, believes the natural knowledge of God begins with apprehensive cognition of features
of the world and is developed by rational argumentation (*Syntagma* 2.4 [135]).

[*notitia*, basic awareness or apprehension of something] from which conclusions both theoretical and practical are deduced."[130] In other words, the "implanted" natural knowledge of God is called such simply because it arises
"spontaneously, without ratiocinations." It includes certain "common notions"
acknowledged intuitively or by direct apprehension by all human beings.
Some of these "notions" are theoretical or related chiefly to the apprehension
of the real, and others are practical or related chiefly to things that must be
done.[131] In this connection, the human person is created with a natural law
written on the conscience that "includes a knowledge of God the lawgiver,
by whose authority [conscience] obligates men to obedience." Accordingly,
there is in human beings a "sense of the divine" and "propensity toward
religion."[132] Additionally, the natural knowledge of God involves "common
notions" about God in the sense that these notions are not "proper." Though
they teach us that there is a God to be worshiped, they do not "teach

---

[130]On the one hand, the "first principles" of thinking (e.g., the law of noncontradiction, the existence of an effect assumes the existence of a cause) are regarded as "self-evident" (*per se nota*)
or known "by their own light." They are indemonstrable, unquestionable, and basic to scientific
demonstration (so Turretin, *Inst.* 1.9.5 [1:33]; 2.4.22 [1:76]; 6.18 [1:101]; cf. Thomas, *De hebdomadibus* 1 [269]). On the other hand, if the first principles (also called "common conceptions" or *dignitates*) are not only a feature of the power or faculty of knowing but in fact items
of knowledge, then it would be consistent to say that they too are engendered by experience of
outward reality (see Thomas, *In Post. An.* 2.15.20 [397-403]; cf. Gisbertus Voetius, *Selectarum
disputationum theologicarum* (Utrecht, 1648) 1.1 [1-2]; 10 [140-42]). It seems to me that one
could easily moor this point in Turretin's line of thinking where he speaks of reason as signifying either a faculty of the soul or a natural light "externally proposed" and "internally impressed
on the mind" that disposes the mind toward forming certain concepts and drawing certain
conclusions (*Inst.* 1.8.1 [1:26]).

[131]Voetius, *Select. disp.* 1.10 (140-41).

[132]Turretin, *Inst.* 1.3.2, 4-5, 8-9, 11 (7-10); 8.1 (26); John Owen, *The Works of John Owen*, vol. 17,
Theologoumena pantodapa, ed. William H. Goold (Edinburgh: T&T Clark, 1862), 1.5.2, 6 (45,
47); Mastricht, *TPT* 2.2.18 (70). Richard Muller observes that talk of "innate" knowledge of God
"indicate[s] neither an unmediated act of God by which knowledge is implanted nor an inward
illumination, but rather that fundamental sense of the divine mediated by the created order
and known by the mind's apprehension of externals, rather than by the process of logical deduc-
tion" (*Dictionary of Latin and Greek Theological Terms: Drawn Principally from Protestant Scholastic Theology* [Grand Rapids: Baker, 1985], 70-71). This implanted knowledge of God may be
called "intuitive" in the sense that it is not derived from ratiocination, but not in the sense that
it bypasses the creaturely media of revelation altogether—a bypassing that is experienced only
by the blessed in heaven (see Polanus, *Syntagma* 1.8 [11]). Per Polanus, if "intuitive" describes
a knowledge not mediated by forms of revelation, then our apprehensive knowledge of God in
this life by the media of his effects and his word is an "abstractive" knowledge in which the
object is not directly present to the intellect (compare also John Owen, *Christologia*, in *The
Works of John Owen*, vol. 1, *The Glory of Christ*, ed. William H. Goold [Edinburgh: Banner of
Truth, 1965], 5 [65-69]).

singularly" or "point out" that *this one* is the true God. Even in the state of integrity before the fall, this knowledge of God was limited and needed to be perfected by ratiocination and especially by the grace of supernatural revelation.[133] The "common notions" are "increased" and "drawn out" by consideration of God's works of creation and providence. For John Owen, the "common notions" implanted by God and the external, revelatory works of creation and providence are a "twofold font" (*duplex fons*) by which humanity after the fall still retains some natural knowledge of God's eternal power, deity, and justice. God's works of creation and providence are thus "media" of a "catholic revelation."[134]

Humanity's fall into sin yields a holistic corruption of the human subject and therefore a corruption of the human subject's natural knowledge of God. The fall also involves a rejection of the supernatural knowledge of God initially made available to Adam and Eve. In this sense, Franciscus Junius invokes the scholastic dictum that "the natural gifts are corrupted and the supernatural gifts are lost."[135] Whatever truth remains in the natural theology of fallen humanity is mixed with error and is available in its discursive mode to only the few who devote themselves to the practice of reasoning about the divine.[136] Moreover, it is not sufficient to bring us to salvation and right

---

[133]Junius, *De vera theologia* 9 (74-77); 10 (69-82). As Polanus puts it, "It is not enough to know that there is one God, but it is necessary to know who that one is." Polanus of course asserts that this one God is the God of Israel (*Syntagma* 2.5 [137]).

[134]Owen, *Theologoumena pantodapa*, 1.5.9-10 (51); 6.2 (28, 30, 55, 67-68); 7.2 (78). It is important to underscore that, broadly speaking, in Reformed orthodoxy the implanted knowledge of God (or the *sensus divinitatis* or *semen religionis*) is neither a purely noncognitive feeling nor a body of theological propositions built into the mind. There is no pristine *sensus divinitatis* separable from common human experience of outward reality and insulated from the operations of the intellect and their incomplete apprehensions of God (*pace* the impression given by Van Til, *Defense of the Faith*, 120, 136-37, 173-74, 191, where he aims to preserve for Christianity a point of contact with the unbelieving world, while [1] keeping it free of the partial character and the corruption of the natural knowledge of God and [2] suggesting that its intelligibility depends entirely on being viewed with reference to the dicta of supernatural theology). The *sensus divinitatis* or *semen religionis* includes cognitive content, and while the native power and propensity of arriving at that content is itself prior to acts of cognition, that content arises from the active engagement of the natural faculty of knowing with the facts of God's world. After the fall, it is not untouched by error. Yet, happily, it is connected to outward reality and part of the field of common experience. It is also (at least to some degree) intelligible and exerts cognitive and moral pressure on human persons even apart from supernatural revelation.

[135]Junius, *De vera theologia* 10 (78).

[136]Junius, *De vera theologia* 10 (78-80); Owen, *Theologoumena pantodapa* 1.7.2-8 (78-81). Turretin notes that the self-evident principles of reason (e.g., the law of noncontradiction) remain

fellowship with God, for it does not bring us Christ the mediator.[137] Nevertheless, there is an ongoing use for natural theology in the divine economy. Johann Alsted identifies a twofold use: (1) "to render man inexcusable" and (2) "to prepare him for the school of grace" and enable him to read the "book of grace" with prior awareness of the majesty of God and the imperfection of nature that anticipates grace.[138] Turretin comments that natural theology still attests the goodness of God toward sinners (see Jn 1:5; Acts 14:16-17), encourages us to await further revelation of God (see Acts 17:27), and preserves a certain "subjective condition" in the human person preparatory for the "admission of the light of grace" since God in the gospel "addresses not brutes . . . but rational creatures."[139]

The renewal of supernatural theology after the fall is not opposed to nature or natural theology as such—indeed it was present in harmony with natural theology before the fall—but it is opposed to the corruption of human nature and natural theology. It comes to us from beyond nature and restores and perfects nature. The supernatural theology present before the fall transcended nature in that it was a gift of God from beyond any principles intrinsic to the created order.[140] It transcends nature after the fall both in this way and in that it must reform the corrupted natural knowledge of God, for the subject in possession of natural theology lacks the right *habitus* or disposition to assimilate and salvifically receive the truth of supernatural theology.[141] Supernatural theology is given by testimony (i.e., by the word of God) and received by faith, a *habitus* (a determination of a power or capacity toward a particular action) that is granted and infused by the Holy Spirit's regenerative work. Faith is, in Turretin's words, a "composite habit" present and active in both the intellect and the will.[142] The *habitus* of faith is infused

---

certain, but the fallen mind's use of them to draw various conclusions about divine matters is riddled with error (*Inst.* 1.8.21 [1:31]).

[137] E.g., Turretin, *Inst.* 1.4 (1:10-17); Owen, *Theologoumena pantodapa* 1.6 (54-78).

[138] Johann Alsted, *Theologia naturalis* (Frankfurt, 1615), 1.1 (3).

[139] Turretin, *Inst.* 1.4.4 (1:11). In other words, reason provides some "presupposed articles" that can help one come to faith in Christ (1.8.1, 4 [1:26-27]).

[140] Junius, *De vera theologia* 9 (65-66); cf. 11 (84-87).

[141] Junius, *De vera theologia* 10 (80-82); cf. Polanus, *Syntagma* 1.10 (12). As Owen phrases it, the unregenerate are "incapable of evangelical theology" in that such theology involves fear of and communion with God and yields and is enriched by obedience and holiness (*Theologoumena pantodapa* 6.5.5 [432]; 6.1-4, 14-16 [438-40, 444-47]; 9.3-9 [469-71]).

[142] Turretin, *Inst.* 1.6.2 (1:20); 15.8.13 (2:616).

"immediately" in the intellect and will by the Holy Spirit, for it cannot arise in fallen persons mediately through the outward presentation of its object alone (i.e., through "moral suasion" alone) (see, e.g., Jer 31:31-34; Ezek 36:26). Nevertheless, when the Spirit incites the exercise of faith on the part of the human person, he does so not by bypassing the mind but by utilizing the instrument of the word of God (so Rom 10:14)—a word with intelligible content—so that the exercise of faith includes apprehensive knowledge of God's gracious promises (*notitia*).[143] The "natural power of understanding and willing" remains in the human person after the fall and enables him or her to understand the meaning of the gospel, but that faculty is without a disposition to honor and desire God. The supernaturally infused habit of faith is thus a restoration of that natural power's "moral disposition of judging and willing well."[144] This new habit and the theological content apprehended in its act can thus renew the intellect and its ratiocinative activity, the *lumen naturae* that functions as an internal cognitive principle of natural theology. As Alsted puts it, with the advent of grace, reason does not "lose its native force" (*vis insita*) but is "made firm" by the support of Christian faith and illumined by it like the moon by the sun.[145]

Renewed and healed by supernatural grace, reason becomes active in the practice of dogmatic theology, not in a principial role but in an instrumental or ministerial role, which is to say as an instrument by which we understand scriptural truth. It is employed as a "handmaiden" (*ancilla*) for drawing conclusions from principles, clarifying the teaching of Scripture, comparing theological claims with the teaching of Scripture, and setting forth

---

[143]Turretin, *Inst.* 15.4.13, 16-17, 23, 28-31, 36, 50, 54 (2:569-70, 571, 573-74, 577-80, 582-83, 589, 590-91); 9.3-15 (617-20). The external cognitive principle of supernatural theology is thus the word of God, and the internal cognitive principle is the Spirit, who gives faith (*Inst.* 1.7.6 [1:24]). Owen acknowledges that the meaning of biblical propositions is accessible to the unregenerate mind as well. However, the unregenerate person without the Spirit's sanctifying work will not receive and enjoy the spiritual things signified by those propositions (*Theologoumena pantodapa* 6.3.2-6 [418-21]). In light of that reality, the Reformed orthodox distinguish between *fides historica* (a recognition of the truth of the gospel) and *fides salvifica* (*notitia* and *assensus* with *fiducia*, trust or persuasion of the truth and goodness of the gospel whereby one receives Christ and his benefits) (e.g., Turretin, *Inst.* 15.8.6-7 [2:613-14]).

[144]Turretin, *Inst.* 15.3.21 (2:561-62); 4.13, 23, 29-31, 49 (2:569-70, 574, 577-80, 589). In other words, the Spirit enables us to grasp not only the truthfulness of the gospel but also its goodness and desirability (cf. 15.8.7 [2:613]). Otherwise, Turretin comments, the intellect is affected by corruption and cannot be corrected merely by its own judgment (15.4.56 [2:591]).

[145]Alsted, *Theologia naturalis* 1.1 (5-6).

arguments against opponents of orthodoxy.[146] Basic rational principles like the law of noncontradiction apply in both the sphere of nature and the sphere of grace. As grace perfects nature, so faith perfects and utilizes reason in the formulation of doctrine.[147] Accordingly, for Turretin, rational proofs for the existence of God are not essential to theology; instead, proving the existence of God takes place only *"per accidens* by an adventitious necessity, namely, for confuting profane men and atheists."[148]

On the one hand, the supernatural theology communicated by divine revelation enables us to "run past" created things and "fly over" to the subject of true wisdom, namely, God himself and all things as ordered to God.[149] On the other hand, reason, under the guidance of faith and supernatural theology, can also revisit the book of nature and correctly grasp its teaching about God. Alsted thus calls Holy Scripture a "mixed principle" of natural theology (one taken not purely from the sphere of nature per se but from within the sphere of salvific grace as it treats God as Creator as well as Redeemer). Alsted's application of Reformed thinking about the dynamics of theological knowledge in his system of natural theology leads him to commend not a *theologia naturalis nuda* (natural theology of fallen humanity left to itself) but rather a *theologia naturalis vestita et exaltata* (natural theology "clothed" and "exalted" in the illumined mind of the regenerate believer), though he still grants to unregenerate humanity some natural knowledge of God.[150] Such expressions of the principles and function of natural theology will influence our distillation of the role of natural theology in Christian *theologia* at the end of the chapter, but not before we consider some objections raised by more recent authors.

---

[146]Turretin, *Inst.* 1.8.3-7 (1:27-28). It is worth noting here that the term *reason* can be used in different senses. It can signify, objectively, a body of facts or truths that are discoverable by the mind unaided by supernatural revelation or that are already impressed on the mind and by which it will draw various conclusions about reality. It can also signify subjectively the faculty of knowing or, more particularly, the mind's capacity or activity of inferring hitherto unknown conclusions from known principles (cf. Turretin, *Inst.* 1.8.1 [1:26]). In either usage, it is not so much the faculty itself but the outside world that generates the content of natural knowledge.

[147]Turretin, *Inst.* 1.9.4-5, 15 (1:32-33, 35); cf. 1.10 (36-39). Theology may therefore draw insights from the lower sciences (1.6.8 [1:22]).

[148]Turretin, *Inst.* 1.5.6 (1:19).

[149]Junius, *De vera theologia* 11 (86).

[150]Alsted, *Theologia naturalis* 1.1 (2, 7). Cf. Turretin, *Inst.* 1.3.10 (1:9), where he remarks that something (e.g., that God exists) can be known with more certainty by the light of faith and yet also still knowable by the light of reason (albeit less perfectly in this respect).

Modern Challenges

Objections. Now that we have examined some key representations of the natural knowledge of God through the early modern period, there are many angles from which we could view criticism of natural theology. I will focus on four in this section. The first is a criticism founded on the work of authors like Immanuel Kant and Martin Heidegger regarding the mind's ability to make contact with objective (and divine) reality. The second is Barth's development of something like the first criticism in an overtly theological direction in light of his understanding of sin and grace. In contemporary theology, Barth's name is, perhaps more than any other, readily linked with opposition to natural theology, but only part of his criticism will appear here. His discussion of the *analogia entis* in particular will be addressed in more detail in chapter five. The third criticism in this section is from Herman Bavinck, who, while quite open to the reality of a natural knowledge of God, is critical of what he regards as a "dualistic" version of it in Thomas and Roman Catholicism. Finally, the fourth criticism is from the contemporary Christian philosopher Alvin Plantinga, according to whose "Reformed epistemology" the justification of belief in God does not require rational demonstration of God's existence.

First, there is a characterization of natural theology as "ontotheology" that is associated with Kant and Heidegger, ontotheology being, roughly, an application of the laws of human thought to the development of a concept of "being," which could be used to posit a supreme being (i.e., God) that would ground and organize human thinking about the mind's various objects. In other words, natural theology as ontotheology is a matter of securing a concept of a first being in light of which one can legitimize and structure reason's investigation of the world as it appears to us.[151]

---

[151]Treatments of Kant and Heidegger on the relevant points can be found in, e.g., Michelle Grier, *Kant's Doctrine of Transcendental Illusion* (Cambridge: Cambridge University Press, 2001), esp. chap. 7; Nicholas Wolterstorff, "Is It Possible and Desirable for Theologians to Recover from Kant?," in *Inquiring About God: Selected Essays*, ed. Terence Cuneo (Cambridge: Cambridge University Press, 2010), 1:42-55; Merold Westphal, "The Importance of Overcoming Metaphysics for the Life of Faith," *MT* 23 (2007): 253-60; Martin Westerholm, "Kant's Critique and Contemporary Theological Inquiry," *MT* 31 (2015): 403-27; Burkhard Nonnenmacher, "Natürliche Theologie und Offenbarung," *Neue Zeitschrift für Systematische Theologie und Religionsphilosophie* 59 (2017): 311-30; Iain Thomson, "Ontotheology? Understanding Heidegger's *Destruktion* of Metaphysics," *International Journal of Philosophical Studies* 8 (2000): 297-327; Merold Westphal, *Transcendence and Self-Transcendence: On God and the Soul* (Bloomington: Indiana University Press, 2004), 15-40; Timothy Stanley, *Protestant Metaphysics After Karl Barth and Martin Heidegger*

For Kant, human reason seeks to obtain a kind of knowledge that is characterized by necessity and universality and is thus a priori (i.e., independent of the contingent dynamics of experience and perception and of worries about whether the mind's content conforms to external reality). This compels him to claim that there are in the mind a priori concepts and judgments that shape or determine the "raw material" of sense perception.[152] The true objects of human knowledge are thus appearances or mental representations given shape by a priori judgments, not external things in themselves, even if external things may still exist outside the mind and may be thought about (though not truly cognized). Space and time and various features of the objects of the mind pertain to the mind's mental representations (the phenomenal), not outward reality in itself (especially that which transcends sensory experience) (the noumenal). Kant can even say that "objects in themselves are not known to us at all." This view he calls "transcendental idealism," as opposed to "transcendental realism."[153] Included in the human subject's a priori resources that pertain to the laws of the mind rather than the structure of reality itself are the concepts and categories of the classical metaphysical tradition (e.g., substance, quantity, quality, action, passion), which, in Kant's view, precede and facilitate experience of objects and cannot be based on experience of external things.[154]

(Eugene, OR: Cascade, 2010); Kevin W. Hector, *Theology Without Metaphysics: God, Language and the Spirit of Recognition* (Cambridge: Cambridge University Press, 2011), 3-15.

[152]Immanuel Kant, *Critique of Pure Reason*, ed. and trans. Paul Guyer and Allen W. Wood (Cambridge: Cambridge University Press, 1998), A1-2.

[153]Kant, *Critique of Pure Reason*, Bxxxix, A30/B45, A36/B53, A104, B146, A368-76, A490-91/B518-19. In using the word *transcendental* here, Kant signals that his argument is aimed at determining the conditions that make something possible, in this case the necessary and universal character of human knowing.

[154]Kant, *Critique of Pure Reason*, A77-83/B102-9, A92-95/B125-29, B406-13; Kant, *Prolegomena to Any Future Metaphysics*, in *Prolegomena to Any Future Metaphysics, with Selections from the Critique of Pure Reason*, ed. and trans. Gary Hatfield, rev. ed., Cambridge Texts in the History of Philosophy (Cambridge: Cambridge University Press, 2004), 4:265-66. Kant notes that David Hume believed the categories were derived from experience, but without this ensuring that the categories actually pertain to realities themselves and their relations to one another. Such a view, Kant points out, leads to skepticism. Hume's epistemology had problematized reasoning from effects to knowledge of a cause because he suggested that the mind's impressions of causal relations do not apply to external things themselves, particularly when the purported effect and cause are radically dissimilar to one another (e.g., Hume, *A Treatise of Human Nature: A Critical Edition*, vol. 1, *Texts*, ed. David Fate Norton and Mary J. Norton [Oxford: Oxford University Press, 2007], 1.3.14 [105-16]; Hume, *Dialogues Concerning Natural Religion*, in *Dialogues Concerning Natural Religion and Other Writings*, ed. Dorothy Coleman, Cambridge Texts in the

Without giving grounds for affirming the extramental reality of causation, the concepts and judgments of pure reason compel the human person naturally to posit the existence of an absolutely necessary and unconditioned supreme being, a ground of conditioned, limited beings that makes such beings possible and intelligible in their various determinations. Reason inevitably posits this supreme being but cannot justifiably assert its extramental reality. It is a "transcendental illusion" or "ideal being" providing a mental basis on which reason can undertake explanation of its objects. It is "the immovable rock of the necessary" and the "resting place in the regress from the conditioned," containing in itself the "because" that answers every "why." In other words, God becomes a mental "regulative principle," "taking care of nothing but the formal interest of reason." Reason proceeds *as if* God were actually there even as it strives not to let the limiting concept of God restrain its pursuit of knowledge. This is the way of "ontotheology" (on which any "cosmotheology" or cosmological argument for God would depend). Though reason is driven to hypostatize its divine regulative principle and posit it as though it were an actual "something subsisting," its concept of God is ultimately without content: a hypothetical organizing principle or empty placeholder.[155]

While Kant thought "ontotheology" to be at least an expedient philosophical move, Heidegger argues, in the words of Merold Westphal, that it "involves the sacrifice of divine alterity."[156] Heidegger's critique of ontotheology takes place within his assessment of metaphysics in the Platonic and Aristotelian tradition. Metaphysics, Heidegger writes, has an "ontotheological constitution" in that it attempts to study both "beings" as such and also, in pursuit of a full description of reality, the highest being by reference to which all other beings can be grounded and understood.[157] In

History of Philosophy [Cambridge: Cambridge University Press, 2007], 5 [41-45]). For Kant's response to Hume, see *Prolegomena*, 4:310-13.

[155] Kant, *Critique of Pure Reason*, A290-2/B347-49, A296/B352-53, B593-95, A578-91/B606-19, A592-620/B620-48, A632/B660, A845-46/B873-74; *Prolegomena*, 4:350-60.

[156] Westphal, *Transcendence*, 16.

[157] Martin Heidegger, "Introduction to 'What Is Metaphysics?' (1949)," trans. Walter Kaufmann, in *Pathmarks*, ed. William McNeill (Cambridge: Cambridge University Press, 1998), 287; Heidegger, *Identity and Difference*, trans. Joan Stambaugh (New York: Harper and Row, 1969), 54-61. On Heidegger's view of the analogy or univocity of being in this connection, see the discussion in Philip Tonner, *Heidegger, Metaphysics and the Univocity of Being* (London: Continuum, 2010). "Ontotheology" is thus the positing of a notion of being that can be used

its focus on beings and ultimately on the highest (but still particular) being, metaphysics or ontotheology neglects the difference between a particular being (*das Seiende*) and the being (*das Sein*) that is not itself a particular being but rather the underlying ground of all particular beings.[158] The Western philosophical tradition has lacked an awareness of the important and mysterious question of *das Sein* that emerges from recognition of the radical contingency of beings and has slipped into presumptuously thinking that it can capture all things in its mental representation of objects.[159] Metaphysics as ontotheology prioritizes understanding what things are, in accord with the mind's ability to grasp and categorize them in their essential determinations. In this way, the human subject, made central in philosophies like those of Descartes and Kant, objectifies and "pictures" both finite beings and any purported deity meant to ground their existence, which entails a loss of divine transcendence.[160] For Heidegger, metaphysics is compelled to do this by Leibniz's principle of sufficient reason that always seeks after causal explanations of things by which the human subject can, so to speak, epistemically conquer the world. The principle of sufficient reason enlists God, the ultimate causal explanation, to complete the

---

to capture and characterize the being of both finite beings and God himself as its primary instance and as that which legitimizes our assertions about other beings. Understood thus, "ontotheology" (1) assumes a Creator-creature parity in which both participate in being at the cost of God's transcendence and (2) instrumentalizes outward realities (including God) in the interest of intellectual accomplishment.

[158] Martin Heidegger, *Introduction to Metaphysics*, rev. and trans. Gregory Fried and Richard Polt, 2nd ed. (New Haven, CT: Yale University Press, 2000), 7-9. The difference is sometimes expressed in a distinction between the "ontic" and the "ontological."

[159] Martin Heidegger, *Being and Time*, trans. John Macquarrie and Edward Robinson (Oxford: Blackwell, 1962), 25-26; Heidegger, "What Is Metaphysics? (1929)," trans. David Farrell Krell, in *Pathmarks*, 90-91, 95-6; Heidegger, "Introduction," 288-89.

[160] Martin Heidegger, "The Age of the World Picture," in *The Question Concerning Technology and Other Essays*, trans. William Lovitt (New York: Harper and Row, 1977), 127-30, 134; Heidegger, "European Nihilism," in *Nietzsche*, vol. 4, *Nihilism*, ed. David Farrell Krell, trans. Frank A. Capuzzi and David Farrell Krell (San Francisco: HarperSanFrancisco, 1991), 83-84, 119-22, 159-66; Heidegger, "The Word of Nietzsche: 'God Is Dead,'" in *Question*, 100, 107; Heidegger, "Metaphysics as the History of Being," in *The End of Philosophy*, trans. Joan Stambaugh (Chicago: University of Chicago Press, 2003), 2-4, 24-32, et passim; Heidegger, "Postscript to 'What Is Metaphysics?' (1943)," in *Pathmarks*, 231-32, 234-37; Heidegger, "Overcoming Metaphysics," in *End of Philosophy*, 87-89; Heidegger, "Introduction," 288-89; Heidegger, "The Question Concerning Technology," in *Question*, 26; Heidegger, *The Principle of Reason*, trans. Reginald Lilly (Bloomington: Indiana University Press, 1991), 23, 27, 54-55; Heidegger, "The End of Philosophy and the Task of Thinking," in *Basic Writings*, ed. David Farrell Krell (New York: HarperCollins, 1977), 377.

metaphysical project.[161] Heidegger comments that a god called on merely
to satisfy reason's demands is not a god before whom one can pray or "play
music and dance."[162] Though not an advocate of Christian theology charting
the course of philosophy, Heidegger prods Christians to break free from
ontotheology and to "resolve to take seriously the word of the apostle" char-
acterizing philosophy as "foolishness."[163]

Second, Barth also registers concerns about the ability of the natural
human intellect to come to know God, but he moors those concerns in a set
of theological commitments. For example, in *Church Dogmatics* III/1, he
writes that on our own we cannot "cross the bridge from mere consciousness
to the apprehension of the truth of being, to the recognition of existence."
Ultimately, we have no inherent capacity that can, by the way of negation,
eminence, or causality, form a reliable idea of a perfect being and guarantee
that this idea corresponds to the reality of God. God alone can come to us
from the outside in his self-authenticating revelation and affirm the real
existence of the world by declaring himself to be its Creator. God alone can
break the "vicious circle of consciousness and being (which might equally
well be a matter of appearance)" and does so in the event of his self-revelation
in Christ.[164] Barth is critical of the notion that we have direct epistemic
access to God by observation of the world, a notion that he, not unlike Kant,
characterizes as a naive "realism." Of course, Barth does hold that the human
subject can come into contact with the reality of God (*pace* a strong "idealism"), but this takes place only by God's initiative in revelation.[165] For

---

[161]Martin Heidegger, "On the Essence of a Ground," in *Pathmarks*, 100-102; Heidegger, "Letter on
Humanism," in *Pathmarks*, 242-43; Heidegger, *Identity and Difference*, 56; Heidegger, *Principle
of Reason*, 3-4, 20-28, 32-33, 100-101, 117-21, 125.

[162]Heidegger, "Word of Nietzsche," 105; Heidegger, *Identity and Difference*, 72.

[163]Heidegger, "Introduction," 288; Heidegger, *Introduction to Metaphysics*, trans. Gregory Fried
and Richard Polt, 2nd ed. (New Haven, CT: Yale University Press, 2000), 7-9. For an account
of Heidegger's relationship to Christian theology, see Judith Wolfe, *Heidegger and Theology*
(London: Bloomsbury, 2014).

[164]Barth, *CD* III/1, 346-49. Barth goes on to associate the "vicious circle of consciousness and
being" (or "appearance") with the work of Descartes in particular (III/1, 350-63).

[165]Karl Barth, "Fate and Idea," in *The Way of Theology in Karl Barth: Essays and Comments*, ed. H.
Martin Rumscheidt (repr., Allison Park, PA: Pickwick, 1986), 32-60; Barth, *CD* I/1, 167-69, 173,
175. On Barth's "critical realism," see Bruce L. McCormack, *Karl Barth's Critically Realist Dialectical Theology: Its Genesis and Development 1909-1936* (Oxford: Clarendon, 1995), 129-30,
225-26, 245-62; McCormack, *Orthodox and Modern: Studies in the Theology of Karl Barth* (Grand
Rapids: Baker Academic, 2008), 109-65; Keith L. Johnson, *Karl Barth and the Analogia Entis*
(London: Bloomsbury, 2010), 98-106. However, for a more recent reassessment of Barth's

Barth, there is a danger in taking a "neutral" concept of being and using it as a cipher to be filled in "arbitrarily" "with every conceivable superlative" and then applied to God. For the human knower is a "sinner who of himself can only take wrong roads" and will never fill in that concept of being with the proper trinitarian content revealed in the incarnation.[166]

Before looking more directly at how Barth's view of sin and grace shapes his view of analogy, it is worth considering a relevant treatment of Barth's understanding of causation by Archie Spencer. Following Eberhard Jüngel's account of causation and the analogical relationship between causes and effects in Aristotelian and Neoplatonic philosophy,[167] Spencer argues that a traditional practice of moving from knowledge of created effects to knowledge of a divine cause involves both agnosticism and, according the logic of Barth's thought, an unwarranted presumption of "cause-effect-resemblance" (CER). On the one hand, according to Spencer, the pursuit of knowledge by causation yields agnosticism because Kant's restriction of our knowledge of causal dynamics to the empirical world (indeed, the empirical world as shaped by a priori mental determinations) entails that we cannot come to a knowledge of God himself as cause. On the other hand, it is wrong in assuming CER in the first place because Barth was right in rejecting an automatic cause-effect resemblance in the case of God and creatures. Spencer anchors this in Barth's refusal to reduce God's omnipotence to his "omnicausality" (or his outward activity) and his desire to underscore the freedom of God in preserving creation, a freedom informed by God's manner of working in the salvific covenant of grace. Spencer stresses that, for Barth, God is not caught up in a Platonic emanationist framework in which he must produce beings other than himself and give them perfections distinct from his own by degree only. Within such an emanationist framework, God would be located under an overarching "master-concept" of being or causality encompassing both God and creatures.[168]

---

conception of theological reason in relation to Kant and modern thought, see Martin Wester-holm, *The Ordering of the Christian Mind: Karl Barth and Theological Rationality* (Oxford: Oxford University Press, 2015).

[166] Barth, *CD* II/1, 260-62, 288, 329. Cf. I/1, 131-32.

[167] Eberhard Jüngel, *God as the Mystery of the World*, trans. Darrell Guder (Grand Rapids: Eerdmans, 1983), 261-81.

[168] Archie J. Spencer, "Causality and the *Analogia entis*: Karl Barth's Rejection of Analogy of Being Reconsidered," *Nova et Vetera* 6 (2008): 347-70; Spencer, *The Analogy of Faith: The Quest for God's*

Ultimately, Barth believes that the problem of natural theology is rooted in the problem of sin. Natural theology is, according to Barth, an attempt to find a manifestation of God in creation that serves as an entrance into the "inner circle of true theology grounded in *revelatio specialis*." However, that attempt is viable only in Roman Catholicism or in a Protestant "theology of glory." For a genuinely Protestant recognition of the "extent of sin" entails that any "direct discernment" of God in relation to creation is lost in the fall and restored only by the gospel.[169] Thus, for Barth, "the theology and the church of the antichrist can profit from [natural theology]," but "the Evangelical Church and Evangelical theology would only sicken and die of it."[170] Humanity has lost its "capacity for God" or "point of contact" with God. The *imago Dei* is "totally annihilated" in the fall.[171] Natural theology is therefore a matter of seeking in vain a source of theological knowledge or a "knowability of God" apart from the only true knowability of God in Jesus Christ. In seeking this knowability, natural theology disregards the unity of God, imagining it is possible to find some truth of God disconnected from his triune grace and lordship. It produces idolatrous conceptions of God that look suspiciously like what sinful humanity would want God to be. In this way, it is humanity's attempt to justify itself before God, to claim that "man is not really needy, that he is already rich and self-secure and therefore that he is not dependent on God's grace." Not surprisingly, the political climate in Europe shaped Barth's concerns: he diagnosed German nationalism as fundamentally a "new combination of Christian and natural theology."[172]

Barth is prepared to base this assessment of natural theology on his exegesis of particular biblical texts, insisting that no biblical author as a witness to God's revelation will "dare to incorporate into his proclamation, or to place side by side with it, statements which he derives from another

---

Speakability, Strategic Initiatives in Evangelical Theology (Downers Grove, IL: IVP Academic, 2015), 193-212. Spencer draws especially from Barth, *CD* II/1, 526-32; III/3, 66-67, 97-107.

[169]Barth, *CD* I/1, 130-31.

[170]Karl Barth, "No!," in *Natural Theology: Comprising "Nature and Grace" by Professor Dr. Emil Brunner and the Reply "No!" by Dr. Karl Barth*, trans. Peter Fraenkel (repr., Eugene, OR: Wipf and Stock, 2002), 128.

[171]Barth, *CD* I/1, 238-39.

[172]Barth, *CD* II/1, 79-80, 84, 125-78. Stanley Hauerwas puts it bluntly: "The denial of natural theology as well as the discovery of the Christological center in theology were of a piece with [Barth's] opposition to Hitler" (*With the Grain of the Universe: The Church's Witness and Natural Theology* [Grand Rapids: Baker Academic, 2013], 170).

source" (i.e., from nature, without reference to God's grace in Christ).[173] In expounding Psalm 8, Barth holds that the expression "O YHWH, our Lord, how majestic is your name in all the earth" in Psalm 8:1, 9 is based on the intervening content in Psalm 8:2-8, about the place of humanity in the cosmos. But, Barth asks, how could humanity's sinful exercise of dominion teach us about the glory of God? "What an unreliable witness!" The key to understanding this psalm lies in the author of Hebrews (Heb 2:5-9) identifying Jesus as the "man in the cosmos of Ps. 8": "in the mouth of this man" the declaration of Psalm 8:1, 9 rings true.[174] Similarly, in his comments on Psalm 104, Barth denies that in the brokenness of the world there is a "direct seeing" of God's glory. It is "blatantly evident" that it is not the "world picture" of the natural human being that witnesses to God; rather, "through this picture" the psalmist "causes the picture of the future world to speak, in which the divinity and wisdom and goodness of creation again come to us, although here and now they are completely concealed from us." In light of the new heavens and the new earth in Revelation 21, one can "read *into* the cosmology of natural man" creation's testimony to the glory of God.[175] In Barth's view, Job 38–41 confirms that God's works in the world are "dark and strange." There is no "direct understanding of God's works," so God makes himself known by addressing us in his Word.[176]

Barth's exegesis of Romans 1 continues on this trajectory. Early in his career he stated in his Romans commentary that there is a possibility of humanity's finding God and eternal life, but that possibility exists as "God's possibility and as His possibility only."[177] In Barth's comments on Romans 1 in the *Church Dogmatics*, he argues that the passage is not a "summons" to natural theology. Instead it is "a constituent part of the apostolic kerygma" and not to be read in isolation from "the event which took place between God and man in Christ." Because of Christ's death and resurrection for the salvation of both Jews and Gentiles, "Paul does not know . . . Gentiles in themselves and as such," for they too are placed under the judgment and

---

[173]Barth, *CD* II/1, 109-10.
[174]Barth, *CD* II/1, 113-14.
[175]Barth, *CD* II/1, 114.
[176]Barth, *CD* II/1, 115.
[177]Karl Barth, *The Epistle to the Romans*, trans. Edwyn C. Hoskyns, 6th ed. (Oxford: Oxford University Press, 1968), 62.

grace of God given in the incarnation.[178] In other words, "the Jews and the heathen of whom he speaks are very definitely characterised as Jews and heathen objectively confronted with the divine ἀποκάλυψις in the Gospel (1:15-16)." Paul therefore discusses the wrath of God and its connection to the Gentiles' knowledge of God simply because it is the "shadow side" of the gospel. He is still speaking as an apostle of Christ in Romans 1:18-32 and not drawing on another (i.e., strictly natural) source of knowledge. Paul is explaining why the Gentiles are placed under God's judgment, but he is not appealing to a preexisting "point of contact" in a natural knowledge of God already possessed by the Gentiles. Rather, he is helping the Gentiles to understand God's judgment and grace by providing a point of contact that is in fact "newly instituted in and with the proclamation of the Gospel."[179]

Third, Bavinck is critical of what he calls a "dualistic" account of the natural knowledge of God in Thomas's writings and in Roman Catholicism.[180] On the one hand, Bavinck emphasizes that God has revealed himself in the created order and asserts that this is a "preamble" to Christianity that preserves humanity for "healing" in Christ and provides epistemic common ground on which Christians may meet non-Christians. This view of the natural knowledge of God is, for Bavinck, a catholic commitment that his own Reformed tradition has heartily upheld.[181] In light of this, Bavinck can on the whole be regarded as an ally in maintaining a place for natural theology. On the other hand, Bavinck does draw attention to certain problems he sees in Roman Catholic teaching about natural theology. According to Bavinck, Roman Catholicism places the knowledge of God from nature alongside the knowledge of God from supernatural revelation without sufficiently integrating the two. This framework encourages a "rationalism in the sphere of

---

[178]Barth, *CD* I/2, 306-7.

[179]Barth, *CD* II/1, 119-21.

[180]As I read him, Bavinck holds Thomas in high esteem and does not think Thomas is to blame for all the faults that he (Bavinck) perceives in Roman Catholicism. Nevertheless, Bavinck does associate Thomas with certain problematic elements he identifies in Rome's approach to the natural knowledge of God.

[181]Bavinck, *RD* 1:307, 310-11, 321-22. However, Bavinck's appropriation of traditional theological epistemologies is critical and conducted with willingness to learn from various modern epistemologies (on which, see Cory Brock and Nathaniel Gray Sutanto, "Herman Bavinck's Reformed Eclecticism: On Catholicity, Consciousness and Theological Epistemology," *SJT* 70 [2017]: 310-32; Nathaniel Sutanto, "Herman Bavinck and Thomas Reid on Perception and Knowing God," *Harvard Theological Review* 111 [2018]: 115-34).

natural revelation" that downplays the effects of sin on the human mind in its pursuit of God. It also implies that the knowledge gained from supernatural revelation so exceeds the natural human intellect (not merely the *fallen* intellect) that the result is (though Bavinck does not explicitly use the term here) a fideism about Christian dogma that would logically undermine rational exploration of the truth of supernatural revelation. In Bavinck's view, the Reformed tradition stresses the need for the illumination of the truths of natural revelation by God's revelation in Scripture and by the renewing work of the Holy Spirit. Thus Reformed theology, at least in the earlier expressions of it in the seventeenth century, circumvents an autonomous natural theology and places natural theology firmly under the tutelage of Christian dogmatics. It also insists that while the truths of supernatural revelation cannot be produced or legislated by reason, their content eludes or reproves not reason as such but only fallen reason in its hostility to the truth of God.[182]

What, in Bavinck's assessment, gives rise to this dualism about natural and supernatural theology? He connects it to what he views as a Roman Catholic dualism about the nature and destiny of the human race. Humanity is created *in puris naturalibus* (in a purely natural state), lacking the image of God but still able to possess an intact natural knowledge and love of God. However, humanity's destiny (the beatific vision and mystical union with God) cannot be obtained by what humanity is given *in puris naturalibus*. The image of God, together with the higher virtues of faith and charity, is then construed as a "superadded gift" (*donum superadditum*) by which humanity can obtain its destiny. In light of this, if only a superadded gift is lost in the fall, without nature itself being corrupted, then the natural knowledge and love of God would logically remain intact after the fall, allowing natural theology to function independently of supernatural theology. Further, within this system grace is implicitly opposed to nature (not just to sin) so that supernatural revelation would consequently be inaccessible to the natural human intellect.[183]

Finally, Plantinga objects to a form of natural theology that he links to "classical foundationalism." In this foundationalist natural theology,

[182]Bavinck, *RD* 1:304-5, 321, 620-21; 2:74-75, 78, 90-91.
[183]Bavinck, *RD* 1:358-62. For his more detailed exposition of issues surrounding the image of God, see 2:539-53.

exemplified (for Plantinga) by Thomas, some beliefs are regarded as "properly basic" (not justified on the basis of other beliefs). These beliefs are self-evident, meaning that they are either rooted in sense perception of present sensible objects or simply incorrigible. All other beliefs must be justified by evidence and rational argumentation. According to Plantinga, Thomas essentially accepts this epistemological approach and holds that belief in God is not a properly basic belief and therefore must be justified by rational demonstration.[184] However, Plantinga observes, there are many "properly basic beliefs" that do not meet the criteria laid down by classical foundationalism. Furthermore, Reformed thinkers—Plantinga mentions Calvin, Bavinck, and Barth—have ably made the case that the rationality of belief in God does not require a demonstration of God's existence.[185] Human beings possess a *sensus divinitatis*, a disposition to form certain beliefs about God when they encounter God's handiwork in the world. Plantinga clarifies, though, that this is not a matter of fideism, for belief in God is "grounded" in one's experiences of, for example, a beautiful flower or one's own sense of guilt after acting wrongly.[186] One can still offer arguments for God's existence, but in this approach they are not needed in order for belief in God to be rational.

Responses. In this section I will attempt a brief response to each of these critiques of natural theology. This will clear the way for a distillation of the role of the natural knowledge of God in Christian *theologia* in the conclusion to this chapter.

1. It should be noted that Kant's discussion of ontotheology is less a criticism of natural theology than a matter of making peace with a thoroughgoing apriorism and epistemic disconnection from external reality. However, the authors drawn on in the constructive work of this book emphasize that

---

[184]Alvin Plantinga, "Reason and Belief in God," in *Faith and Rationality: Reason and Belief in God*, ed. Alvin Plantinga and Nicholas Wolterstorff (Notre Dame, IN: University of Notre Dame Press, 1983), 46-48, 55. Like Plantinga, Wolterstorff has critiqued what he regards as the overreaching demands of "evidentialism" with respect to belief in God (e.g., "Can Belief in God Be Rational If It Has No Foundations?," in Plantinga and Wolterstorff, *Faith and Rationality*, 135-86).

[185]For an integration of Barth and Plantinga on theological epistemology and natural theology, see Kevin Diller, *Theology's Epistemological Dilemma: How Karl Barth and Alvin Plantinga Provide a Unified Response*, Strategic Initiatives in Evangelical Theology (Downers Grove, IL: IVP Academic, 2014).

[186]Plantinga, "Reason and Belief in God," 60, 63-73, 78-80.

human knowledge, including natural theological knowledge, emerges from encountering external features of the world. Accordingly, they do not posit a Kantian apriorism or Cartesian doubt and introspection as the basis for cognition or understanding cognition.[187] Kant's attempt to secure necessary, a priori knowledge minimizes true apprehension of the world and of God and ultimately runs contrary to humanity's natural and ineradicable realist disposition to believe in the existence of the external world and to believe that we apprehend truth (if not *all* the truth) about its various objects and causal structures.[188] The inclination toward this belief may be chastened by the recognition of our fallibility, but this is no reason to deny its general import. However one might wish to modify or supplement the epistemological nuances of the premodern Christian tradition, the Kantian suggestion that we cannot encounter and reliably apprehend external reality is neither binding for nor consistent with Christian theology. For the veracity of the natural realist belief in the existence of the world and our capacity to obtain truth about it is an implicate of the Christian doctrines of creation and humanity, according to which God the Creator has made the world and the human mind and ordained that we would steward (and therefore presumably understand) his world and obtain knowledge of himself.

Within such a framework, the origin of a natural knowledge of God does not lie in an anthropocentric attempt to validate and systematize subjective laws of thought. It lies in the human encounter with the things of God's world, which encounter, acting on our innate and God-given capacity for knowing, is what engenders in us a responsive subscription to the laws of thought (e.g., the law of noncontradiction, the notion that a whole is greater than any of its individual parts).[189] The natural knowledge of God, then, does not turn on looking *at* such principles of thought and self-servingly positing

---

[187] Augustine and Thomas of course precede Kant's and Descartes's time, but for a Reformed orthodox critique of Descartes's epistemological approach, see Peter van Mastricht, *Novitatum Cartesianarum gangraena* (Amsterdam, 1677), 1.2 (13-33).

[188] The notion of a "natural realism" reflects emphases in Bavinck, *RD* 1:223-33.

[189] See, e.g., Thomas Aquinas, *In Metaphysicorum* 4.6.599 (167); Thomas, *Opera omnia*, vol. 47/2, *Sententia libri Ethicorum*, Leonine ed. (Rome: ad Sanctae Sabinae, 1969), 6.3.1139b25-35 (341). Cf. White, *Wisdom in the Face of Modernity*, 192-93. I am sympathetic to Alister McGrath's statements about the difficulty of constructing a "'neutral' or 'tradition-free' natural theology" and about the importance of constructing one informed by Scripture (*Re-imagining Nature: The Promise of a Christian Natural Theology* [Oxford: Wiley Blackwell, 2017], 33 et passim). Still, I would maintain that basic rational principles like those just mentioned are indeed universally

an inward organizing principle for them. Rather, it turns on looking *with*
these principles at outward features and causal structures of God's world
that witness to his existence and glory. That we human beings can do this is
not a mere figment of sinful reason but, fundamentally, an implicate of divinely given biblical teaching.

Heidegger speaks negatively about Kant's a priori epistemological orientation, and we do well to agree with him on this point. At the same time,
Heidegger's critique of ontotheology does not actually undermine accounts
of the natural knowledge of God like those found in Thomas and the Reformed orthodox.[190] This is where the excursus above, on Thomas's work,
comes into play. Without stipulating that we must appropriate every detail
of Thomas's epistemology, an account of the natural knowledge of God that
draws from his work will emphasize that human knowledge begins with
sense experience, not concepts or propositions embedded in the mind prior
to such experience. The likeness of a thing in human sense or the human
intellect is transparent to the object of knowledge (i.e., an external existent)
and is not itself the object of knowledge.[191] Knowledge of the essences of

---

(if very often only implicitly) upheld in all human cultures and conduce to naturally apprehending the existence of a divine cause.

[190]John Caputo in a study of Heidegger and Thomas suggests that Thomas's philosophy does not
evade Heidegger's critique of the Western metaphysical tradition but does still, despite its scholastic form, allow for a mystical experience of "Being" that Heidegger would find commendable
(*Heidegger and Aquinas: An Essay on Overcoming Metaphysics* [New York: Fordham University
Press, 1982], 8-9). In my view, Heidegger does not provide normative desiderata that contemporary Christian theologians must satisfy, but it is worth noting that, to the extent that Heidegger had a point in warning against "essentialist" ontotheology, the natural knowledge of
God described here is not that sort of undertaking (cf. Turner, *Faith, Reason and the Existence
of God*, 23, 238-39, 249, 254; Merold Westphal, "Aquinas and Onto-theology," *American Catholic
Philosophical Quarterly* 80 [2006]: 173-91; Reinhard Hütter, "Attending to the Wisdom of God—
from Effect to Cause, from Creation to God: A *Relecture* of the Analogy of Being According to
Thomas Aquinas," in *The Analogy of Being: Invention of the Antichrist or the Wisdom of God?*, ed.
Thomas Joseph White [Grand Rapids: Eerdmans, 2011], 216-17, 240-44; White, *Wisdom in the
Face of Modernity*, 25-27, 97, et passim; James Dominic Rooney, "Being as Iconic: Aquinas on
'He Who Is' as the Name of God," *IJST* 19 [2017]: 163-74; John R. Betz, "After Heidegger and
Marion: The Task of Christian Metaphysics Today," *MT* 34 [2018]: 565-97; Liran Shia Gordon
and Avital Wohlman, "A Constructive Thomistic Response to Heidegger's Destructive Criticism: On Existence, Essence and the Possibility of Truth as Adequation," *Heythrop Journal* 60
[2019]: forthcoming). For an interesting account of the questions that Heidegger's work has left
open on the relationship between God and being, see George Pattison, *God and Being: An Enquiry* (Oxford: Oxford University Press, 2011).

[191]Discussion of the various theories of perception is beyond the bounds of this chapter and can
be found in standard epistemology texts (e.g., Robert Audi, *Epistemology: A Contemporary Introduction to the Theory of Knowledge*, 3rd ed. [New York: Routledge, 2010], chap. 2). Without

things arises from the intellect's coming into contact with real existents and apprehending what constitutes them in their various kinds, not from projecting antecedent mental constructs onto things and then claiming that those constructs are constitutive of them. The account of human knowing and the natural knowledge of God advocated here is not "essentialist" in this respect. Indeed, the Thomistic essence-existence distinction mentioned above is a stark expression of an awareness of the radical contingency of creatures and of the fact that the essential determinations of things do not exhaust the mystery of being. The Thomistic notion of the identity of essence and existence in God is an indication that God is not in any way determined by or located under a genus he might share with creatures.[192] It is thus also an indication that human beings can never comprehend God or know his essence as such and in its entirety. We therefore cannot presume to speak of God by straightforwardly applying created perfections to him in something like their maximum degree on a Creator-creature continuum.[193] For there is no traversable number of degrees of perfection between us and God. There is no abstract *ens* that might be exemplified by creatures and God alike. He does not participate in perfections that extend beyond himself but is himself the infinite fullness of wisdom, love, and so on. He transcends the system of created being altogether. The attributes that we predicate of God never "capture" what God is but instead serve as inadequate (but still truthful!) descriptions of God that both facilitate ectypal knowledge of him and combat delusions about obtaining archetypal knowledge of him. Such a construal of the knowledge of God rules out the univocity of theological

---

going into detail, my own inclination would be to hold that both the human senses and intellect do receive some impression of an external object, but without that impression becoming itself the object of knowledge or a barrier between the mind and the world. On the distinction between the "phantasm" in Thomas's epistemology and the idea of a "sense datum" in later theories of perception, see Pasnau, *Thomas Aquinas on Human Nature*, 186-89, 274-95; Anthony Lisska, *Aquinas's Theory of Perception: An Analytic Reconstruction* (Oxford: Oxford University Press, 2016).

[192]As te Velde puts it, "God cannot be approached in a line of 'more of the same'" (*Aquinas on God*, 117).

[193]Such a misstep is sometimes associated with projects of "perfect-being theology" (whether rightly or wrongly should be decided on a case-by-case basis). For examples of work on perfect-being theology, see Kathrin A. Rogers, *Perfect Being Theology* (Edinburgh: Edinburgh University Press, 2000); Daniel J. Hill, *Divinity and Maximal Greatness* (New York: Routledge, 2005); Yujin Nagasawa, *Maximal God: A New Defence of Perfect Being Theism* (Oxford: Oxford University Press, 2017).

speech that Heidegger (rightly) seems to resist when he cautions against what Kevin Hector aptly calls "attempting to speak of God by speaking of human persons in a loud voice."[194]

Heidegger also says that ontotheology allows the principle of sufficient reason to dictate God's place in our thinking. While the "principle of sufficient reason" is, strictly speaking, typically associated with philosophers like Leibniz and Christian Wolff,[195] it is worth noting that the talk here of causation, act, potency, and so on does not imply that causality itself is above God. It does not assign God a role to which he must acquiesce. According to Scripture, God himself, the absolute and first cause, has established the world in all its order and causal dynamics and intends that this order should point us back to himself. Certainly Scripture does not explicitly delineate all the causal dynamics that have been employed in fine-tuned proofs of God's existence, but it does invite us to see in creation an order and dependence on the Creator that is arguably open to being explicated in the kinds of analyses found in an author like Thomas or Turretin. Moreover, in this study, while the natural knowledge of God provides some rudimentary preparation for the reception of the gospel, Aristotelian causal analysis does not function as a *principium* or norm of the Christian doctrine of God. With Alsted, one can commend a regenerate natural theology undertaken by the illumined mind pondering creation as a gift of our heavenly Father.[196] In addition, though Heidegger has a point in warning against an arid consideration of God as a being who fills a slot in reason's schematic of the world, the natural knowledge of God affirmed here in fact possesses great spiritual significance, making sinners aware of their accountability to God before their conversion and making believers stand in awe of God afterward.

---

[194]Hector, *Theology Without Metaphysics*, 13.

[195]On the principle of sufficient reason, see, e.g., Alexander R. Pruss, *The Principle of Sufficient Reason: A Reassessment* (Cambridge: Cambridge University Press, 2006); Edward Feser, *Five Proofs of the Existence of God* (San Francisco: Ignatius, 2017), 148, 163-64.

[196]In this connection, though I would insist on the genuinely natural character of such knowledge (its openness to discovery by the natural intellect, its development by logical principles known and practicable by the natural intellect), I can appreciate the emphasis of Nicholas Healy, for example, that once we have received supernatural revelation, our understanding of natural revelation is enriched in various ways ("Natural Theology and the Christian Contribution to Metaphysics: On Thomas Joseph White's *Wisdom in the Face of Modernity*," *Nova et Vetera* 10 [2012]: 556-62).

2. Barth's concerns about natural theology remind us of the danger of subsuming the triune God under a central philosophical theme of our own choosing or invoking God to justify our own social agendas. They also draw attention to the problem of aiming to make the gospel look "respectable" according to the intellectual trends or cultural aesthetics of any given age. One could ponder, for example, how "natural theology" in the negative Barthian sense might be at work in both the decline of mainline Protestantism and the development of "seeker-friendly" evangelicalism. However, in the light of Scripture and with the grain of the catholic Christian tradition, one can also speak of a natural knowledge of God that is not reducible to human self-absorption and oppression.

The extent to which Barth was influenced by Kant's epistemology is a matter that I am content to leave in the hands of Barth scholars, so I will only reiterate that Christians have good reason to believe that Kant's epistemology is flawed.[197] In addition, Spencer's development of Barth's assessment of the theological knowledge available by causal analysis is open to critique. As mentioned above, the Christian is not bound to accept the Kantian claim that causal knowledge pertains to empirical reality alone or to immanent structures of thought alone. A premodern figure like Thomas certainly did not accept that view and cannot be charged with having a theological program whose own inner logic would terminate in agnosticism.[198] Indeed, Thomas held that knowledge of created effects yields knowledge of God not just as the cause of those effects but also as the one who has in himself and in a simple and eminent way the perfections

---

[197]Indeed, given Kant's aversion to knowledge of the supersensible and to theological realism, his epistemology would preclude even Barth's "Christocentric" approach to knowing God (so Thomas Joseph White, "How Barth Got Aquinas Wrong: A Reply to Archie J. Spencer on Causality and Christocentrism," *Nova et Vetera* 7 [2009]: 244, 248; Westerholm, "Kant's Critique," esp. 423). White in particular points out that it would be odd for Barthians to "import wholesale Kantian *philosophical presuppositions* into their theology without sufficient justification" given "their prohibition on an 'autonomous philosophy' that is distinct from revelation" ("How Barth Got Aquinas Wrong," 261-62). At any rate, McCormack, for example, argues that Barth's agreement with Kant is driven by his view of the centrality of the incarnation. According to McCormack, Barth could dispense with Kant's epistemology if another philosophical option proved stronger (*Orthodox and Modern*, 125-26).

[198]*Pace* Spencer, "Causality"; cf. Lawrence Dewan, "St. Thomas and the Principle of Causality," in *Form and Being: Studies in Thomistic Metaphysics,* Studies in Philosophy and the History of Philosophy 45 (Washington, DC: Catholic University of America Press, 2006), 74-80; White, "How Barth Got Aquinas Wrong."

discerned in those effects. Further, one need not choose between cause-effect resemblance, on the one hand, and divine freedom and transcendence, on the other. The freedom of God is adamantly upheld by authors like Thomas, Turretin, and Peter van Mastricht. They reject an emanationist framework, not least where they deny that God creates by a "necessity of nature" and where they affirm a divine "liberty of indifference" with respect to creation.[199] Thomas and the Reformed orthodox also explicitly affirm that God's causal activity is radically distinct from that of creatures. Given God's plenitude, his effects can reflect him in only a profoundly limited way and are never adequate to him or distinct from him by mere degree. Given God's absoluteness and primacy, he is never "like" his effects: they are like him.[200] Yet with these authors one can reject an emanationist view without abandoning the notion that God's effects will in some way reflect their divine cause. For even as God enjoys a liberty of indifference, there is no source of perfection or archetype other than God himself according to which God would establish the natures and perfections of his creatures. To be sure, God does not have to create, and he can and does allow creatures themselves to effect various things, but given God's free decision to create and act in the world, there will be a hypothetically necessary (and inevitably faint) resemblance of God's effects to God.[201] Indeed, it is precisely the fact that God's effects will ultimately resemble God and not something else that dispels the problem of a larger system of being's supposedly encompassing both God and creatures.

Any response to Barth's concerns must ultimately address his exegesis of biblical texts traditionally taken to affirm the reality of a natural knowledge

---

[199]For more on this, see Steven J. Duby, "Election, Actuality and Divine Freedom: Thomas Aquinas, Bruce McCormack and Reformed Orthodoxy in Dialogue," *MT* 32 (2017): 325-40. A "necessity of nature" is a propensity intrinsic to the nature of something on account of which it seeks some end or performs some action, while a "liberty of indifference" is a freedom to do or not to do something without detriment to the being or completeness of the acting subject.

[200]E.g., Thomas Aquinas, *Scriptum super libros Sententiarum*, ed. R. P. Mandonnet (Paris, 1929), 1.35.1.4 sol. and ad 6 (1:819-21); *De Trin.* 4.1 corp. (120-21); *ST* Ia.3.4 ad 1 (42); 7.1 ad 3 (72); 8.1 ad 1 and 3 (82); 11.3 corp. (111); 13.5 (146-47); Turretin, *Inst.* 3.8.3 (1:213-14); Mastricht, *TPT* 2.5.7-8 (94-95); 9.6 (118). For pointed discussion of the "clumsiness" and rhetorical "redherrings" with which Barth and some Barthians have engaged Thomas on causation, and of the way in which understanding divine causation is integral to understanding the incarnation, see White, "How Barth Got Aquinas Wrong," 251-69.

[201]In scholastic discourse, a "hypothetical" or "suppositional" necessity is one that arises only after a free decision is made.

of God.[202] In my view, Barth's exegesis has significant weaknesses, particularly his treatment of Romans 1. While Paul of course writes as an apostle and as one who already knows the gospel, this does not entail that all the Gentiles about whom he is writing in Romans 1 also know the gospel. Nor does it entail that all of the Gentiles about whom he is writing have just been given the gospel in Romans 1:16-17. Certainly Paul brings up humanity's awareness of and accountability to God in Romans 1:18-32 to help the church at Rome understand the need for the gospel, but when sketching this accountability Paul speaks broadly about humanity, giving us no reason to suppose that he is limiting his statements to those who already know Christ or belong to the church. This section of the epistle explains why the saving righteousness of God is now being revealed: "For the wrath of God is being revealed from heaven on all the ungodliness and unrighteousness of human beings, who suppress the truth in unrighteousness" (Rom 1:18-19). Before and after this section, Paul uses second-person pronouns and verbs to address his readership (Rom 1:15; 2:1), but here he is speaking broadly in the third person about "human beings who suppress the truth." Such persons already know of God's eternal power and deity and of their own wrongdoing—and they know these things by the created order (τοῖς ποιήμασιν), with no indication that this knowledge is given only in an evangelistic explanation of creation and human guilt. This is why such persons are culpable before God, and that is why the proclamation of the gospel is so urgent. To take up a distinction noted above from Thomas, humanity's ignorance of God in Romans 1 is not theoretical but "affective," meaning they do not know God in that they do not love and worship him as they ought.[203] In this connection, natural knowledge of God is not, as Barth worried, a means of human self-justification before God but rather the exact opposite: an awareness that none of us is righteous before God, even if that awareness might be temporarily pushed aside. It is precisely humanity's possession of at least some theoretical knowledge of God that is assumed in

---

[202]Perhaps it is worth noting that a total skepticism about natural human perception could be used to critique even a theological epistemology like Barth's, insofar as hearing the word of God preached (or seeing and reading the word written) is itself an act of perception whose reliability would be suspect.

[203]It can be called a theoretical ignorance relative to the articles of faith given in biblical revelation, but not relative to the knowledge of God communicated by nature.

Paul's claim that they "suppress" what they know when they go astray. Barth also comments that Paul no longer regards Gentiles "in themselves and as such" since they are an object of God's saving work through Christ. Yet whatever one might wish to say about an objective change taking place in the Gentiles' spiritual status when the death and resurrection of Christ occurred, it simply does not follow that this would negate the existence of some natural knowledge of God prior to Gentile reception of the gospel. Ultimately, although the occasion of Paul's discussion in Romans 1 is the exposition of the gospel for the church at Rome, this fact does not entail that all those whom he mentions in his writing must share all of his own epistemological bearings. Indeed, he explicitly indicates otherwise where he states that these persons know something of God τοῖς ποιήμασιν.

Barth's exegesis of Psalm 104 also is problematic. While it is true that the brokenness of the world affects human perception of God's glory in it, this does not logically lead to the claim that the present "world picture" is so void of God's glory that only an understanding of the world's eschatological fullness can enable us to know something of God from the created order. The psalmist recognizes that the present creation attests God's providential beneficence even while acknowledging that God sometimes "hides his face" (Ps 104:29). There should be no doubt that the eschatological restoration of the world will effect an even richer awareness of God's wise and generous provision, but biblical prophecy about the world to come hardly prompts us to say that the present state of creation in its own right teaches us nothing about God. In his exposition of Psalm 8, Barth concentrates on humanity as the focal point of God's majesty in the world, but the psalmist also presents the handiwork of God in the heavens as the ground of the declaration, "O YHWH, our Lord, how majestic is your name in all the earth" (Ps 8:1, 3; cf. Ps 19:1-6). This leads the psalmist to recognize the relative smallness of humanity (Ps 8:4), whose divine commission to rule is then perhaps by the end of the psalm part of the ground on which the opening declaration is reiterated (Ps 8:9). In view of this, it is not *only* humanity's (now sinful) dominion that is a medium of divine revelation, for the heavens declare the glory of God. Furthermore, even given that after the fall human dominion is marred by sin and must be fulfilled by Christ, that does not entail that human dominion prior to its renewal in Christ conveys absolutely nothing about the wisdom or power of God. In sum, it seems to me that Barth's exegesis is beset by two key problems: (1) having to assume that all persons about whom the biblical authors write must share the epistemological orientation that the authors themselves possess at the time of writing and (2) having to assume that the fulfillment of creation in Christ's saving work entails that creation bears witness to God's glory only when one already knows of that saving work. Neither of those principles is tenable when one attempts to deal with particular biblical texts like Roman 1 and the Psalms.

Barth's warnings about sinners' misuse of natural theology should be taken seriously. But throughout this chapter we have already encountered strong warnings about the distortion and insufficiency of natural theology from Scripture itself and from authors like Augustine, Thomas, and the Reformed orthodox. In the end, though he has become a remarkably influential figure in Protestant discussion of natural theology, Barth is but one voice in the discussion, one who knew he had taken up a minority position. Indeed, he called the church's pre- and post-Reformation doctrine of a natural knowledge of God a "hydra" that kept returning.[204] Barth should have allowed the church's consensus (a word he himself uses) with its biblical moorings to chasten his rejection of the natural knowledge of God.[205] In light of all this, we need not make Barth's work *the* point of reference or criterion for our account of the natural knowledge of God in the present chapter.

Third, something must be said of Bavinck's concern about the prospect of a "dualistic" vision of nature and grace, natural and supernatural theology. A full response would require discussing both the relationship between Thomas's teaching and later developments in the official teaching of the Roman Catholic Church, and certain recent debates among interpreters of

---

[204]Barth, *CD* II/1, 127-28.

[205]Keith Johnson notes that Barth still has a way of upholding a "natural" knowledge of God in that Barth can read the created order as a "function of God's decision to reconcile sinful humans in and through Jesus Christ" ("Natural Revelation in Creation and Covenant," in *Thomas Aquinas and Karl Barth: An Unofficial Catholic-Protestant Dialogue*, ed. Bruce L. McCormack and Thomas Joseph White [Grand Rapids: Eerdmans, 2013], 145; cf. George Hunsinger, *Evangelical, Catholic, and Reformed: Doctrinal Essays on Barth and Related Themes* [Grand Rapids: Eerdmans, 2015], 90 105). I will explore this more in chap. 5 in connection with Barth's view of the *analogia entis*. On Barth engaging non-Christian material and finding in it "secular parables of the truth," see Hunsinger, *How to Read Karl Barth: The Shape of His Theology* (Oxford: Clarendon, 1993), 234-80.

Thomas.[206] From a Reformed Protestant perspective that seeks to be appreciative of Thomas and also forthright about relevant differences between Reformed and Roman Catholic anthropology, I would argue that although Bavinck is right to caution against a "dualistic" account of the natural and supernatural knowledge of God, his opposition of Reformed theology to Thomas's theological epistemology is problematic. Thomas's description of natural theology as a "preamble" to *sacra doctrina* indicates an awareness of the unity of natural and supernatural theology, the former prodding humanity to anticipate the latter. In addition, as noted above, in Thomas's commentaries on Romans and John he clearly recognizes the effects of sin on the natural intellect and natural knowledge of God.[207] That recognition is part of the reason why Thomas holds that it is beneficial for the content of the natural knowledge of God to be given again in Scripture and that rational demonstration of theological truths is not necessary to justify the practice of *sacra doctrina*. Furthermore, *sacra doctrina* begins with a Christian faith that does involve knowledge: a *cognitio* (a general term for knowledge that might apply to different kinds of knowing) of the articles of faith and then a *scientia* (discursive knowledge of necessary consequences) about conclusions drawn from the articles of faith by working with the ordinary structures of logical inference.[208] A Reformed catholic approach to natural theology should therefore feel free to employ the insights of Thomas. At the same time, there are still differences between Reformed and Roman Catholic theology over the underlying anthropological framework in which concrete natural and supernatural knowledge of God is actualized. In particular, the Reformed tradition has historically argued that the Roman

---

[206]See Henri de Lubac's *Surnaturel* (Paris: Aubier, 1946), and *The Mystery of the Supernatural*, trans. Rosemary Sheed, Milestones in Catholic Theology (New York: Herder and Herder, 1998), as well as those in the opposing *natura pura* camp who believe Thomas affirms a purely natural knowledge of God with an integrity and telos of its own in human existence (e.g., Lawrence Feingold, *The Natural Desire to See God According to St. Thomas Aquinas and His Interpreters*, Faith and Reason: Studies in Catholic Theology and Philosophy, 2nd ed. (Ave Maria, FL: Sapientia, 2004); Steven A. Long, Natura Pura: *On the Recovery of Nature in the Doctrine of Grace* (New York: Fordham University Press, 2010); White, *Wisdom in the Face of Modernity*, 291-322. In my judgment, while both sides make points worth considering, the *natura pura* reading is generally the more accurate interpretation of Thomas.

[207]This recognition, however, does take place within an understanding of the state of integrity and the fall that is somewhat different from a Reformed approach (see, e.g., *ST* Ia.95.1 [420-21]; IaIIae.85.1 [110-11]).

[208]So Thomas, *De Trin.* 2.1-3 (92-100); 3.1 corp. (107); *SCG* 4.1 (4-5).

Catholic affirmation of the *donum superadditum* implies that human nature as created by God—if it needed an additional, supernatural gift to be upright before God—would tend toward evil. By implication, would God then initially be the author of sin? In this regard, the Reformed stress that Adam was not created *in puris naturalibus* with a conflict between his corporeal and spiritual parts, for he was originally given a natural righteousness or "rectitude" of nature by virtue of which he was inclined to the good (cf. Eccles 7:29).[209] Yet, as discussed above, there is still room for a genuine and distinct natural knowledge of God, though such natural knowledge was implemented to help lead humanity to its appointed end of communion with the triune God and was always accompanied by supernatural revelation even before the fall. In short, a Reformed Protestant description of the natural knowledge of God can learn much from Thomas, bearing in mind its historical disagreement with Rome on the *donum superadditum* in humanity's progression from creation to heavenly glory.

Fourth, Plantinga's criticism of "foundationalism"—in this context an insistence that belief in God must be rooted in prior rational demonstration of God's existence—may be worth taking into account when dealing with a rationalist demand for philosophical argumentation always to precede and authorize Christian faith. However, Plantinga's concern is also not necessarily opposed to the conception of natural theology under development here from Scripture and with the help of Thomas and the Reformed orthodox.[210] As Plantinga himself notes, Thomas acknowledges in *SCG* 3.38 an "immediate" natural knowledge of God ("immediate" in the sense of not being dependent on ratiocination) wherein we grasp from the order and motion of the world that it has a divine cause and guide.[211] Indeed, as I read him, when Thomas affirms that few can undertake rational demonstration of God's existence and that it is fitting for the content of the natural knowledge of God to be given again in *sacra doctrina*, he conveys that there is no absolute requirement for Christian faith to be

---

[209]So, e.g., Johannes Maccovius, *Loci communes theologici*, ed. Nicolaus Arnoldus, 2nd ed. (Amsterdam, 1658), 44 (369); William Ames, *Bellarminus enervatus* (Amsterdam, 1628), 1.3 (4:10-12); Turretin, *Inst.* 5.11 (1:517-21); Mastricht, *TPT* 3.9.43 (384).

[210]The sort of program to which Plantinga's critique would apply is typically associated with an author like Descartes or the Lutheran philosopher Christian Wolff.

[211]Cf., e.g., Thomas, *ST* IIa.IIae.85.1 corp. (215).

justified by ratiocination and that *sacra doctrina* is not built on the proofs of God' existence.[212] Furthermore, it is worth recalling that Thomas does not deny that faith itself involves true knowledge (*cognitio*). In fact, he emphasizes that faith's knowledge of God is "firmer" and more certain than reason's knowledge of God since it is based on God's own infallible testimony in Scripture.[213] Finally, I take it that something like Plantinga's emphasis on experience (e.g., experience of beauty or guilt) grounding belief in God's existence is already present in Reformed orthodox description of the *cognitio Dei insita* as spontaneously generated by human encounter with the created order.

Conclusion: Natural Theology and Christian *Theologia*

After beginning with scriptural teaching on the natural knowledge of God in the divine economy, we have explored the reflections of major thinkers from the patristic into the post-Reformation or early modern period (Augustine, Thomas, Scotus, Ockham, the Reformed orthodox). Within that largely historical work I began to indicate some ways in which such authors could help us articulate the role and limitations of the natural knowledge of God in Christian *theologia* today. I also took into consideration important objections raised against the practice of natural theology. These objections provided some salutary warnings about potential abuses of the natural knowledge of God but ultimately afforded an opportunity to clarify rather than abandon the approach advocated here. Taking into account the ground covered in these previous sections, it is now time to conclude this chapter with a summative expression of the role of natural theological knowledge in Christian *theologia*.

1. The ultimate origin or efficient cause of the natural knowledge of God is God the Creator himself, who purposefully makes himself known by the created order to the human race as a whole. *God* gives this knowledge. Themes in Kant, Heidegger, and Barth notwithstanding, natural theology in the sense that I have in mind here is not fundamentally a matter of human

---

[212]Cf. Thomas, *ST* IIaIIae.1.5 ad 3 (17); 2.4 corp. (30). See also Dewan, "Existence of God," 735-37. Thomas is, however, still prepared to identify signs by which the supernatural origin of biblical revelation can be confirmed (*SCG* 1.6 [17]).

[213]Thomas, *SCG* 1.4 (11); *ST* Ia.1.1 corp. (6); 1.2 corp. (9); 1.6 (17-18); 1.8 ad 2 (22); 12.13 ad 3 (138); IIaIIae.2.4, corp. (30); 4.8 (52-53). Pace Diller, *Theology's Epistemological Dilemma*, 200n96.

beings of their own resolve trying to climb up to God rather than depend on and receive from God.[214] The natural knowledge of God rightly conceived is communicated by God's own self-revelation—a "natural" revelation but no less divine or true for that reason. Indeed, it is communicated and impressed on us by God not in order to enable us to justify our epistemic prowess before him but in order to render us aware of and accountable to him, which in fact places us in the rather disquieting position of having no excuse for our sin and hubris. If it is a "way of ascent" (as Thomas puts it), it is so not because it is intrinsically a matter of self-exaltation but because we apprehend effects of God and then arrive at knowledge of a cause that is higher than these (i.e., God).[215] Given that this knowledge is available from observation of the created order (Ps 8:1, 3; 19:1-6; Rom 1:20) and continually accessible to the human race as a whole, it is reasonable to conclude that the subjective "light" by which natural revelation is grasped is not wholly external or only occasionally given to human persons. The divine "illumination" by which human persons receive natural knowledge of God is God's gift of a natural capacity of understanding resident in the human person, though God actively sustains and intimately oversees the exercise of this capacity in the ordinary course of human life and thought. As the Reformed orthodox point out, this knowledge of God can be characterized as either "implanted" or "acquired," the former being primary and the latter being a developed version obtained by some through ratiocination. Accordingly, the

---

[214]That is, natural theological knowledge is first given and impressed on us by God himself. This fact, coupled with the fact that natural knowledge of God is not adequate to secure sinners' right fellowship with God, entails that upholding this natural knowledge is not a matter of "epistemological Pelagianism" (as Hunsinger puts it in *Evangelical, Catholic, and Reformed*, 92).

[215]Put differently, the understanding of the natural knowledge of God advocated here does not stipulate that human beings are able or authorized to develop an entirely a priori set of criteria to which the biblical God must conform or else be cast aside. Instead, human beings encounter what the biblical God has himself given in the created order. Human beings have impressed on them by God's own handiwork a sense that there is one who is eternal and wise and immeasurably powerful. Our initial awareness that the true God must be eternal, wise, powerful, and so forth is implanted by the God of Holy Scripture, who is the true God and maker of heaven and earth and who wills that recipients of his supernatural revelation would perceive how that revelation resonates with their prior awareness of there being an all-powerful Creator. God himself has arranged that we would hear the gospel with the assumption that there is a first cause who governs the world. While sinful humanity does distort this knowledge and create false expectations about what the true God must be, this knowledge nevertheless does originate from without and does remain in its basic elements (God is powerful, God is to be worshiped, etc.) even when it is suppressed.

natural knowledge of God is not dependent on the use of formal syllogisms, though it can certainly be enriched by discursive reasoning and by the ongoing refinement of arguments for Christian theism.[216]

2. The content or object of the natural knowledge of God is God the Creator under the aspect of various attributes like wisdom, power, righteousness, and goodness. In this connection, Scripture compels us to recognize that natural knowledge includes positive knowledge of God, not just a knowledge of what God is not. At the same time, it is limited in scope and specificity. As Thomas expresses it, it is like knowing someone is coming toward us without yet seeing who it is. A Reformed author like Junius helpfully adds that natural theological knowledge is "common" rather than "proper," recognizing that there is a God but not "pointing out" for us precisely who this God is. In other words, it does not include a knowledge of all that distinguishes God as God (insofar as this is knowable by creatures) or a knowledge of God's economic acts (e.g., the exodus, the episode of Elijah and the prophets of Baal) by which he helps us to distinguish him from false gods.[217] Of course, as writers like Thomas, Scotus, and Junius note, natural theological understanding is indirect in that it is an apprehension of God from created effects and does not directly or immediately tell us of God in himself, as Holy Scripture does.[218] Still, though it is an indirect knowledge, its content ultimately pertains to God himself and not just God's relationship

---

[216]There are a number of recent analytical and creative developments of arguments for God's existence that could be explored in a full study of natural theology: Alister E. McGrath, *The Open Secret: A New Vision for Natural Theology* (Oxford: Blackwell, 2008); and McGrath, *Reimagining Nature*; Feser, *Five Proofs*. See also parts 4 and 5 of Manning, ed., *Oxford Handbook of Natural Theology*, and Rowan Williams, *The Edge of Words: God and the Habits of Language* (London: Bloomsbury, 2014). Perhaps some readers will be disappointed that such works do not receive further attention here. However, this chapter has aimed to provide only a basic account of the role of natural theology in the Christian doctrine of God, leaving it to others to continue making proposals about how this role might be developed.

[217]As Wolfhart Pannenberg notes, a relatively "vague" knowledge of God (e.g., "a vague sense of infinitude") can be interpreted and filled out by subsequent growth in theological understanding (*Systematic Theology*, trans. Geoffrey W. Bromiley [Grand Rapids: Eerdmans, 1991], 1:116-17).

[218]Whereas Barth claims that a knowledge of God from nature would be a presumptuous "direct" seeing of God, these authors are clear that it is an *indirect* knowledge relative to that of Scripture. Of course, even the knowledge gained from Scripture is still mediate in the sense that its locutions draw on our knowledge of created effects, which can have only a very limited similarity to God and do not afford the beatific sight of God promised in the eschaton (see Thomas, *ST* Ia.88.2-3 [367-68]).

to the world or his outward effects.[219] God does not merely cause created existence or created perfections: he himself is, he is wise, he is just, and so on, which takes us into the territory of *theologia* (not just *oikonomia*). Further, if natural theological knowledge begins in the human encounter with external objects of the world—not our own prior ("essentialist") assumptions about things—it is not necessarily a matter of apotheosis or conceptual idolatry. Indeed, the natural theology described in Romans 1 includes an awareness of the Creator-creature distinction and of human culpability for mistaking creatures for the immortal God. Unless one is (like Hume or Kant) convinced of the need to be skeptical about human apprehension of outward causal dynamics, natural knowledge of the Creator-creature distinction can be profitably set forth in a causal analysis of the sort found in Thomas's work.

3. The purpose of the natural knowledge of God lies in God's upholding humanity's ongoing awareness of himself and of our need of him and his mercy. It is a "preamble" to the supernatural revelation that culminates in the incarnation and is transmitted in the biblical canon. It is what enables Paul in Acts 14, for example, to establish a point of contact for the preaching of the gospel when he directs his hearers to God's beneficence in nature. Given that his listeners had just sought to deify him, Paul is certainly not suggesting that their knowledge of God was pure or complete, but he does readily appeal to God's self-attestation in the created order to help the crowd understand that the Creator and ruler of the world is now calling on them to repent and believe the good news. In Alsted's words, this natural knowledge of God is a "preparation for the school of grace."[220] Such knowledge does not entail that there are two Gods or two conflicting parts or versions of God. Nor does it entail, on the subjective level, that there are two conflicting knowledges of God. Natural theological knowledge is incomplete, but its incompleteness does not mean that it necessarily negates or contradicts the teaching of supernatural revelation. Not-knowing is not

---

[219]In other words, the mode of communication is more indirect, even if the content that is communicated ultimately concerns God himself.

[220]The "preamble" language helpfully expresses that within the plan of God nature and natural theology are organically connected to grace and supernatural theology. *Pace* rationalism, nature and natural theology are not sufficient in themselves to lead humanity to its end (everlasting fellowship with the triune God and the people of God). *Pace* fideism, faith in Christ and supernatural theology do not arise *ex nihilo* or detached from human experience and knowledge about the external world. In other words, nature anticipates grace, and grace perfects nature.

the same as denying or knowing-not. One can apprehend truth about the one God without apprehending *all* truth about the one God. One can understand that there is a God who is wise or powerful without yet understanding that he is triune, for example.[221] With Bavinck, we can clarify that natural theology should not be configured in a "dualistic" manner, but drawing from authors like Thomas, Junius, and Turretin does not require such a configuration. Indeed, we can (and, I think, should) maintain that humanity was not created *in puris naturalibus* in the sense the phrase typically bore in post-Reformation polemics with Roman Catholic authors, but we can also still affirm the reality of a genuinely natural knowledge of God distinct (but ultimately not separate) from supernaturally given knowledge.

4. In light of texts like Romans 1 and in accord with various statements in Augustine, Thomas, and early Reformed authors, the natural knowledge of God is limited objectively in its content and also distorted subjectively in its suppression and abuse by sinful humanity. Indeed, knowledge of God in its fullest sense includes love and worship of God. In these respects, the world does not know God (Jn 17:25; Rom 1:21, 28). Here it is fitting to recognize that the tone or level of optimism with which we speak of natural theology should be sensitive to context. In a context (Barthian or otherwise) marked by emphatic denial of any positive role for the natural knowledge of God, we should underscore the reality and positive function of it. In a different context (one pervaded by a *theologia gloriae*, we might say) where philosophical investigation is brought out from under the guidance of scriptural theology and allowed to develop ideas of God to which Scripture supposedly must conform, we should be ready to criticize resultant claims about God, not least those that exalt a favorite philosophical theme and posit God as simply the maximal instance of that theme.[222] Thus, according to the present study, natural knowledge of God merely provides some basic and incomplete awareness of God's existence, primacy, and justice prior to reception of the gospel, without ever being propped up as a foundational norm and criterion for dogmatic theology. The content of this natural knowledge is

---

[221]Compare Turner, *Faith, Reason and the Existence of God*, 17-20, 226.

[222]In this connection, White helpfully comments that natural theology rightly understood actually discourages a theology of glory by exposing our need for further revelation of God (*Wisdom in the Face of Modernity*, 290).

republished in Holy Scripture and illumined by verbal revelation, but even then it does not of itself bring salvation and reconciliation with God, for it does not bring us Christ the mediator. Thus in the plan of God it is ordered to the supernatural revelation of the person and work of the incarnate Son. Salvific reception of that supernatural revelation is initiated by the Spirit's enabling sinners to believe in Christ. The Spirit restores the human person's disposition to judge rightly the things of God and to receive Christ. This grace does not eliminate the light of natural reason but heals it and commissions it to see and love the glory of God in the created order. And while Christian meditation on the natural works of God involves greater understanding of those works, it also involves greater understanding of the one who brought them about (*theologia*).

Natural theology is thus caught up in the overarching purpose of God to lead us to everlasting communion with himself. It retains a positive role even after the fall, but it does not stand alone as an independent agenda for human inquiry. It must be viewed in its relationship to the supernatural revelation that culminates in the incarnation, which is the subject of the next chapter.

THREE

Incarnation in Context

Christology's Place in Theology Proper

T HE PREVIOUS CHAPTER EXAMINED how natural revelation and
the natural knowledge of God contribute to the outworking of God's
plan to communicate knowledge of himself to us. It also stressed the insufficiency of the natural knowledge of God. Without at all diminishing
its positive role, we can recognize that natural theology will not enable
reconciliation with God or the beatific vision. It must be reformed by
supernatural revelation and the illumination of the Spirit. Indeed, the
primary purpose of natural knowledge of God is to preserve in us an
awareness of our Creator and prepare us for the supernatural revelation
of the gospel. But the fact that supernatural revelation culminates in the
coming of Jesus Christ is taken by some to mean that the incarnation itself
is the starting point or even the exclusive basis on which the doctrine of
God must stand. Some go beyond this and argue that the incarnation is
constitutive of God's being and, consequently, that it is entirely misguided
to pursue a knowledge of God in his transcendence of the economy and
the incarnation.

Here I will contend that the incarnation should be understood within the
broader context of the supernatural revelation given by God in Holy
Scripture. The incarnation must inform our doctrine of God without being
its first or only epistemological principle. Moreover, this chapter will argue
that the incarnation itself confirms that God's being is not constituted by the
incarnation and that God wills to communicate knowledge of himself in his
transcendence of the economy. First, I will take note of some recent

assertions about the centrality of the incarnation in our knowledge of God and then respond by qualifying the role of the incarnation in light of scriptural teaching. Then we will explore the incarnation's positive contribution to our knowledge of God. For concerns about the hypertrophy of Christology in relation to theology proper should not cause us to lose sight of the fact that God's self-revelation truly does culminate in Jesus Christ. The next section will broaden our look at Christ's role in the communication of theological knowledge, considering the sense in which Christ is the source of our theology even before the incarnation and the sense in which the manifestation of God's glory in Christ is central to the fulfillment of God's plan and to our theological knowing. The final section of the chapter will then examine more closely a potential challenge that centers on the notion of the *Logos asarkos* and *extra Calvinisticum* in Barth's theology.

QUALIFYING CHRISTOLOGY'S ROLE

Christology and theology proper in Barth and other recent theologians. I have already noted Barth's concerns about natural theology and his emphasis on the "knowability of God" in Christ alone in the previous chapter. He does still affirm that God is who he is even without respect to his outward works.[1] God enjoys a "supreme and utter independence," in which "He would be no less and no different even if [created beings] all did not exist or existed differently."[2] At the same time, Barth contends that God's essence is "something which we shall encounter either at the place where God deals with us as Lord and Saviour, or not at all." "God is who He is in the act of His revelation" (i.e., in the incarnation of the Son), and that is where we must seek him.[3] Regarding his commitment to understanding God's being on the basis of the economy and ensuring that God's being and economic action are aligned with each other, Barth declares that

> we have consistently followed the rule, which we regard as basic, that statements about the divine modes of being [Father, Son, Spirit] antecedently in themselves cannot be different in content from those that are to be made about their reality in revelation. All our statements concerning what is called

---

[1]Barth, *CD* II/1, 259-60.
[2]Barth, *CD* II/1, 311.
[3]Barth, *CD* II/1, 261-62.

the immanent Trinity have been reached simply as confirmations or under-linings or, materially, as the indispensable premises of the economic Trinity.[4]

Later in the *Church Dogmatics* Barth is critical of claims about God's supremacy that seem to conflict with his condescension in Christ. He writes,

> The meaning of His deity . . . cannot be gathered from any notion of a su-preme, absolute, non-worldly being. It can be learned only from what took place in Jesus Christ. . . . Who the one true God is, and what He is, i.e., what is His being as God, and therefore His deity, His "divine nature," which is also the divine nature of Jesus Christ if He is very God—all this we have to dis-cover from the fact that as such He is very man and a partaker of human nature, from His becoming man, from His incarnation and from what He has done and suffered in the flesh.[5]

For Barth, the Logos *in abstracto* or the eternal Son without reference to the incarnation is a conceptual placeholder reminding us that there was a "free basis in the inner being and essence of God" in light of which he under-takes his reconciling work. We are not to seek him as the Logos *in abstracto*:

> Since we are now concerned with the revelation and dealings of God, and particularly with the atonement, with the person and work of the Mediator, it is pointless, as it is impermissible, to return to the inner being and essence of God and especially to the second person of the Trinity as such, in such a way that we ascribe to this person another form than that which God Himself has given in willing to reveal Himself and to act outwards.[6]

God has made the election and work of Jesus Christ the content of his eternal will, and we "cannot go back on it." We cannot "bracket that which God has actually done" in pursuit of an abstract *Logos asarkos* whose "content and form" are other than the incarnate Christ. Failure at this point displays a lack of "real faith and obedience."[7] More emphatically,

> The election of Jesus Christ is the eternal choice and decision of God. And our first assertion tells us that Jesus Christ is the electing God. We must not ask concerning any other but Him. In no depth of the Godhead shall we

---

[4]Barth, *CD* I/1, 479.
[5]Barth, *CD* IV/1, 177.
[6]Barth, *CD* IV/1, 52.
[7]Barth, *CD* IV/1, 52-53.

encounter any other but Him. There is no such thing as Godhead in itself. Godhead is always the Godhead of the Father, the Son and the Holy Spirit. But the Father is the Father of Jesus Christ and the Holy Spirit is the Spirit of the Father and the Spirit of Jesus Christ.[8]

With such statements Barth sounds as though he is going beyond the epistemological claim (taking the incarnation as the exclusive basis for the doctrine of God) and making an ontological claim (God could not have been God without election and the incarnation), though this may be counterbalanced by other statements he makes about God's freedom in election.[9]

Barth's influence can be seen in similar claims made by various Protestant theologians after him. T. F. Torrance highlights the correspondence between God's being and his economic action: "God is who he is in the Act of his revelation, and his Act is what it is in his Being." When Torrance speaks of God's action in this regard, he seems to have in mind the particular action of God in the incarnation. He winsomely writes that "there is no God behind the back of Jesus Christ."[10] Accordingly, Torrance criticizes a "metaphysical conception" of God's being and instead advocates a "powerful soteriological approach to the doctrine of God."[11] Likewise, Paul Molnar holds that the incarnation is the starting point for the doctrine of God while still maintaining that the incarnation does not constitute God's being: "I believe that we are indeed limited to the human Jesus as the incarnate Word to know who God is, but that the God we know in him is constituted eternally within the immanent Trinity and not by his relation to us in history, just as I believe his being is not realized through his humiliation on our behalf."[12]

---

[8]Barth, *CD* II/2, 115.

[9]See, e.g., Barth, *CD* II/2, 155, where God is not "submerged in his relationship to the world" or "tied in Himself to the universe." For debate on this, see Bruce L. McCormack, *Orthodox and Modern: Studies in the Theology of Karl Barth* (Grand Rapids: Baker Academic, 2008), esp. part 3; Paul Molnar, *Faith, Freedom and the Spirit: The Economic Trinity in Barth, Torrance and Contemporary Theology* (Downers Grove, IL: IVP Academic, 2015); George Hunsinger, *Reading Barth with Charity: A Hermeneutical Proposal* (Grand Rapids: Baker Academic, 2015). On aseity in Barth, see Brian D. Asbill, *The Freedom of God for Us: Karl Barth's Doctrine of Divine Aseity* (London: Bloomsbury, 2016).

[10]Thomas F. Torrance, *The Christian Doctrine of God: One Being, Three Persons* (Edinburgh: T&T Clark, 1996), 4-5, 206, 243.

[11]Torrance, *Christian Doctrine of God*, 248.

[12]Paul D. Molnar, "Can Jesus' Divinity Be Recognized as 'Definitive, Authentic and Essential' if It Is Grounded in Election? Just How Far Did the Later Barth Historicize Christology?," *Neue Zeitschrift für systematische Theologie und Religionsphilosophie* 52 (2010): 73.

Others after Barth move in the direction of affirming the idea that God in fact constitutes his being with reference to the incarnation. Developing Barth's thought in the Lutheran tradition, Eberhard Jüngel focuses on God's "unity with perishability" in his identification with "the man Jesus." Jüngel is concerned to articulate how God's love is enacted in the incarnation through his opposition to the death and "nothingness" that threaten created being. The love of the Father and Son "takes place as the radical relatedness of God to an other which is absolutely opposite to him, that is, to the human essence which he creates for that reason." In other words, "The self-relatedness of the deity of God takes place in an unsurpassable way in the very selflessness of the incarnation of God. . . . For that reason, the 'economic' Trinity is the 'immanent' Trinity, and vice versa. And thus the Crucified One belongs to the concept of God." This yields a "correction" and "destruction" of the "classical doctrine of God" with its insistence on God's absoluteness, immutability, and impassibility. Since the "thought of God" should "correspond to the being of God," the "place of [God's] thinkability" is "the man Jesus."[13] Jüngel thus speaks of the incarnation's establishing an "analogy of advent," in which there is a correspondence or similarity between God and humanity and, consequently, the possibility of a correspondence between our language and God's being.[14]

Robert Jenson is even more direct in his contention that God's being is established by his economic works. According to Jenson, God is "identified with" (not just "by") events like the exodus and the resurrection. God constitutes his identity by way of the "dramatic coherence" of such events. God is God not by continuing to be something he already was but by "anticipat[ing] an end in which he will be all he ever could be."[15] At one time Jenson acknowledged that "God could have been himself on different terms, established his identity without reference to us," though "we can assert only the sheer contrafactual." We would not know "*how* God would then have been the same God we now know."[16] Later in his work, however, Jenson

---

[13]Eberhard Jüngel, *God as the Mystery of the World: On the Foundation of the Theology of the Crucified One in the Dispute Between Theism and Atheism*, trans. Darrell L. Guder (Grand Rapids: Eerdmans, 1983), 191-92, 199, 209-10, 371-73.

[14]Jüngel, *God as the Mystery of the World*, x, 277-98.

[15]Robert Jenson, *Systematic Theology*, vol. 1, *The Triune God* (Oxford: Oxford University Press, 1997) 59, 66.

[16]Jenson, *Systematic Theology*, 1:65.

concluded that the question of how God would be God apart from creation and the incarnation is beholden to an "unbaptized notion of time" according to which God could not be initially determined by an identity that is accomplished eschatologically. For Jenson, the contrafactual question is simply "nonsense." There is nothing in God's life that ontologically precedes the mission and obedience of the Son.[17]

Finally, Bruce McCormack builds on Barth's theology by advancing the claim that God constitutes his own essence by his eternal decision for the incarnation. According to McCormack, there is no divine essence behind this decision. The traditional "essentialist" ontology must in this regard be exchanged for an "actualist" ontology wherein God "gives himself being" by the act of election. Thus there is no "metaphysical gap" between God *in se* and God *pro nobis*. God as such and in himself is also God *pro nobis*.[18] In this way, "the Son is already, by inclination and disposition, that which He will become."[19] McCormack is clear that he makes this assertion for christological reasons, particularly in order to affirm the full deity of Christ and the fact it is the Son himself (not a another person) who suffers and atones for sin.[20]

[17]Robert W. Jenson, "Once More the *Logos Asarkos*," *IJST* 13 (2011): 130-33.

[18]Bruce L. McCormack, "Grace and Being," in *The Cambridge Companion to Karl Barth*, ed. John Webster (Cambridge: Cambridge University Press, 2000), 98-99; McCormack, "The Actuality of God: Karl Barth in Conversation with Open Theism," in *Engaging the Doctrine of God: Contemporary Protestant Perspectives*, ed. Bruce L. McCormack (Grand Rapids: Baker Academic, 2008), 188, 221; McCormack, "Election and the Trinity: Theses in Response to George Hunsinger," *SJT* 63 (2010): 208, 210; McCormack, "Why Should Theology Be Christocentric? Christology and Metaphysics in Paul Tillich and Karl Barth," *Wesleyan Theological Journal* 45 (2010): 75, 79; McCormack, "The Lord and Giver of Life: A 'Barthian' Defense of the Filioque," in *Rethinking Trinitarian Theology: Disputed Questions and Contemporary Issues in Trinitarian Theology*, ed. Robert J. Wozniak and Giulio Maspero (London: T&T Clark, 2012), 231, 244; McCormack, "Processions and Missions: A Point of Convergence Between Thomas Aquinas and Karl Barth," in *Thomas Aquinas and Karl Barth: An Unofficial Catholic-Protestant Dialogue*, ed. Bruce L. McCormack and Thomas Joseph White (Grand Rapids: Eerdmans, 2013), 121.

[19]McCormack, "Lord and Giver of Life," 252.

[20]See Bruce L. McCormack, "Karl Barth's Christology as a Resource for a Reformed Version of Kenoticism," *IJST* 8 (2006): 243-51; McCormack, "Seek God Where He May Be Found: A Response to Edwin Chr. van Driel," *SJT* 60 (2007): 79; McCormack, "'With Loud Cries and Tears': The Humanity of the Son in the Epistle to the Hebrews," in *The Epistle to the Hebrews and Christian Theology*, ed. Richard Bauckham et al. (Grand Rapids: Eerdmans, 2009), 37-68; McCormack, "Divine Impassibility of Simply Divine Constancy? Implications of Karl Barth's Later Christology for Debates Over Impassibility," in *Divine Impassibility and the Mystery of Human Suffering*, ed. James F. Keating and Thomas Joseph White (Grand Rapids: Eerdmans, 2009), 150-86; McCormack, "The Only Mediator: The Person and Work of Christ in Evangelical Perspective,"

Some of the technical christological issues here will be explored in the last section of this chapter ("The *Logos Asarkos* and *Extra Calvinisticum*"). For now, the epistemological implications must be considered. In light of his discussion of God's self-determination by election and the incarnation, McCormack eschews "metaphysical thinking" about God, or any approach to God that might "take up a starting point 'from below' in some creaturely reality or magnitude and proceed through a process of inferential reasoning to establish the nature of divine reality." According to McCormack, such an approach claims to know "what God is before a consideration of Christology": "At the point at which Christology is finally introduced, its central terms ('deity' or 'divinity,' the divine 'nature' or 'person') have already been filled with content. The result is that the content of Christology will be made to confirm a prior understanding of God." One such method is that of "classical theism," which operates with a "robust Creator-creature distinction" independent of Christology and attempts to "deny to God any similarity to created reality through a process of negating the limits thought to belong to the creaturely." It assumes we must talk of something else before speaking of God. This leads to a denial of God the Son's direct suffering in the incarnation and to an "abstract" view of God since it is a matter of "looking away from the knowledge of God given in Jesus Christ." In McCormack's "postmetaphysical" doctrine of God, "the event in which God gives himself being" (i.e., his decision for the incarnation) "is the event which founds our knowledge of him, there divine reality and human language do not fall apart." In short, McCormack advocates "resolving never to speak about God on any other basis than that of the incarnation."[21] In relatively recent essays, McCormack describes this as a matter of "transcendental" thinking about God's being that "works exclusively from the economy to the so-called immanent Trinity." A transcendental approach "does not find in God anything more than is necessary to explain the missions." This is different from what one finds in Thomas Aquinas, for example, who is willing also to "speculate" about God's being via "metaphysics" and "natural theology." For

in *Renewing the Evangelical Mission*, ed. Richard Lints (Grand Rapids: Eerdmans, 2013), 250-69; McCormack, "Atonement and Human Suffering," in *Locating Atonement: Explorations in Constructive Dogmatics*, ed. Oliver D. Crisp and Fred Sanders (Grand Rapids: Zondervan, 2015), 202-3.
[21]McCormack, "Actuality of God," 186-88, 211-12.

McCormack, the transcendental move upholds a correspondence or identity of the "economic Trinity" and the "immanent Trinity." Otherwise, McCormack writes in dialogue with Karl Rahner, the incarnation would tell us nothing "specific to the Son," nothing about the "Logos as such." It would be a purported revelation of God that fails to disclose the order of God's own triune life. At that point, the only thing linking the economy to the "immanent Trinity" would be "the concept of verbal revelation": "We know that God is triune in and for Himself because He tells us He is."[22]

Response. Barth and the other authors mentioned here argue that the incarnation is the proper basis for the Christian doctrine of God, its first and even exclusive epistemological principle. Some go further by grounding this in the ontological claim that it is the incarnation (or God's decision for it) that constitutes God's being. Though I cannot respond to each individual statement brought forward by Barth and the others considered here, I will offer the following comments to address key issues highlighted by their arguments. These will deal primarily with the epistemological question of whether the incarnation is the starting point of theology proper, while my response to the ontological question of whether the incarnation constitutes God's being will appear in the course of the next section of the chapter.

1. It is important to make the straightforward—but sometimes neglected—point that we cannot access the person of Christ apart from the Bible. We may sometimes be tempted to speak as if we do have a knowledge of Christ that is independent of the witness of Scripture with all its particularity and concreteness. However, there is no true access to the meaning of Christ apart from what the prophets and apostles have handed down to us in the biblical canon, even if the average person encounters the biblical portrayal of Christ first through the proclamation of the word by another. The way to the knowledge of Christ runs through God's own exposition of the person, work, and teaching of the Savior given in the Old and New Testaments. And this is not a matter of subordinating Christ to Scripture. Indeed, it was Christ's Spirit who directed the Old Testament prophets to deliver their

---

[22]McCormack, "Lord and Giver of Life," 230-31, 238-39; McCormack, "Processions and Missions," 115, 117-18, 124-25; McCormack, "Atonement and Human Suffering," 201-2. For the statements from Karl Rahner, see his *The Trinity*, trans. Joseph Donceel (London: Burnes and Oates, 1970), 11.

message (1 Pet 1:10-11; 2 Pet 1:20-21). It was Christ's Spirit who spoke from
Christ to teach the apostles and enable them to bear witness to him in
preaching and in writing (Jn 16:12-15; Acts 1:8). In fact, while the eternal
Word, being true God, exists with an absolute necessity, the early Protestant
writers correctly point out that Scripture exists in God's economy with just
a "hypothetical" or "suppositional" necessity (i.e., on the basis of God's sovereign decision to govern and edify the church by this authoritative written
word).[23] Thus, taking Scripture (not Christ or the incarnation per se) as the
external cognitive principle and "immediate" or "formal object" of supernatural theology is simply a matter of recognizing how God has chosen to
grant us knowledge of himself and, in particular, knowledge of the incarnate
life and work of the Son.[24]

2. If we were left to treat the incarnation just as an event or datum, without
recourse to God's own verbal explanation of it, we would be left trying to do
dogmatic theology under limitations that are characteristic of natural theology. First, like the human observer of the world developing an "acquired"
natural theology, we would encounter an object (here, a man named Jesus
who was born in the first century, performed miracles, and so forth) and
then have to depend on our fallible ratiocination to posit various inferences
with the aim of arriving indirectly at a knowledge of God's triune being.
Second, like the practitioner of acquired natural theology, we would follow
what Thomas calls a *via inventionis* (way of discovery) moving backward
from consequent things (in this case, the Son's enfleshment and human obedience and suffering) to higher principles (the eternal processions and the
divine decree), without the benefit of a *via iudicii* (way of judgment) along
which to apprehend the higher principles by divine testimony and then understand the consequent things more adequately in their light.[25] In these
respects, beginning with the incarnation and relying on transcendental reasoning to posit or get back to a knowledge of God's triune being bears

---

[23]E.g., William Whitaker, *Disputations on Holy Scripture* (repr., Orlando: Soli Deo Gloria, 2005),
1.6.7 (516-17); Mastricht, *TPT* 1.2.20 (22-23).

[24]E.g., Polanus, *Syntagma* 1.14 (16); Turretin, *Inst.* 1.5.4 (1:18); 7.6 (1:24). On the relationship
between Christ and Scripture as an object of knowledge, see esp. John Owen, *Christologia*, in
The Works of John Owen, vol. 1, *The Glory of Christ*, ed. William H. Goold (Edinburgh: Banner
of Truth, 1965), 5 (74).

[25]See Thomas, *ST* Ia.79.8 corp. (274).

methodological resemblance to the work of natural theology, which, though not altogether invalid, is beset with significant weaknesses. By contrast, if the external cognitive principle of dogmatics and of theology proper is Holy Scripture, we begin with God's own infallible description and can contemplate God from above in what Thomas calls a "way of descent,"[26] understanding God himself (in an ectypal manner) and then with God's own guidance framing his outward works in the light of his eternal triune life.[27]

Obviously, the economy is the context in which we encounter God. Our very existence and our knowledge of God by God's revelation cannot take place outside the economy. In this regard, our knowledge of God begins with the economy of God's outward works, which culminate in the incarnation. Nevertheless, the *context* of divine revelation and the knowledge of God does not exhaust the *content* of that revelation and knowledge. The material content of scriptural revelation transcends the economy. It not only invites us to consider how the missions reveal the processions in God but also provides direct (albeit brief) description of the eternal processions themselves (e.g., Jn 5:25-30; 6:45-46; 7:28-29; Heb 1:3).[28]

To be sure, the Scriptures (and traditional theology proper) do not preclude some form of transcendental reasoning from the economy to God's being.[29] For example, in John 5:19-30 Jesus speaks of his acting from the Father and being sent from the Father and ultimately roots this in his procession from the Father wherein he receives from the Father "life in himself." We are invited to trace how the incarnate work of the Son corresponds to

---

[26]Thomas, *SCG* 4.1 (3-4).

[27]Supernatural theology thus provides what Keckermann calls a "primary order of cognition" or a "cognition according to the nature of things," which follows the order of being (as opposed to a "secondary order of cognition," which considers first things that are more readily perceived by us and are in fact secondary in reality) (*Scientiae metaphysicae brevissima synopsis et compendium*, in *Operum omnium quae extant* [Geneva, 1614], 1.5 [1:2020]).

[28]Compare Gilles Emery, "*Theologia* and *Dispensatio*: The Centrality of the Divine Missions in St. Thomas's Trinitarian Theology," *The Thomist* 74 (2010): 515-61.

[29]The Christian tradition supplies a variety of explorations of the fittingness of the Son's incarnation and (in some cases) even of his being the only divine person who could take on flesh (e.g., Augustine, *De Trinitate, libri XV*, ed. W. J. Mountain, 2 vols., CCSL 50-50A [Turnhout: Brepols, 1968], 4.28-29 [1:198-200]; Peter Lombard, *Sententiae in IV libris distinctae*, 3rd ed., Spicilegium Bonventurianum 5 [Rome: Grottaferrata, 1981], 3.1.1-2 [2:24-26]; Thomas, *ST* Ia.43.4 [449]; IIIa.3.5 corp. and ad 1 and 3 [63]; Girolamo Zanchi, *De incarnatione Filii Dei* [Heidelberg, 1593], 2.2 [95-98]; Turretin, *Inst.* 13.4.5-6 [2:331]. See also Matthew Levering, "Christ, the Trinity, and Predestination: McCormack and Aquinas," in *Trinity and Election in Contemporary Theology*, ed. Michael T. Dempsey [Grand Rapids: Eerdmans, 2011], 252-71).

and thus reveals the eternal order of the persons. We then confess the Son's eternal generation to be the ultimate ground of his mission and incarnation, not just something stipulated by Scripture without any ontological moorings. But a text like John 5:19-30 does not leave us to take the initiative and tentatively posit an eternal procession of the Son. It tells us that there is such a procession. And in so doing it gives us an ectypal glimpse of God's immanent richness that is more than a conceptual placeholder instrumentalized and put to use for other ends in the development of a dogmatic system. Scripture's direct description of God himself means that we are not limited to transcendental reasoning.[30] Indeed, even in the place that perhaps most powerfully underscores the epistemological importance of the incarnation—John's prologue—the text does not begin with the event of the incarnation itself but by first telling us that the Word already was God in eternal fellowship with the God the Father (Jn 1:1).

3. Since Scripture is the divinely appointed source of our knowledge of the incarnate Son, we have to recognize that within Scripture Jesus is presented as the culminating moment in God's revelation, not the first or only moment. It is possible that someone might hear of the God of the Bible for the first time in the context of the proclamation of the gospel, but that proclamation will at least implicitly include or presuppose an understanding of God as ontologically prior to the world and as the Creator of it. A new believer's catechetical training would then involve a study of Scripture and Christian doctrine that locates the incarnation in relation to God and in the broader arc of God's dealings with creatures. In this connection, Herman Bavinck fittingly comments that Christ is the "midpoint of Scripture" and therefore "cannot be its starting point. Christ presupposes the existence of God and humanity. . . . It is, moreover, undoubtedly true that Christ revealed the Father to us, but this revelation of God through the Son does not nullify the many and varied ways he spoke through the prophets."[31]

---

[30]Compare Bruce D. Marshall, "The Trinity," in *The Blackwell Companion to Modern Theology*, ed. Gareth Jones (Oxford: Blackwell, 2004), 193-97; Marshall, "The Unity of the Triune God: Reviving an Ancient Question," *The Thomist* 72 (2010): 1-32; Emery, "*Theologia* and *Dispensatio*." Note also Nicholas M. Healy, "Karl Barth, German-Language Theology, and the Catholic Tradition," in Dempsey, *Trinity and Election*, 240-43.

[31]Bavinck, *RD* 1:110. Kevin Vanhoozer similarly remarks that "Jesus Christ reveals God neither *de novo* nor *ex nihilo*" since his identity is "inextricably tied up" with the identity of the God of

4. This is borne out concretely in the way Scripture deals with the incarnation. If someone unfamiliar with Christ attempted to go straight to the New Testament in order to study Christ and his revelation of the Father, they would quickly find that the Evangelists assume some knowledge of the God of the Old Testament, the one who made heaven and earth and chose Israel to be his covenant people. Matthew's Gospel begins with a genealogy of Christ and presupposes that the reader will understand the significance of names like Abraham and David. The discussion of how Jesus was born presupposes a knowledge that the God of Israel is sovereign over angels and performs miraculous works (Mt 2:18-25). Mark's Gospel begins by quoting Malachi 3:1, saying, "Behold, I send my messenger before your appearance, who will prepare your way" (Mk 1:2). The "I" here is YHWH, who already is who he is and has already made himself known to his people (if only incompletely under the old covenant). Luke's Gospel begins with the promise of John the Baptist's birth and assumes the reader will know that it is good news that he will bring people back to the God of Israel (Lk 1:15-17). When the angel addresses Mary it is expected that the reader will know something of this "Most High" and "Lord God" of whom Jesus is the Son (Lk 1:32). John's Gospel begins by revealing that the Logos existed in eternal fellowship with God the Father and is himself true God (Jn 1:1). The Logos has the divine life by which he created and sustains the world (Jn 1:3-4). Even here in John's prologue, where the subject of the first clause in the entire Gospel is the person of the Son, John has chosen to begin with a description of the life of the Son that has no immediate reference to the incarnation and echoes the opening words of Genesis in order to identify Jesus as the true God who transcends the created order.

The speeches in Acts follow a similar pattern. Though not everything in the narrative of Acts should be taken as normative, its record of early Christian proclamation shows that a grasp of the broader sweep of supernatural revelation is necessary for hearers to understand the meaning of God's revelation in Christ. This is evident in the proclamation of the gospel to both Jews and Gentiles. Peter begins his sermon at Pentecost by speaking about God's promises in Joel 2 (Acts 2:16-21). Shortly after this, he preaches

---

Israel (*Remythologizing Theology: Divine Action, Passion and Authorship*, Cambridge Studies in Christian Doctrine [Cambridge: Cambridge University Press, 2010], 418).

at Solomon's portico and from the outset declares that the God of Abraham, Isaac, and Jacob has glorified his servant Jesus (Acts 3:13). Stephen's speech in Acts 7:2-53 begins with God appearing to Abraham and recounts major acts of God in Israel's history (compare Paul's speech in Acts 13:16-52). The tendency to set the incarnation in the broader context of supernatural revelation remains when the gospel goes out to the Gentiles. When Philip meets the Ethiopian eunuch, the latter is reading from the prophet Isaiah. Given his economic standing and several other features of the passage, it is reasonable to infer that the Ethiopian man was reading from a full copy of this Old Testament book.[32] He has some knowledge of the God of Israel—the self-sufficient, sovereign Creator in Isaiah's prophecy (e.g., Is 40:12-31)—when he inquires about the one who would be led like a sheep to the slaughter (Acts 8:26-40). Cornelius too already has a knowledge and fear of God before Peter preaches the gospel to his household (Acts 10:1-8).

Paul's preaching to the Gentiles follows this pattern. After healing a man in Lystra, Paul begins his instruction of those tempted to deify him by emphasizing that they must turn to the living God who made heaven and earth (Acts 14:8-18). Paul appeals to the Gentiles' natural knowledge of God the Creator in Athens before coming to the fact that God has raised up and appointed one man through whom he will judge the world (Acts 17:22-31).[33] The apostle's speeches before Gentile rulers and under house arrest in Rome also place Christ's incarnate work within the context of a knowledge of the God of Israel (Acts 24:10-21; 26:2-29; 28:23-31). Affirming this order of teaching in the witness of the early church does not necessarily require us to neglect the surprising nature of God's revelation in the incarnation.[34] There is a coherence to God's self-revelation across the development of salvation history even as the incarnation and the

---

[32]So, e.g., Darrell L. Bock, *Acts*, BECNT (Grand Rapids: Baker Academic, 2007), 342.

[33]See Eckhard J. Schnabel, *Paul the Missionary: Realities, Strategies and Methods* (Downers Grove, IL: IVP Academic, 2010), 104, on the point that Paul's preaching does produce converts in Athens and is not presented as an example of how not to preach.

[34]The disruptive character of God's revelation in Christ is emphasized in recent discussion of "apocalyptic" in New Testament studies (on which, see, e.g., Ben C. Blackwell, John K. Goodrich, and Jason Maston, eds., *Paul and the Apocalyptic Imagination* [Minneapolis: Fortress, 2016]; Philip G. Ziegler, *Militant Grace: The Apocalyptic Turn and the Future of Christian Theology* [Grand Rapids: Baker Academic, 2018]). For a level-headed assessment of the issues, see Grant R. Macaskill, "History, Providence and the Apocalyptic Paul," *SJT* 70 (2017): 409-26.

"foolishness" of the cross break up human misconceptions of God. Affirming this order of teaching does not require us to deny that the incarnation would have prompted the apostle Paul (and others) to revisit and modify previously held theological commitments.[35] The present line of argument is not committed to negating or identifying any particular degree to which the advent of Jesus pressed the early Christians to reason backward and adjust the theology they had inherited in the context of Second Temple Judaism. However that matter might be addressed, it remains the case that those who had some contact with the theology of Old Testament Scripture did already know things about God. They were not beginning *ex nihilo* when Jesus came.

5. Once we have granted that we have no access to Jesus apart from the Bible, we are thrown back to the supernatural revelation of the Old Testament that frames his identity. And the Old Testament narrative begins with God the Creator who, unlike other would-be deities of the ancient Near East, does not have to overcome anything or receive anything in order to actualize himself.[36] He is not one more feature of the world that must obtain an identity in relation or opposition to other things. His being and completeness are simply not hanging in the balance as he creates, orders, and commissions his creatures. He is the God who is and who generously gives (Gen 1:1, 28-30).[37] As noted in chapter two, God's aseity and the Creator-creature distinction are often neglected under the corruption of our natural knowledge of God. They are recapitulated and fleshed out in the supernatural revelation of the Bible from Genesis 1 onward. Barth is right to stress the uniqueness and ultimacy of the true God and to deny

---

[35]Various New Testament scholars explore how the coming of Jesus led Paul to do this (e.g., N. T. Wright, *Paul and the Faithfulness of God*, 2 vols. [Minneapolis: Fortress, 2013]).

[36]Cf., e.g., Bill T. Arnold, *Genesis*, New Cambridge Bible Commentary (Cambridge: Cambridge University Press, 2009), 32. Even if Israel's "foundational experience of YHWH" in some sense primarily concerned his saving action (Neil B. MacDonald, *Metaphysics and the God of Israel: Systematic Theology of the Old and New Testaments* [Grand Rapids: Baker Academic, 2006], xiii-xv, drawing from Gerhard von Rad), Israel's Scriptures framed God's saving action by his work in creation narrated in Gen 1.

[37]This is sometimes overlooked in treatments of Old Testament theology, which can yield literalistic interpretations of texts that speak of God's jealousy and repentance, for example, as though God were made to suffer some loss by creatures' behavior (see, e.g., Terence E. Fretheim, *What Kind of God? The Collected Essays of Terence E. Fretheim*, ed. Michael J. Chan and Brent A. Strawn [Winona Lake, IN: Eisenbrauns, 2015]). For a response to this, see Steven J. Duby, "'For I Am God, Not a Man': Divine Repentance and the Creator-Creature Distinction," *JTI* 12 (2018): 149-69.

that he might be merely an instantiation of some broader universal.[38] But this truth is set forth by God from the beginning of Scripture's narrative, well before the incarnation takes place. Throughout the Old Testament God underscores his plenitude and self-sufficiency. He is who he is and acts in freedom toward us (Ex 3:14; 33:19).[39] He makes it clear that he does not need his people's worship (Ps 50:9-15). He is not upheld by another but upholds the needy and satisfies the desires of his creatures (Ps 145:14-16). According to Isaiah's prophecy, YHWH requires no help or instruction. He never faints or grows weary. He transcends the entire created order, the inhabitants of which are like "grasshoppers" before him (Is 40:12-31). The idols are created, dependent beings, but YHWH is the living and everlasting God (Jer 10:1-16).

Thus, according to the Old Testament's description of God, we can neither provide God with nor deprive him of some good that he must acquire. This is in fact good news for us creatures who are unfit to bear the burden of having to complete God or serve as the foundation of his happiness. God loves his covenant people though they have no great strength or virtue with which to impress others (Deut 7:7-8). As the Reformed author Johannes Coccejus notes, human beings form covenants for "mutual benefits," but God makes his covenant with us for our benefit. His covenant is "nothing other than the divine declaration of the way [*ratio*] of receiving the love of God and obtaining union and communion with him."[40] Within this covenantal context, the Lord is called "jealous" (e.g., Ex 20:5; 34:14; Deut 32:21), but his jealousy is an inflection of a divine love and holiness that are free from the fear of deprivation or "missing out" found in creaturely jealousy.[41] He invites the thirsty and poor to drink and eat without payment. Because his thoughts and ways are higher than ours, he brings mercy and renewal for his covenant people when offended human companions would refuse to do so (Is 55:1-13; cf. Hos 11:9). Such is the revelation of God in the Old

---

[38]E.g., Barth, *CD* II/1, 310-12.

[39]See the reflection on Ex 3 in chap. 1.

[40]Johannes Coccejus, *Summa doctrinae de foedere et testamento Dei*, 5th ed. (Amsterdam, 1683), 1.5 (5).

[41]On God's jealousy, compare Polanus, *Syntagma* 2.35 (193-94); John Owen, *The Works of John Owen*, vol. 12, *The Mystery of the Gospel Vindicated*, ed. William H. Good (Edinburgh: Banner of Truth, 1966), 113-14; Peter van Mastricht, *Idea theologiae moralis* (Utrecht, 1724), 1.7 (1207-8).

Testament that forms the context and backdrop to the Bible's account of the incarnation. This God is not constituted as the God that he is by his relationship to us. He is the perfect and living one over against lifeless idols, and he insists that we know it for our own good. He communicates this knowledge not least by drawing our attention to the Creator-creature distinction, which brings into focus what he is and what he is not. As the external cognitive principle for Christian theology proper, God's revelation in Scripture employs the Creator-creature distinction. That distinction is a divinely consecrated means of instructing the people of God and appears in Scripture prior to the narrative of the incarnation.

If this breaks up certain assumptions we might have about what the epistemological decisiveness of the incarnation *must* entail, then so be it. It is not the business of dogmatic theology to isolate or absolutize a particular theme found in Christian doctrine and then deduce a system of thought from it alone at the expense of other relevant material. It is the business of dogmatic theology to take into account the full sweep of Scripture's concrete teaching however disruptive that may be to our own thinking. None of this is meant to downplay that God's revelation truly does culminate in the coming of Christ. Indeed, there will be much more to say on that in the next section. It is meant only to remind us of how the Bible itself frames the incarnation. It is meant to defuse a potentially stifling "Christocentrism" that would keep us from availing ourselves of the Bible's capacious pedagogy and use of various means to communicate the truth of God.

So far I have emphasized that supernatural revelation and supernatural theology do not begin with the incarnation and do not present it as an exclusive foundation for the doctrine of God. I noted in the last chapter that natural knowledge of God is "common" and not yet "proper" or inclusive of an identification of the true God as the God of Israel who has undertaken a particular course of action in the economy. The supernatural knowledge of God given in the Old Testament begins to grant us a "proper" knowledge of the true God as the God of Israel. The knowledge of God given in the New Testament then offers a rich development of Old Testament revelation, not least in its account of the incarnation. After qualifying the role of Christology in the doctrine of God, it is vital not to understate its positive contribution. Indeed, as we will see below, it is a contribution that in fact reinforces our

understanding of God's aseity and prevenient completeness and, consequently, the need for Christian *theologia*.

CHRISTOLOGY'S POSITIVE CONTRIBUTION

The basis of Christology's positive contribution. I will now explore both the
basis of the incarnation's being the culminating moment of supernatural
revelation and the content of this locus of revelation. First, with respect to
the basis of this climactic moment, the Gospels emphasize that Christ has a
unique authority to reveal the Father. Mark comments that Jesus' listeners
were amazed, "for he was teaching them as one having authority and not as
the scribes" (Mk 1:21-22). When Christ thanks the Father that he has hidden
spiritual truth from the wise but revealed it to little children, he says that the
Father has entrusted all things to him. Indeed, as the Son, he alone knows
the Father (Mt 11:25-27). "Jesus thus has a unique role as the mediator of the
knowledge of God to humankind. The role is directly linked with the person
of Jesus, his identity as the unique representative of God. The relationship
between Jesus and God is accordingly *sui generis*."[42] The world does not
know the Father; only the Son does (Jn 17:25-26). Thomas's exegesis of John
17 captures well how this statement, while not in conflict with the teaching
of Romans 1:19-20, accentuates the deficiency of the world's theological understanding apart from Christ. Thomas points out that although the world
has some "speculative" knowledge of God the Creator, that speculative
knowledge is mixed with error and does not include knowledge of God as
"Father of the only-begotten and consubstantial Son." Furthermore, the
world lacks the "affective" knowledge of God that involves delight in him.[43]
So decisive is the Son's revelation of the Father that he can identify himself
as "the truth" and declare that no one comes to the Father except through
him (Jn 14:6). In Pauline terms, Christ is "our wisdom" in whom "all the
storehouses of wisdom and knowledge are hidden" (1 Cor 1:30; Col 2:3).

The veracity and authority of Jesus' words arises from the fact that he
teaches as the one sent of the Father (Jn 7:16-18; 8:26-29; 12:49-50; 17:6-8).
But, more fundamentally, the Son's having authority from the Father and

---

[42]Donald A. Hagner, *Matthew 1–13*, WBC 33A (Dallas: Word, 1993), 320.
[43]Thomas Aquinas, *Super Evangelium S. Ioannis lectura*, 5th ed., ed. P. Raphael Cai (Turin-Rome:
Marietti, 1952), 17.6.2.2265 (426).

having perfect knowledge of the Father are entailments of his eternal procession from the Father. The Son was eternally "with" the Father (Jn 1:1). He has received the divine life ("life in himself") from the Father (Jn 5:26). In receiving the divine life from the Father, he receives divine knowledge. Jesus says, "It has been written in the prophets, 'And they will all be taught of God.' Everyone who hears and learns from the Father comes to me. Not that anyone has seen the Father, except the one who is from God, he has seen the Father" (Jn 6:45-46). Again, "I have not come from myself, but the one who sent me is true, whom you do not know. I myself know him, for I am from him and he sent me" (Jn 7:28b-29). Since the Son coming from the Father in John 6:45-46; 7:28-29 is put forward as the reason he has full knowledge of the Father, it does not stand in synonymous parallelism with the statement that he was temporally sent by the Father. The statement "I am from him" references an eternal procession from the Father by which the Son receives the divine essence and knowledge. "The Son has the perfect similitude of the Father because he is of the same essence and power with him, and therefore he knows [him] perfectly. . . . But in order that this would not be referred to the mission by which he comes into the world, he adds, 'And he sent me.'"[44] In addition, the Son is uniquely positioned to reveal the Father because he is in the Father and the Father is in him and works in and through him (Jn 14:10-11). The perichoresis of the divine persons also is an entailment of the Son's procession from and consubstantiality with the Father. The mutual indwelling is "not according to grace or participation . . . but because the Son's own being is the offspring of the Father's essence." "Thus the things that the Son does are works of the Father. . . . Thus the one seeing the Son sees the Father."[45] Accordingly, the Son is the "image of the invisible God" (Col 1:15) and the radiance of the Father's glory and "expression" or "representation" of his *hypostasis* (Heb 1:3).

Of course, the preeminence of Christ's revelation of God is rooted not just in the fact that he is the consubstantial Son but also in the fact that in his incarnation God has drawn near in an unparalleled way. The Logos who was with God and was God has taken on flesh and dwelt in our very midst

---

[44]Thomas, *Super Ioannem* 7.3.7.1065 (202).

[45]Athanasius, *Athanasius Werke*, vol. I/1.3, *Oratio III contra Arianos*, ed. Karin Metzler and Kyriakos Savvidis (Berlin: de Gruyter, 2000), 6 (312).

(Jn 1:14). Echoing Exodus 33:18–34:7, where God proclaims his steadfast love and faithfulness to Moses, John writes, "We have seen his glory, glory as of the only Son of the Father, full of grace and truth."[46] In Exodus, God only briefly passed by and allowed Moses to glimpse him "from behind," but the enfleshed Son has exhibited the divine glory, grace, and truth over the course of his whole earthly ministry. This is the glory not of any mere prophet but of God's proper Son.[47] On the one hand, John says, "no one has ever seen God" (Jn 1:18a). Creatures, especially fallen ones, do not have the capacity to behold the glory of God in its infinite fullness and holiness. The people of Israel, John Chrysostom recalls, could not tolerate even the illumined countenance of Moses (Ex 34:29-35). How, then, could we behold "bare Godhead" (θεότης γυμνή).[48] On the other hand, John continues, God the Son has made God known (Jn 1:18b). He is, in John Owen's words, the "immediate author of evangelical theology."[49] According to Paul, in him "all the fullness of deity dwells bodily" (Col 2:9). The Son's assumption of a human nature and ongoing corporeal subsistence brings the knowledge of God to us in a manner suited to the conditions of our way of knowing in this life. We now behold the glory of God in the person of the Son "through a body like ours."[50] Elaborating on John 1 in dialogue with Chrysostom, Thomas draws a suggestive analogy: "Weak and infirm eyes are not able to see the light of the sun, but then they are able to see it when it shines in a cloud or in some opaque body."[51] Accordingly, in the Son's incarnate works, we can see the Father (Jn 14:9-11). And in the Son's incarnate teaching, the early disciples heard the audible voice of God himself. In the Old Testament God spoke predominantly through his servants, but now he has done so

---

[46]On the connection between Jn 1:14 and Ex 33–34, see, e.g., Craig A. Evans, *Word and Glory: On the Exegetical and Theological Background of John's Prologue*, Library of New Testament Studies (Sheffield: Sheffield Academic, 1993), 79-83; Richard Bauckham, *Gospel of Glory: Major Themes in Johannine Theology* (Grand Rapids: Baker Academic, 2015), 46-52.

[47]See John Chrysostom's explanation of the particle "as" ("glory *as* of the only Son . . .") in *Homiliae CXXXVIII in Johannem*, in PG 59 (Paris, 1862), 12 (82).

[48]Chrysostom, *In Johannem* 12 (81).

[49]John Owen, *The Works of John Owen*, vol. 17, *Theologoumena pantodapa*, ed. William H. Goold (Edinburgh: T&T Clark, 1862), 6.1.2 (411).

[50]Chrysostom, *In Johannem* 12 (81). As Bauckham states, "Precisely the visibility of the flesh is the point. If we take 'we have seen' to refer to something purely spiritual, we negate the incarnation" (*Gospel of Glory*, 51).

[51]Thomas, *Super Ioannem* 1.8.1.181 (36).

"through himself." The Old Testament saints had Moses for a teacher; we have Moses' Lord.[52]

Furthermore, as noted in the discussion of the kinds of ectypal theology in chapter one, the theology of Christ's human soul surpasses that of all rational creatures.[53] In union with the person of the Son, the humanity of the Son is uniquely endowed with wisdom by the one who is the Spirit of the Son as well as the Father (Rom 8:9; Gal 4:6; 1 Pet 1:11).[54] The Spirit of YHWH, the Spirit of wisdom and understanding, is on him, anointing him to preach good news to the poor (Is 11:2; 61:1-2; Lk 4:17-21). Because the Son is from heaven and has the Spirit "without measure," he is above all and delivers the word of God in a preeminent manner (Jn 3:31-35). "To the immeasurable gift of the Spirit corresponds the perfection of the revelation through him."[55] Thus in the discharge of his prophetic office as the God-man, the Son's revelation of God surpasses all others in its (relative, not beatific) immediacy and in its content and spiritual efficacy. He is the prophet like Moses but greater, for he is faithful in God's house not merely as servant but as Son (Deut 18:15; Heb 3:5-6). He is the Messiah who explains all things pertaining to salvation and the worship of God (Jn 4:25-26). He rectifies incomplete or inaccurate understandings of God's prior revelation: "You heard that it was said, but I say to you . . ." (Mt 5:21-22; 27-28, 31-34, 38-39, 43-44). He alone is the true teacher (Mt 23:8-10). Accompanied by the powerful working of the Spirit, his words are "spirit and life" (Jn 6:63). In short, "Never did a man speak like this" (Jn 7:46).

Accordingly, there is an important sense in which no additional revelation will occur in redemptive history. In the upper room, Christ did not

---

[52]Chrysostom, *In Johannem* 15 (99-100).

[53]So Thomas: "By this, that the Son is from the Father, he has perfect knowledge of the Father. So also by this, that the [human] soul of Christ is singularly united with the Word, it has singular and more excellent knowledge of God above all creatures, although it does not comprehend him" (*Super Ioannem* 7.3.7.1065 [202]).

[54]Framing the matter this way—in terms of the hypostatic union entailing the Spirit's communication of graces to Christ's human nature (see, e.g., Turretin, *Inst.* 13.12.1-2 [2:377])—circumvents the problem of placing the deity of Christ and the work of the Spirit in competition with one another. Compare Ian A. McFarland, "Spirit and Incarnation: Toward a Pneumatic Chalcedonianism," *IJST* 16 (2014): 143-58.

[55]George Beasley-Murray, *John*, 2nd ed., WBC 36 (Nashville: Thomas Nelson, 1999), 54. On this reading of Jn 3:34, cf. Marianne Meye Thompson, *The God of the Gospel of John* (Grand Rapids: Eerdmans, 2001), 170-71.

tell his disciples all that he might have, but the coming of the Spirit as another Paraclete involves not so much a supplementing but an unfolding of God's revelation in the incarnate Son: "When he comes, the Spirit of truth, he will lead you into all truth. For he will not speak from himself, but as many things as he will hear he will speak, and he will declare to you things to come. He will glorify me, for from me he will receive and will declare to you" (Jn 16:13-14). The apostle Paul knows and declares many things in his epistles, but in a sense he knows only "Christ and him crucified" (1 Cor 2:2). The church should therefore never be enticed by worldly wisdom and philosophy, for believers have the sum of wisdom in Christ (Col 2:8-10). Believers have an anointing from the holy one (the Son) and "all know" or "know all things" (1 Jn 2:20). They are anointed with the word made effectual by the Spirit.[56] They know the truth that is an "encapsulation of the God-given understanding of God and of what God has done."[57] Though they need teachers who minister the truth of Christ, they do not need teachers who claim to be masters offering new content to augment or supplant the revelation of the incarnate Son. The epistemological imperative for the Christian is not to chase after new teaching but to "remain in him" (1 Jn 2:27).

The content of Christology's positive contribution. The content of God's revelation in the incarnate Son may be ramified under three aspects.

1. Christ reveals the plan and will of God. He is the central and decisive figure in the outworking of that plan. Though the Old Testament prophets in their time could not identify the person of Jesus (so 1 Pet 1:10-12), their writings anticipate his coming to fulfill God's promises for the good of the world. He is the Son of David and Son of God who will inherit the earth (Ps 2:7-12). He is the light of the nations and the one whose universal government and peace will continue for eternity (Is 9:1-7; 49:1-7). He is the servant of YHWH whose suffering will secure the justification of many (Is 52:13-53:12). Texts from the Old Testament could be multiplied here, but the point is, as Jesus himself puts it, he is the one who fulfills the law and the prophets (Mt 5:17; cf. Lk 24:27, 44). He does so in both his actions and his

---

[56]On this reading of the anointing in 1 Jn 2:20, 27, see I. Howard Marshall, *The Epistles of John*, NICNT (Grand Rapids: Eerdmans, 1978), 155.

[57]Judith M. Lieu, *I, II, & III John: A Commentary*, New Testament Library (Louisville: Westminster John Knox, 2008), 104.

words. He brings to their appointed end various typological events and institutions (e.g., Passover, the sacrificial system) as well as direct prophecies about the coming Messiah.[58] As Paul has it, Christ is the one in whom God is "recapitulating" or "summing up" all things in heaven and on earth (Eph 1:10). With his words, Christ explains God's work in the past, present, and future.[59] In this way, he discloses the decretive will of God. But he also gives the ultimate revelation of God's preceptive will, calling for repentance and faith in himself and, in the Sermon on the Mount and other places, setting out the moral theology of the kingdom of God.

2. The incarnation provides the fullest revelation of God's relationship to the world and to the people of God. Christ's actions and words disclose God's many perfections in relation to us. Though it ought not to be sentimentalized or detached from Christ's revelation of the divine wisdom, holiness, and so forth, his revelation of God's love and mercy has a special significance. Christ is God in the flesh healing the sick and socializing with sinners and outcasts. He announces that God so loved the world that he gave his only Son to bring us eternal life (Jn 3:16). As God incarnate, he gives his flesh for the life of the world (Jn 6:51). He loved his own who were in the world and "loved them to the end," illustrating that great and condescending love for his disciples by washing their feet (Jn 13:1-20). Rarely would someone die even for a righteous person, but God demonstrates his love in the death of Christ for sinners living in open rebellion against him (Rom 5:6-8; cf. 1 Jn 4:10). When we were dead in transgressions and "children of wrath," God, who is rich in mercy, made us alive together with Christ and seated us with him in the heavenly places. This he did in order to show the riches of his kindness and grace throughout the coming age (Eph 2:4-7). The self-giving love of God in Christ then becomes the pattern we must imitate in the church (Eph 5:1-2).

The love of God revealed in Christ has a distinctly fatherly character. Though some elements of the Lord's Prayer resemble an ancient Jewish prayer used in the time of Jesus, his instruction to call God "our Father" is

---

[58]G. K. Beale, *A New Testament Biblical Theology: The Unfolding of the Old Testament in the New* (Grand Rapids: Baker Academic, 2011), 805.

[59]Turretin, for example, treats the material content of Christ's prophetic office in terms of his exposition of the law of Moses, the gospel, and the future consummation of the kingdom (*Inst.* 14.7.6-11 [2:432-34]).

a new development. Even if such language is not entirely without precedent, Jesus' way of filling out its meaning throughout his teaching ministry invests it with a peculiar sense of the nearness of God.[60] He is our Father to whom we may pray in secret (Mt 6:6). He knows our needs, and his fatherly care addresses our anxieties (Mt 6:25-33). If we sinners know how to give good gifts to our children, how much more does our heavenly Father (Mt 7:11). In union with Christ, we are caught up in the love of the Father for his Son (Jn 17:20-26). In Christ we have the Spirit of God and of Christ, the Spirit of sonship who testifies with our spirit that we are the children of God (Rom 8:9-17). God sent his Son in the fullness of time to make us sons and daughters who, by the Spirit, call God "Abba, Father" (Gal 4:4-6). The coming of Christ and of our salvation is the appearance of the "kindness and philanthropy" of God by which we receive regeneration, justification, and adoption (Tit 3:4-7).

3. In addition to God's outward relation to us, the incarnation reveals something of God in himself. Perhaps drawing this distinction here between God's outward action and his inward life will seem like begging the question to someone inclined to think that the incarnation shows that God's outward action is in some sense constitutive of his inward life. However, the claim being made here is not that the incarnation reveals something about God that might be located by us under an artificially constructed doctrinal heading called "God in himself." The claim is in fact much stronger: along with other scriptural teaching about God, the incarnation itself actually informs us that there is an objective basis for distinguishing between God's outward works and God's own inward life. That is, the incarnation itself reveals that God is *a se* and self-referentially complete, and that he wants us to have knowledge of him in that completeness.

The incarnation shows in at least three ways that God's being transcends his economic works, the first of which will receive most of the attention here.

1. In the biblical description of the incarnation, its significance turns on the fact that God is already God and thus that the incarnation was not necessary for him to become God. Its decisiveness, efficacy, and wonder derive

---

[60]Compare, e.g., R. T. France, *The Gospel of Matthew*, NICNT (Grand Rapids: Eerdmans, 2007), 243-45; Craig S. Keener, *The Gospel of Matthew: A Socio-rhetorical Commentary* (Grand Rapids: Eerdmans, 2009), 638-39.

from the triune God's prevenient fullness, according to which the incarnation was undertaken freely by him. In John's prologue, the Logos already was with the Father and already was true God (Jn 1:1). His identity and deity are not presented as though they were constituted by historical events. The incarnation of the Logos in John 1:14 is then set up to be understood as an act of gracious condescension. John writes that "from his fullness we all have received grace upon grace" (Jn 1:16). We *receive* from this plenitude. It is not something to which we contribute. It is not something established by reference to us. It is an antecedent plenitude and life, a rich font from which God gives us gifts and not a fund to which our anticipated or actual existence adds. Throughout John's Gospel, Christ makes his famous "I am" statements that hearken back to God's use of that phrase in the Old Testament (see esp. Jn 8:58; 13:19; 18:5).[61] In employing these statements Christ is emphasizing to his hearers that he is not just one more individual whose identity is established within the history of the world. He is the self-existent, eternal God who reveals himself to be such in Isaiah by repeatedly declaring "I am he" (Is 41:4; 43:10-13; 46:4; 48:12; 51:12). Christ claims to be worthy of total trust and reverence because he is the God who transcends the economy. The moment we attempt to make the incarnate, historical life of the Son constitutive of God's being, we forego the distinct gravity of this history as the history of *this one*.[62]

Paul's characterization of the incarnation exhibits the same logic. To inspire the Corinthians to give generously to believers in need, he writes, "For you know the grace [or "gift," χάρις] of our Lord Jesus Christ, that on account of us he became poor though he was rich, in order that we by his poverty might become rich" (2 Cor 8:9).[63] The dependent clause "though he was rich" is a translation of two words in the Greek: πλούσιος ὤν. Because

---

[61]On which, see Richard Bauckham, *The Testimony of the Beloved Disciple: Narrative, History, and Theology in the Gospel of John* (Grand Rapids: Baker Academic, 2007), 246-50; Grant Macaskill, "Name Christology, Divine Aseity, and the I Am Sayings in the Fourth Gospel," *JTI* 12 (2018): 217-41.

[62]Barth rightly notes that the weight and efficacy of God's economic works derives from his transcendence of them (*CD* II/1, 260). That is, "the good news of Christ is only as good as its 'whence'" (Christopher R. J. Holmes, "The Aseity of God as a Material Evangelical Concern," *JRT* 8 [2014]: 64).

[63]On Paul's use of "gift" language, see John M. G. Barclay, *Paul and the Gift* (Grand Rapids: Eerdmans, 2015).

Paul is observing a contrast between Christ's voluntary "poverty" and his antecedent richness, the participle ὤν is typically taken to have a concessive function ("though . . .") in the English translations (e.g., NRSV, NIV, ESV).[64] The poverty in view is not merely Christ's lack of material wealth during his earthly sojourn but, more broadly, his full identification with the lowliness of human life beginning with his assumption of a human nature.[65] In other words, the poverty here is "the total event of incarnation."[66] This means that the richness of Christ that is contrasted with his human lowliness and suffering is something he has prior to the incarnation.[67]

Accordingly, the flow of Paul's thought requires a recognition of Christ's divine fullness in light of which his voluntary humiliation in the incarnation and crucifixion can have its intended effect on the reader.[68] If Christ the divine Son has humbled himself to give to others, so too should Christian believers. If God or God the Son were actualized and perfected through the incarnation, the logic of the incarnation would collapse. Instead of the Son's being "rich" (true and complete God in joyous fellowship with the Father and Spirit) and voluntarily assuming a lowly human nature, he would be originally poor and procuring riches for himself through his human life, suffering, and glorification. The incarnation would not be an act of

---

[64]This does not mean that Christ somehow must have left behind the richness he had. To draw from the hymn of Phil 2, it means that he took on himself the *forma servi* and in it became obedient to death. This alleviates the recent concern about the concessive use of the participle in Mark A. Seifrid, *The Second Letter to the Corinthians*, Pillar New Testament Commentary (Grand Rapids: Eerdmans, 2014), 329-30, where the author seeks to avoid a "kenotic" Christology by positing a modal use of the participle.

[65]Cf. Murray J. Harris, *The Second Epistle to the Corinthians: A Commentary on the Greek Text*, New International Greek Testament Commentary (Grand Rapids: Eerdmans, 2005), 578-79; Ralph P. Martin, *2 Corinthians*, 2nd ed., WBC 40 (Grand Rapids: Zondervan, 2014), 441; Seifrid, *Second Letter to the Corinthians*, 330.

[66]Margaret E. Thrall, *The Second Epistle to the Corinthians*, International Critical Commentary (London: T&T Clark, 2000), 2:532.

[67]Cf. Thrall, *Second Epistle to the Corinthians*, 2:534.

[68]It will not suffice to posit that the surprising nature of the incarnation might be accounted for by (mistaken) human assumptions about divine transcendence. The humiliation and striking practical implications of the incarnation are thrown into relief not merely by what we assume God would or would not do but by the fact that God in himself is not poor. Though he could and did assume a lowly human nature by the power of his rich essence, the poverty of that human nature stands in ontological contrast to the richness of his antecedent divine life. If the Son's human limitations and suffering were built into his divine subsistence, the incarnation ultimately could not be regarded as a truly gratuitous act of humility. It would be implicitly just an extension or outworking of God's eternal life, in which case the Pauline call for self-humbling in 2 Cor 8–9 would be bereft of its theological basis.

humiliation but of divine development. And if God would not be fully himself without the incarnation, the ultimate reason for the incarnation would be a deficiency in God, which would then imply that the incarnation was something undertaken out of necessity for God.[69] But if the incarnation truly is grace or a "gift," as Paul says, then it implies that the Son did not have to take on flesh but did so freely.[70] If he did so freely and from a position of antecedent richness, the incarnation teaches us that God truly is *a se* and wants us to know that he is. Hence Athanasius fittingly insists that in the incarnation the Son is not "straining toward something" or "advancing" but rather leads us to "advance" to eternal life, which reinforces the distinction between *theologia* and *oikonomia*.[71]

The antecedent richness of the Son is corroborated by Philippians 2:6-8, where Paul writes that Christ,

> being in the form of God, considered it not ἁρπαγμὸν [variously translated as "robbery," "something to be grasped," etc.] to be equal with God, but he emptied himself [ἑαυτὸν ἐκένωσεν], taking the form of a servant, being made in the likeness of human beings. And, being found in appearance as a man,

---

[69] A further implication of this would be that evil and suffering are a necessary counterpart to God and in some sense an outworking of his being. McCormack, for example, states that "what happens to [the Son] on the cross and the descent into hell constitutes the realization in time of who and what He is in Himself eternally" ("Atonement and Human Suffering," 206). Against such a view, see David Bentley Hart, "No Shadow of Turning: On Divine Impassibility," *Pro Ecclesia* 16 (2002): 191-92.

[70] One might ask whether God's grace could still be grace as long as God had a freedom from external compulsion (a freedom from "coaction" or a freedom of "spontaneity" in scholastic terms) even if he acted in the incarnation with a "necessity of nature" and did not have a freedom to be the God that he is without choosing to be incarnate (a freedom of "indifference" or "contradiction"). McCormack in fact suggests that positing the latter, stronger freedom in God results from a penchant for Enlightenment "voluntarism." He also argues (without using the specific phrase) that a necessity of nature on God's part with respect to election and the incarnation is compatible with holding that God lacks nothing in himself ("Processions and Missions," 109, 123; "Atonement and Human Suffering," 207-8). However, in my estimation, positing a necessity of nature on God's part vis-à-vis the incarnation has built into it the implication that God is unfulfilled or deficient without the incarnation (and therefore without the existence of creatures), which would entail that he undertakes the incarnation as a matter of self-fulfillment— and self-fulfillment conflicts with the nature of generosity and grace. Furthermore, a theological commitment to the communicative or self-diffusive nature of the divine goodness can find expression in the doctrine of the processions in the Trinity without positing a necessary creation (see below).

[71] Athanasius, *Oratio III* 52 (363). Here Athanasius's overarching argument is that in Lk 2:52 the Son is not advancing in his deity but in his humanity and enables other human beings to "advance" to their appointed end in God.

he humbled himself [ἐταπείνωσεν ἑαυτὸν], becoming obedient until death, even death on a cross.

Biblical scholars have put forward a variety of proposals for understanding the *forma Dei* in this text,[72] but ultimately, within the context of the Bible's Creator-creature distinction, to speak even generally of an exalted state in which Christ existed prior to living as a human being is to speak of him with reference to his deity (not as a tertium quid between God and the creature).[73] However one views the use of the participle in the phrase "being in the form of God" and the meaning of the noun ἁρπαγμός,[74] there is a contrast between the *forma Dei* in which Christ subsisted before the incarnation and the *forma servi* he assumes in the incarnation. Given this contrast, his prevenient subsistence in the *forma Dei* is a rich subsistence, for his assumption of and activity in the *forma servi* is characterized as a κένωσις and ταπείνωσις. As in 2 Corinthians 8:9, if the logic of the incarnation is to stand, the Son must be seen to have abundant life prior to the incarnation.

---

[72]For example, a status or position Christ had (e.g., Stephen E. Fowl, *The Story of Christ in the Ethics of Paul: An Analysis of the Function of the Hymnic Material in the Pauline Corpus* [Sheffield: Sheffield Academic, 1990], 54; Gerald F. Hawthorne, "In the Form of and Equal with God (Philippians 2:6)," in *Where Christology Began: Essays on Philippians 2*, ed. Ralph P. Martin and Brian J. Dodd [Louisville: Westminster John Knox, 1998], 98, 104), or a "realm" or "sphere" in which Christ initially lived (e.g., Ernst Käsemann, "A Critical Analysis of Philippians 2:5-11," *Journal for Theology and the Church* 5 [1968]: 61; John Reumann, *Philippians: A New Translation with Introduction and Commentary*, Anchor Yale Bible [New Haven, CT: Yale University Press, 2008], 341). Some have contended that the *forma Dei* refers back to the *imago Dei* and describes Christ's being like Adam (e.g., Oscar Cullmann, *The Christology of the New Testament*, trans. Shirley C. Guthrie and Charles A. M. Hall, rev. ed. [Philadelphia: Westminster, 1963], 176-77; James D. G. Dunn, "Christ, Adam, and Preexistence," in Martin and Dodd, *Where Christology Began*, 74-79), but that view does not adequately account for (1) the fact that the *forma Dei* is construed as a being "equal with God," (2) the fact that Christ is not presented as human until Phil 2:7, and (3) the contrast between Christ's being in the *forma Dei* and Christ's being in the *forma servi* that is materially appositional to his being human in Phil 2:7 (see C. A. Wanamaker, "Philippians 2.6-11: Son of God or Adamic Christology?," *New Testament Studies* 33 [1987]: 183; Gerald F. Hawthorne and Ralph P. Martin, *Philippians*, rev. ed., WBC 43 [Grand Rapids: Zondervan, 2004], 110-11, 114).

[73]Of course, a number of exegetes (justifiably, in my view) maintain that the phrase μορφή θεοῦ itself directly denotes the divine essence or nature (e.g., Gordon D. Fee, *Paul's Letter to the Philippians*, NICNT [Grand Rapids: Eerdmans, 1995], 204; Dennis W. Jowers, "The Meaning of ΜΟΡΦΗ in Philippians 2:6-7," *Journal of the Evangelical Theological Society* 49 [2006]: 739-66).

[74]Influential studies include C. F. D. Moule, "Further Reflexions on Philippians 2:5-11," in *Apostolic History and the Gospel: Biblical and Historical Essays Presented to F. F. Bruce on his 60th Birthday*, ed. W. Ward Gasque and Ralph P. Martin (Grand Rapids: Eerdmans, 1970), 264-76; Roy W. Hoover, "The HARPAGMOS Enigma: A Philological Solution," *Harvard Theological Review* 64 (1971): 95-119; N. T. Wright, *The Climax of the Covenant: Christ and the Law in Pauline Theology* (Minneapolis: Fortress, 1992), 56-98.

Furthermore, the Son's divine fullness is not threatened by his κένωσις and ταπείνωσις. Biblical scholars have offered a variety of suggestions regarding the meaning of Christ's κένωσις,[75] but the text includes no "genitive of content" to specify something "of which" Christ emptied himself.[76] Indeed, the self-emptying is explained by the instrumental participles that follow it: Christ empties himself *by* taking the form of a servant and *by* being made in the likeness of human beings.[77] In other words, κένωσις here is not subtraction but addition. And the ταπείνωσις comes after he is "found in appearance as a man." It is explained by the instrumental participle that follows it: Christ humbles himself or becomes poor in Philippians 2:8 *by* becoming obedient to death. Insofar as Christ as immortal God cannot die, he does not undertake such τάπεινωσις and obedience as God but as human.[78] Thus the ταπείνωσις in view pertains to the Son's human life, activity, and suffering, entailing that Son's divine fullness remains intact throughout his earthly humiliation and that the *theologia-oikonomia* distinction remains vital in the doctrine of God.

The end of the Philippians hymn does raise the question of whether or in what sense the Son undergoes development through his resurrection and exaltation: "Therefore, God also exalted him and gave him the name that is above every name, in order that at the name of Jesus every knee might bow in heaven and on earth and under the earth and every tongue confess that Jesus Christ is Lord to the glory of God the Father" (Phil 2:9-11). On the one hand, the divine completeness of the Son would be called into question if this is a bestowal of something that the Son as God did not already have. On the other hand, it seems that more than the humanity of Christ is in view if

---

[75]For example, an outright exchange of the *forma Dei* for the *forma servi* (e.g., Käsemann, "Critical Analysis," 74, 76; Fowl, *Story of Christ*, 58, 64-65), a renunciation of certain prerogatives or rights (e.g., Markus Bockmuehl, *The Epistle to the Philippians*, Black's New Testament Commentaries [repr., Peabody: Hendrickson, 1998], 129; Hawthorne, *Philippians*, 118, 121) or a cessation of the exercise of certain divine attributes on the part of Christ (e.g., David J. MacLeod, "Imitating the Incarnation of Christ: An Exposition of Philippians 2:5-8," *Bibliotheca Sacra* 158 [2001]: 318-19, 329-30; Thomas R. Schreiner, *New Testament Theology: Magnifying God in Christ* [Grand Rapids: Baker Academic, 2008], 326).

[76]Hawthorne, *Philippians*, 117.

[77]This is often recognized by recent commentators, even if they are still tempted to posit something Christ must have given up (e.g., Bockmuehl, *Philippians*, 133-35; Hawthorne, *Philippians*, 118, 121).

[78]Cf. Zanchi, *De incarnatione Filii Dei* 2.3.9 (248-49).

this text echoes Isaiah 45:23 and describes Christ as YHWH receiving the honor due to YHWH alone.[79] In what sense might the Son be glorified and receive from the Father a preeminent name?

This is a question that in fact pertains to a broad swath of New Testament material that includes texts like John 17, Acts 2:36, Romans 1:4, and Hebrews 1:4-5. In John 17, Christ himself prays that the Father would glorify him and that he would glorify the Father (Jn 17:1). He asks the Father to glorify him with the glory he shared with the Father before the world existed (Jn 17:5). A number of earlier commentators take the object of this glorification to be the Son according his human nature in which he is raised from the dead and ascends to the Father, perhaps with the additional claim that the Son *qua homo* having this glory before the incarnation pertains to his predestination.[80] But even if the object of the Father's glorification is also the Son according to his *divine* nature, the glory that the Son receives is, according to Jesus' description of it, materially the same as the glory he had before the existence of the world. It is simply now manifested in his exaltation after a period of relative concealment under his flesh and humiliation.[81] Thus, according to John 17:5, it is not a glory that enhances or completes the Son's prevenient deity.

The same applies in Philippians 2:9-11. The Son moves from a state of humble suffering and death to a state of exaltation in which he will receive worship from others. The redemptive-historical development of the hymn by itself already suggests that the glorification of the Son concerns not so much his deity as such but his economic office, in which the Son acts according to both his natures for our salvation. Furthermore, the Son is identified as YHWH by the allusion to Isaiah 45:23, and YHWH is marked out as the true God in Isaiah's prophecy by never having to acquire his divinity (e.g., Is 43:9-13). It is unreasonable to think that Paul would claim Jesus had to perfect his deity immediately before identifying him with the God of

---

[79]There is some debate about whether the name given by the Father in Phil 2:9b is simply the name of Jesus or the name YHWH (see Fee, *Philippians*, 221-22; Bockmuehl, *Epistle to the Philippians*, 142). Yet, whatever the referent of the "name" in Phil 2:9b is, Christ is identified with YHWH in this text by the allusion to Is 45:23.

[80]See Augustine, *In Ioannis Evangelium, tractatus CXXIV*, ed. Lucas Verheijen, CCSL 27 (Turnhout: Brepols, 1954), 114-15-V (601-8); Chrysostom, *In Johannem* 80 (435); Thomas, *Super Ioannem* 17.1.1.2181 (411-12); 4.2191-92 (413-14).

[81]Cf. Turretin, *Inst.* 13.9.7 (2:363); Owen, *Christologia* 4 (55-56).

Isaiah. Yet it also seems unreasonable to say that the Son's reception of the name above all names pertains to his humanity alone. Without it completing his deity (if that were possible), the Father's economic glorification of the Son and his giving of the name must in some way pertain to the Son according to his deity. To integrate all of this: the Father exalts the Son in his economic office (1) according to his humanity by his resurrection and ascension and (2) according to his deity by an outward manifestation of the divine majesty that the Son always had with the Father. Owen summarizes the point here:

> The advancement and exaltation of Christ as mediator to any dignity whatever, upon or in reference to the work of our redemption and salvation, is not at all inconsistent with the essential honour, dignity, and worth, which he hath in himself as God blessed for ever. Though he humbled himself, and was exalted in office, yet in nature he was one and the same.[82]

For our purposes, the upshot is that the divine fullness ingredient in the logic of the incarnation as sheer gift is unchanged throughout the Son's humiliation and exaltation. In this way, the incarnation remains consistent in its witness to the importance of God's aseity and our knowledge of God in his transcendence of the economy.

2. The incarnation reveals God's aseity by setting forth the immanent triunity and love of God. The events of the Son's incarnate life (e.g., his baptism, his transfiguration) reveal that there are distinct persons in God. In the Son's elaboration on his relationship to the Father in John 17, he discloses that there is love among the persons "before the foundation of the world" (Jn 17:20-24). God is not a "solitary" or "lonely" God.[83] On the one hand, since God is the highest and absolute good (Lk 18:19), and since created things are not ends in themselves but are ordered to the manifestation of God's goodness (e.g., Rom 11:35-36), it is legitimate to speak of God's willing himself or being entirely satisfied in his own goodness without making direct reference to the plurality of persons in God. God himself is the primary and

---

[82]John Owen, *A Brief Declaration and Vindication of the Doctrine of the Trinity*, in *The Works of John Owen*, vol. 2, *Communion with God*, ed. William H. Goold (Edinburgh: Banner of Truth, 1965), 389. For comparable statements restricting the development here to Christ's office, see Käsemann, "A Critical Analysis," 76-77; Fee, *Philippians*, 220; Bockmuehl, *Philippians*, 144.

[83]Hilary of Poitiers, *La Trinité*, ed. G. M. de Durand et al., 3 vols., Sources Chrétiennes 443, 448, 462 (Paris: Éditions du Cerf, 1999–2001), 5.39 (2:168); 7.3 (2:282), et passim.

adequate object of God's will. Being satisfied with his own goodness, God does not need to fulfill himself by creating the world; he does not act *pro nobis* by what the scholastics call a "necessity of nature" (an inexorable propensity that would be included in God's essence).[84] On the other hand, the divine self-satisfaction and consequent freedom *pro nobis* are opened up to us further by the incarnation's making known the eternal love of the divine persons. The Father already has an eternal effulgence and hypostatic image of himself in his Son, in whom he beholds the all fullness of deity (Jn 5:26; Col 2:9; Heb 1:3). Thus Thomas writes that the doctrine of the Trinity deepens our understanding of creation: the processions of the Word and Spirit manifest that God did not create out of any lack in himself.[85] "Contemplative men of old did always admire love," Owen remarks, and could understand that "God necessarily loved himself" with an "eternal acquiescence in the holy, self-sufficing properties of his nature." But they did not know the love of the divine persons for one another: "The divine nature in the person of the Son is the only full, resting, complete object of the love of God the Father" and "everything else of love is but a free act of the will of God."[86]

This point is even more crucial if one follows the theological tradition of understanding the good (particularly God as the highest good) to be intrinsically communicative (see, e.g., Ps 107:1-9; 119:68; 145:7-9; Tit 3:4-7).[87] In treating this matter theologians have often clarified that God in his goodness

---

[84]Thomas Aquinas, *De potentia*, in *Quaestiones disputatae*, vol. 2, ed. P. M. Pession, 10th ed. (Rome-Turin: Marietti, 1965), 3.15 (82-85); *SCG* 2.23 (324-25); *ST* Ia.19.3 (234-35); Stephen Charnock, *The Existence and Attributes of God*, 2 vols. in 1 (Grand Rapids: Baker, 1996), 2:223-27; Mastricht, *TPT* 2.17.8 (179). Intriguingly, Thomas is quite confident that the infinite goodness of God (without reference to the plurality of persons) can explain God's freedom. For Thomas, if the good in question is absolutely perfect, the principle that "without sharing there cannot be a pleasing possession of any good" does not necessarily apply (*ST* Ia.32.1 ad 2 [350]).

[85]Thomas, *ST* Ia.32.1 ad 3 (350-51). According to Thomas, the (communicative) goodness of God discoverable by natural reason does not prove or establish the doctrine of the Trinity, but it does fit with and confirm the doctrine (*Scriptum super libros Sententiarum*, ed. R. P. Mandonnet [Paris: P. Lethielleux, 1929], 1.2.1.4 [73-74]; *ST* Ia.32.1 ad 2 [350]). Cf. Athanasius, *Oratio I contra Arianos*, in *Athanasius Werke*, vol. I/1.2, *Oratio I et II contra Arianos*, ed. Karin Metzler and Kyriakos Savvidis (Berlin: de Gruyter, 1998), 12 (121).

[86]John Owen, *Posthumous Sermons*, in *The Works of John Owen*, vol. 9, *Sermons to the Church*, ed. William H. Good (Edinburgh: Banner of Truth, 1965), 22 (613-14). See also Bavinck, *RD* 2:331.

[87]See John of Damascus, *Exp. fid.* 2.2 (45); 4.13 (191-92); Thomas, *In librum Beati Dionysii De divinis nominibus expositio*, ed. Ceslai Pera (Turin-Rome: Marietti, 1950), 4.1.261-91 (87-91); *ST* Ia.19.2 (233); Polanus, *Syntagma* 2.20 (162); 5.3 (263); Charnock, *Existence and Attributes of God*, 2:218, 220, 223-24; Mastricht, *TPT* 2.16.4, 6-7 (171-72).

is communicative not as a mere "natural agent" who does things automatically but as an agent with understanding and will who communicates or shares his goodness in accordance with his freedom to choose what he will do.[88] But God's communicative freedom *pro nobis* is underscored all the more if there is already an internal communication present in God's own triune being. For the processions of the Son and Spirit involve a communication or sharing of the divine life with them (so esp. Jn 5:26).[89] The Dutch Reformed author Johannes Maccovius explicitly connects the freedom of God to intratrinitarian communication. After treating the good as "communicative of itself," he raises the question whether God in his goodness necessarily created the world. He responds that there is a *duplex communicatio* on God's part: one *ad intra*, the other *ad extra*. The former is necessary, while the latter is free either to be or not to be.[90] In other words, the internal communication renders the external gratuitous. Furthermore, while the communication within God's triune life corroborates the contingency of creation and the *theologia-oikonomia* distinction, it also illumines how creation is possible and fitting. Athanasius makes this point in combating Arianism: God can create the world since his essence itself is "fecund" (καρπογόνος) in the generation of the Son and not a "dry fountain."[91] Creation is not "unnatural" for God or in conflict with God's being.[92] In fact, Thomas argues, the processions in God are *rationes* ("reasons," "ways," fitting precedents or archetypes) for the production of the world.[93] So too Bavinck: "Creation cannot be conceived as mere happenstance, nor as the outcome of a divine self-development. It must have its foundation in God, yet not be a phase in the process of his inner life. How can these two concerns be

---

[88]E.g., Thomas, *ST* Ia.19.3 (234-35); Polanus, *Syntagma* 5.3 (263-64); Owen, *Christologia* 4 (59); Charnock, *Existence and Attributes of God*, 2:224-27; Mastricht, *TPT* 2.16.14 (173); 17.4, 12 (179-80). Another way in which Thomas avoids a Platonic emanationist schema is by tying the communicative nature of the good to final causality (rather than efficient causality) (*ST* Ia.19.2 [233]; cf. John F. Wippel, "Norman Kretzmann on Aquinas' Attribution of Will and of Freedom to Create to God," *Religious Studies* 39 [2003]: 295-97).

[89]On this communication, see, e.g., Thomas, *ST* Ia.39.5 ad 6 (405); Polanus, *Syntagma* 3.6 (219); Mastricht, *TPT* 2.26.29 (259).

[90]Johannes Maccovius, *Metaphysica*, ed. Adrianus Heereboord, 3rd ed. (Leiden, 1658), 1.8 (54-57). Maccovius understands communication in the Trinity differently from authors like Thomas, Polanus, and Mastricht, but that is an issue for another time.

[91]Athanasius, *Oratio II contra Arianos*, in *Oratio I et II contra Arianos*, 2 (178).

[92]Thomas, *ST* Ia.19.3 ad 3 (235).

[93]Thomas, *ST* Ia.45.6 (474-75).

satisfied if not by the confession of a triune God?" While God does not need creation, his inward "fecundity" is its ground.[94] And because of the perfection of God's triune goodness, his activity toward us is rich in pure generosity. "Were he not first infinitely blessed, and full in himself, he could not be infinitely good and diffusive to us." But since God is the "highest goodness," he does not "act for his own profit, but for his creatures' welfare, and the manifestation of his own goodness. He sends out his beams, without receiving any addition to himself, or substantial advantage from his creatures." Again, "He is not covetous of his own treasures. . . . He is incapable of envy; his own happiness can no more be diminished, than it can be increased. . . . What God gives out of goodness, he gives with joy and gladness. He did not only will that we should be, but rejoiced that he had brought us into being; he rejoiced in his works" (Ps 104:31).[95]

3. Finally, the Son's assumption of a human nature in the unity of his person and without compromise to either his divinity or the human nature assumed implies God's aseity and transcendence of the economy. That the Son can take up this nature in his own person and not have to allocate it to another in order to remain truly God or to keep the human nature intact implies that the Son according to his divinity does not occupy a common order of being with creatures. For if he did occupy a common order of being with the creature, he would be determined and distinguished by having some negative relation and opposition to other (created) beings. That is, he would be constituted as the God that he is by not having something that is constitutive of another. He would have to keep his distance from other terms in this distinction (e.g., humanity) in order to remain what he was (i.e., God). What he willed to assume and what he already was would be caught in a zero-sum game so that he could not be true God and true man. But he can be and is true God and true man. He does not need to forego something of his divinity in order to accommodate his humanity. He is "capable of presence in [the created order] in such a way that no corresponding absence of created being is required."[96] Thus he does not occupy a common genus

---

[94]Bavinck, RD 2:309, 332-33, 420.
[95]Charnock, Existence and Attributes of God, 2:218-19, 227.
[96]Christopher A. Franks, "The Simplicity of the Living God: Aquinas, Barth, and Some Philosophers," MT 21 (2005): 296.

with us and is not constituted or determined as the God that he is by some reference to us. And if he is not constituted or determined as the God that he is by reference to another, then he is *a se* and complete in himself. God is distinct from us positively by having in himself a plenitude of perfection that no other can have.[97] This distinction by absolute plenitude means that God is incorruptible and transcends the order of creatures altogether, which is precisely what enables God to be immediately present in the created order. Maintaining God's aseity over against pantheism and panentheism, Barth provocatively writes,

> Now the absoluteness of God strictly understood in this sense means that God has the freedom to be present with that which is not God, to communicate Himself and unite Himself with the other and the other with Himself, in a way which utterly surpasses all that can be effected in regard to reciprocal presence, communion and fellowship between other beings. It is just the absoluteness of God properly understood which can signify not only His Freedom to transcend all that is other than Himself, but also His freedom to be immanent within it, and at such a depth of immanence as simply does not exist in the fellowship between other beings. No created being can be inwardly present to another, entering and remaining in communion with him in the depths of its inner life. . . . The essence of every other being is to be finite, and therefore to have frontiers against the personality of others and to have to guard these frontiers jealously. It lies in the nature of created being to have to be true to itself in such a way that with the best will in the world it simply cannot be true to another. It is its very nature that it cannot affirm itself except by affirming itself against others.[98]

More specifically, as the God who is *a se*, the Son can even assume a created nature in the unity of his person without any threat to his divinity or the integrity of his humanity. Such prevenient fullness and transcendence

---

[97]See further the subsection "Scriptural Teaching on Transcendence and Communication" in chap. 5.

[98]Barth, *CD* II/1, 313. For other explorations of the noncompetitive nature of the God-world relation, see Kathryn Tanner, *God and Creation in Christian Theology: Tyranny or Empowerment?* (Minneapolis: Fortress, 1988); Michael J. Dodds, "Ultimacy and Intimacy: Aquinas on the Relation Between God and the World," in *Ordo Sapientiae et Amoris: Hommage au Professeur Jean-Pierre Torrell, O.P.,* ed. Carlos-Josaphat Pinto de Oliveira (Fribourg: Éditions Universitaires, 1993), 211-27; Robert Sokolowski, *God of Faith and Reason: Foundations of Christian Theology* (Washington, DC: Catholic University of America Press, 1995).

of the created order dispels both Nestorianism and Eutychianism. On the one hand, it obviates any need of a second person in the incarnation. On the other hand, it ensures that the divinity of the true God never could be mixed up with a created nature. It is the divine aseity of the Son which ensures that his Godhead remains unchanged in hypostatic union with his passible humanity, which is critical for the efficacy of the Son's atoning work. Without this, the apostle could not truly say that it was *God* who bought the church with his own blood (Acts 20:28).

In sum, after initially qualifying Christology's role in our knowledge of God, I have sought to unfold the sense in which the incarnation is indeed the culminating moment of supernatural revelation. It is the culminating moment because of the stark nearness and bodily subsistence of God in Christ. The actions and teaching of Jesus reveal the will of God, God's relationship to the world, and God's prevenient richness from which he approaches us in an emphatically free and gracious manner. Our next task is to examine the sense in which Christ is the origin and telos of all theological knowledge and how this fits with an emphasis on the knowability of God in his transcendence of the economy.

CHRIST THE SOURCE AND TELOS OF THEOLOGICAL KNOWLEDGE

According to a number of biblical texts, the person of the Son communicates theological understanding even before the incarnation takes place. In addition, the manifestation of God's glory in Christ is revealed to be central to God's plan for the world, including our theological knowing. How might an argument for the practice of Christian *theologia* take into account this broader role of Christ? By now, I have already made the case that God's being is not constituted by the incarnation and that God acts in freedom in deciding to take on human flesh for our salvation. Therefore, we are engaging the pertinent biblical material in this section not to construct an argument for God's aseity or the practice of *theologia* but to show how our conception of the knowledge of God *in se* can be shaped and enriched by the broader biblical teaching on the Son's role in the economy. The point of this section is not nervous polemicizing but positive development. I will first examine the Son's preincarnate mediation of the knowledge of God and then, widening the lens a little more, examine the Son's place in the divine counsel and the eschatological fulfillment of God's plan.

Preincarnate mediation of the knowledge of God. God the Father created the world through his Son, the Logos.[99] This truth is adumbrated in the Old Testament in a text like Psalm 33:6: "By the word of YHWH the heavens were made, and by the breath of his mouth all the starry host" (cf. Ps 148:5). In Proverbs 8, wisdom is "brought forth" by God before the existence of creation and active in the work of creation like a "craftsman" (Prov 8:24-25, 30). The New Testament identifies the word and wisdom through which God created the world as God's own Son, Jesus Christ: "All things were made through him, and nothing that has been made was made without him. In him was life, and that life was the light of human beings. And the light shines in the darkness, and the darkness has not overcome it" (Jn 1:3-5).[100] Augustine comments that the life and light of the Logos is the *ratio* (reason, design, way) of creation.[101] Indeed, while an artisan exists "outside" whatever he makes, the divine Logos dwells within what he makes and inwardly governs it.[102] John's construal of life as light connects the Logos's activity in creation to his activity in revelation. As the one who provides the rationale and order in creation, he illumines the world. He is the "true light that enlightens every human being" (Jn 1:9). Thomas observes that the enlightening work of the Logos in John 1 could pertain to an "influx of natural cognition" or a "communication of grace" and "restoration of the rational creature wrought by Christ."[103] It would be wise not to set the two options against each other, for the passage both echoes the creation account in Genesis 1 and anticipates the moral use of light and darkness terminology that appears later in the Gospel (Jn 3:19-21; 8:12; 12:35-36, 46).[104] The Logos through

---

[99]He acted with and through the Spirit too (e.g., Gen 1:2; Ps 33:6), but the focus here is on the Son.

[100]This handling of the punctuation differs from that of some older exegetes (e.g., Augustine, *In Ioannis Evangelium* 1.16 [9]), but it is found in Chrysostom, *In Johannem* 5.2 (55-56), and in translations like the NIV and ESV.

[101]Augustine, *In Ioannis Evangelium* 1.16 (9-10).

[102]Augustine, *In Ioannis Evangelium* 2.10 (16).

[103]Thomas, *Super Ioannem* 1.3.1.95 (20); 2.102-7 (21-22).

[104]Cf., e.g., Matthew E. Gordley, *New Testament Christological Hymns: Exploring Texts, Contexts, and Significance* (Downers Grove, IL: IVP Academic, 2018), 155-57. On light as an epistemological concept in John—"the means to knowing that which is ultimate"—see Marianne Meye Thompson, "'Light' (φῶς): The Philosophical Content of the Term and the Gospel of John," in

whom the world was made is the source of humanity's natural knowledge of God in the order and majesty of the universe (though that knowledge is corrupted by sin) and the one who has taken on flesh to be the light of the world bringing the salvific knowledge of God (Jn 8:12; 17:3, 25-26).

The apostle Paul also teaches that God the Father created the world through the Son. In his development of the Shema in 1 Corinthians 8:6, Paul writes, "There is one God, the Father, from whom all things exist, and we exist for him. And there is one Lord, Jesus Christ, through whom all things exist, and we exist through him." The Father created all things through the Lord Jesus without this entailing the existence of a second or secondary deity alongside the Father. Paul emphasizes this again in Colossians 1, where he picks up the sort of wisdom theology found in Proverbs 8:22-31.[105] The apostle calls the Son the "image of the invisible God, the firstborn of all creation. For in him all things were created in the heavens and on earth, things seen and things unseen, whether thrones or dominions or rulers or authorities. All things were created through him and for him. And he is before all things and in him all things hold together" (Col 1:15-17; cf. Heb 1:2-3; Rev 3:14). As the image of the invisible God, Christ shares what the Father has and reveals that divine fullness to others (cf. Col 1:19; 2:9).[106] When Paul adds that Christ is the "firstborn of all creation," he explains what he means: "for in him all things were created in the heavens and on earth."[107] The term "firstborn" here does not mean that Christ is some great creature but rather that creation was brought into being in, through, and for him. According to Paul, then, creation and, by implication, its divinely instituted communication of a natural knowledge of God, originates and persists in and through the Son. Christ's agency in creation and providence is then joined to his agency in salvation: "And he is the head of the body of the

---

The Prologue of the Gospel of John: Its Literary, Theological, and Philosophical Contexts; Papers read at the Colloquium Ioanneum 2013, ed. Jan G. van der Watt, R. Alan Culpepper, and Udo Schnelle (Tübingen: Mohr Siebeck, 2016), 273-83.

[105]On this connection, see, e.g., Gordley, New Testament Christological Hymns, 126-30.

[106]For the emphasis on the Son revealing the Father here, see Hilary, La Trinité 8.48-9 (2:454-58); Owen, Christologia 5 (70-73); James D. G. Dunn, The Epistles to the Colossians and to Philemon: A Commentary on the Greek Text, New International Greek Testament Commentary (Grand Rapids: Eerdmans, 1996), 87-90; Marianne Meye Thompson, Colossians and Philemon, Two Horizons New Testament Commentary (Grand Rapids: Eerdmans, 2005), 28-30.

[107]Cf. Athanasius, Oratio II 63-64 (239-41); Hilary, La Trinité 8.50 (2:458).

church." He is the "firstborn from the dead" who reconciles us to God (Col 1:18-20). Thus Hilary of Poitiers writes, Christ is "firstborn" with respect to both the origin of the entire world and the *dispensatio* of his ecclesial body.[108] He is "head in the works of both nature and grace."[109] The coordinating conjunction "and" linking Colossians 1:17 and John 1:18 is noteworthy. On the one hand, there is a distinction to be drawn between (1) creation and providence and (2) salvation and ecclesiology. On the other hand, in the unity of God's plan, there can be no separation of Christ's work in nature and in supernatural grace. He is the second person of the Trinity, through whom God the Father works in creation and providence, and he is the mediator of our salvation and ecclesial life.

Since the Father has created and sustained the world through his Son, the Son is (with the Father and Spirit) the source of humanity's natural knowledge of God. In this regard, some theologians are prepared to call Christ the "mediator" of creation, natural theology, and humanity's supralapsarian relation to God,[110] though it could be added that the term *mediator* is used more strictly with reference to the ethical enmity between God and sinful humanity. To frame this in relation to the triune life of God, the outward works of the Trinity are undivided, which is to say that they are accomplished by all three divine persons acting together. For such works are accomplished by God's one essential power that is common to the three. Creation in particular is thus accomplished by the Father, Son, and Spirit. Each of God's actions is also characterized by the order of subsistence among the three persons, breaking forth from the Father, through the Son, in the Spirit.[111] The Son who *is* from the Father (e.g., Jn 5:26; 6:46; 7:29) accordingly *acts* from the Father (see esp. Jn 5:19-30). Thus the works of creation and

---

[108]Hilary, *La Trinité* 8.50 (2:458).

[109]Herman Witsius, *De oeconomia foederum Dei cum hominibus* (Leeuwarden, 1685), 1.2.8 (11).

[110]See John Calvin, *Institutes of the Christian Religion*, ed. John T. McNeill, trans. Ford Lewis Battles, LCC 20-21 (Philadelphia: Westminster, 1960), 1.12.1 (1:464-65) (though see also the counterbalancing statements of 12.4-5 [467-70]); Bavinck, *RD* 4:685; Stefan Lindholm, "Would Christ Have Become Incarnate Had Adam Not Fallen? Jerome Zanchi (1516–1590) on Christ as Mediator," *JRT* 9 (2015): 19-36; Edwin Chr. van Driel, "'Too Lowly to Reach God Without a Mediator': John Calvin's Supralapsarian Eschatological Narrative," *MT* 33 (2017): 275-92. Compare also Turretin, *Inst.* 14.2.10 (2.414).

[111]For a classic statement of this, see Gregory of Nyssa, *Ad Ablabium, Quod non sint tres dei*, in *Gregorii Nysseni opera*, vol. 3/1, *Opera dogmatica minora*, ed. Fridericus Mueller (Leiden: Brill, 1958), 47-48 (55).

providence are accomplished through the Son. Hence the knowledge of God available via humanity's encounter with the cosmos is given through the Son.

Yet, according to God's description of it in the Bible, the content and apprehension of natural revelation are indeed natural. The content is what can be known of God from observing the world, without reference to the supernatural revelation of Scripture (though Scripture ultimately helps believers to understand natural revelation better). The apprehension of it can take place by the human person's use of the natural faculty of knowing, even without regeneration or the special illumination of the Spirit (though the inward action of the Spirit will help believers to understand and receive natural revelation rightly). None of this is overturned by the biblical teaching that natural revelation is given through the Son.[112] It is not the content or the mode of apprehension but our understanding of how the natural knowledge is communicated that is shaped in a fresh way by glimpsing the trinitarian structure of creation, providence, and revelation. From within an awareness of God's triune life and action, the believer can know and praise the holy Trinity as the efficient cause of true natural theology, an incomplete knowledge that in its own material content still does not involve proper cognition of the Father, Son, and Spirit.

The Son also communicates supernatural knowledge of God prior to the incarnation. For he is the mediator of God's gracious covenant even before he actually takes on flesh. While Moses was the direct human mediator of the Sinaitic covenant and Jesus the mediator of the new covenant (Deut 5:5; Gal 3:19; Heb 3:1-6; 9:1-28; 12:24), it remains the case that Jesus acts as the primary, overarching covenantal mediator of salvation throughout all of history (so Gal 3:8-18; cf. Jn 8:56; Rom 4:1-25; 1 Tim 2:5; Heb 11:39-40). His mediatorial work encompasses and utilizes the "typological interlude" of the old covenant instituted through Moses to direct the people of God toward his future atoning work and toward his gospel.[113] Early Reformed authors often explicate the prophetic aspect of this preincarnate mediation by identifying the angel of YHWH as God the Son offering counsel to God's people

---

[112]This differs from the trajectory of Barth's exegesis of texts like John 1:3 (see *CD* II/2, 95-99; III/1, 29-31)

[113]Michael S. Horton, "The Church," in *Christian Dogmatics: Reformed Theology for the Church Catholic*, ed. Michael Allen and Scott R. Swain (Grand Rapids: Baker Academic, 2016), 320.

of old and by pointing out that it is the Son who, by his Spirit, authors the Old Testament's prophetic material (1 Pet 1:10-11).[114]

Often it is said to be the Holy Spirit who speaks through the human authors in the text of the Old Testament (e.g., Heb 3:7a; 2 Pet 1:20-21). But the Spirit is the Spirit of the Son (Rom 8:9; Gal 4:6; 1 Pet 1:11), the one through whom the Son acts. With the Father, the Son acts through his Spirit to guide the Old Testament prophets to grant God's people theological understanding, some of which pertains to God himself. This certainly does not mean that Old Testament teaching on God himself has the Son's incarnation as its primary or exhaustive content. It does not mean that it can be understood at all only by looking at it backward from the incarnation. Thus, in taking the full range of scriptural teaching on God (not the incarnation by itself) to be the cognitive principle of theology proper we are not seeking a way to God that is not authorized by the Son. Rather, we are following the way given by the Son (with the Father) through the Spirit. We may add that when the Son is considered to be the (preincarnate) source of theological knowledge, the biblical passages sometimes include a reference to his being the incarnate Christ (e.g., Jn 1:9-11; Col 1:14, 18-20, 22; Heb 1:2, 3b; 1 Pet 1:11; Rev 3:14, 21). But we do not have to posit that the Son was constituted as Son by anticipation of the incarnation in order to make sense of this. Instead, because the Son and Jesus Christ are one and the same person, it should not surprise us that the biblical authors would call him Son, Logos, and Christ somewhat interchangeably in describing his preincarnate and incarnate work. The hypostatic identity and the deity of the Son remain constant: Prior to the incarnation the Son is the Son ἀσύνθετος (as a "noncomposite" person); in and after the assumption of a human nature, in light of which he bears many additional names, like Immanuel and Jesus Christ, the Son is the Son σύνθετος (as a "composite" person).[115] The enduring hypostatic identity of the Son, taken together with the eternal divine counsel according to which the Son will be incarnate, explains why he can be called "Christ" (and other names that

---

[114]E.g., Johannes Maccovius, *Loci communes theologici*, ed. Nicolaus Arnoldus, 2nd ed. (Amsterdam, 1658), 60 (509-10); Turretin, *Inst.* 12.2.15 (2:195); 14.7.12 (2:434-35); Owen, *Christologia* 7 (87-90); Witsius, *De oeconomia*, 2.3.3 (112); Mastricht, *TPT* 5.6.5-6 (556).

[115]For the use of this language, see, e.g., John of Damascus, *Exp. fid.* 3.7 (123); Polanus, *Syntagma* 6.12 (362). Note also Turretin, *Inst.* 14.2.14 (2:415).

signify him with his two natures) in description of his work prior to the incarnation, without us having to posit an eternal constitution of the person of the Son by the incarnation.

Christ in the decree and its eschatological fulfillment. This treatment of the knowledge of God in himself should also consider that the manifestation of God's glory in Christ is in some sense what Owen calls the "foundation of all the counsels of God."[116] I will discuss the significance of this for the practice of *theologia* under the following three points.

1. A number of scriptural texts may be invoked to substantiate the claim that the manifestation of God's glory in Christ is the central content and telos of the divine decree. Ephesians 1 is particularly important in this regard, where Paul says that God has "blessed us with every spiritual blessing in Christ, just as he chose us in him before the foundation of the world in order that we should be holy and blameless before him in love" (Eph 1:3-4). God's lavish blessings in Christ that are given in time correspond to and are grounded in God's eternal election of us in Christ. In predestining us to be his sons and daughters (Eph 1:5), he united us with Christ decretively and pledged in due course to unite us with Christ in act, by his calling and through our faith.[117] Even if the prepositional phrase "in him" in Ephesians 1:3 does not also carry the meaning "by him," Scripture as a whole conveys that the Son himself acts in election (esp. Jn 13:18; 15:16, 19). Moreover, when Paul teaches that we are chosen "in him" in Ephesians 1:4, the referent of the pronoun "him" is "Christ" in Ephesians 1:3. We were chosen not just in the Son but in the Son with reference to his eventual assumption of a human nature. The Son is eternally (though still freely) the *Logos incarnandus,* predestined to be the *Logos incarnatus.* The work of Christ, then, is not an afterthought in the plan of God. It is central to the content of God's eternal decree. Paul adds that God has made known to us the mystery of his will, according to his good pleasure, which he set forth in Christ, the one in whom all things in heaven and on earth are to be "summed up" (Eph 1:9-10). The eternal will of God has established that all things would find their

---

[116]Owen, *Christologia* 4 (54).

[117]For a study of Christology and predestination in early Reformed thought, see Richard A. Muller, *Christ and the Decree: Christology and Predestination in Reformed Theology from Calvin to Perkins* (Grand Rapids: Baker Academic, 2008). See also David Gibson, *Reading the Decree: Exegesis, Christology and Election in Calvin and Barth* (London: Bloomsbury, 2009).

appointed end in relation to the God-man, Jesus Christ. "The significance of the cosmos is made known in him."[118]

Other scriptural texts reiterate these points. Christ is the Lamb "foreknown before the foundation of the world" (1 Pet 1:20). He is the Lamb "slain from the foundation of the world" (Rev 13:8). While the crucifixion obviously did not take place at the beginning of history, "the death of Christ was a redemptive sacrifice decreed in the counsels of eternity."[119] Christ is the telos of creation, the one "appointed to be heir of all things" (Col 1:16; Heb 1:2). With respect to the goal of our theological knowledge, it is significant that Christ prays that we would ultimately be with him and behold his glory (Jn 17:24). God's goal in our salvation is that he would display for all eternity "the surpassing richness of his grace in kindness to us in Christ Jesus" (Eph 2:7). At the end of the book of Revelation, our eschatological destiny is to dwell with and to see God and the Lamb (Rev 22:1-5). There the person of Christ himself is called "the Alpha and the Omega, the first and the last, the beginning and the end" (Rev 22:13).

2. In light of these biblical passages, there are different ways in which one could express the role of Christology in the practice of *theologia*. Though he is reticent to say much about the logical order of the divine decree, Owen, for example, begins his discussion of it with an alertness to God's completeness and consequent freedom in choosing to create the world. He argues that God freely chose to create the world and then, "upon a prospect of the ruin of all by sin," foreordained that Christ would be the incarnate Savior who restores all things.[120] For Owen, it is within this free, infralapsarian schema that the goal of the decree is the Father's delight in his incarnate Son and, derivatively, our love to God "by and in Christ" (cf. 1 Pet 1:21).[121] While refusing to speculate about whether the Son would have assumed a human nature apart from the fall, another Puritan author, Thomas Goodwin, exhibits a somewhat different approach by arguing that in foreordaining the incarnation God "had not Christ in his eye only or chiefly as a redeemer, but withal looked upon that infinite glory of the

---

[118]Ernest Best, *Ephesians*, International Critical Commentary (Edinburgh: T&T Clark, 1998), 142.
[119]Robert H. Mounce, *The Book of Revelation*, rev ed., NICNT (Grand Rapids: Eerdmans, 1997), 252.
[120]Owen, *Christologia* 4 (61-62).
[121]Owen, *Posthumous Sermons* 2 (615).

second Person to be manifested in that nature through his assumption." Indeed, the glory of the person of Christ had the "greater sway" in the decree; to it "redemption itself was subordinated."[122]

Barth is more emphatic and argues that Christ is the "electing God himself." For Barth, it is not sufficient to state that the Trinity is the electing God and that the person of Christ is the "organ which serves the electing will of God." It will not do to say that election "precedes the being and will and word of Christ" or that it is "independent of Jesus Christ and only executed by him." Otherwise we would have to contemplate a God hidden "behind his revelation," a God who is "above and beyond Jesus Christ." In that act of looking away from God's revelation, the loss of a "christological reference" in election would leave "man to be the instructor in the things concerning God and himself."[123] It seems that in insisting on this "christological reference" Barth posits that in election the Son acts not only according to his divinity but also in some anticipative way as hypostatically constituted by his humanity. This is different from saying only that the Son, who would be incarnate given the free decree of God, acted in election, or that the same person who is contingently the man Jesus Christ acted according to his divinity in election.[124] Rather than allow fallen humanity to consider God without this "christological reference" in election, Barth reasons that there is "no such thing as Godhead in itself," "no such thing as a will of God apart from the will of Jesus Christ." Christ, then, is both the subject and object of election.[125] In harmony with this insistence that Christ is not an afterthought in the divine counsel, later in the *Church Dogmatics* Barth ends up arguing that the covenant of grace is the "internal basis" and presupposition of creation. Indeed, according to Barth, "created being as such needs salvation."[126]

---

[122]*The Works of Thomas Goodwin*, vol. 1, *An Exposition of the First Chapter of the Epistle to the Ephesians* (repr., Grand Rapids: Reformation Heritage, 2006), 99-100.

[123]Barth, *CD* II/2, 64-65.

[124]According to a traditional Reformed Christology, such statements are legitimate on the basis of the unity of the person of Christ and the *communicatio idiomatum*, by way of what Turretin calls an "indirect predication," in which something pertaining to Christ according to one of his natures (e.g., the divine) may be predicated of Christ even when he is denominated by a concrete name derived from the other nature (e.g., "man") (*Inst.* 13.8.3 [2:350]).

[125]Barth, *CD* II/2, 115.

[126]Barth, *CD* III/1, 43-46, 94-97, 229-32; IV/1, 8-10. This line of thinking is addressed later, in chap. 5.

To the extent that Barth's approach implicitly—and against some of Barth's own theological instincts—ends up compromising God's aseity and freedom in the incarnation, I would suggest that something like the approach of Owen is better suited to expressing the role of Christ in the divine counsel and its eschatological fulfillment. Owen is content to acknowledge that God has mysteriously chosen to permit the fall and that it is with that permission in place that God has determined to display his rich glory in the incarnate Son for all eternity. If one adheres to a more traditional understanding of God's aseity but is still inclined to think that God would have decreed the incarnation whether humanity had fallen or not, then something like Goodwin's view is an option. Yet that view does not necessarily conflict with the work of Christian *theologia*. For what is revealed in the incarnate life and work of the Son and enjoyed in our eternal fellowship with him is a divine richness that pertains to God's own being, not merely his works *ad extra*. It is a richness displayed for us (even for God himself) in this particular way, but its content is not reducible to what takes place in the economy. The locus of the beholding and the plenitude of what is beheld should not be confused. At any rate, I would point out that Scripture does not teach that the incarnate Son alone is the telos of God's plan. Paul can identify God (without reference to any one divine person) or God the Father as the telos of God's plan, the one whose glory will be manifested (Rom 11:36; 1 Cor 8:6; 15:28).

3. As mentioned in chapter one, Owen argues that the focal point or perhaps even the content of the beatific vision is Christ: "The blessed and blessing sight which we shall have of God will be always 'in the face of Jesus Christ.'" If the finite cannot grasp the infinite, then according to Owen, we will see the "manifestation of the glory of God, in his perfections, and all their blessed operations" in Christ the God-man.[127] This brings up the question of whether or in what way Christ might be considered the mediator of the knowledge of God even in the new creation. That question in turn can be situated within earlier debates about whether the mediatorial kingdom of Christ (as distinct from the "essential" kingdom or rule of the Father, Son, and Spirit) endures for all eternity.[128]

---

[127] John Owen, *Meditations and Discourses on the Glory of Christ*, in *The Works of John Owen*, vol. 1, *The Glory of Christ*, ed. William H. Goold (Edinburgh: Banner of Truth, 1965), 292-93.

[128] For Reformed discussions, see Calvin, *Institutes of the Christian Religion* 2.14.3 (485-86); Turretin, *Inst.* 14.17 (2:534-38); Mastricht, *TPT* 8.4.9, 20 (1196-97, 1200). Note also Polanus, *Syntagma* 1.5 (3), where he comments that "[God] himself alone without any mediator or medium

It is not possible to address all the relevant christological and eschatological details here, but I do think it fitting to hold that Christ's mediatorial
kingdom does endure eternally in a certain way (see 2 Sam 7:16; Is 9:6-7;
Rev 7:17; 11:15; 12:10; 21:22-23). To use some of the distinctions found in
Francis Turretin and others, its mode of administration will be changed (see
esp. 1 Cor 15:24-28). It will no longer be administered by word and sacrament
and no longer require active opposition to the enemies of Christ and the
church. It will involve an immediate vision of God and everlasting peace. But
the substance of the benefits granted to us by Christ the mediator will remain
the same. Moreover, as Turretin notes, while the acquisition and application
of those benefits are finished, Christ's preservation of those benefits abides
forever. Christ remains the "bond of our eternal communion with God"
(*vinculum perpetuae nostrae communionis cum Deo*). This arguably pertains
to the prophetic aspect of his mediatorial office: "And the city has no need
of the sun or moon that they should shine on it, for the glory of God illumines it, and its lamp is the Lamb" (Rev 21:23).[129] At the same time, while
our sight of God is secured by Christ and actualized only in union with
Christ, the Apocalypse (with other scriptural texts) informs us that we will
not behold Christ the mediator alone but "God and the Lamb" (Rev 22:3-4;
cf., e.g., Mt 5:8; 1 Cor 13:12). Although we will behold God only in union with
Christ, and while we will behold Christ himself as the God-man, we will
enjoy an immediate vision of the triune God, Father, Son, and Spirit. On the
one hand, someone like Owen could maintain within the logic of his view
that Christ is the focal point of the beatific vision while God's immanent
richness is its ultimate content.[130] On the other hand, I would suggest that
there is no choice that must be made between seeing Christ the mediator in
his economic glory and seeing the triune God in his essential glory. In the
city of God, we may see both Christ the mediator's peculiar display of God's
abundant grace (Eph 2:7) and, in union with Christ, God's very essence.

To sum up, the Son is the one through whom the Father created the world
and has given the human race a natural knowledge of God. The Son was also

---

will be for eternity the immediate cause and author of all our good and felicity" and the "immediate object" of our felicity.

[129]Turretin, *Inst.* 14.17.4, 8 (2:535-36).

[130]See his *Christologia* 4 (56-60); 5 (73).

the mediator of the supernatural knowledge of God even prior to his incarnation. The Son was predestined to be the incarnate mediator and to be given the name Jesus Christ. The triune God (including the Son himself) determined that all things would have their end and meaning in the Son's fulfillment of the plan of God. But, according to texts like Romans 11:36 and 1 Corinthians 8:6; 15:28, the fulfillment of that plan ultimately orients all things to the triune God (not Christ alone). The Son continues to mediate his benefits (not least the beatific vision) in preserving them for the saints throughout eternity. Yet even as the blessed will live and know and rejoice only in union with Christ, we will see not only Christ the God-man but also the triune God in his essential glory. Christology does not shape the doctrine of God as though the incarnation constituted the being of God or as though it were the sole basis or content of the knowledge of God. However, it does shape our understanding of the knowledge of God when we consider the trinitarian structure of divine action and the fact that it is only in union with Christ the mediator that we will see God face-to-face. Moreover, if we recall from chapter one that the work of Christian dogmatics is but an elaboration on the infused theology given in our reception of the gospel, we will do well to remember that we practice dogmatic theology in the first place only in Christ. Even if we do not take the incarnate Christ by himself to be the epistemic principle of scientific theology, we begin our growth in theological understanding as those already united to him by faith.

THE *LOGOS ASARKOS* AND *EXTRA CALVINISTICUM*

Challenge from Barth. In this chapter we have already noted various statements from Barth about the *Logos asarkos* and *extra Calvinisticum*.[131] His

---

[131]Traditionally, the concept of the *Logos asarkos* signifies the person of the Logos or Son "without flesh," that is, in ontological priority to his assumption of a human nature. The concept of the *extra Calvinisticum* expresses that the Son according to his deity subsists "outside" his human nature or is not contained under the limitations of his human nature. For the (material if not formal) presence of the *extra* in patristic sources, see, e.g., Athanasius, *De incarnatione*, in *Contra Gentes and De incarnatione*, ed. and trans. Robert W. Thomson (Oxford: Clarendon, 1971), 17; Augustine, *In Ioannis Evangelium* 13.8 (125); John of Damascus, *Exp. fid.* 3.7 (122-26). For more recent literature, see E. David Willis, *Calvin's Catholic Christology: The Function of the So Called* Extra Calvinisticum *in Calvin's Theology* (Leiden: Brill, 1966); Christina Aus der Au, "Das Extra Calvinisticum—mehr als ein reformiertes Extra?," *Theologische Zeitschrift* 64 (2008): 358-69; Myk Habets, "Putting the 'Extra' Back into Calvinism," *SJT* 62 (2009): 441-56; Cornelis van der Kooi, "The Identity of Israel's God: The Potential of the So-Called Extra Calvinisticum,"

treatment of these concepts in fact involves a range of claims about the eternal subsistence of God the Son, the divine decree, the role of Christ in election, and so forth. To this point I have not directly addressed his contention that talk of the Son's prevenient identity (without reference to his decision to be incarnate) may involve positing one sort of Logos prior to the act of election and another after it, which would yield an implicitly Nestorian Christology.

Addressing this challenge will require summarizing some of Barth's key statements, but first I should mention that I do not intend to adjudicate which contemporary interpreters of Barth (Bruce McCormack, Paul Molnar, George Hunsinger, and others) have offered the correct interpretation of Barth's work on this subject. It seems to me that one can find in Barth some statements that tend toward a more traditional account of God's aseity vis-à-vis election and the incarnation and other statements which imply that God is constituted as God by his determination to be God for us in the incarnation. For instance, Barth can say that "the divine essence of the Son does not, of course, need actualization" or that "the divine essence of the Son . . . did not need His incarnation."[132] However, in discussing Jesus Christ as the electing God, he says, "There is no such thing as Godhead in itself."[133] Indeed, Barth can even make comments about the incarnation itself bringing about a *novum* for God, a "special" or "new actualization" of the divine essence in union with Christ's humanity, even if the divine essence already was "actual in itself" and undergoes no "inherent change."[134] Sorting all this out is a complicated task that I will not undertake here. Without attempting to integrate all of Barth's thinking, I will simply focus on the challenge presented by his contention that a robust affirmation of the *extra Calvinisticum* may compromise the unity of the person of Christ.

---

in *Tradition and Innovation in Biblical Interpretation*, ed. W. Th. van Peursen and J. W. Dyk (Leiden: Brill, 2011), 209-22; Darren O. Sumner, "The Twofold Life of the Word: Karl Barth's Critical Reception of the *Extra Calvinisticum*," *IJST* 15 (2012): 42-57; Andrew M. McGinnis, *The Son of God Beyond the Flesh: A Historical and Theological Study of the* Extra Calvinisticum (London: Bloomsbury, 2014); James R. Gordon, *The Holy One in Our Midst: An Essay on the Flesh of Christ* (Minneapolis: Fortress, 2016).

[132]Barth, *CD* IV/2, 113. Cf. I/1, 83; I/2, 136; IV/2, 47.

[133]Barth, *CD* II/2, 115.

[134]Barth, *CD* IV/2, 113-14.

Barth insists that we are not authorized to seek a knowledge of God apart from his revelation in Christ. We cannot allow "man to be his own instructor" and seek a God hidden "behind his revelation" or "above and beyond Jesus Christ."[135] For Barth, this means that in an important sense there *is* no God to be sought behind or beyond Christ. If Christology is to remain decisive for our understanding of God, the "christological reference" in the divine decree in particular cannot lack an ontological basis. Thus there is no God acting in the decree that is already constituted without reference to the decision for the incarnation. "There is no such thing as Godhead in itself." Even in election the Father, Son, and Spirit act as the Father of Jesus Christ, Jesus Christ himself and the Spirit of Jesus Christ.[136] The eternal Logos just is Jesus Christ.[137] To say otherwise is ultimately to posit some "'other' god" and a "second person of the Trinity as such" with "another form than that which God Himself has given in willing to reveal Himself and to act outwards."[138] To bring this into relation to some earlier material in *Church Dogmatics*: If the person and deity of the Son transcend his decision to be united with his human nature or if he can be known without reference to his human nature, this will lead to a "dissolution of the unity of the natures and hypostatic union, and therefore a dissolution of the unequivocal Emmanuel and the certainty of faith and salvation based thereon." It will generate a "twofold Christ."[139] For Barth, whether it results from positing an eternal Son behind Jesus Christ or from a nineteenth-century kenotic Christology, a double Christ would mean that the Christ who acts in the incarnation is not the true God and, consequently, not able to atone for sin and reconcile us to God.[140]

Within this framework, the legitimacy of the concept of the "immanent Trinity," which Barth early on had called an "indispensable premise" for talk about an "economic Trinity," requires significant qualification. The "second 'person' of the Trinity as such" ("the eternal Word of God *in abstracto*," "the so-called λόγος ἄσαρκος") functions as a "necessary and important concept"

---

[135]Barth, *CD* II/2, 64-65; IV/1, 52, 177, 181; IV/2, 21, 45.
[136]Barth, *CD* II/2, 63-67, 115; IV/1, 52-53.
[137]Barth, *CD* II/2, 95-99; IV/1, 51. Cf. IV/2, 45.
[138]Barth, *CD* IV/1, 52, 181.
[139]Barth, *CD* I/2, 170.
[140]Barth, *CD* IV/1, 133, 183-86; IV/2, 21.

that underscores the "free basis" of God's self-revelation, but, especially in treating the works of God, it is "pointless" and "impermissible" to attempt to "reckon with any Son of God in himself, with any λόγος ἄσαρκος, with any other Word of God than that which was made flesh."[141]

This then has bearing on Barth's approach to the *extra Calvinisticum*. On the one hand, he recognizes both earlier and later in the *Church Dogmatics* that the *extra* has an important role. God the Son was ἄσαρκος before the incarnation. Furthermore, he is not limited by or absolutely "included" in his humanity in the incarnation and remains Lord in his incarnate life. His divinity remains distinct from his humanity—and the distinction (rather than separation) of the natures was the point for the early Reformed authors, who held that the Son still truly subsists *intra carnem* as well as *extra carnem*. On the other hand, Barth worries that the if the notions of the *Logos asarkos* and the *extra Calvinisticum* imply that there is a Son whose identity transcends the union with his human nature, a Son whose *forma Dei* does not "[consist] in the grace in which God Himself assumes and makes His own the *forma servi*," then there will be a "twofold Christ": an exalted one about whom we could only speculate and an attenuated and lowly one who is not mighty to save.[142]

What is the basis of Barth's concern that a Logos constituted without reference to the incarnation would have a lesser version of deity when he does come into union with his human nature? It seems the answer lies in Barth's understanding of the way in which the lowly human experience of the Son must be aligned with the divine subsistence and nature of the Son (and vice versa).[143] The Son humbles himself in and after taking on flesh. He lives a life of human lowliness, suffering, and obedience to the Father. But Barth is not content to say that this is characteristic of the Son's humanity alone. In order for the Son's lowliness, suffering, and obedience not to conflict with his Godhead and to be positively resonant with it, such lowliness must be a "possibility included in His unalterable [divine] being."

---

[141]Barth, *CD* I/1, 479; IV/1, 52.

[142]Barth, *CD* I/2, 165-71; IV/1, 180-81, 188, 196, 198. Cf. IV/2, 64-69.

[143]For more on the significance of Christ's humanity in Barth's thought, see Paul Dafydd Jones, *The Humanity of Christ: Christology in Karl Barth's "Church Dogmatics"* (London: T&T Clark, 2008); Darren O. Sumner, *Karl Barth and the Incarnation: Christology and the Humility of God* (London: Bloomsbury, 2014).

Hence "for God it is just as natural to be lowly as it is to be high."[144] Accordingly, Barth posits that the Son's humility is "not alien to Him, but proper to Him." If the Son's humility and obedience belonged only to the "divine dispensation," then the economy would not "bring us into touch with God Himself." Thus that God truly was in Christ reconciling the world to himself (2 Cor 5:19) entails that the Son's "subordination" (though not "inferiority") and obedience "belongs to the inner life of God." In this way, the Son's incarnation is not an abrogation of his divine subsistence or Godhead since he already is in his divine mode of subsistence "the One who is obedient in humility."[145] With such a schema in place, where the Godhead of the Son itself has to align with and anticipate the humility and obedience of his incarnate life, one can see why Barth would suggest that a Logos constituted without reference to the incarnation would be an abstract concept with no real being or knowability. One can also see why Barth would argue that if there were such a Logos, and if, under the divine decree, the Godhead of this Logos would have to be recalibrated to allow for his incarnate suffering, then that Logos under the decree and in union with his human nature would have a secondary version of deity lacking salvific efficacy.

Response. One can appreciate certain theological instincts found in Barth's reasoning here even if one does not agree with his conclusions. In particular, upholding the full deity of the incarnate Son and the unity of the person of Christ is vital in any exposition of Christian doctrine. However, in my view, Barth's aversion to "natural theology" and his insistence on there being no God to be known "behind" Christ have led him to make some problematic moves in his efforts to uphold Christ's deity and hypostatic unity. My response will offer some criticism of Barth and attempt to clarify that affirming a divine subsistence (and knowability) of the Son without reference to his incarnation does cohere with Christ's hypostatic unity.

First, it seems to me that Barth's rejection (at least in some parts of his work) of the existence of a divine Son constituted without respect to the incarnation and his claim that the affirmation of such a Son entails a "twofold Christ" are ultimately built on his conception of the mode of union involved

---

[144]In this section of *Church Dogmatics*, Barth is attempting to answer the question *Quo iure Deus homo* ("by what right did God become man?").
[145]Barth, *CD* IV/1, 183-210. Cf. IV/2, 84.

in the incarnation.[146] The way in which Barth treats the union that takes place in the incarnation suggests that he envisions the two essences themselves (not just the *hypostasis*) to be the focal point of the union. For he contends that the dynamics of the human existence of the Logos must have precedent in his divine mode of subsisting and, in turn, that the divine mode of subsisting must anticipate these human dynamics (humility, subordination, obedience), lest the incarnation involve a renunciation of the Son's eternal subsistence and Godhead and thus a lessening of the divine being of the Son in his incarnate work. In other words, Barth's approach to securing the hypostatic unity of Christ seems to be rooted in his sense that the Son's humanity must correspond to the Son's Godhead and that the Son's divine subsistence must have all along contained in itself those features that mark his human life. While clearly not advocating a Eutychian confusion of the two natures, Barth has advocated a certain correspondence or similarity between the two, without which, according to Barth, the Son would have to give up his antecedent Godhead in light of the divine decree and exist with a lesser version of it in the incarnation.

But what if the assimilation of the two natures is simply not necessary? What if it is sufficient to affirm that the *hypostasis* himself is the locus of union? The work of Christ as the second Adam certainly involves obedience, humility, and suffering, but in order to avoid this conflicting with Christ's eternal Godhead (and entailing a subsequent diminution of the Godhead and a double Christ) all that needs to be said is that the Son's Godhead allowed for (even enabled) the Son's assumption of a lowly human nature into immediate union with himself. There is no need to say that the Son's divine subsistence or his Godhead itself must be characterized by obedience and humility. One could respond that what Barth would consider an inflexibly "high" or "exalted" divine essence would preclude the assumption of a humble human nature, but such a response would betray a failure to take seriously the noncompetitive relation between divinity and humanity. By virtue of his divine completeness, incorruptibility, and transcendence of

---

[146]For traditional consideration of the sort or mode of union in the incarnation, see, e.g., Thomas, *ST* IIIa.2.1 (22-23); Bartholomäus Keckermann, *Systema s.s. theologiae*, in *Operum omnium*, 3.2 (2:175); Turretin, *Inst.* 13.6.3, 8 (2:337, 339); Mastricht, *TPT* 5.4.7 (538). Levering also notes this issue while engaging Barth ("Christ, the Trinity, and Predestination," 269-70).

created being, the Son's Godhead neither requires nor precludes his assumption of a created nature—a nature that has no prospect of being in competition with his deity.[147] The Son can assume a human nature with all its limitations without that scenario's requiring discussion of whether the human nature is sufficiently comparable to his divinity.[148] One could also respond that this approach, where the mode of union is strictly hypostatic, assumes a separation of the Son from the divine essence.[149] However, while it is true that the Son can never be separated from the divine essence, it is also the case that it is only the Son himself and not the divine essence as such that is immediately incarnate.[150] If the essence as such were immediately incarnate, or if there were no distinction observed here between person and essence in God, that would mean the Father and Holy Spirit also would be incarnate. For they are persons of the same essence, persons whose real identity with the essence is no less than that of the Son. Indeed, at a more fundamental level, rejecting any distinction whatsoever between person and essence in God would entail Sabellianism, for, if each person is really identical with the essence and without any distinction at all from the essence, each would be identical with the others. Accordingly, there is a distinction between person and essence that must be observed. Given that what

---

[147]I would add that one thing that God's essence (by its unity and simplicity) does preclude is the importing of obedience back into the eternal subsistence of the Son. To be sure, Barth does work to distinguish his understanding of subordination from subordination*ism* (see Darren O. Sumner, "Obedience and Subordination in Karl Barth's Trinitarian Theology," in *Advancing Trinitarian Theology: Explorations in Constructive Dogmatics*, ed. Oliver D. Crisp and Fred Sanders [Grand Rapids: Zondervan, 2014], 130-46). However, even though Barth endeavored to distinguish his position from Arianism, there is still a problem in suggesting an eternal subordination and obedience of the Son when he and the Father share the one essential divine will. For relevant literature on this, see, e.g., Paul D. Molnar, "The Obedience of the Son in the Theology of Karl Barth and Thomas F. Torrance," *SJT* 67 (2014): 50-69; Steven J. Duby, "Trinity and Economy in Thomas Aquinas," *Southern Baptist Journal of Theology* 21 (2017): 29-51; D. Glenn Butner, *The Son Who Learned Obedience: A Theological Case Against the Eternal Submission of the Son* (Eugene, OR: Wipf and Stock, 2018). In particular, while the Son wills *a Patre* just as he subsists *a Patre*, he and the Father will in one and the same act, so the Son according to his deity never has to acquiesce to something the Father has already determined.

[148]This does not preclude arguments in favor of the impeccability of the Son (or a pneumatic "communication of graces" to the Son's humanity), but that is an issue for another time.

[149]Compare McCormack's critique of a "real" communication of human *idiomata* to the person and not to the other nature in "With Loud Cries and Tears," 43-44, 47.

[150]On which, see Lombard, *Sententiae* 3.5.2 (46); Polanus, *Syntagma* 6.16 (376); Turretin, *Inst.* 13.4.7-9 (2:331-32); Mastricht, *TPT* 2.24.9 (238); 5.4.5 (537); 9 (539); 15-16 (540-41); 23 (543-44).

constitutes the Father, Son, and Spirit as distinct persons is their proper modes of subsisting, I would submit that it is suitable to take up the scholastic expression that each person is distinct from the essence as a mode from that of which he is a mode.[151] Given the presence of such a distinction, the person of the Son is immediately incarnate, while the essence is mediately incarnate. Put differently, the divine essence is incarnate only as restricted in the person of the Son or under his proper mode of subsisting.[152]

That there is no immediate union of Godhead as such to the human nature of Christ corroborates the point that the mode of union in the incarnation is not essential but hypostatic or personal, which then corroborates the point that there is no need to posit a similarity between the two natures themselves. Barth's initial concern about a knowability of God apart from the incarnation need not keep us from affirming that God (or God the Son) is complete in himself without reference to the economy, and it need not keep us from saying that God wants us to have a knowledge of God *in se* that does not have the incarnation as its epistemological principle. After addressing this in chapter two and in the second section of this chapter ("Qualifying Christology's Role"), here I have now clarified that our belief in an eternal Son who is constituted as such without reference to the incarnation does not yield a "twofold Christ" (one with an antecedent Godhead and then another with a diminutive Godhead). For we need not accept Barth's premise that the divine nature and the human nature of the Son must have the sort of correspondence to one another that Barth envisions. It is sufficient that the Son by the power of his divine nature can assume a lowly human nature that is quite unlike his divine nature. If the union that takes place is not essential but hypostatic, the Son's divine transcendence of the union with his human nature and a proportionately robust affirmation of the *extra Calvinisticum* will not entail the existence of a double Christ.[153]

---

[151]So Johann Alsted, *Metaphysica* (Hebornae Nassoviorum, 1613), 1.29 (240); Turretin, *Inst*. 3.27.11 (1:307-8); 13.4.9 (2:332); Mastricht, *TPT* 2.24.9 (238).

[152]Barth himself operates with an understanding that it is not Godhead as such but the person who acts and lives in the human nature (*CD* IV/2, 65-66).

[153]As some of the early Reformed put it, the union in the incarnation is a "union of natures, but not natural," a "union not of persons, but personal" (see Turretin, *Inst*. 13.6.3 [2:337]; Mastricht, *TPT* 5.4.7 [538]). More could be said about some of the early modern debates between the Lutherans and the Reformed on the *extra*, but my goal here has been to address Barth's concerns in particular.

Second, having addressed what is, I think, the hinge on which Barth's approach ultimately turns, it is possible to offer a number of additional clarifications regarding why a more traditional understanding of God's aseity in relation to the decree does not yield a Nestorian Christology. I will, however, have to be briefer here. Among other things, as noted in chapter one (and discussed later in chapter five), the divine decree does not produce a new actuality of God or a new version of God. Instead, the divine decree involves just an application or direction of God's essential actuality to the establishment of the divine counsel and the eventual unfolding of history.[154] In addition, the approach taken here does not require any great investment in talk of an "immanent Trinity" and an "economic Trinity."[155] There is, after all, only one Trinity. Certain actions of this unique triune God have no *terminus ad quem* outside himself, while others do have a *terminus ad quem* outside himself (i.e., the creature).[156] The former, particularly the processions of the persons, are constitutive of the divine persons' respective identities and are necessary. The latter (e.g., creation, judgment, the divine missions) are nonconstitutive on God's side and are free. The latter require no new actuality on God's part, so there is no chance of God's outward actions producing two versions of the Trinity, one lacking (*per impossibile*) what the other would have. Divine action *ad extra* is just God's essence with a relation to the creature. In particular, as Thomas describes it, a divine mission is just the procession with the addition of a created, temporal *terminus ad quem* (e.g., the Son's human

---

[154]From a traditional Reformed perspective, it does not involve (as McCormack worries in "Processions and Missions," 108-9, 116) a "two-act drama" with a resultant new actuality and being of God other than his original actuality and being. See Steven J. Duby, "Election, Actuality and Divine Freedom: Thomas Aquinas, Bruce McCormack and Reformed Orthodoxy in Dialogue," *MT* 32 (2016): 325-40.

[155]For cautions regarding this manner of speaking, see Marshall, "Trinity" and "Unity of the Triune God"; Emery, "*Theologia* and *Dispensatio*," 557-61; Thomas Joseph White, "'Through Him All Things Were Made' (John 1:3): The Analogy of the Word Incarnate According to St. Thomas Aquinas and Its Ontological Presuppositions," in *The Analogy of Being: Invention of the Antichrist or the Wisdom of God?*, ed. Thomas Joseph White (Grand Rapids: Eerdmans, 2011), 252n7. A more positive assessment can be found in certain works of Emery ("Essentialism or Personalism in the Treatise on God in Saint Thomas Aquinas?," *The Thomist* 64 [2000]: 531; "The Personal Mode of Trinitarian Action in Saint Thomas Aquinas," *The Thomist* 69 [2005]: 66; *The Trinitarian Theology of St Thomas Aquinas*, trans. Francesca Aran Murphy [Oxford: Oxford University Press, 2007], 40-4) and in Fred Sanders, *The Triune God*, New Studies in Dogmatics (Grand Rapids: Zondervan, 2016), 144-53.

[156]Polanus is exemplary here (*Syntagma* 4.1-5 [236-38]).

nature).[157] Focusing our attention on these points without letting talk of an "immanent Trinity" and an "economic Trinity" predominate can help to circumvent potentially anxious discussion about how these two Trinities must relate to one another. It can obviate moves that would read features of the economy back into God's eternal triune life in order to secure a correspondence between an economic Trinity and an immanent Trinity. At the same time, taking the path of simply talking about what the Trinity does *ad intra* and what the Trinity does *ad extra* still invites us to see how the economy reflects the processions described in the Bible, where, for example, a person's mission and mode of acting in the economy expresses his eternally coming forth from another (e.g., Jn 5:16-30; Gal 4:4-6).[158]

As for the notion of the *extra Calvinisticum* itself, we should bear in mind, as Barth himself wished to do, that the *extra* does not stipulate a subsistence of the Son that is separate from his human nature. The Son does not withdraw from his humanity and certainly does not assign it to another *hypostasis*. In this sense, there is no longer a *Logos asarkos* that might live alongside a *Logos ensarkos*. The only Logos there is now subsists and forevermore will subsist as both God and man at the same time.[159] He is "no less true man than he is true God."[160] But the Logos does subsist in two eternally distinct natures. Thus he has (or is) one subsistence but with a "twofold *ratio* of subsisting."[161] That is, he subsists in the divine essence as the one generated by the Father and in the humanity that he has individuated with that humanity's accidents, its proper act of existing, and so forth. The divine essence in which he subsists cannot be circumscribed or contained under the local presence of his humanity. It always exceeds that humanity, and he in it exists and is present beyond the space in which he dwells in his

---

[157]Thomas, *ST* Ia.43.1 corp. and ad 1 (445); 43.2 corp. and ad 3 (446).

[158]I have fleshed out more thoughts on this in Duby, "Trinity and Economy."

[159]This point could be obscured if one speaks of two *divine* modes of subsisting on the part of the Logos (as in George Hunsinger, "Election and the Trinity: Twenty-Five Theses on the Theology of Karl Barth," *MT* 24 [2008]: 194). While I appreciate Hunsinger's arguments for the contingency of creation, his statements about the Trinity having two "forms" also seem to invite unnecessary questions about how these "forms" hold together (*Evangelical, Catholic, and Reformed: Doctrinal Essays on Barth and Related Themes* [Grand Rapids: Eerdmans, 2015], 21-22).

[160]Zanchi, *De incarnatione Filii Dei* 2.2 (82, 84).

[161]Polanus, *Syntagma* 6.16 (377); William Ames, *Medulla theologica*, 2nd ed. (Amsterdam, 1659), 1.18 (73).

humanity. Used and understood properly, the concept of the *extra* upholds the indissoluble union of the two natures in the one person of Christ while also reinforcing the need for Christian description of God in his transcendence of the economy.

Conclusion

In this chapter I have sought to give an account of the role of supernatural revelation and especially the incarnation in the practice of *theologia*. The first section took note of various statements from Barth and others on the decisiveness of the incarnation as an external cognitive principle for theology proper. I then went on to discuss that Holy Scripture is in fact the external cognitive principle for theology proper and how this requires us to qualify Christology's role in obtaining knowledge of God. The next section then treated Christology's positive contribution to the knowledge of God, emphasizing, among other things, that the incarnation is the culminating moment of supernatural revelation and actually underscores God's aseity and the need to ground God's economic activity in his preveniently complete being. After this, I examined the role of the Son in communicating knowledge of God even prior to his incarnation, as well as the role of the Son in the divine decree and the beatific vision. Finally, I considered a challenge from Barth regarding whether the affirmation of a divine identity of the Son that transcends the union with his human nature will yield a "twofold Christ" and an implicitly Nestorian Christology. I argued in response that Barth's underlying rationale is not compelling and that his concerns ought not to determine how we think of the relationship between Christology and theology proper. Yet some authors, considering approaches to the doctrine of God in which Christology's role is relativized, have described the kind of approach advocated here as "metaphysical" in a pejorative sense. The task of the next chapter is to consider whether this is so and how *theologia* relates to metaphysics.

FOUR

Theology and Metaphysics Revisited

S O FAR WE HAVE EXAMINED the scriptural rationale for the Christian practice of reasoning about God in himself and taken into consideration how both natural revelation and the supernatural revelation that culminates in Christ and is handed down in Scripture contribute to that task. Already in my exposition of Christology's place in theology proper we encountered certain claims that set a Christ-centered approach to God in opposition to a "metaphysical" approach.[1] The development of these claims in recent theology can be traced back to the work of figures like Albrecht Ritschl, Wilhelm Herrmann, and Hermann Cremer in the nineteenth and early twentieth centuries.[2] In the sense intended here, a metaphysical approach is often presented as a matter of mistakenly speaking about God by inferring from created being and its limitations what must be true of God, rather than beginning from the economy or the incarnation in particular. In some cases, "metaphysics" may be shorthand for any doctrine of God according to which God is complete in himself

---

[1]See, e.g., Thomas F. Torrance, *The Christian Doctrine of God: One Being, Three Persons* (Edinburgh: T&T Clark, 1996), 248; Eberhard Jüngel, *God as the Mystery of the World: On the Foundation of the Theology of the Crucified One in the Dispute Between Theism and Atheism*, trans. Darrell L. Guder (Grand Rapids: Eerdmans, 1983), 184, et passim; Wolf Krötke, *Gottes Klarheiten: Eine Neuinterpretation der Lehre von Gottes "Eigenschaften"* (Tübingen: Mohr Siebeck, 2001), 49-59, et passim; Bruce L. McCormack, "The Actuality of God: Karl Barth in Conversation with Open Theism," in *Engaging the Doctrine of God: Contemporary Protestant Perspectives*, ed. Bruce L. McCormack (Grand Rapids: Baker Academic, 2008), 188, 211-12.
[2]See Albrecht Ritschl, *Theology and Metaphysics*, in *Three Essays*, trans. Philip Hefner (Philadelphia: Fortress, 1972); Wilhelm Hermann, *Die Metaphysik und Theologie* (Halle: Max Niemeyer, 1876); Hermann Cremer, *Die christliche Lehre von den Eigenschaften Gottes*, 2nd ed. (Gütersloh: Bertelsmann, 1917).

without reference to the economy. In addition, questions about the relationship between metaphysics and the doctrine of God arise because various concepts from classical metaphysics ("being," "essence," "substance," and so on) have been incorporated in traditional descriptions of God *in se*.

In the previous chapter, I argued that we must begin with Scripture as the epistemological principle for the doctrine of God, a move that affords use of the Creator-creature distinction as a means of knowing God and does not require us to take the incarnation as the exclusive starting point for theological understanding. In this chapter, we will look more carefully at how some authors claim that the practice of *theologia* is a matter of doing "metaphysics" and a matter of compromising a distinctly Christian account of God. First, I will explore some of the criticisms of "metaphysical" accounts of God and focus on three main concerns that emerge (i.e., that it renders God merely a larger version of the creature, that it obstructs God's economic condescension and interaction with us, and that it creates a rift between God *in se* and God *pro nobis*). Second, in light of these criticisms, this chapter will examine what metaphysics really is according to some of its actual practitioners in history, including some of the older theologians whose views of God are sometimes taken to be "metaphysical." The result of this section will be the drawing of a firm distinction between metaphysics properly understood and the Christian practice of *theologia*. Third, having addressed the mistaken conflation of metaphysics and *theologia*, the next section will offer an account of theology proper's positive use of metaphysical concepts, which will enable me to finish addressing the first of the three aforementioned concerns (i.e., that a "metaphysical" theology proper collapses the Creator-creature distinction). Finally, the fourth section will address the latter two concerns about metaphysics by arguing that it is precisely the knowledge of God in his aseity that can help us to understand the freedom of God for economic action and the sameness of God *in se* and *pro nobis*.

Criticism of Metaphysics in Theology Proper

Recent concerns about the influence of metaphysics in theology proper are often connected to concerns about the natural knowledge of God. Key objections to natural theology—some of which involve claims made after David Hume and Immanuel Kant about the natural intellect's inability to know the external world and its causal structures—were addressed in chapter two. Elements of those objections come into play here, but for the most part I will consider other aspects of the criticism of metaphysics in theology proper. In such criticism, three significant concerns emerge. First, some authors argue that "metaphysical" reflection on God in his aseity and transcendence of the economy will jeopardize the Creator-creature distinction. For, the argument goes, God becomes simply a more exalted version of the creature positioned above the vicissitudes of the world.[3] Second, God is posited as the unchanging ground of created being and then is no longer free to humble himself and draw near to us in the economy and in the passion of the Son. Third, if metaphysics gives us a God in himself who cannot draw near to us or suffer for us, then there is an ontological rift between God *in se* and God *pro nobis*, which imperils the true Godhead of Christ and the efficacy of his saving work. Each of these concerns will now be fleshed out in turn.

First, there is the concern that in a metaphysical doctrine of God he will become simply a counterpart or correlate to created being. Though sympathetic to a number of themes in classical theism that are sometimes now deemed "metaphysical" (God's simplicity and God's transcendence of time, for example), Friedrich Schleiermacher criticizes the use of certain metaphysical language in his treatment of the person of Christ. Without explicitly labeling it a problem with "metaphysics," Schleiermacher emphasizes that the concept of "nature" introduces considerable confusion when applied to God. "Nature" denotes either "the aggregate of all finite existence" or "mutually conditioned" entities of the corporeal world. Accordingly, "nature" implies "some restricted being, which is engaged in some contrast." Talk of a "divine nature" in Christian dogmatics would therefore entail an "aggregate of modes of conduct or a body of laws according to which life circumstances not only change but are also contained within a distinct course

---

[3]In the words of Thomas Joseph White, there is a worry that God will become merely the "archetypal instantiation" of created beings (*Wisdom in the Face of Modernity: A Study in Thomistic Natural Theology*, 2nd ed., Faith and Reason: Studies in Catholic Theology and Philosophy [Ave Maria, FL: Sapientia, 2016], 23).

of life." In the incarnation, such a "nature" would compete and conflict with Christ's human nature in a manner that would compromise Christ's "unity of life."[4] Thus, in Schleiermacher's work, there is a worry about the language of a divine "nature" positioning God within the realm of finite being and, in turn, hindering proper description of the person of Christ.

Ritschl makes explicit reference to the problem of "metaphysics" and warns against the use of metaphysical concepts in describing God. For Ritschl, the use of metaphysical concepts is typically undertaken to harmonize divine revelation and Hellenistic philosophy. It is meant to demonstrate the universality of the Christian worldview, but in fact it "[diminishes] the value of the knowledge of God that we obtain from revelation." It reduces God to a correlate of created being and reverts Christian theology to a paganism that identifies God as something that "in the judgment of Christians properly belong[s] to the world."[5]

Barth too is wary of taking a generic notion of being as the starting point for the doctrine of God. His concern can be seen in his assessment of Philip Melanchthon, "the first dogmatician of the Evangelical Church." On the one hand, he chides Melanchthon for initially omitting the *locus de Deo* in his *Loci communes* and proceeding too quickly to the benefits of Christ without first considering God himself. After all, God is who he is even without his outward works. On the other hand, Barth also criticizes Melanchthon (along with the medieval scholastics and the Protestant orthodox) for later including a theology proper in the *Loci communes* that was built on a "doctrine of being" or "general idea of God."[6] For Barth, the problem is that a "common" and "neutral" concept of being that is filled in "arbitrarily" "with every conceivable superlative" and applied to God by "a sinner who of himself can only take wrong roads" will ultimately lead us away from the particular "concretion" of God's being in his trinitarian revelation.[7] This particularity compels Barth to criticize Thomas Aquinas's (putative) willingness to "fall back upon a concept of being which comprehends God and what is not God"

---

[4]Friedrich Schleiermacher, *The Christian Faith: A New Translation and Critical Edition*, trans. Terrence N. Tice, Catherine L. Kelsey, and Edwina Lawler, ed. Catherine L. Kelsey and Terrence N. Tice, 2 vols. (Louisville: Westminster John Knox, 2016), §96 (584-85); §97 (604-6).
[5]Ritschl, *Theology and Metaphysics*, 157-58, 170.
[6]Barth, *CD* II/1, 259-60.
[7]Barth, *CD* II/1, 260-62, 288, 329.

and to use this to explain God and his relationship to the created order. For Barth, there is no "master-concept" that includes both God and other beings and provides a foundation for theology proper: *Deus non est in genere*.[8] Positively, it is vital to recognize that God's being is "in act." His being is in act in his eternal triune life and in his revelation in time. It is a "specific act with a definite content," and this specificity is essential for a right understanding of God.[9]

A number of contemporary authors also voice the concern about metaphysics eliding the Creator-creature distinction. Jürgen Moltmann states that metaphysics involves finding a "support and stay" against the threats of suffering, death, and chaos. Because of the "religious need of finite, threatened and mortal man for security in a higher omnipotence and authority," metaphysics conceives of God "for the sake of finite being," having "all the determinations of finite being" and excluding "those determinations which are directed against being."[10] According to Bruce McCormack, classical Christian theism claims to "know what God is before a consideration of Christology" and develops a "metaphysical" account of God by examining created being and proceeding through a number of negations and analogies in the hope of eventually obtaining knowledge of God's being. For McCormack, however, this undertaking yields only statements about us creatures, not true knowledge of the God revealed in the incarnation.[11]

A second criticism of "metaphysical" portrayals of God is that they inhibit God's freedom to condescend to us in the economy, particularly in the incarnation. God is seen to be stuck, so to speak, in his inflexible transcendence and unable to act in new ways in the world and undergo suffering in the person of the Son. Isaak Dorner, for example, is critical of "the metaphysics of the old dogmatics" in which God is an "absolutely simple" pure act whose attributes can never be accidents but must all be really identical

---

[8]Barth, *CD* II/1, 310-12. Here Barth is also critical of Kant and any pantheistic or panentheistic attempts to place God and creatures in the same order under abstract concepts like freedom or immortality.

[9]Barth, *CD* II/1, 262-64, 272-74. For more on Barth and "metaphysics," see Kenneth Oakes, *Karl Barth on Theology and Philosophy* (Oxford: Oxford University Press, 2012), 37-39, 45, 53-54, 101-2, 130.

[10]Jürgen Moltmann, *The Crucified God: The Cross as the Foundation and Criticism of Theology*, trans. R. A. Wilson and John Bowden (Minneapolis: Fortress, 1993), 214.

[11]McCormack, "Actuality of God," 188, 211-12.

with his essence. According to Dorner, if this is the case, then God cannot will or do anything new. His causal power cannot be differentiated or applied in different ways to the various circumstances of the world. All change belongs on the side of the creature, which is disastrous for the doctrine of the incarnation. For this implies that God is not truly active and present in a special way in Christ. There could be only a special "receptivity" of Christ's human nature to the universal presence of God. For Dorner, though, given that God is indeed active in "the actual emergence of the new," there must be "change in his living self-exercise." In the incarnation, then, there is a change on God's side in the God-world relation. In fact, the incarnation is a "new being of God himself in the world, which previously existed according to potence or decree, and first achieves actuality in Christ." If it were otherwise, the incarnation would be merely a docetic phenomenon.[12]

Barth contrasts a notion of God derived by metaphysical "apotheosis" (considering our own "limits" and inferring from our "non-being" what God as "true being" must be) with the biblical notion of God. With the former, the aseity of God is parsed primarily in terms of independence, and the transcendence of God is regarded as "God's opposition to the reality distinct from Himself." But this yields a lopsided view of God's freedom, in which God's transcendence must be upheld by a diminishing of his immanence. In the biblical notion of God, however, his aseity is first a positive concept: God is "self-moved" or "self-determined." "Within the sphere of His own being He can live and love in absolute plenitude and power." The transcendence of God then means that he is free not just *from* external conditioning but also *for* "giving Himself" to fellowship with creatures: "Without sacrificing His distinction and freedom, but in the exercise of them, He enters into and faithfully maintains communion with this reality other than Himself in His activity as Creator, Reconciler and Redeemer." Again, God's freedom is "His freedom not merely to be in the differentiation of His being from [creation's] being, but to be in Himself the One who can have and hold communion with this reality (as in fact He does) in spite of His utter distinction from it."[13]

---

[12]Isaak A. Dorner, *Divine Immutability: A Critical Reconsideration*, trans. Robert R. Williams and Claude Welch (Minneapolis: Fortress, 1994), 101-2, 107-10, 123-29, 142-43, 145-47, 186-88.
[13]Barth, *CD* II/1, 301-4.

In line with his contention that metaphysics advocates a God removed from the realities of suffering and death, Moltmann reasons, "In the metaphysical concept of God . . . the being of the Godhead, of the origin of all things or the unmoved mover, as the zone of the impossibility of death, stands in juxtaposition to human beings as the zone of the necessity of death." "If this concept of God is applied to Christ's death on the cross, the cross *must* be 'evacuated' of its deity, for by definition God cannot suffer and die. . . . But Christian theology must think of God's being in suffering and dying and finally in the death of Jesus, if it is not to surrender itself and lose its identity." Because of this, the cross introduces "something new and strange" into the "metaphysical world." It positions itself as the true point of departure for understanding God's being. "God cannot suffer, God cannot die, says theism. . . . God suffered in the suffering of Jesus, God died on the cross of Christ, says Christian faith." The cross therefore "effects liberation" from the metaphysical practice of projecting human needs onto a "divinized father-figure."[14]

While generally more optimistic about theology's engagement with metaphysics, Wolfhart Pannenberg thinks that not all Christian theologians in the history of the church have carried out the necessary "critical revision" of Hellenistic philosophy. Taking God to be the metaphysical "world principle" conflicts with God's being the "free Lord of history." Since God acts in new ways in the contingent events of the world, he can "assume properties into his eternal essence through such deeds in that he chooses these and no other events as the form of his contingent operation."[15] According to Pannenberg, this has been undermined by a concept of divine immutability learned from Greek philosophy. For such a concept locates God outside of time and excludes the possibility of divine faithfulness within the history of the world. Indeed, it renders the incarnation meaningless for God: "Whether this event takes place or not makes no difference so far as he is concerned. He could not be affected by the passion of the Son."[16] Finally, Eberhard Jüngel argues

---

[14]Moltmann, *Crucified God*, 214-16.

[15]Wolfhart Pannenberg, "The Appropriation of the Philosophical Concept of God as a Dogmatic Problem of Early Christian Theology," in *Basic Questions in Theology: Collect Essays*, trans. George H. Kehm (Philadelphia: Fortress, 1971), 2:179-83.

[16]Wolfhart Pannenberg, *Systematic Theology*, trans. Geoffrey Bromiley (Grand Rapids: Eerdmans, 1991), 1:436-38.

that classical Christian theism is plagued by a metaphysical conception of God that describes God as pure act and wrongly removes all potency from God's being. The notions of absoluteness, immutability, and apathy are "unsuitable axioms for the Christian concept of God" and must be exchanged for a doctrine of God informed by the incarnation. So emphatic is Jüngel that the metaphysical notion of an absolute God should not blind us to God acting and suffering in Christ that Jüngel identifies God's essence as God's (historical) existence in the sense that God's essence is constituted by the work of Christ.[17]

A third related concern about the doctrine of God taking a metaphysical form is that it leads to an ontological gap or opposition between God *in se* and God *pro nobis*, which, if present, would of course raise questions about the genuineness of our knowledge of God. If the metaphysical God *in se* cannot condescend to us and suffer in the incarnation, then it would appear that Christ, who has indeed humbled himself in the incarnation and even suffered death for us, is other and less than what God originally and eternally is in himself. As I have noted previously, elements of this line of thought can be found in Barth and are developed by Robert Jenson and McCormack.

Barth holds that God is who he is without his outward works, but he still draws attention to the danger of a "cleavage" between God's being and his revelation. Sometimes Barth addresses the problem of evacuating God's essence of its richness and assigning the glory of God's various attributes to the economy alone.[18] He also addresses the opposite problem, namely, ascribing the fullness of God to his eternal essence alone and removing that fullness from God's economic activity and presence. Barth insists that God does not deny or lose what he eternally is when the Son assumes a human nature. God will countenance no "gulf in God himself, between His being and essence in Himself and His activity and work as the Reconciler of the world created by Him." That sort of "gulf" would entail that God would "give Himself away" in the incarnation. If God had done that, "how could he reconcile the world with Himself? Of what value would His deity be to us if—instead of crossing in that deity the very real gulf between Himself and us—He left that deity behind Him in His coming to us, if it came to be

---

[17]Jüngel, *God as the Mystery of the World*, 100-101, 191-92, 209, 213-14, 217, 371, 373.
[18]Barth, CD II/1, 324-25, 329.

outside of Him as He became ours?" Therefore, instead of presupposing that God must deny or impoverish himself to enter the weakness of the human condition in Christ, we must submit to his revelation in Christ and recognize that it is "within his nature" to do exactly that.[19]

In their own distinct ways, Jenson and McCormack also emphasize that God's condescension and economic activity must correspond to what he is in himself and argue that this correspondence is undermined by metaphysical speculation. Jenson speaks of what he calls "the old dissonance between the metaphysical principles of the Greeks and the storytelling of the gospel" and suggests that, on the metaphysical conception of God, there can be no "temporal contamination of God himself."[20] Integral to "pagan antiquity's metaphysical prejudice" is the teaching of divine impassibility ("immunity to suffering and temporal contingency in general").[21] This places God's essence in conflict with his economic condescension and, in turn, compromises our knowledge of God. For Jenson, the essence-economy discrepancy means that God is not authentically present in his revelatory action, which is a problem that must be overcome by rethinking the way in which God's being is determined by his acts in history. According to Jenson, it is not just that God must be identified *by* events in history (e.g., the exodus or the resurrection) but that he must be identified *with* those events, lest the cleft between God *in se* and God *pro nobis* require us to impose our "idolatrous projections" on God *in se* if we are to claim any knowledge of his being.[22] God is constituted by the "dramatic coherence" of his action in history. "The biblical God is not eternally himself in that he persistently instantiates a beginning in which he already is all he ever will be; he is eternally himself in that he unrestrictedly anticipates an end in which he will be all he ever could be."[23] Formerly, Jenson thought that "God could have been himself on different terms" (though we could never know *how* God would have been God in that case),[24] but more recently he has written that even

---

[19]Barth, *CD* IV/1, 184-86.

[20]Robert W. Jenson, *Systematic Theology*, vol. 1, *The Triune God* (Oxford: Oxford University Press, 1997), 112.

[21]Jenson, *Systematic Theology*, 1:95, 103, 107, 234.

[22]Jenson, *Systematic Theology*, 1:59.

[23]Jenson, *Systematic Theology*, 1:66.

[24]Jenson, *Systematic Theology*, 1:65.

raising the contrafactual question wrongly assumes that God cannot be constituted by future events.[25]

Taking a different approach, McCormack believes that God the Son himself (and, in McCormack's logic, therefore God the Son *as God*) must suffer on the cross to secure the efficacy of the atonement.[26] The being of God in the incarnation thus undergoes suffering, which, if suffering were not originally included in God's being, would entail an alteration and diminution of God's being in the Son's incarnation and passion. In light of this, for McCormack, the being of God is constituted in (and is not in any way prior to) God's eternal decision for the incarnation and anticipatively includes the suffering of Christ, ensuring the sameness of God's being *in se* and *pro nobis* and, therefore, the full deity of Christ. McCormack argues that, by contrast, a "metaphysical" approach to theology proper, in which there is a God *in se* whose essence is constituted without respect to the incarnation, leaves a "metaphysical gap" between God *in se* and God *pro nobis* and weakens the church's affirmation of Christ's deity.[27]

To sum up, there are three significant concerns here: (1) that claiming to know God *in se* by drawing inferences from a general concept of "being" collapses the Creator-creature distinction; (2) that metaphysical reasoning robs God of his freedom to condescend to us in the economy and especially in the incarnation; and (3) that metaphysical reasoning leaves us with a discrepancy between God in himself and God for us, undermining our knowledge of God and the efficacy of Christ's saving work. In the next

---

[25]Robert W. Jenson, "Once More the *Logos Asarkos*," *IJST* 13 (2011): 131.

[26]See, e.g., Bruce L. McCormack, "'With Loud Cries and Tears': The Humanity of the Son in the Epistle to the Hebrews," in *The Epistle to the Hebrews and Christian Theology*, ed. Richard Bauckham et al. (Grand Rapids: Eerdmans, 2009), 43-44, 47, 50-51; McCormack, "The Only Mediator: The Person and Work of Christ in Evangelical Perspective," in *Renewing the Evangelical Mission*, ed. Richard Lints (Grand Rapids: Eerdmans, 2013), 262-64.

[27]Bruce L. McCormack, "Seek God Where He May Be Found: A Response to Edwin Chr. van Driel," *SJT* 60 (2007): 68; McCormack, "Election and the Trinity: Theses in Response to George Hunsinger," *SJT* 63 (2010): 208, 210; McCormack, "The Lord and Giver of Life: A 'Barthian' Defense of the *Filioque*," in *Rethinking Trinitarian Theology: Disputed Questions and Contemporary Issues in Trinitarian Theology*, ed. Robert J. Wozniak and Giulio Maspero (London: T&T Clark, 2012), 231; McCormack, "Processions and Missions: A Point of Convergence Between Thomas Aquinas and Karl Barth," in *Thomas Aquinas and Karl Barth: An Unofficial Catholic-Protestant Dialogue*, ed. Bruce L. McCormack and Thomas Joseph White (Grand Rapids: Eerdmans, 2013), 115-16.

sections of this chapter, I will outline a rather different view of the place of metaphysics in the work of knowing and speaking of God in himself, which will in turn enable us to respond to these objections. I continue by exploring how some actual Christian practitioners of metaphysics through church history have conceived of its subject matter and its relationship to theology. This survey will begin to help us grasp the distinction (and relationship) between metaphysics and *theologia*.

THE SUBJECT OF METAPHYSICS:
ARISTOTLE TO THE EARLY MODERN PERIOD

While the fathers and medieval doctors of the church interact with a range of non-Christian philosophers and certainly cannot all be characterized as devout Aristotelians, they pay significant attention to the metaphysical grammar set forth by Aristotle. "The Philosopher" offers a taxonomy of ten kinds or modes of being in the *Categories* (substance, quantity, quality, and so on) and in the *Metaphysics* gives an account of that science which treats being qua being (τὸ ὄν ᾗ τὸ ὄν). In this work Aristotle makes clear that it is the task of metaphysics to describe being and whatever properly pertains to it as such. From another angle, metaphysics investigates principles and causes, which must pertain to something not just accidentally but according to itself (μὴ κατὰ συμβεβηκὸς ἀλλ᾽ ᾗ ὄν), and that is being.[28] Being concerns "substance" (οὐσία) fundamentally and concerns other things (accidents, genus and species, whole and part, for example) only with some reference to substance.[29] Later in his *Metaphysics*, Aristotle develops the argument that, in view of what he takes to be the eternal motion of the world, some substance must exist that is the eternal, immutable, active cause of this motion. This substance is immaterial (matter is susceptible to change) and is identified as God.[30] Thus metaphysics or "first philosophy," categorized

---

[28]Aristotle, *Aristotelis Metaphysica*, ed. W. Jaeger, Oxford Classic Texts (Oxford: Clarendon, 1957), 4.1003a (59).

[29]Aristotle, *Metaphysica* 4.1003b-1005a (60-64); 5.1017a-1017b (98-100). Aristotle famously identified two predominant meanings of the word "substance": (1) a subject (ὑποκείμενον) that cannot be predicated of another and (2) a "such-something" (τόδε τι) that is "separable" and is the form (μορφή, εἶδος) of a substance in the first sense.

[30]Aristotle, *Metaphysica* 12.1071b-1073a (249-54). While making the argument for the first mover, Aristotle identifies three kinds of substances: the sensible and eternal, the sensible and destructible, and finally, the unmoved divine substance (12.1069a [243]).

as a theoretical science alongside physics and mathematics, can be construed as theology insofar as the first substance or deity is the ground of all other substances.[31]

On the one hand, Aristotle does recognize differences between the unmoved, purely actual divine substance and other, moved substances. Indeed, Thomas Aquinas (whether too optimistically cannot be decided here) is prepared to attribute to Aristotle a doctrine of creation in which God is the universal efficient cause of the existence (*esse*) of all things and, by implication, is uniquely his own *esse*.[32] Yet, on the other hand, given that Aristotle holds to the idea of an eternal universe while Christianity affirms the doctrine of *creatio ex nihilo*, Christian theology draws a sharper and more forceful distinction between God and the world of created, contingent being.[33] Though not speaking with regard to Aristotle in particular, Athanasius captures the point well in commenting that it is a "Greek" or "Gentile" thought (Ἑλληνικὸν τὸ φρόνημα) rather than a Christian one that God might merely shape eternally coexistent matter to fashion the world rather than make the world out of nothing.[34] The God of Holy Scripture, Athanasius insists, is not part of a greater whole or the whole universe itself but

---

[31] Aristotle, *Metaphysica* 6.1026a (122-23).

[32] See Thomas Aquinas, *De potentia*, in *Quaestiones disputatae*, vol. 2, ed. P. M. Pession, 10th ed. (Rome-Turin: Marietti, 1965), 3.5 corp. (49); *De substantiis separatis*, in *Opera omnia*, vol. 40/D-E, Leonine ed. (Rome: ad Sanctae Sabinae, 1968), 9 (57). In this connection, White emphasizes that Thomas's development of the distinction between essence and *esse* is an unfolding of Aristotle's own understanding of the divine. In White's estimation, an interpreter of Thomas like Etienne Gilson exaggerates the discontinuity between Thomas and Aristotle on the distinction between essence and existence (*Wisdom in the Face of Modernity*, 124-29).

[33] As Thomas himself points out, the recognition that the universe is not eternal highlights that God did not act with a "necessity of nature" in creating it (*SCG* 2.38 [356]). In my view, whatever Aristotle may have thought about the world's ontological dependence on God, Thomas and other Christian theologians go beyond Aristotle in clearly setting forth the radical contingency of creation through developing the distinction between essence and *esse* with the concepts of act and potency (cf. Rudi te Velde, *Aquinas on God: The "Divine Science" of the "Summa Theologiae"* (repr., New York: Routledge, 2016), 88-89; White, *Wisdom in the Face of Modernity*, 34, 76, 81-83, 124-28, 226-27n51). To borrow the language of Robert Sokolowski, Christian thought emphasizes that the distinction between God and the world is not a distinction within a greater "whole." It is rather a distinction between God and the "whole" itself as one distinct term (*God of Faith and Reason: Foundations of Christian Theology* [Washington, DC: Catholic University of America Press, 1995], 41-46; cf. Gregory Rocca, *Speaking the Incomprehensible God: Thomas Aquinas on the Interplay of Positive and Negative Theology* [Washington, DC: Catholic University of America Press, 2004], 218-20, 224-31).

[34] Athanasius, *Oratio II contra Arianos*, in *Athanasius Werke*, vol. I/1.2, *Oratio I et II contra Arianos*, ed. Karin Metzler and Kyriakos Savvidis (Berlin: de Gruyter, 1998), 22 (198).

instead transcends the whole as "the Maker of the constitution of all things."[35] In the work of various Christian theologians this emphasis comes through in reservation about calling God a "substance"—even after the Nicene invocation of "substance" terminology (οὐσία, ὑπόστασις)—and in related clarifications about the relationship between God and metaphysics.

Augustine, for example, remarks that *substantia* is a word properly applied to things that function as subjects in which other things exist. *Substantia* indicates something that "subsists" under accidents and is composite and changeable. With God, however, it is "wickedness" to say that his *substantia* (or, preferably, his *essentia*) is other than his goodness, for example, as though his goodness were merely a quality added to his essence. For, with God, to be is the same as to be good, omnipotent, and so on. For he is the one who truly and immutability is: *Ego sum qui sum* (Ex 3:14). Therefore, *essentia* (a word derived from *esse*) is more suited to God than *substantia*. According to Augustine, if *substantia* is applied to God, it can be done only "improperly" (*abusive*).[36]

Later in the patristic period, Boethius reiterates Aristotle's threefold division of the theoretical sciences (physics, mathematics, and theology), joining metaphysics and theology as the study of that which is separable from both motion and matter.[37] Yet Boethius also asserts that when any categories of being are used in "divine predication," "all are changed." The category of substance would be the most likely candidate for locating God within an inventory of being, but, Boethius states, substance in God's case "is not truly substance but beyond substance" (*ultra substantiam*).[38] In *De Trinitate*, Boethius fleshes out this claim by way of the teaching of divine simplicity. Other substances are composed of parts and depend on those parts (particularly matter and form), but God is without matter and, indeed, is his own form or essence. Insofar as matter is required to enable the accrual

---

[35] Athanasius, *Contra Gentes*, in *Contra Gentes and De incarnatione*, ed. and trans. Robert W. Thomson (Oxford: Clarendon, 1971), 28 (76).

[36] Augustine, *De Trinitate, libri XV*, ed. W. J. Mountain, 2 vols., CCSL 50-50A (Turnhout: Brepols, 1968), 7.4 (1:260). Given recent aversion to the purported prevalence of "substance" metaphysics in older theology proper, Augustine's words might be unexpected for some.

[37] Boethius, *De Trinitate*, in *The Theological Tractates. The Consolation of Philosophy*, trans. H. F. Steward, E. K. Rand, and S. J. Tester, LCL 74 (Cambridge, MA: Harvard University Press, 1973), 2 (9).

[38] Boethius, *De Trinitate* 4 (16).

of accidents, God is also without accidents, distinguishing him all the more from created substances.[39] Boethius's description here does not fully distinguish God from what are called "separate" substances (substances separate from matter, like angels) since these also are without matter and materially grounded accidents. Yet a little later Boethius does mention that substances ordinarily have the sort of accidents that clearly are immaterial. While substances can have the quality of justice, for example, God does not possess such as an accident. With God it is not one thing to be and another to be just: "God himself is the same as what is just."[40] Indeed, in another work, Boethius writes that a being or substance (*id quod est*) is different from its existence (*esse*) and, in order to be, must participate in the God who in fact is *ipsum esse* and *ipsum bonum* (being itself and the good itself).[41]

Toward the end of the patristic period, John of Damascus also underscores the Creator-creature distinction while speaking about the concepts of being (τὸ ὄν) and substance or essence (οὐσία). According to John, being can be distinguished into substance (οὐσία) and accident (συμβεβηκός). The former he takes to be a "self-subsisting thing not needing another for constitution." As self-subsisting, such a thing does not have its existence in another or through another. It is, rather, the subject of those things that must inhere in another in order to exist (accidents).[42] Though the self-subsisting character of οὐσία might give the impression that it is a promising designation for God, John thinks otherwise. He writes that God is not one of the common beings (τῶν ὄντων) that exist. To be clear, this is not to say that God does not exist (οὐκ ὡς μὴ ὤν) but rather that he is above all beings and even above (finite) existence itself (αὐτόδε τὸ εἶναι).[43] Thus God is above substance or "super-essential" (ὑπερούσιος). This is not an illogical claim

---

[39]Boethius, *De Trinitate* 2-3 (8-13).

[40]Boethius, *De Trinitate* 4 (18). Cf. *Contra Eutychen et Nestorium* (in *Theological Tractactes. Consolation of Philosophy*, 90-92), where Boethius articulates that God is not a substance as if he were a subject of other things, though he is the *principium* of other things and gives them subsistence.

[41]Boethius, *Quomodo substantiae in eo quod sint bonae sint cum non sint subtantialia bona*, in *Theological Tractactes. Consolation of Philosophy*, 40-48. In this treatise (also known as *De hebdomadibus*), Boethius is contending that while substances are good by virtue of their very existence, their existence is still different from the underived existence of the first good (God).

[42]John of Damascus, *Dialectica*, in *Die Schriften des Johannes von Damaskos*, vol. 1, ed. P. Bonifatius Kotter (Berlin: de Gruyter, 1969), fus. μ´ (106); μη´ (110).

[43]John of Damascus, *Exp. fid.* 1.4 (13).

that God exists and in the same sense does not exist. It is to say that God himself is "essence itself" (αὐτοουσία), who does not have a derivative, limited existence but is the absolute "fount of existence" for created being.[44]

In the great medieval textbook the *Sentences*, Peter Lombard echoes patristic analysis of the word *substance*. He quotes at length the material from Augustine examined above to reject the notion that *substance* can be in any proper sense applied to God. Drawing from Augustine, Lombard also says that the other categories or *praedicamenta* (quantity, quality, place, and the rest) "do not convene with the nature of God, which is subject to no accidents."[45] While God's essence can be said to "have" many attributes, "there is nothing in [the divine essence] that is not [the essence] itself." "The same is the thing having and what is had" (*idem est habens et quod habetur*).[46]

Thomas develops a more detailed account of the relationship between metaphysics and theology in dialogue with Aristotle and Boethius. He and other medieval scholastics also interact with the Muslim philosophers Avicenna (980–1037), who maintained that the subject of metaphysics is being (without excluding God from the field of being), and Averroes (1126–1198), who argued that the subject of metaphysics is the genus of separate substances, especially God as the first substance, who can be included in the subject matter of metaphysics because his existence is already demonstrated by the discipline of physics.[47]

When Thomas introduces his commentary on Aristotle's *Metaphysics*, he writes in the prologue that there must be some science or division of knowledge that is "most intellectual" and governs other sciences. According to Thomas, this science will be supremely "intellectual" with regard to (1) the

---

[44]John of Damascus, *Exp. fid.* 1.8 (18). That this does not entail a depersonalization of the biblical God is evident in that John still emphasizes that God is the one who knows, sustains, and oversees all things.

[45]Peter Lombard, *Sententiae in IV libris distinctae*, 3rd ed., Spicilegium Bonaventurianum 4B (Rome: Grottaferrata, 1971), 1.8.6-7 (100-101).

[46]Lombard, *Sententiae* 1.8.8.1 (101).

[47]For an excellent account of Thomas's view with comments on Avicenna and Averroes, see John F. Wippel, *The Metaphysical Thought of St. Thomas Aquinas: From Finite Being to Uncreated Being* (Washington, DC: Catholic University of America Press, 2000), chap. 1. On Avicenna and Averroes, see Albert Zimmermann, *Ontologie oder Metaphysik? Die Diskussion über den Gegenstand der Metaphysik im 13. und 14. Jahrhundert* (Leiden-Köln: Brill, 1965), 108-16; Daniel De Haan, "The Doctrine of the Analogy of Being in Avicenna's *Metaphysics of the Healing*," *Review of Metaphysics* 69 (2015): 261-86.

"order of knowing" since it will consider that which yields the greatest certainty for the intellect (causes, especially first causes); (2) the objects toward
which it is directed since it will concentrate not on what the senses apprehend but on what the intellect properly discovers (i.e., universals, especially "being and the things that follow being," like one and many, potency
and act); and (3) the proportion between the immaterial operation of the
intellect and the objects of the science, since these objects will be separate
from all "sensible matter" not just in the human mind (*secundum rationem*)
like mathematical concepts but also in reality (*secundum esse*) like God and
the separate substances.[48] These three marks of the supremely intellectual
science need not be distributed to three different sciences but are in fact all
gathered up into the discipline of metaphysics. For the subject of metaphysics is *ens commune* (common being), which is able to exist without
matter. Moreover, because any science considers not only its subject (viewed
as a genus) but also the causes of its subject, and because the subject of
metaphysics (*ens*) is caused by the separate substances, metaphysics
considers things that are essentially immaterial and are the first and universal causes of all things.[49] On this Aristotelian account, metaphysics can
therefore be called divine science or *theologia* insofar as it also considers
separate substances. However, Thomas states that *ens commune* is metaphysics' only proper subject, while knowledge of the causes of *ens commune*
is metaphysics' "end."[50]

---

[48]Thomas Aquinas, *In duodecim libros Metaphysicorum Aristotelis expositio*, ed. M.-R. Cathala and
Raymund M. Spiazzi (Turin-Rome: Marietti, 1950), prooemium (1).

[49]Thomas, *In Metaphysicorum*, prooemium (1-2). For Aristotle, the causality of the separate substances is final: as good and desirable, they elicit the motion of the universe (*Metaphysica* 12.1072a-b [251-53]). While Aristotle posits a first unmoved mover, he envisions a
number of subsequent unmoved movers as well (see Joseph Owens, *The Doctrine of Being in the
Aristotelian Metaphysics: A Study in the Greek Background of Mediaeval Thought* [Toronto: Pontifical Institute of Mediaeval Studies, 1951], 442-54). In the prologue to his commentary on the
Metaphysics, Thomas chooses not to critique Aristotle on this point. However, as Owens
comments, Thomas himself of course differs from Aristotle in his view of God and the origin of
the universe because Thomas is "conditioned by the reading of the sacred Scriptures" that present God as the first and decisive efficient cause who "bestows existence" on all things ("Aristotle
and Aquinas," in *The Cambridge Companion to Aquinas*, ed. Norman Kretzmann and Eleonore
Stump [Cambridge: Cambridge University Press, 1993], 45-46).

[50]Thomas, *In Metaphysicorum*, prooemium (2). Thomas confirms elsewhere that "first philosophy"
has a common object (*ens secundum quod est omnibus commune*) but considers a special aspect
(*ratio*) of it, namely, that it does not depend on matter or motion (*Scriptum super Sententiis*,
ed. Maria Fabianus Moos [Paris, 1933], 3.27.2.4, sol. 2 [3:886-87]; cf. *SCG* 2.37 [354]).

The extent to which Thomas would include God in metaphysical inquiry is made clearer in his commentary on Boethius's *De Trinitate*. Given Boethius's Aristotelian reiteration of the threefold division of the theoretical sciences, Thomas takes up the question of whether "divine science" genuinely treats things that are separate from matter and motion. While his answer to this particular question has its importance, it is more relevant to our task that this query leads Thomas to pause and distinguish between two kinds of "divine science." A given science, according to Thomas, will treat both its subject (taken as a genus) and the principles of its subject. However, there are two different sorts of principles. On the one hand, some are distinct natures or entities in their own right (*completae naturae, res in se ipsis*), while also serving as principles of other things, like "simple bodies" are principles of "complex bodies." On the other hand, some principles are not complete *in se* and are only principles of other things, like form and matter are principles of a corporeal substance. Principles of the former sort must be studied not just in the science in which they are principles but also in a distinct science of their own.[51] Significantly, it is in this former sense that God is a principle of the subject of metaphysics (*ens*). Metaphysics may therefore be called "divine science" not because it gives direct or adequate description of God but only because God is the cause of its subject.[52] Though he does not expressly characterize metaphysics as a form of "natural theology" here, Thomas does invoke Romans 1:20 to point out that visible things make known the "invisible things of God." Yet the knowledge of God available to the philosophers does not set forth God as he is in himself (*res divinae secundum quod in se ipsis subsistunt*) or apart from a causal analysis of created being. Such is the prerogative of the theology "passed down in sacred Scripture," according to God's revelation by the Spirit, who knows the deep things of God (1 Cor 2:10-12).[53]

A different approach to the question of God and metaphysics can be found in the works of John Duns Scotus and Francisco Suárez. Scotus

---

[51]Thomas, *De Trin.* 5.4 (153).

[52]Thomas notes that philosophers have taken not only God but also other separate substances or "intelligences," which Thomas identifies as angels, to be the principles of common being (*De Trin.* 5.4 ad 3 [155]). By contrast, on the logic of Thomas's teaching, separate substances are in fact included within common being (see Robert Sokolowski, "The Science of Being as Being in Aristotle, Aquinas, and Wippel," in *The Science of Being as Being: Metaphysical Investigations*, ed. Gregory T. Doolan [Washington, DC: Catholic University of America Press, 2011], 21-29).

[53]Thomas, *De Trin.* 5.4 (154).

engages Avicenna and Averroes at length in his *Questions on the Metaphysics of Aristotle* as he discusses the subject of metaphysics.[54] He prefers Avicenna's view of the subject of metaphysics to Averroes's view, not least because physics, Scotus says, can establish God only as first mover (not first being) and because the field of separate substances lacks the unity requisite for the subject of a science.[55] Without committing himself to the position, Scotus is willing to suggest some ways in which God might still be considered the subject of metaphysics.[56] However, according to Scotus, like the notion of God as first mover in physics, the notion of God as first being in metaphysics still does not disclose God's essence or "quiddity" as such. Metaphysics can therefore describe God only *per accidens*.[57]

Like Thomas, Scotus sheds more light on his own position in his theological writing. First, God "in particular and properly" is not known naturally or apart from supernatural revelation by the intellect of the "pilgrim" (*viator*). That is, God is not known "naturally . . . under the aspect of this essence as this and in itself" (*sub ratione huius essentiae ut haec et in se*).[58] Therefore, God "under the proper aspect [*ratio*] of deity" and per se is the object of the theology of supernatural revelation alone. Thus God is not the subject of metaphysics.[59] Second, however, while no "simply simple" concept of God (one that is not composite and does not reduce to other concepts) is naturally present in the pilgrim intellect, the concept of *ens* may be modified and joined to other concepts (e.g., "necessary being" or "highest being") to yield a complex concept of God proper to or distinctly pertaining

---

[54]On Scotus's view, see, e.g., Joseph Owens, "Up to What Point Is God Included in the Metaphysics of Duns Scotus?," *Mediaeval Studies* 10 (1948): 163-77; Zimmerman, *Ontologie oder Metaphysik*, 271-74; Peter King, "Scotus on Metaphysics," in *The Cambridge Companion to Duns Scotus*, ed. Thomas Williams (Cambridge: Cambridge University Press, 2002), 16-18.

[55]Duns Scotus, *Opera philosophica*, vols. 3-4, *Quaestiones super libros Metaphysicorum Aristotelis*, ed. R. Andrews et al. (St. Bonaventure: St. Bonaventure University, 1997), 6.4, nn. 6-12, (4:86-88); cf. 1.1, n. 145 (3:65-66); n. 163 (3:71-72).

[56]See Duns Scotus, *Metaphysicorum* 1.1, nn. 25-26 (3:25); n. 32 (3:28); nn. 131-36 (3:60-63); n. 153 (3:68); n. 160 (3:71).

[57]Duns Scotus, *Metaphysicorum* 1.1, n. 163 (3:71-72).

[58]John Duns Scotus, *Opera omnia*, vols. 1-4, *Ordinatio*, ed. P. Carolo Balić (Vatican City: Typis Polyglottis Vaticanis, 1950–1956), 1.3.1, ad q. 1, nn. 56-57 (3:38-39). Scotus comments that while God can create in our intellect a proper concept of God, contemplation of creatures cannot do this (*The Examined Report of the Paris Lecture: Reportatio I-A*, trans. Allan B. Wolter and Oleg V. Bychkov [St. Bonaventure: St. Bonaventure University, 2004], 1.3.1, ad q. 3, n. 43 [196-97]).

[59]Scotus, *Reportatio I-A*, prol., q. 1, a. 4, nn. 110-16 (41-44); q. 3, a. 1, n. 218 (76-77).

to God (though not one that expresses his deity as such).[60] *Ens*, in Scotus's estimation, is a univocal concept equally applicable to both the creature and God.[61] In itself, the concept of being contains no built-in differentiation between the creature and God and is differentiated only when joined to additional concepts. Consideration of *ens* can thus include God as "infinite being," which then means that the subject matter of metaphysics ultimately includes God.[62]

Writing after the dawn of the Reformation, the Roman Catholic philosopher Francisco Suárez considers the opinions of various authors on the subject ("object," in his language) of metaphysics, including Avicenna, Averroes, and Thomas, with the aim of ensuring that nothing is wrongly excluded from or included in this science.[63] Suárez is critical of Averroes and does not believe that God alone can be the object of metaphysics, for metaphysics has historically treated other things too. Furthermore, metaphysics cannot attain to God as he is in himself, since it proceeds "by natural discourse" (rather than divine revelation) and attains to God just "insofar as he is able to be manifested from creatures by the light of nature." Indeed, no "natural science" can contain God as its "adequate object," for it could grasp God only under a *ratio* he would have in common with creatures. Thus God

[60]Scotus, *Reportatio I-A*, 1.3.1, ad q. 3, nn. 45-46 (197).

[61]Scotus's view of the univocity of being will be considered in the next chapter.

[62]Scotus, *Ordinatio*, 1.3.1, ad q. 1, nn. 26-55 (3:18-38); *Reportatio I-A*, 1.3.1.2, nn. 28-40 (193-96). Scotus's discussion of God as infinite being contains an apparent tension. On the one hand, while the subject or object of theology is God under the aspect of his essence, this pertains strictly to *theologia in se* (the knowledge of God possessed by God himself) rather than *theologia nostra* (knowledge of God accommodated to the capacity of our intellect). The object of *theologia nostra* is God as infinite being, the most perfect concept of God possible for us in this life. On the other hand, the subject of metaphysics also includes God as infinite being. It seems, then, that the concept of God as infinite being in *theologia nostra* encompasses more fully all that God is (e.g., that he is triune) and is in an important sense more suitably called a knowledge of God as God. By contrast, the concept of God as infinite being in metaphysics is less particular. To be sure, it is not indicative of a mere extrinsic relation God has; it does signify God absolutely. Yet, *ens infinitum* does not express God's quiddity or even the fullness of *ens infinitum* in *theologia nostra* and thus remains in one sense a *per accidens* concept of God derived from contemplation of creatures. See Scotus, *Opera omnia*, vol. 16, *Lectura in librum primum Sententiarum*, ed. P. Carolo Balić (Vatican City: Typis Polyglottis Vaticanis, 1960), prol., pars 2, ad qq. 1 and 2, nn. 71-88 (27-32); *Ordinatio*, prol., pars 3, ad q. 1, nn. 168 (1:190); 1.3.1, ad q. 1, n. 25 (3:16-17); nn. 58-60 (3:40-42). On this tension in Scotus's thinking, see Owens, "Up to What Point?," 171-72.

[63]Francisco Suárez, *Opera Omnia*, vol. 25, *Disputationes metaphysicae* (Paris: Vivès, 1861), 1.1.1 (2). For an overview of Suárez's approach to metaphysics, see Rolf Darge, "Suárez on the Subject of Metaphysics," in *A Companion to Francisco Suárez*, ed. Victor M. Salas and Robert L. Fastiggi (Leiden: Brill, 2014), 91-123.

cannot be the "adequate" object of this science, though this is not to say that he cannot be the first or special object of it.[64] Suárez therefore agrees with Avicenna, Thomas, and others that being (*ens in quantum ens reale*) is the "adequate" object of metaphysics, but he also argues that this object "ought to comprehend God." In Suárez's view, this is possible because one can consider God and the creature together under a common *ratio*. In God's own being (*in suo esse, et secundum se*) he is more distinct from creatures than any creatures are distinct from one another, but, in those things manifested of God by creatures, he has a greater "proportion and agreement" with creatures than some creatures have among themselves. However, Suárez emphasizes, this does not mean that there must be some entity or *ratio entis* that would be "prior in nature to God" and would in reality encompass both him and the creature. Rather, there is just something (*ens* in this case) that is prior to God "according to abstraction or the consideration of the intellect." That is, by virtue of a certain "imperfect similitude" between the creature and God—a similitude owing to the creature participating in God's being—there are common concepts applicable to both the creature and God, like "being," "substance," and "spirit," that are prior to God in the course of human predication without having any ontological priority or independence with respect to God himself.[65] Thus, for Suárez, God as known by creation is both the cause of the object of metaphysics and a part of the object as well (indeed, the primary part of it). Metaphysics, then, discusses God as principle and, in addition, studies God "absolutely" or with respect to his own nature and attributes known by creation.[66]

Various influential Reformed authors advocate a more Thomistic approach to the relationship between metaphysics and God. For the Reformed philosopher and theologian Bartholomäus Keckermann, metaphysics is "the science of being . . . absolutely and generally accepted," where a being (*ens*) is taken to be "that which is" (*id quod est*) or "what has essence" (*quod habet essentiam*). *Ens* as the "most general genus" applies primarily to substance

---

[64]Suárez, *Disputationes metaphysicae* 1.1.11 (5). Cf. 1.1.12 (6).

[65]Suárez, *Disputationes metaphysicae* 1.1.13 (6); 2.2.14 (74).

[66]Suárez, *Disputationes Metaphysicae* 1.1.19 (8-9). Strangely, having recognized that Thomas refuses to include God as part of the object of metaphysics, Suárez still wants the Angelic Doctor on his side and thus insists that Thomas never explicitly *excluded* God from being the special object of metaphysics (1.1.18, 20 [8-9]).

and secondarily to accidents. Significantly, God is *aliquid supra ens* (something beyond being) and *supersubstantia* (beyond substance). This is because God is his own essence and *esse* and does not strictly speaking "have essence" or actuate a delimited (creaturely) form of being. God is called *ens* only on account of the weakness of our intellect. Therefore, metaphysics treats only those things that depend on God—created beings—not God himself.[67] Johann Alsted likewise identifies the subject of metaphysics as "being insofar as it is being," and he distinguishes it from natural theology. Metaphysics is a "universal science," Alsted argues, but "the ambit of philosophy" does not "contain" theology.[68] Metaphysics is a "most general wisdom," according to Alsted, and has no business treating God, who is a "most singular being."[69] Johannes Maccovius also identifies "being in general" or being as a quasi-genus (*genus analogum*) as the subject of metaphysics. But God exists "outside the order of creatures" and is not treated under metaphysics except as a cause of created being.[70]

In view of this (admittedly fast-paced) survey of various premodern and early modern Christian approaches to the question of metaphysics and God, what should be said in connection with the argument of this chapter? Three things in particular merit our attention. First, it is a mistake to assume that the patristic and medieval theologians take up the concept of "being" as a genus under which they could place both God and the creature. Barth, for example, is right to resist a "master-concept" like *ens* that might be applied in a univocal manner to both God and the creature. Yet the historical judgment that an author like Thomas is guilty of promoting such a practice is ill-founded. In their observations on the concepts of *ens* and *substantia*, authors like Augustine, Boethius, John of Damascus, Thomas, and Keckermann insist that it is emphatically not appropriate to treat God as though he were just one more instance of "being." It may be worth asking whether the approaches of Scotus and Suárez might imply an infelicitous blurring of the Creator-creature distinction, but Scotus and Suárez themselves would

---

[67]Bartholomäus Keckermann, *Scientiae metaphysicae brevissima synopsis et compendium*, in *Operum omnium quae extant* (Geneva, 1614), 1.1-2 (1:2013-16).

[68]Johann Alsted, *Metaphysica* (Hebornae Nassoviorum, 1613), praecognita, 18-19 (23-24).

[69]Johann Alsted, *Theologia naturalis* (Antonius Hummius, 1615), 1.1 (8).

[70]Johannes Maccovius, *Metaphysica*, ed. Adrianus Heereboord, 3rd ed. (Leiden, 1658), 1.1 (1-3); 2.1, 6 (180, 265).

not approve of blurring the distinction and retain in the material content of their theology various means of upholding that distinction. Indeed, it may be worth asking whether certain modes of discourse in contemporary philosophical theology presume a common structure of being in which God and the creature are both situated. It is misguided, however, to posit a thoroughgoing deference to a generic concept of being in the history of Christian reflection on God. "Metaphysics" in this sense—utilizing a generic concept of being to determine what God is—is quite different from a recovery of Christian *theologia* that would appropriate insights from authors like Augustine, John of Damascus, and Thomas.

Second, metaphysics taken not just in a pejorative sense (allowing a generic concept of being to govern theological discourse) but also in a classical sense (the study of being as such) differs greatly from the Christian practice of *theologia*. Metaphysics as the study of that which is or that which "has" or actuates essence restricts itself to the treatment of created being, while *theologia* focuses on God in his unique plenitude and transcendence of created being. Metaphysics properly understood has no authority to dictate the content of *theologia*. To be sure, if one follows the path of Boethius, Thomas, or Maccovius, for example, then causal analysis of *ens* does yield some limited knowledge of God as cause. Importantly, though, for such authors, that causal analysis will proceed in an a posteriori manner and underscore that God is not a cause within the field of common being but rather the transcendent Creator, the one who is really identical to his own essence and existence and therefore called *ens* in only an analogical way. With Alsted, though, we might take the additional step of distinguishing between metaphysics and natural theology. Strictly speaking, the former is the study of created being as such and remains focused on created being and its principles and modes, while the latter is the study of the created order under the particular aspect of its revelation of God the Creator, from whom and to whom all things exist and to whose eternal power and deity creation bears witness. Where that distinction is made, metaphysics properly speaking does not deliver the content of theology at all, even if natural theology does provide a limited knowledge of God himself that is reoriented and refined by Christian dogmatics.

Third, in light of the firm distinction between metaphysics and theology proper, the practice of *theologia* is precisely what is needed to avoid the problem of Christian dogmatics becoming nothing more than meta-physics. Precisely by thinking and speaking of the triune God in his self-referential completeness and independence of the economy, we can resist the temptation to locate this God within the field of common being. Conversely, a Christian doctrine of God that neglects description of him in his aseity and independence will risk treating God as but another part of the whole of reality. On the one hand, there are various projects in contemporary theology that speak of the "metaphysics" of God, creation or the incarnation, for example. Typically this means that the author in-tends to deal with not just the outward relations or effects of the subject but rather the thing in itself (God himself, the one person of Christ in his two natures, etc.). Given that such a project regularly involves taking up common terms in metaphysics ("being," "nature," etc.), it is not surprising that it might be taken to offer a "metaphysics" of its subject. On the other hand, in an important sense metaphysics strictly speaking is exactly what *theologia* (discourse about God himself) does not do and is exactly what *theologia* relativizes by reminding us that there is one, the triune God, who lives *a se* and transcends the whole world. Authors like Friedrich Schleiermacher, Ritschl, and Barth are right to push back against locating God within the created order and presuming to speak about him as though he were a great creature, but what is sometimes missed today is that rec-ognition and description of God *in se* without primary reference to the economy is in fact the necessary pathway to ensuring that metaphysics does not take over theology proper.

To this point I have begun to underscore that the Christian practice of *theologia* is not metaphysics and does not entail that God should become just an exalted version of created being. After stressing that theology proper is not to be confused with metaphysics, the next section will discuss why and how it can still make use of metaphysical concepts without compro-mising the Creator-creature distinction.

THEOLOGIA AND THE REFRACTION OF METAPHYSICAL CONCEPTS

If Christian theology proper is distinct from metaphysics, why should it still incorporate metaphysical concepts from the Aristotelian tradition? And, if their use is retained, how can these concepts be applied to God without reducing God to one more instance of common being? Both of these questions deserve a careful answer and can help us fill out our understanding of theology's positive use of metaphysics.

In answering the "why" question before the "how," my contention here is that while using Aristotelian metaphysical language is not absolutely necessary for articulating the Christian doctrine of God, it is at least expedient for the following reasons. First, our exegesis of Scripture's teaching on the triune God—if it is going to be exegesis and not bare, verbatim repetition of biblical locutions—requires the use of extrabiblical concepts that enable us to expound and summarize the sense of the relevant passages. John Owen is instructive here on the task of biblical interpretation:

> Use is to be made of words and expressions as, it may be, are not literally and formally contained in the Scripture, but only are, unto our conceptions and apprehensions, expository of what is so contained. And to deny the liberty, yea, the necessity hereof, is to deny all interpretation of the Scripture—all endeavours to express the sense of the words of it unto the understandings of one another; which is, in a word, to render the Scripture itself useless.[71]

Presumably this by itself is a fairly uncontroversial point to make, but it is an important step in making a case for retaining some use of metaphysical concepts in the doctrine of God.

Second, given God's aseity and transcendence of the economy, expounding the Bible's account of God will require a set of elaborative concepts that can help us speak of God himself, not just God's relations and works *ad extra*. Because they are designed to facilitate understanding of things in themselves, concepts like essence, *esse*, actuality, and so on can help us to contemplate God *in se*, even if the concepts must undergo significant analogical modification for the work of theology proper. To make this claim is not to presume that this is the only set of concepts that could be serviceable in discourse about God himself. It is simply to highlight one important reason that this metaphysical grammar may continue to be useful.

Third, because Holy Scripture itself anticipates the church's later use of terms like *essence*, *nature*, and *substance*, there is reason to hold that the

---

[71]John Owen, *A Brief Declaration and Vindication of the Doctrine of the Trinity*, in *The Works of John Owen*, vol. 2, *Communion with God*, ed. William H. Good (Edinburgh: Banner of Truth, 1965), 379.

work of *theologia* benefits from commandeering broadly Aristotelian meta-physical concepts. While the New Testament authors do not intend to supply us with a technical ontology and can use words like φύσις (nature) and ὑπόστασις (substance), for example, in various ways, some of these uses do overlap with usage in the Aristotelian tradition and in subsequent ecclesiastical use of that tradition's resources. In Galatians 4, Paul reminds Christians that when they did not know God they were enslaved "to those who by nature are not gods" (τοῖς φύσει μὴ οὖσιν θεοῖς). By implication, the true God is the one who is God "by nature"—by what he is—rather than by any spurious claim to supremacy (Gal 4:8; cf. 1 Cor 8:6). Surveying the uses of φύσις in Hellenistic, Jewish, and New Testament writings, Scott Ha-femann comments that in Galatians 4:8 "the ontological meaning is clearly marked," with φύσις and a form of εἰμί (οὖσιν) appearing together.[72] In Romans 1:20, the apostle remarks that all human beings understand something of God's "eternal power and θειότης," the latter term denoting "di-vinity," or, in the words of one lexicon, "the nature of God," "what God is," "the fact that he is God."[73] Paul utilizes the related term θεότης as well, an abstract form of the noun θεός: "in [Christ] all the fullness of deity [θεότητος] dwells bodily" (Col 2:9).[74] James Dunn writes that the term denotes "the nature or essence of deity, that which constitutes deity," and became a "principal building block of subsequent Christology."[75] In Philip-pians 2, Paul speaks of Christ subsisting "in the form of God" (ἐν μορφῇ τοῦ θεοῦ) and yet taking on the "form of a servant" (μορφὴν δούλου). If the language here denotes not just the outward appearance but that which constitutes something as what it is,[76] this passage represents another bridge

---

[72]Scott J. Hafemann, "'Divine Nature' in 2 Pet 1,4 Within Its Eschatological Context," *Biblica* 94 (2013): 91. Throughout this article, Hafemann is hesitant to separate "nature" from action and is particularly interested in arguing that the divine φύσις in 2 Pet 1:4 signifies God's eschatologi-cal activity. While it cannot be discussed at length here, it is worth mentioning that older meta-physicians also affirm the close connection between nature and action, the former being the principle of the latter (so, e.g., Alsted, *Metaphysica* 1.3 [43]).

[73]Johannes P. Louw and Eugene A. Nida, *A Greek-English Lexicon of the New Testament Based on Semantic Domains* (New York: United Bible Societies, 1988), 1:140. Cf., e.g., C. E. B. Cranfield, *A Critical and Exegetical Commentary on the Epistle to the Romans* (Edinburgh: T&T Clark, 1975), 1:115.

[74]See BDAG, 452.

[75]James D. G. Dunn, *The Theology of Paul the Apostle* (Grand Rapids: Eerdmans, 1998), 205-6.

[76]So, e.g., Gordon D. Fee, *Paul's Letter to the Philippians*, NICNT (Grand Rapids: Eerdmans, 1995), 202-4.

between biblical thought and the metaphysical grammar taken up by the likes of Boethius, John of Damascus, Thomas, Keckermann, and others. The writer of Hebrews uses the term ὑπόστασις in several places (Heb 1:3; 3:14; 11:1). The first appearance of it has a meaning that overlaps with metaphysical usage, where the Son is called the "representation of [God the Father's] ὑπόστασις" (1:3). A number of older theologians argue that this occurrence of ὑπόστασις pertains to the Father as one individual "substance" or distinct person in the divine essence,[77] though recent lexica often translate it as something like "substantial nature" or "essence."[78] At any rate, the point is that Hebrews 1:3 is another place in the biblical canon that provides not just a material but even a formal basis for using the metaphysical terminology in view here.

It may seem that the language of "actuality" is farther afield of biblical categories, but it too has a certain connection with Scripture. In traditional metaphysical analysis, "primary actuality" or *actus primus* is just the essence of a thing as existing, while "secondary actuality" or *actus secundus* is the action or operation (ἐνέργεια) of one such thing.[79] On a mundane level, the biblical authors are certainly cognizant of the existence of things. For example, in Revelation 4:11, the heavenly creatures praise God, saying, "You created all things and through your will they existed [ἦσαν] and were created." The writer of Hebrews asserts that everyone coming to God "must believe that he exists [ἔστιν]" (Heb 11:6). The point may seem prosaic and in fact is prosaic: the biblical authors know of the existence of things. Yet, because of potential suspicion that invoking terms like *actuality* will subvert scriptural exegesis or properly Christian reasoning about God, the point, banal as it sounds, does need to be made that Holy Scripture speaks of the existence of things and that this is what *actuality* (more precisely, *primary actuality*) expresses. In addition, the biblical authors frequently discuss the ἐνέργεια (action, operation, working[80]) of creatures and God. For example, Paul calls

---

[77] E.g., Polanus, *Syntagma* 3.1 (198-99). For discussion of the issue, see *The Works of John Owen*, vol. 20, *An Exposition of the Epistle to the Hebrews, with Preliminary Exercitations*, ed. William H. Good (Edinburgh: T&T Clark, 1862), 3:85, 88-95.

[78] E.g., BDAG, 1040; Verlyn D. Verbrugge, ed., *New International Dictionary of New Testament Theology*, abridged ed. (Grand Rapids: Zondervan, 2000), 582-83.

[79] See, e.g., Keckermann, *Scientiae metaphysicae* 1.2 (1:2016).

[80] See, e.g., BDAG, 335.

for faith "operating [ἐνεργουμένη] through love" (Gal 5:6). While there are different "operations" or "workings" (ἐνεργημάτων) of the Holy Spirit in believers, "the same God is the one working [ὁ ἐνεργῶν] all things in all" (1 Cor 12:6; cf. 1 Cor 12:11). Paul prays for the saints to know "the working [ἐνέργειαν] of the might of [God's] strength, which he worked [ἐνήργησεν] in Christ by raising him from the dead" (Eph 1:19-20; cf. Eph 3:7, 20). For Paul, God is "the one working" (ὁ ἐνεργῶν) in believers to enable them to "work" (ἐνεργεῖν) (Phil 2:13; cf. Phil 3:21). Given that such language is already explicitly present in Scripture itself, it is especially defensible in theology proper to employ the notion of actuality as in *actus secundus*.

Fourth, and finally, the metaphysical concepts in view here not only intersect with the language of Scripture but also can and should be used in a ministerial manner. If deployed in a magisterial manner, these concepts would dictate what practitioners of Christian *theologia* should say about God, but if their function is ministerial, they simply help to declare and illumine for us what Holy Scripture already teaches about the triune God.[81] It is true that there is always a risk that we might allow a term's generic meaning, derived purely from analysis of created things, to cloud our understanding when we apply it to God. This is to do "metaphysics" in the infelicitous sense, which hinders our alertness to the uniqueness and transcendence of God. However, in addition to taking some encouragement from the fact that we are employing language with precedent in Scripture itself, we can be confident that the Spirit is always addressing us in Scripture and working to renew our minds and refine our understanding of God and, consequently, our understanding of whether we are suitably using various concepts in theological description. Such conceptual ascesis will require work on our part to uphold the primacy of exegetical judgments in Christian *theologia* above any philosophical apparatus we might utilize. Francis Turretin puts it nicely when he comments that in our use of philosophical terminology the words must be "consecrated according to ecclesiastical custom" and applied to the mystery of God in an "eminent" manner (κατ' ἐξοχήν).[82] This brings us to the "how" question regarding our decision to use this language without compromising the Creator-creature distinction.

---

[81]On the magisterial-ministerial distinction, see, e.g., Turretin, *Inst.* 1.8.6-7, 11-12 (1:28, 29).
[82]Turretin, *Inst.* 3.23.9 (1:282).

If there is no need to avoid words like *being, essence, substance*, and so forth, there is still a need to clarify that they can be applied to God in only an analogical manner. There is a need to take up the caution found in earlier Christian writers about calling God a "being" or "substance" in any ordinary sense. For, strictly speaking, the being discussed in metaphysics is something that "has" a limited (created) essence differentiated from the essences of others within the same order of being. Furthermore, the *esse* or actuality of that essence is (contingently) given by another. In a sense, an *ens* is "really" distinct from its own essence—not as one "thing" (*res*) from another thing but in reality as a constituted thing from its constitutive principle.[83] Such a being's essence and *esse* also are in a sense "really" distinct. While they are not two distinct "things" strictly so called, essence is what something is and existence is the actuality and restriction of that essence in an individual being.[84] In the case of created beings, what they are (essence) does not automatically include their act of existing (*esse*), which is why they are contingent. They exist by a participation in the triune God that is freely ordained by him.[85]

By contrast, the God revealed in Scripture has no beginning or dependence on another. There is no theogony in Genesis. Unlike other gods of the ancient Near East, YHWH is not delimited by having a certain role or relation to others.[86] There was no god "before" or "after" YHWH, whereas the idols are derivative "no-gods" (Deut 32:17, 21, 39; 17:7-8; 43:10-13). YHWH is not individuated or demarcated within a company of similar beings. He sits enthroned above all creation. "To whom will you compare me," he asks, "or who is my equal?" (Is 40:25). The question is rhetorical, but the appropriate

---

[83]Compare Thomas Aquinas, *Opera omnia*, vol. 25/2, *Quaestiones de quolibet*, Leonine ed. (Rome: Commissio Leonina; Paris: Éditions du Cerf, 1996), 2.2.2 [4] (215-18); Keckermann, *Scientiae metaphysicae* 1.2 (1:2015-16); Alsted, *Metaphysica* 1.3 (43-44); Turretin, *Inst.* 3.7.5 (1:211).

[84]See Thomas, *Quaestiones de quolibet* 2.2.1 [3] ad 2 (215); Keckermann, *Scientiae metaphysicae* 1.2 (1:2016-17); Alsted, *Metaphysica* 1.3-4 (45-48). Mastricht sums up the distinction nicely in stating that essence is "that by which anything is what it is" while existence is essence "in act, or outside its own causes" (*TPT* 2.24.6 [237]). On medieval discussion of the essence-*esse* distinction, see John F. Wippel, "Essence and Existence," in *The Cambridge History of Later Medieval Philosophy: From the Discovery of Aristotle to the Disintegration of Scholasticism 1100–1600*, ed. Norman Kretzmann, Anthony Kenny, and Jan Pinborg (Cambridge: Cambridge University Press, 1988), 392-407.

[85]See Thomas, *ST* Ia.3.4 corp. (42); Turretin, *Inst.* 3.7.5 (1:210).

[86]John H. Walton, *Ancient Near Eastern Thought and the Old Testament: Introducing the Conceptual World of the Hebrew Bible* (Grand Rapids: Baker Academic, 2006), 87-88, 104-5.

response is simply *Deus non est in genere*. He is the God who eternally and absolutely is, the one in whom all things find their ultimate point of reference (Ex 3:14; Acts 17:24-28; Rom 11:33-36). He is the one with fullness of life in triune fellowship, from which he "abounds" toward us in power and love (Eph 1:8, 18-21, 23; 2:4-7; 3:8, 14-19; 4:10).

The sharp distinction between God and created being necessitates an adjustment or refraction of any metaphysical concepts that we might use to describe God. A responsible treatment of the doctrine of God will have to make this point explicit, either in an initial discussion of how our words are predicated of God or in specific cases when they are predicated of him along the way. Christian theologians using concepts like "being" will have to acknowledge that God is not limited within a field of being shared by other (divine or created) entities. He does not receive a specific determination of essence in order to be a certain kind of being. Nor does he receive a particular determination of some divine essence extended beyond himself in order to be *this* God. Framed positively, God is his own essence. Further, as he is not brought into being or actuated by another, God's essence is identical with his own existence. It is still possible to call God "a being" or perhaps even "a particular being" in order to clarify that he is and that he is distinct from others (i.e., creatures).[87] But such a statement immediately requires the clarification that God's "particularity" (if it is permissible to speak in that way) lies in his having all perfection in himself in an eminent manner, not in partially having something and then lacking something that others have in order to be individuated within a field of common being.[88] The unavoidable clumsiness ingredient in calling God a "being" is vividly expressed by Barth:

> If we think and speak of God as an element juxtaposed with others in a series, the very idea or view of the series as such must be fundamentally disturbed (which in this case means reinterpreted) by the fact that the element God is in such a way independent of all the other elements and of the series as such, that, whatever may be the common denominator, God will not be embraced by it, but will remain detached and independent in regard to both these

---

[87]Cf. the pertinent material in John of Damascus, *Exp. fid.* 1.4 (13); Thomas, *ST* Ia.13.1 ad 2 (139-40); Keckermann, *Scientiae metaphysicae* 1.2 (1:2015).

[88]This point will come up below in my discussion of God's freedom in the economy.

associated elements and to the common factor which binds them together. *Deus non est in genere.*[89]

Correspondingly, it is possible to speak of God's "essence" or "nature," but the use of such language comes not from God's existing under a delimiting principle that constitutes his being within a genus or species but from the need to articulate that God is God and that what God is as God is common to the three divine persons and distinguishes him from false gods.[90] It is possible to speak of God's *esse* not because he participates in a source of life other than himself but simply because he is in act (not merely a potential deity).[91]

Given reactions against "substance metaphysics" in recent theological discussion,[92] the concept of "substance" may seem particularly difficult to employ. But skeptics of its use in theology proper will do well to remember that they are not the first to question it. Indeed, as noted above, the likes of Augustine and John of Damascus—the sort of theologians often accused of indulging in "substance metaphysics"—voiced trenchant objections to it. Earlier theologians were concerned that calling God a "substance" would give the impression that he "stands under" accidents and that his essence must be completed by the addition of qualities. For, classically speaking, substances are susceptible to undergoing dramatic changes and being shaped by relations with others. Thus, for reasons opposite to those who misunderstand the classical terminology today and worry that calling God a "substance" would suggest that he is inactive or aloof, proponents of a doctrine of God with a strong accent on God's aseity have already initiated the critical reception of these concepts that is necessary for theology proper today.

If the term *substance* is applied to God in what is historically its secondary sense (the essential constitution of a thing, eventually designated by the Greek οὐσία according to catholic custom), then, as in the case of the term

---

[89]Barth, *CD* II/1, 310.

[90]In the case of God, then, *ens* and *essentia* are identical (compare Keckermann, *Scientiae metaphysicae* 1.2 [1:2015]).

[91]Thus, with God, Thomas points out, *id quod est* and *esse* are one and the same (Thomas, *Expositio libri De hebdomadibus*, in *Opera omnia*, vol. 50, Leonine ed. [Rome: Commissio Leonina; Paris: Éditions du Cerf, 1992], 2 [273]).

[92]E.g., Jenson, *Systematic Theology*, 1:215-16; and Jenson, *Systematic Theology*, vol. 2, *The Works of God* (Oxford: Oxford University Press, 1999), 39-40; McCormack, "Actuality of God"; Chris Tilling, *Paul's Divine Christology* (Grand Rapids: Eerdmans, 2015), 34, 36, 39, 47, 103-4.

essence itself, this is permissible because we have to affirm that God is God, that what God is subsists equally in the three divine persons, and that God is entirely distinct from false gods. With an author like McCormack, the chief concern with the term *substance* used in this sense is that it will signify a divine essence that is not open to being constituted by God's action (particularly the act of election).[93] However, if God's essence is wholly actual in the fellowship of the Father, Son, and Spirit and not established or filled out by God's action *pro nobis*, then that objection to substance language loses its force. On a related note, it is permissible to distinguish between God's *actus primus* (his essence in act) and God's *actus secundus* (his action) not as if he passes from idleness to activity like creatures when they perform actions but because he does apply his essential actuality to produce new outward effects at different times.[94] Finally, with respect to the doctrine of the Trinity, if the term *substance* is applied to God to designate a distinct divine person in what is historically the term's primary sense (one that subsists per se and without needing to inhere in another as a part of it, eventually designated by the Greek ὑπόστασις according to catholic custom), then this is permissible because the Father, Son, and Spirit do indeed subsist in their own right and are not merely parts of something else.

More could be said about the specific analogical changes needed for utilizing metaphysical concepts in theology proper, but I hope to have shown that a commitment to a Christian understanding of the Creator-creature distinction and a commitment to working (ministerially) with conceptual resources from classical metaphysics can fit together in the practice of *theologia*. It is likely that some will wonder whether the terms in view still need more revision than I have suggested here. In particular, should God's essence be taken to denote what God is irrespective of his activity in the economy? Would that not imply that God cannot truly humble himself to engage us in the economy, and would that not imply a conflict between God *in se* and God *pro nobis*? In previous chapters, I have already argued that God is indeed complete in himself without reference to us, which entails that

---

[93]McCormack, "Actuality of God," 221-23.

[94]Cf., e.g., Thomas, *SCG* 2.9 (284). For more on the relationship between divine action and the divine essence, see Steven J. Duby, "Divine Immutability, Divine Action and the God-World Relation," *IJST* 19 (2017): 144-62. This was also discussed in the section "Pilgrim *Theologia* and the Hiddenness of God," in chap. 1.

it is proper to speak of God's essence as what God is, without this being determined by what he does *pro nobis*. In the next section of this chapter, I will flesh out a little more the argument that God's complete aseity is in fact what enables God's genuine condescension in the economy and what grounds the sameness of God in his inward and outward activity.

Theologia and God's Freedom for Us

So far I have distinguished *theologia* from metaphysics and yet also argued that Christian reasoning about God in himself can make use of metaphysical concepts without necessarily blurring the Creator-creature distinction. Now I hope to exhibit that the practice of *theologia* also circumvents the other worries about a metaphysical approach to God, namely, that it inhibits the freedom and authenticity of God's economic condescension and that it produces a rift between God in himself and God for us, which might ultimately imperil the true deity of Christ, the one who is Immanuel. I will aim to do this under four points.

1. In his completeness God does not have to undergo any actualization in order to accomplish his outward works. God is already wholly active and fulfilled in his own triune life and beatitude even without reference to the world, so his outward action does not require a transition from passive potency to actuality. Furthermore, the Bible indicates that when God acts in creation and providence, salvation, and judgment, he does so without the exertion that is characteristic of creaturely action (Ps 33:6-9; 148:5; Heb 1:3; Jn 5:28-29; 2 Thess 2:8). Indeed, he is never idle, even if he may appear so to the limited understanding of human beings (Ps 44:23; 121:4; Hab 1:2-6). If God is already in act in himself and requires no exertion or motion (passing from inactivity to activity) to perform his outward works, then in God's case the relationship between *actus primus* and *actus secundus* is quite different from that of creatures. In creaturely action, finite beings strive toward some end and pass from inactivity to activity: *actus primus* (their essential actuality) is in an important sense really distinct from *actus secundus* (their action). In fact, creatures act by qualities added to essence ("mediating accidental forms") that they acquire and by actuating the inactive power of those qualities.[95] How they are in themselves is always distinct from how

---

[95]See Thomas Aquinas, *Scriptum super libros Sententiarum*, ed. R. P. Mandonnet (Paris, 1929), 1.8.3.1 corp. and ad 4 (1:211-12); 2.1.1.5 ad 11 (2:37); *De potentia* 1.1 ad 11 (10).

they are after rousing themselves to bring about their intended effects. In divine action, the infinite God need not pass from idleness to activity in order to perform his works. His primary actuality is already adequate to the accomplishment of all his works. He brings about his effects by the actuality of his eternal essence.[96] In other words, according to Thomas, divine action is just "God's essence with a relation toward the creature."[97] Or, as Peter van Mastricht phrases it, God's operation is nothing but "the essence operating." Divine operation "encompasses two things: the active essence of God and the relation of it to the work."[98]

This has significant implications for the genuineness with which God meets us in the economy, but perhaps putting the matter this way will raise questions about whether this approach aligns with the essence-energies distinction often associated with Eastern Christianity and, at the constructive level, whether it would entail that God's outward works are necessary emanations of his essence, which would compromise the entire aim of this study. It may be fitting to comment briefly on the historical question and then the constructive question as well.[99]

Within the Eastern tradition John of Damascus can speak of plural divine "energies" in talking about God performing diverse actions. Yet at the same time he writes that God acts "without motion" (δι' ἀκινησίας). God has "one simple energy" (μίαν ἁπλῆν . . . ἐνέργειαν) with which he "energizes differently" in the various circumstances of the world. On the one hand, John can speak of positive attributes of God signifying not "what he is according to essence" but "either what he is not, some relation toward some contrasting

---

[96] Alsted observes that God's action is not "motion" in one common sense of that term (a reduction of inactive potency to actuality). In Alsted's words, it is called "motion" only "hyperphysically" (in a manner that transcends the creaturely, natural pattern of motion). On the one hand, God does indeed bring about diverse effects, but, on the other hand, he does so only by the one eternal act of his own essence (Theologia naturalis 1.16 [141-42, 148]).

[97] Thomas, ST Ia.25.1 ad 2 (290); 45.3 ad 1 (467).

[98] Mastricht, TPT 3.1.4 (273). This means it is quite misguided to say that in a more traditional account of God he is an inactive subject standing behind a forthcoming activity. In the sort of account commended here, God in fact just is his eternal act of knowing, willing, and loving in the fellowship of Father, Son, and Spirit.

[99] For recent reflections on Eastern perspectives, see Torstein Theodor Tollefsen, Activity and Participation in Late Antique and Early Christian Thought (Oxford: Oxford University Press, 2012); Constantinos Athanasopoulos and Christoph Schneider, eds., Divine Essence and Energies: Ecumenical Reflections on the Presence of God in Eastern Orthodoxy (Cambridge: James Clarke, 2013).

thing, something following his nature or an energy."[100] On the other hand, Thomas offers a plausible interpretation of John that, if correct, would facilitate an agreement between their approaches. He argues that John is hesitant to identify these attributes with God's essence because he is underscoring that God's essence is not defined by them and because they arise formally from our speech about what are, in creatures, accidents added to substance—not because John would deny that what they signify is essential in God.[101] It may be more difficult, however, to harmonize authors like Thomas and Mastricht with the theology of Gregory Palamas. Palamas reasons that the divine energies manifest and in some sense constitute God's essence, but he also says that God is their "cause" (αἴτιος). Moreover, in Palamas's description, the energies are not just divine operations *ad extra* but include attributes like knowledge, will, and goodness.[102]

If the approach to divine actuality commended here does conflict with Palamas it can be said in its favor at the constructive level that it alleviates the ontologically awkward implication (which Palamite theologizing itself might resist) that God is the cause of his own perfections. Moreover, this approach positively follows from God's triune actuality. To clarify that it does not render God's outward works necessary emanations of his essence (in which case they would be included in the constitution of that essence), a few points may be carefully made. The following line of reasoning is not meant to *prove* God's full actuality or the contingency of his outward action. For here I am taking these to be necessary consequents of God's aseity and plenitude in the fellowship of the Trinity and therefore as givens with which we are bound to work in the doctrine of God. My task here is simply to shed some light on their coherence and address a potential objection regarding this coherence.[103]

---

[100]John of Damascus, *Exp. fid.* 1.4 (13); 9 (31); 10-11 (33-34).

[101]Thomas, *De potentia* 7.4 ad 1 (196); 5 ad 1 (199).

[102]Gregory Palamas, *Défense des saints hésychastes: Introduction, text critique, traduction et notes*, trans. Jean Meyendorff (Louvain: Spicilegium Sacrum Lovansiense, 1959), 3.2.6-14 (653-59). See further Tollefsen, *Activity and Participation*, 185-200, 215-17; D. Glenn Butner Jr., "Communion with God: An Energetic Defense of Gregory Palamas," *MT* 32 (2016): 20-44.

[103]I have attempted to develop this line of thought with help from the Reformed orthodox in Steven J. Duby, "Election, Actuality and Divine Freedom: Thomas Aquinas, Bruce McCormack and Reformed Orthodoxy in Dialogue," *MT* 32 (2016): 336-39; Duby, "Divine Immutability," 144-62; Duby, "Divine Action and the Meaning of Eternity," *JRT* 11 (2017): 362-75.

God enjoys fullness of life in himself and is complete without reference to another. His being neither entails nor precludes the existence of the world.[104] Any potential relation to that which is other than himself will thus be nonconstitutive on his side. Accordingly, God has, in scholastic terms, a liberty of "indifference" with respect to creation: not an indecisive or unstable disposition but a freedom either to create or not to create without detriment to his own completeness.[105] Since God is already complete and active in triune fellowship, his action toward the creature (whether in his decree or its execution *ad extra*) thus involves merely an application or direction of his essential actuality toward a created object. In his decree, God applies or directs his essential actuality toward a created object that he will bring into being. That there is this application or direction entails that the attendant relation God assumes toward the creature is not itself included in God's essence or characterized by the necessity of God's own act of being.[106] In his action *ad extra*, God applies or directs his prevenient actuality in diverse "egressions" that terminate on created objects.[107] The actuality or force of the action is nothing other than God's essential actuality, but the egression

---

[104]Phrased in scholastic terms, God is "naturally indifferent" to the world's being: he could have willed that it not exist without detriment to his own triune being and beatitude (see Turretin, *Inst.* 3.2.13 [1:346]; Mastricht, *TPT* 3.1.21 [276]). This, of course, is no denial of the fact that given God's will to create he loves his creatures.

[105]See again Turretin, *Inst.* 3.14 (1:241-43); 4.2.13 (1:346); Mastricht, *TPT* 3.1.21 (276).

[106]One might ask whether even an "application" of God's prevenient actuality would still entail a transition from passive potency to actuality. "Application" is, after all, an action noun. My response is that, insofar as there is anything in act at all it follows that there is a first cause who acts without having to transition from passive potency to actuality, lest there be an infinite regression of such transitions without an original actuality that produces the actuality in the world. In other words, strange as it might sound, the actuality of things in the world implies that there is an original actuality brought to bear on (or applied to) an object without requiring a transition from idleness to activity. One could then infer either (1) that this primary actuality is just God's essential actuality without including the actuality of his action or (2) that this primary actuality is God's essential actuality as inclusive of the actuality by which he decrees, creates, and effects things in the world. Given that the former would require (1) a diversity of parts in God by virtue of which passive potency and actuality could both be resident in God and (2) some primordial idleness on God's part that is at odds with the doctrine of the Trinity, the second inference obtains (i.e., that the original actuality applied without an underlying reduction of potency to act includes the actuality whereby God accomplishes his works *ad nos*).

[107]The language of "egression" and "termination" is drawn from Reformed orthodox authors like Alsted, *Theologia naturalis* 1.17 (150-51); Gisbertus Voetius, *Selectarum disputationum theologicarum* (Utrecht, 1648), 1.13 (233); Turretin, *Inst.* 3.10.15 (1:225); 5.3.16 (1:484-85); John Owen, *A Dissertation on Divine Justice*, in *The Works of John Owen*, vol. 10, *The Death of Christ*, ed. William H. Goold (Edinburgh: Banner of Truth, 1967), 1.1 (498-500).

of that actuality is located under a free application and relation of it toward us. Divine action in the former respect is God's essence and is thus eternal and necessary. Divine action in the latter respect (i.e., as egression) is contingent and diversified according to the circumstances of creatures. Furthermore, the effects wrought by various egressions of God's essential actuality—for example, the act of creation itself or the Spirit's communication of Christ and his benefits in the Lord's Supper—are never adequate to the fullness of God's power or essence.[108]

For the purposes of this section, the significance of God's prevenient actuality is that when God acts in the life of his creatures, he is not acting by something added to his own being or by changing from who he is *in se* to who he is *pro nobis*. He does not have to develop himself in any way in order to meet us in the economy. He simply exercises outwardly what he himself is as God in accomplishing his good works in our midst. We therefore never encounter a secondary iteration of God but rather only the one true God himself freely turned toward us in his holiness and love. Perhaps unexpectedly, then, the old inflection of God's aseity as pure actuality serves to corroborate and emphasize that God is fully himself in all his activity *ad extra*.

2. Following on the previous point, God in his aseity and transcendence of the economy is not "really" related to the creature, a statement that has often been misinterpreted. To understand its meaning and its import for the argument here, it is helpful to consider Thomas's explanation of it.[109] Thomas presents three ways in which two things might be related to each other. In one scenario, two things are related to one another only in the mind. For example, if we say that a thing is identical to itself, in this case the *relata* (here, one thing thought twice) are related only rationally. In another scenario, two things are related to one another by a thing that they mutually possess (like a quantity possessed by two things related to one another as great and small) or by some mutual determination (like a father and son).

---

[108]In affirming the contingency of God's action *ad extra* and the important distinction between God's effects and God's essence, the present approach resonates with Michael Horton's recent Reformed appropriation of the essence-energies distinction (*The Christian Faith: A Systematic Theology for Pilgrims on the Way* [Grand Rapids: Zondervan, 2011], 129-32, 159, 612-15, 690-92, 817-18). However, this approach differs from Horton where he appears to reject the real identity of the divine energies and the divine essence and his consequent claim that God's essence is not revealed to us.

[109]See Thomas, *SCG* 2.12 (290-91); *ST* Ia.13.7 corp. (152-53).

In a third scenario, though, the relation is mixed, being "real" on the part of one *relatum* and "rational" on the part of the other. This occurs when the two *relata* do not exist in the same order of being and when the being of one implies the being of the other but not vice versa. For example, in the relation between human sense perception and a sensible object, the relation is "real" on the side of the human subject since the subject's perceiving is in its own being ordered to the sensible object, but the relation is "rational" on the side of the sensible object since it is not in itself ordered to the human subject. Thomas famously concludes that the creature is "really" related to God, while God is "rationally" related to the creature. But this is not a denial of the fact that God is the one who acts to create and sustain the world.[110] Instead, it is a way of reinforcing that the being of God does not imply or require the being of creatures.

In the *Summa contra Gentiles* in particular, it turns out that this has a striking implication for the nearness of God to the creature. If God's relations toward his created effects were "real," the "thing" that they would be would have to be either God's own substance or an accident inhering in God. If such a relation toward the creature were identical with God's own substance or essence, then it would follow that God could not be without the creature, which would entail that God in some sense depends on the creature. Denying that God's relation to the creature is "real" in this sense—it is not what God is—obviously emphasizes God's aseity. Yet, Thomas also points out, neither is God's relation to the creature an accident that begins to inhere in God. If God's relation to the creature were "real" in this sense, then, since it "comes to God *de novo*," it would entail a change in God.[111] Appropriating this construal of the God-world relation means rejecting the thought that some "thing" accedes to God by virtue of which he would stand in relation to us and which would yield a change in him. To say that God is only "rationally" related to the creature is to say not only that he is not necessarily ordered to us but also that he lives in the most intimate and unobstructed relation to us. While creatures relate to one another by various kinds of media and by the acquisition of various accidents and determinations of

---

[110]See, e.g., Thomas, *ST* Ia.45.2-3 (465-67). On the different kinds of relations of reason, see *De potentia* 7.11 (211-12).
[111]Thomas, *SCG* 2.12 (290-91).

being, the triune God in his completeness creates and sustains us by his own essential *actus* without using any instrument to do so. In his immutable plenitude, then, he is immediately connected and present to each one of his creatures. In helping us to glimpse and appreciate God's aseity and his strictly "rational" relation to the world, the practice of *theologia* thus strengthens our understanding of the authenticity with which God lives and works among us in the economy.

3. In his aseity God stands in a noncompetitive relationship to the being of creation. Because he is entirely *a se* and has no correlate, God and creation do not share a common order of being, as though God were one genus or part within the system of the world. When this is overlooked in the doctrine of God, it may be tempting to appeal to some form of divine kenosis to explain God entering into a relationship with something other than himself. The presence of God with us, it may appear, will require a "self-limitation" on God's part in order to "make room" for our existence and causal activity.[112] While this move may seem initially to secure God's capacity to assume a relation to the world, it in fact generates a God-behind-God scenario in which he does not truly come to us in the original fullness of his being.[113] However, if God is complete in himself and is not determined at all by reference to a counterpart, he transcends the world in a manner that robustly facilitates his immanence. For God is not one more finite nature within the field of common being, where a given thing is what it is in part by lacking what other things have and by occupying a different space than other things. He is free to live and act among his creatures in the economy without in any way altering himself to "fit in" or qualifying his presence in order to avoid being assimilated to the world. As Hilary of Poitiers observes, "God is everywhere and whole wherever he is" (*totus ubicumque est*).[114] Such is the plenitude of God that he can be unreservedly with us and yet not at risk of

---

[112]See, e.g., Jürgen Moltmann, *God in Creation: A New Theology of Creation and the Spirit of God*, trans. Margaret Kohl (Minneapolis: Fortress, 1993), 86-89; John C. Polkinghorne, "Kenotic Creation and Divine Action," in *The Work of Love: Creation as Kenosis*, ed. John C. Polkinghorne (Grand Rapids: Eerdmans, 2001), 90-106. For critical assessment of this approach by someone sympathetic to it, see Thomas Jay Oord, *The Uncontrolling Love of God: An Open and Relational Account of Providence* (Downers Grove, IL: IVP Academic, 2015), 151-60.

[113]Compare Dorner, *Divine Immutability*, 158-59.

[114]Hilary of Poitiers, *La Trinité*, ed. G. M. de Durand et al., 3 vols., Sources Chrétiennes 443, 448, 462 (Paris: Éditions du Cerf, 1999–2001), 2.6 (1:285).

foregoing his identity or transcendence. He is at once "whole in all things and whole above everything."[115] Though he will dwell in the midst of Israel in the temple, Solomon recognizes that YHWH still will not be contained there (1 Kings 8:27). Though he dwells in the heavens like a tent, he remains the one who caused the heavens to be and sovereignly commands the stars to come forth by name (Is 40:22-26). In his transcendence and unobstructed immanence God could act in one and the same event as Joseph's brothers when they sold him into slavery, without compromising their integrity as created agents or compromising his own righteousness: "You meant evil against me," Joseph tells his brothers, "but God meant it for good" (Gen 50:20).

Of course, when we speak about God in this manner—as one who is not determined by the being of others or by lacking what others have—it is crucial that we avoid giving the impression of a pantheistic doctrine of God in which he is not really distinct from created beings.[116] For this reason, calling God "a being" or "a substance" (one who subsists in distinction from others) remains warranted.[117] Calling God ὑπερούσιος (super-essential) or *ipsum esse subsistens* (subsisting being itself), for example, underscores that there is no *esse* beyond himself in which God participates in order to be, but that theologoumenon must not be opposed to the distinctness of God. To say that God is *ipsum esse subsistens* is not to negate that he is *this one*. Rather, it is to say that in light of God's aseity the conceptual content of *ens*, when the term is applied to God, must be modified to include the content of absolute existence that is the font of the existence of all other things.[118] On the one hand, John of Damascus, for example, is right that God has "no contrary" (μηδὲν ἐναντίον),[119] for God is not moored within a system of finite, mutually delimiting beings. Yet, on the other hand, precisely because he is infinite—not indefinite (ἀόριστος) but unlimited (ἄπειρος) and eminently containing all perfection and goodness in himself—the Holy One of

---

[115]John of Damascus, *Exp. fid.* 1.13 (38).

[116]For an incisive expression of this concern, see Isaak A. Dorner, *System of Christian Doctrine*, trans. Alfred Cave and J. S. Banks (Edinburgh: T&T Clark, 1880), 1:195-200.

[117]Compare the concerns of Pannenberg, *Systematic Theology*, 1:356-57.

[118]As Thomas has it, in God *id quod est* and *ipsum esse* are one and the same (*De hebdomadibus* 2 [273]; cf. *ST* Ia.13.1 ad 2-3 [139-40]). For helpful discussion of this, see Eleonore Stump, *The God of the Bible and the God of the Philosophers* (Milwaukee: Marquette University Press, 2016), 84-89; Stump, "The Nature of a Simple God," *Proceedings of the ACPA* 87 (2014): 33-38.

[119]John of Damascus, *Exp. fid.* 1.8 (18).

Israel is distinct from his creatures.[120] For to be a creature, a caused being, is to participate in a restricted manner in the life of God and thus to be finite and in this way decidedly other than the Creator.[121] But the perfections granted to creatures are present in God, the one from whom all things exist (Ps 94:8-11; Rom 11:36; 1 Cor 8:6), without limit and in an undivided manner.[122] The infinity of God thus secures his distinction from creatures and yet, given that God is not in the same order of being as creatures, does so in such a way that he need not mitigate his presence or economic condescension in order to uphold that distinction. God therefore has no gap to bridge in order to draw near to us, and in fact we can exist only where he is: "in him we live and move and have our being" (Acts 17:28).

4. The aseity and prevenient completeness of God ensures that the Son remains fully God in the incarnation and is also truly the subject of the work of Jesus Christ.[123] Since the Son is already and incorruptibly established in his deity, he need not keep his distance, so to speak, from the human nature he is to assume. He need not delegate that human nature to another *hypostasis*, nor does he need to modify his deity in order to accommodate his human nature.[124] Thus the Son throughout his incarnate ministry continues to subsist in the original, undiminished fullness of the *forma Dei*, which he shares with the Father and Spirit. As the apostle Paul would have us believe,

---

[120]See Thomas Aquinas, *De ente et essentia*, in *Opera omnia*, vol. 43, Leonine ed. (Rome: Editori Di San Tommaso, 1976), 5 (378); *ST* Ia.3.4 ad 1 (42); 7.1 ad 3 (72); 8.1 ad 1 and 3 (82); Turretin, *Inst.* 3.8.3 (1:213-14); Mastricht, *TPT* 2.9.6 (118), where Mastricht addresses the matter of whether God's infinity coheres with his being in a certain sense a particular being (*hoc aliquid*) distinct from creatures. Cf. Rocca, *Speaking the Incomprehensible God*, 262.

[121]So Thomas, *SCG* 2.45 (372); *ST* Ia.7.2 corp. and ad 1 (74); 47.1 corp. and ad 2 (485-86).

[122]John of Damascus, *Exp. fid.* 1.8 (18); Thomas, *ST* Ia.4.2 (51-52); Turretin, *Inst.* 3.8.15 (1:216); Mastricht, *TPT* 2.3.13 (80); 4.8 (87).

[123]This matter was touched on in chap. 3, under the section titled "Christology's Positive Contribution," but there I was moving along a *via inventionis* from the incarnation to discernment of God's aseity. It also appeared later in the chapter, in the section titled "The *Logos Asarkos* and *Extra Calvinisticum*," but there the aim was to address Barth's concern about a "twofold Christ." Here I am moving along a *via iudicii* from the knowledge of God's aseity to discernment of the nature of the incarnation.

[124]Compare Thomas Joseph White, "How Barth Got Aquinas Wrong: A Reply to Archie J. Spencer on Causality and Christocentrism," *Nova et Vetera* 7 (2009): 260-69. Intriguingly, Jüngel laments that Spinoza believed the God-world distinction prevented God from taking on human flesh (*God as the Mystery of the World*, 280). Jüngel himself aimed to avoid this obstruction of the incarnation by positing that God's being is constituted by the work of the incarnate Son, whereas this section circumvents Spinoza's reasoning by revisiting the implications of God's aseity and Creator-creature distinction.

the Son's kenosis is not a matter of foregoing anything of deity but a matter of positively taking up the *forma servi*, under which his divine glory is typically veiled during his earthly ministry (Phil 2:6-8; cf. Col 2:9). Subsisting in the divine essence that stands in a noncompetitive relation to created being, the Son is immediately the one who exists, acts, and suffers in his human nature. Since the Son has communicated his *hypostasis* to this human nature, it has its own subsistence in him, and in him alone.[125] There is thus a "reciprocation" in which the Son subsists in the human nature and the human nature subsists in him.[126] This entails a "real communication" (not merely "verbal" or predicative communication) of the properties, capacities, and sufferings of the human nature to the person of the Son, a point that is well-marked in classical Reformed Christology. Girolamo Zanchi, for example, aptly comments that the *communicatio idiomatum* is "real" with respect to the person, though it is "verbal" with respect to the other nature *as such*.[127] The Son therefore does not merely wield his human nature as an instrument or detached object; instead, he directly subsists in it and thereby experiences (without sin) the full range of human emotion and hardship.[128] Having one subsistence but with a "twofold *ratio* of subsisting"—"one in the

---

[125]On the communication of the Son's *hypostasis* as the rendering of his person common to his humanity as well as his deity, see Polanus, *Syntagma* 6.16 (375-76); Turretin, *Inst.* 13.6.22 (2:344); John Owen, *Christologia*, in *The Works of John Owen*, vol. 1, *The Glory of Christ*, ed. William H. Goold (Edinburgh: Banner of Truth, 1965), 18 (233). On the subsistence of the human nature in the Son, see, e.g., Polanus, *Syntagma* 6.16 (375).

[126]Johannes Maccovius, *Loci communes theologici*, ed. Nicolaus Arnoldus, 2nd ed. (Amsterdam, 1658), 17 (491). There are two senses of the word *subsist* at work here. On the one hand, there is the subsisting (*hyparxis*) of the *hypostasis* with his own peculiar, individuating character. On the other hand, there is the subsisting (*ousiōsis*) that is just the actuality of the substance or essence in the individual person, without reference to the distinguishing features or incommunicability of the particular person (though the essence is actuated only in conjunction with the incommunicable mode of subsisting of the particular person). On the complexities and different uses of the terminology, see Boethius, *Contra Eutychen* 3 (84-93); Turretin, *Inst.* 3.23.5 (1:280-81).

[127]Girolamo Zanchi, *De incarnatione Filii Dei* (Heidelberg, 1593), 2.2 (86-88). By "verbal" in this case Zanchi means that while the death of Christ, for example, pertains to him as man, it is possible to denominate him by his divine nature and under such a name attribute to him something that pertains to his human nature, as in the statement "God bought the church with his own blood" (Acts 20:28). Cf. Turretin, *Inst.* 13.8.3 (2:350), who calls this "indirect predication."

[128]The Reformed do sometimes call Christ's human nature an "instrument" (e.g., Polanus, *Syntagma* 6.16 [375]; Turretin, *Inst.* 13.6.22 [2:344]), but the language is actually used to stress that the human nature does not become a second person but is rather enhypostatic vis-à-vis the one person of the Son, warding off the problem of Nestorianism.

divine nature from eternity, the other in the human nature after the incarnation"[129]—the Son is "no less true man than true God."[130]

In his divine aseity, then, the Son can subsist immediately in a human nature without forfeiting or adjusting his deity in any way. This is reinforced by the fact that in the incarnation the locus of unity is not the natures (divine and human) but rather the person (the Son, Jesus Christ).[131] The New Testament teaching on the incarnation does not require us to homogenize the Son's divine and human natures to make them compatible with one another but only to acknowledge (1) that the Son operating in his divine essence can assume a lowly human nature (John 1:14; Phil 2:6-7) and (2) that there is just one subject subsisting in these two distinct natures (Acts 20:28; 1 Cor 2:8). It is not the divine essence as such that is incarnate but one of the persons of that essence that takes on flesh. In other words, the divine essence is "mediately" incarnate while the person of the Son is "immediately" incarnate.[132] To be sure, there is no "real" distinction between essence and person in God, where a real distinction is taken to be a distinction between one "thing" and another.[133] Yet given that the singular divine essence subsists in three distinct persons, it is critical to recognize that the essence is in a certain sense "broader" (*latius*) than any one of the persons taken individually.[134] Additionally, given that only the Son is incarnate—not the Father or Spirit, with whom the Son shares the divine essence—it follows that a divine person is in some sense distinct from the essence as such. Each person is "really" God or the divine essence (is one and the same "thing" as the essence), but, since each exists in the Godhead in his own peculiar manner, each is distinct from it as a mode of subsisting of the essence from the essence itself.[135] However, the fact that the divine essence is only "mediately" incarnate is good news for those who wish to affirm the freedom and authenticity of the

---

[129]William Ames, *Medulla theologica*, 2nd ed. (Amsterdam, 1659), 1.18 (73).

[130]Zanchi, *De incarnatione* 2.2 (84).

[131]See the section "The *Logos Asarkos* and *Extra Calvinisticum*" in chap. 3.

[132]So Turretin, *Inst.* 13.4.7 (2:331); Mastricht, *TPT* 5.4.5 (537).

[133]Such a distinction would yield a quaternity, with the essence as a distinct subsistence alongside the Father, Son, and Spirit.

[134]See Turretin, *Inst.* 3.15.24 (1:299).

[135]As Keckermann notes, this is a real distinction just in the sense that it is in reality and outside the human mind (*Systema s.s. theologiae*, in *Operum omnium quae extant* [Geneva, 1614], 1.4 [2:85-86]). Cf. Alsted, *Metaphysica* 1.29 (40), and Mastricht, *TPT* 2.24.9 (238), who call this a "real modal distinction."

Son's economic condescension. For, on the one hand, his deity is in no way changed or lessened in the incarnation, and, on the other hand, it is not communicated to his humanity at the expense of that humanity's genuineness. The Son who subsists in the fullness of deity also in the unmitigated finitude and lowliness of his human nature acts and suffers on our behalf. Christ operates as God in sovereignly laying down his life (John 10:17-18), for example, while he also with costly self-denial exercises his genuinely human will in submitting to the plan of God for salvation (Mk 14:34-36; Phil 2:8; Heb 5:7-10).[136] The human suffering of the Son is not translated back into his deity or distanced from our suffering by his continually subsisting in the form of God. The Son who is God over all experiences unalloyed human anguish in his passion, and this distinctly human suffering is the marrow and consolation of Christ's sympathetic priesthood for believers. Thus the Christian practice of *theologia* helps us to confess that the Son is true God throughout his earthly pilgrimage, to affirm the direct subsistence of his human nature in his singular person, and to retain a firm distinction between his human and divine natures. It helps us to understand and appreciate all the more the Son's radical humility in taking on flesh and blood to rescue the children of Abraham (Heb 2:14-18).

Conclusion

In this chapter, we have examined the relationship between *theologia* in its strict sense and the discipline of metaphysics. We have noted that this is necessary because often discourse about God in himself without reference to the economy is thought to be a matter of "metaphysics" (i.e., inferring from a generic concept of being what God must be like in himself). The identification of what I have been calling *theologia* with metaphysics in this sense gives rise to three concerns in recent literature on the subject: (1) that God will be understood as a mere counterpart to creatures at the expense of the Creator-creature distinction; (2) that it undermines God's freedom to condescend to dwell among us in the economy; and (3) that such a doctrine

---

[136]A point that is distilled in the traditional Protestant teaching of the *communicatio operationum* (viz., the "sharing" of the operations of the two natures of Christ in all his mediatorial works), on which see further Steven J. Duby, "Atonement, Impassibility and the *Communicatio Operationum*," *IJST* 17 (2015): 284-95.

of God will produce a conflict between God *in se* and God *pro nobis* and will therefore call into question the genuine deity of the Son in the incarnation. In light of this, I have argued that metaphysics, historically understood, is actually just the study of created being as such and that it does not include God within its field of inquiry. In fact, metaphysics both in its more traditional sense and in the more pejorative sense (wrongly using a "master-concept" of being to establish what God is) is quite different from the practice of contemplating God in his aseity and transcendence of the economy on the basis of his self-revelation. Indeed, the work of *theologia* is precisely what is needed to ensure that the Christian understanding of God does not degenerate into mere metaphysics and lose sight of the Creator-creature distinction. At the same time, description of God *in se* can make good (analogical and ministerial) use of metaphysical concepts developed in the broadly Aristotelian tradition, particularly in view of the biblical precedent for doing so. To finish the chapter, I then maintained that the practice of *theologia* circumvents the other two concerns about "metaphysical" doctrines of God. Pondering God's self-referential completeness, instead of obscuring God's freedom for economic condescension or his sameness *in se* and *pro nobis*, actually helps us to understand the authentic presence of God in the world and the immediacy and depth of the Son's human experience in the incarnation.

At different points in this chapter there has been occasion to mention the analogical nature of theological language, but I have not yet taken the time to explore the historical or constructive dynamics of a Christian doctrine of analogy. Moreover, I have not yet taken into account notable objections raised against the notion of an ontological similarity between God and creatures and against the analogical (rather than univocal) character of theological predication. Certainly an account of the Christian practice of discourse about God in himself will do well to consider the nature of analogy and theological language more carefully. This will take place in the final chapter of this study.

FIVE

"To Whom Will You Compare Me?"

Retrieving the (Right) Doctrine of Analogy

T HE TASK OF OFFERING DESCRIPTION of God in himself necessarily involves using language that human beings customarily apply to themselves and to fellow creatures. This raises the question of how creaturely language can be applied to God without undermining either God's transcendence or our genuine knowledge of him in that transcendence. Often in the Christian tradition this question has been answered by appealing to an analogy—a similarity that leaves room for significant dissimilarity—that exists between the sense in which our language applies to creatures and the sense in which it applies to God. There is also an important question about the ontological basis on which this semantic analogy depends. What about our ontological relationship to God would justify our application of creaturely language to God himself? Is there an *analogia entis* (analogy of being) between us and God according to which we may use our words to describe him?

In exploring this aspect of the practice of *theologia* I am interested in retrieving a doctrine of analogy for contemporary description of God, but this requires facing several objections raised by systematic and philosophical theologians. Authors like Karl Barth and Wolfhart Pannenberg present serious challenges to the notion of an *analogia entis*. Others like William Alston and some expositors of John Duns Scotus have argued that analogy alone is insufficient to secure the truthfulness of our speech about God. In this chapter I will first consider some pertinent biblical teaching on the relationship between God and creatures, exploring God's otherness or transcendence, on the one hand, and God's communicative activity, on the other. These two realities (divine transcendence and divine communication) require us to navigate between triumphalism and agnosticism in our approach to theological description. This will prompt an exploration of how these issues have been handled in historical treatments of analogy and univocity. After surveying some of the major authors, I will explain why I believe a carefully crafted doctrine of analogy is the way forward. Next I will examine objections found in Barth, Pannenberg, and some proponents of univocity and provide a response to them.

Scripture, Divine Transcendence, and Divine Communication

Scriptural teaching on transcendence and communication. In his rich goodness God has chosen to give life to others. He has chosen to bring about a world of created beings that, on the one hand, are inadequate to express the fullness of his perfection and yet, on the other hand, as *his* effects, cannot help but derive all their perfection and goodness from him as the one from whom, through whom, and to whom all things exist (Rom 11:36; 1 Cor 8:6; Col 1:16). God did not create out of lack or need but with a desire to communicate (i.e., to share and manifest his goodness) and to enter a covenant partnership in which human beings contribute to the development and flourishing of the world.

In revealing himself to humanity, God has underscored his otherness or transcendence that abides even in the midst of creatures sharing in what God has. The divine transcendence is ultimately rooted in his aseity. As the independent and self-sufficient one (Ps 50:7-13; Acts 17:24-25), God enjoys a plenitude of life in himself by virtue of which he cannot be contained by finite reality and cannot be circumscribed by human thoughts or words. The infinite fullness of God is an unsearchable greatness (Ps 145:3). Within that infinite fullness there is a wisdom beyond tracing out, a love beyond understanding, a power capable of more than we could imagine (Rom 11:33; Eph 3:14-21). In light of this positive richness and preeminence, Holy Scripture alerts us to the fact that representing God in human words will not be a straightforward undertaking. In face of God's incomprehensibility, it is fitting, with Job, to put one's hand over one's mouth (Job 40:4). It is fitting to heed the words of the prophet Habakkuk:

> the LORD is in his holy temple;
>> let all the earth keep silence before him! (Hab 2:20 NRSV)

As the underived and immeasurable God before whom all creatures are nothing, YHWH asks,

> To whom then will you compare me,
>> or who is my equal? (Is 40:25 NRSV)

Not because of any emptiness, confusion, or darkness in God himself but because of his plenitude and holiness—his "unapproachable light" (1 Tim 6:16)—the application of human language to God will involve some disruption of its ordinary ways of signifying.

At the same time, the Bible is clear that God's will to communicate something of his perfection to creatures has resulted in a genuine creaturely participation in what God is and does, a participation according to which there is some ontological basis for utilizing words that properly signify created things in our description of God himself. Though YHWH does not give his glory to another in that he does not allow idols to receive credit for his mighty deeds and does not tolerate human arrogance (Is 48:3-11), he does generously enable creatures to partake of and point back toward his glory. The heavens and the earth are filled with his glory—his wisdom, power, and majesty in their outward manifestation (Num 14:21; Ps 8:1, 5; 19:1; 97:6; Is 6:3; Rom 1:20). This participation and reflection of the divine glory is an established reality, even if it would not persist without the constant sustaining activity of trinitarian providence (Col 1:17; Heb 1:3). It is an established reality even if there is an important sense in which the display of God's glory in his miraculous activity and supernatural revelation may come and go (see Ezek 10:18; 43:4-5; 44:4). Accordingly, the biblical authors point out that whatever perfection belongs to the created order must ultimately come from God. He has granted hearing and sight to creatures, so he too possesses understanding and sees what happens in the world (Ps 94:9). He is the archetypal Father, "from whom all fatherhood in the heavens and on earth is named" (Eph 3:15).

God exhibits his communicative purposes especially in the creation of humanity in the image of God. God makes humanity, male and female, "in his image," "according to his likeness," and he blesses them and commands them to fill and subdue the earth, ruling over its many creatures (Gen 1:26-28). The *imago Dei* is thus closely tied to humanity's dominion in the text of Genesis 1, a point that is, according to various studies of the Old Testament's cultural context, corroborated by ancient views of statues representing the rule of kings throughout the land and kings themselves being images of the gods and executing the rule of the gods.[1] The interpretation of the *imago Dei* "as rule" appears to be, one writer notes, "the near consensus of opinion in current Old Testament scholarship."[2] However, this emphasis on the functional aspect of the image of God can be affirmed and yet also set within a broader understanding of relevant scriptural teaching. According to Genesis 1, the exercise of power and authority in action is indeed included in the meaning of the image. Human creatures bear a similitude to God in the earthly exercise of their intellectual and volitional capacities. Without directly applying these insights to the doctrine of the image of God per se, Thomas sheds light on this when he remarks that with God it "agrees especially to act, and to diffuse his own similitude to others."[3] In his providence, God works through his higher creatures to govern his lower creatures, "not because of a defect of his own power, but because of the abundance of his own goodness, that he should communicate the dignity of causality also to creatures."[4] God sustains the nature and powers of human persons in order to enable them to operate in the world. God has ordered the nature of human beings not toward a "static" existence but rather to be perfected in action: "Form, which is *actus primus*, exists for its own operation, which is *actus secundus*, and so operation is the end of a created thing."[5] In Turretin's

---

[1] E.g., J. Richard Middleton, *The Liberating Image: The* Imago Dei *in Genesis 1* (Grand Rapids: Brazos, 2005), 93-184; John H. Walton, *Ancient Near Eastern Thought and the Old Testament: Introducing the Conceptual World of the Hebrew Bible* (Grand Rapids: Baker Academic, 2006), 212-13.

[2] Middleton, *Liberating Image*, 45.

[3] Thomas Aquinas, *De potentia*, in *Quaestiones disputatae*, vol. 2, ed. P. M. Pession, 10th ed. (Rome-Turin: Marietti, 1965), 1.1 corp. (9).

[4] Thomas, *ST* Ia.22.3 corp. (267).

[5] Thomas, *ST* Ia.105.5 corp. (475-76). Of course, in Thomas's theology, the ultimate end of human persons is the restful activity that takes place in the beatific vision (e.g., *Compendium theologiae*, in *Opera omnia*, vol. 42, Leonine ed. [Rome: Editori Di San Tomasso, 1979], 149 [138]).

words, humanity's lordship is a "character" of God's supreme lordship, which is in a limited way "communicated" to humanity.[6]

Nevertheless, given all that the biblical canon teaches on the *imago Dei*, dominion is just one dimension of the image. Christians must "put on the new self which is created to be like God [κατὰ θεὸν] in righteousness and true holiness" (Eph 4:24), which echoes Genesis 1:26-27.[7] This "new self" is "renewed in knowledge according to the image of the one who created him" (Col 3:10). The Ephesians and Colossians texts together signal that our restoration in the image of God includes the restoration of the qualities of righteousness and holiness and of the natural faculty of knowing (cf. Eccles 7:29; Rom 12:2). Such a restoration implies that from the beginning the image of God included not just the exercise of dominion but also a righteousness, holiness, and wisdom that enabled a right dominion in the first place. Furthermore, insofar as our original righteousness, holiness, and wisdom are lost in the fall without the image's being lost entirely (so Gen 9:6; Jas 3:9), it seems that the image includes at a fundamental level the very nature of the human race, whose powers of understanding and willing are now bereft of their original virtues.[8] One can then identify (1) human nature as fundamentally "constitutive" of the image; (2) righteousness, holiness, and wisdom as belonging to the "integrity" or completeness of the image; and (3) the exercise of dominion as a "consequent part" or "emanation" of these two other parts.[9] The doctrine of the *imago Dei* thus entails that there is some resemblance of human action and being to God's action and being.

Since human beings now "fall short of the glory of God" (Rom 3:23), he has endeavored to restore and perfect his communicative work in our redemption. The archetype to which we are conformed is not merely the first Adam but God's own Son, Jesus Christ, the "image of the invisible God" in

---

[6]Turretin, *Inst.* 5.10.22 (1:516-17).

[7]See, e.g., Frank Thielman, *Ephesians*, BECNT (Grand Rapids: Baker Academic, 2010), 306-7.

[8]Since God's own being is incorporeal and spiritual, it is arguably the spiritual part of our nature in which the likeness to God should be located. However, the fact that God is *imaged* implies some visible and bodily representation of this likeness. Further, given that the human person is a composite creature, both spiritual and material, the endowments and workings of the human soul are expressed in bodily action in the world so that the *imago Dei* encompasses in a broad sense the body too (so, e.g., Polanus, *Syntagma* 5.34 [328]).

[9]So Turretin, *Inst.* 5.10.6, 22 (1:513, 516-17).

whom "all the fullness of deity dwells bodily" (Col 1:15, 19; 2:9; cf. 2 Cor 4:4, 6; Heb 1:3). We are predestined to be conformed to his image (Rom 8:29). We are called by the gospel of God to "take possession of the glory of our Lord Jesus Christ" (2 Thess 2:14; cf. 1 Thess 2:12; 2 Tim 2:10; Heb 2:10). This glory will be fully realized in us and revealed at the second coming of the Lord (Rom 8:18-19; 2 Cor 4:17; Col 1:27; 3:4; 2 Thess 1:12; 1 Pet 5:1, 4, 10), at which time the rest of creation too will once more reflect the glory of God without blemish (Rom 8:20-22). Our sight of Christ "just as he is" will render us "like him" (1 Jn 3:2). Even now we behold him (albeit in a limited way) and thus undergo a reordering of our desires and a transformation into his image "from glory to glory" (2 Cor 3:18). We share in God's holiness (Heb 12:10). We are "partakers [κοινωνοί] of the divine nature" in that we escape worldly corruption and acquire virtue, knowledge, self-control, perseverance, godliness, and love (2 Pet 1:4-7). The acquisition of such can hardly entail an inactive kind of participation.[10] The saints exercise Christian virtues in a multitude of actions that reflect the holiness and love of God (Mt 5:43-48; Jn 13:34-35; Eph 4:32-5:2; 1 Pet 1:16; 1 Jn 3:3). As in the sphere of creation and nature, so too in the sphere of redemption and supernatural grace there is a resemblance of human being and action to divine being and action.

Scriptural teaching and the concept of participation. Our understanding of the implications of divine transcendence and divine communication for our speech about God will benefit from a bit of technical analysis of the concept of participation, something that can be undertaken with the help of various authors in the Christian tradition.[11] In this discussion to participate

---

[10]Some have argued that by "sharers of the divine nature" Peter refers to partnership with God in his covenantal or eschatological action (so Al Wolters, "'Partners of the Deity': A Covenantal Reading of 2 Peter 1:4," *Calvin Theological Journal* 25 [1990]: 28-44; Scott. J. Hafemann, "'Divine Nature' in 2 Pet 1,4 within Its Eschatological Context," *Biblica* 94 [2013]: 80-99). That line of thought is certainly not incompatible with the argument of this section (though it is, I think, incomplete). The "sharing" in 2 Pet 1:4 is explained by our growth in knowledge, love, and so on in the subsequent verses (cf., e.g., Gene L. Green, *Jude and 2 Peter*, BECNT [Grand Rapids: Baker Academic, 2008], 186-87), all of which leads to the exercise of Spirit-wrought virtue.

[11]Discussion of "participation" in recent theology is quite complex and for some has generated concerns about whether it may compromise the asymmetrical nature of the Creator-creature relation (see John Webster, "Perfection and Participation," in *The Analogy of Being: Invention of the Antichrist or the Wisdom of God?*, ed. Thomas Joseph White [Grand Rapids: Eerdmans, 2011], 379-93). I hope that the explanation of my use of it here will allay such concerns.

means, in Thomas's words, "to receive partially that which belongs to another wholly,"[12] or as some have said it, "to have partially what another is without restriction."[13] God has what he has (wisdom, justice, goodness, and so on) "without restriction," which is to say, without limitation or derivation from another. As Barth puts it, "God does not borrow what He is from outside."[14] The true God has abundant life, light, and love in himself (Jn 1:4; 5:26; 17:24). His perfection is never a mere instance of something greater or broader than himself, so he can even be called "life" and "light" and "love" (Jn 11:25-26; 1 Jn 1:2; 4:8, 16; 5:20).[15] There is no impersonal form of life, wisdom, or love "out there" from which God must draw in order to be what he is. Indeed, if he is not produced by another or even held in unity by an impersonal, underlying modal structure according to which God would necessarily have distinct parts in himself, the divine attributes do not signify parts composing God's being but rather describe God's whole being from a certain angle. God's being (his essence and *esse*) and his perfections are infinite and really identical (the same *res* or "thing," not multiple "things" brought together). We distinguish among God's perfections not because they are really distinct from one another in God but because we cannot conceive the whole of God's being all at once and because his operations and effects bear diverse characters and indicate that the content of diverse attributes (wisdom, justice, love, and so on) is truly present in the unity of God's being.[16] Thus God's perfections (life, wisdom, love, power, and so on)

---

[12]Thomas Aquinas, *Expositio libri Boethii De hebdomadibus*, in *Opera omnia*, vol. 50, Leonine ed. (Rome: Commissio Leonina; Paris: Éditions du Cerf, 1992), 2 (271).

[13]Bernard Montagnes, *The Doctrine of the Analogy of Being According to Thomas Aquinas*, trans. E. M. Macierowski (Milwaukee: Marquette University Press, 2004), 34; cf. Gregory P. Rocca, *Speaking the Incomprehensible God: Thomas Aquinas on the Interplay of Positive and Negative Theology* (Washington, DC: Catholic University of America Press, 2004), 282-86; Reinhard Hütter, "Attending to the Wisdom of God—from Effect to Cause, from Creation to God: A *Relecture* of the Analogy of Being According to Thomas Aquinas," in White, *Analogy of Being*, 230.

[14]Barth, *CD* II/1, 334.

[15]John of Damascus expresses this by calling God αὐτοζωή, αὐτοαγαθότης, αὐτοφῶς (*Exp. fid.* 1.8 [18]).

[16]Thomas Aquinas, *Scriptum super libros Sententiarum*, ed. R. P. Mandonnet (Paris, 1929), 1.2.1.2-3 (1:61-72); Johann Alsted, *Metaphysica* (Herbornae Nassoviorum, 1613), 1.29 (242); Gisbertus Voetius *Selectarum disputationum theologicarum* (Utrecht, 1648), 1.13 (233); Mastricht, *TPT* 2.5.7 (93-94); 6.23 (104). This is often expressed in terms of a "virtual" distinction among God's attributes: a distinction located in the operations and effects of God brought about by God's multifaceted power (*virtus*). On such a view, it is not the case that the divine attributes pertain to "varying creaturely projections, reflecting varying creaturely states, none of which touch the

"preexist" in God in an eminent way in that they are infinite and really one in him.[17] God is therefore the one who possesses in himself the perfections of all created genera and is their *principium* (foundation, beginning).[18]

In his work of creation, God gives being to that which is other than God, that which "receives partially" what he is "without restriction." The being and perfections of creatures are derived. Their being and perfections are finite, limited in degree and restricted under various genera. Created effects are, after all, necessarily finite since finitude is requisite to being other than the infinite God in the first place. If distinction presupposes that something is not found in one that is found in another, it would be illogical to posit two absolute infinites that would both (if truly absolutely infinite) comprehend all perfection without limit.[19] As Thomas would put it, the being or *esse* of

---

vicious abstraction [*ipsum esse subsistens*] in its ineffable bliss" (Paul R. Hinlicky, *Divine Simplicity: Christ the Crisis of Metaphysics* [Grand Rapids: Baker Academic, 2016], 158). Rather, the content of the diverse attributes (if not the diversification of the attributes) is present in God himself in the most immediate and striking way: as his very essence, not as something consequent or added to his essence.

[17]Thomas, *De ente et essentia*, in *Opera Omnia*, vol. 43, Leonine ed. (Rome: Editori Di San Tommaso, 1976), 5 (378); *ST* Ia.4.2 (51-52).

[18]Thomas, *De potentia* 7.7 ad 4-6 (204-5); *ST* Ia.4.3 ad 2 (54). Cf. Polanus, *Syntagma* 2.9 (144); Mastricht, *TPT* 2.3.13 (80); 4.8 (87). In Thomas's understanding, a created essence limits the *esse* and perfection that a creature possesses, while in God's case his essence and abundant *esse* are one and the same, which entails that he uniquely enjoys a fullness of perfection. In this connection, since it is essence (rather than *esse*) that is taken to be a limiting factor, Thomas regards *esse* as the "perfection of all perfections" (*De ente et essentia* 5 [378]; *ST* Ia.4.2 corp. [52]). In this regard, Thomas says that the name "He who is" (*Qui est*) is the most fitting for God because it does not apply any particular (limiting) form to him (*De potentia* 7.5, corp. [199]). Cf. John Wippel, *The Metaphysical Thought of Thomas Aquinas: From Finite Being to Uncreated Being* (Washington, DC: Catholic University of America Press, 2000), 170-75. Rudi te Velde construes the role of essence somewhat differently, but he helpfully presents the logic of *esse* as the "perfection of all perfections" in *Aquinas on God: The "Divine Science" of the "Summa Theologiae"* (repr., New York: Routledge, 2016), 87-90. Related to this understanding of *esse* is Thomas's insistence that God as *ipsum esse subsistens* can have nothing added to his *esse*, while *esse commune* does not conceptually require but in reality always has some addition or further determination (*ST* Ia.3.4 ad 1 [42]).

[19]Thomas argues that the ultimate "principle of plurality" is an *ens* including in itself the "negation" of another *ens*. One *ens* has something by virtue of which it imitates the first cause (God), something that is lacking in another *ens*, and it lacks something that the other *ens* has by virtue of which that other *ens* in its own way imitates the first cause (*De Trin.* 4.1 corp. [120-21]). To be clear, though, this approach does not entail a reification of *non ens* as a positive differentiating or individuating factor but only a recognition that one created being lacks something that another has (and that God the first cause also has in an unlimited way) (cf. Wippel, *Metaphysical Thought of Thomas Aquinas*, 177-92). On the impossibility of more than one absolute infinite, see Thomas, *ST* Ia.11.3 corp. (111) and also Turretin, where he takes it as axiomatic that an infinite created effect is simply impossible (*Inst.* 3.8.9 [1:215]; 5.2.5, 9 [1:478, 479]). Scotus stresses

every creature is determined by its essence, an essence that can be expressive of the divine perfection in only a limited degree and manner.[20] This is a rationale for the multiplicity of creatures:

> The distinction and multitude of things is from the intention of the first agent, which is God. For he has produced things in being for his own goodness to be communicated to creatures and represented by these. And because it is not able to be sufficiently represented by one creature, he has produced many and diverse creatures, so that what is lacking to one with respect to the divine goodness to be represented should be supplied by others. For the goodness which is in God simply and uniformly is in creatures multiply and dividedly.[21]

To recall some of the material on "being" in chapter four, the essences or natures of creatures are not only finite but also really distinct from their *esse*. The essence of a creature does not automatically include its existing. The creature is not really identical with its own *esse* and therefore must "have" or participate in *esse* according to the generous will of God.[22] Furthermore,

---

that a thing cannot be finite (and distinct) by virtue of a relation to something else (including God) but must be finite by virtue of what is essential to it (*Opera omnia*, vols. 1-4, *Ordinatio*, ed. P. Carolo Balić [Vatican City: Typis Polyglottis Vaticanis, 1950–1956], 1.2.1.2, nn. 140-44 [2:211-13]; Scotus, *The Examined Report of the Paris Lecture: Reportatio I-A*, trans. Allan B. Wolter and Oleg V. Bychkov [St. Bonaventure: St. Bonaventure University, 2004], 1.2.1.3, nn. 52-57 [130-31]; cf. Daniel P. Horan, *Postmodernity and Univocity: A Critical Account of Radical Orthodoxy and John Duns Scotus* [Minneapolis: Fortress, 2014], 181). However, Thomas's view set out in the commentary on *De Trinitate* and appropriated here does not entail that one created thing is finite and distinct from another (or from God) by a mere accident or extrinsic relation (cf., e.g., *De potentia* 7.7 corp. [203-4], where it is the intrinsic "mode of existing" of things that produces diversity). For the claim here is that the essence itself of one created thing lacks what another created thing essentially has and lacks the plenitude that is essential in God and distinguishes him from all others. Still, it is true that no creature would have what it has apart from its relationship to the God in whom we participate and by whose providence we continue in existence. What a creature has and lacks is explicable only with reference to God. To anticipate later discussion in this chapter, this is an inflection of the point that what is often called an "analogy of proportionality" is situated within the context of an underlying Creator-creature "analogy of attribution" (on which see, e.g., Rocca, *Speaking the Incomprehensible God*, 124-27).

[20]E.g., Thomas, *ST* Ia.7.2 corp. and ad 1 (74). Here I favor Wippel's interpretation of the essence-*esse* relation in Thomas's thought (see his *Metaphysical Thought of Thomas Aquinas*, 124-31; cf. Montagnes, *Doctrine of the Analogy of Being*, 87-88) over that of Rudi te Velde, *Participation and Substantiality in Thomas Aquinas* (Leiden: Brill, 1995), 150-54. In my view, what something is (essence) need not (illogically) exist before the thing has *esse* in order to limit that *esse*. It can be a limiting principle in God's knowledge of how he may be imitated by created effects and then function as a real or actual limiting factor only from the inception of the creature's *esse*.

[21]Thomas, *ST* Ia.47.1 corp. and ad 2 (485-86).

[22]See Thomas Aquinas, *Opera omnia*, vol. 25/2, *Quaestiones de Quolibet*, Leonine ed. (Rome: Commissio Leonina; Paris: Éditions du Cerf, 1996), 2.2.1 [3] (214-15).

unlike God, for whom to be just is to be wise, good, and so on, creatures' have their various perfections (e.g., wisdom, justice, mercy) as qualities added to essence.[23] In this regard, all of God's attributes are incommunicable in that their absoluteness and real identity with essence cannot be replicated in anything other than God.[24] In this sense, creatures do not share God's perfections and are always inadequate to the power of God, their efficient cause.[25] At the same time, whatever perfection or goodness creatures do have can come from God alone (Rom 11:36; 1 Cor 8:6). There is no other fount of perfection or goodness. God's plenitude under its many aspects is the archetype according to which he endows creatures—especially his redeemed people—with their various virtues and perfections that they enact in the world. Just as there is no other ultimate efficient or final cause of things, there is likewise no other ultimate exemplar cause.[26]

On the one hand, then, God remains radically distinct. He does so not by entering into a system of demarcation where distinctions occur by one individual's lacking something that another has but by having all perfection without lack or limit and thus transcending the order of creatures altogether.[27] Accordingly, God infinitely exceeds the things properly and

---

[23]As Polanus writes, such perfections are in creatures accidentally but are in God essentially: "God by himself or by his own essence lives, knows, is wise and good etc." (*Syntagma* 2.14 [154]).

[24]See Turretin, *Inst.* 3.6.2, 4 (1:208). Put differently, there is no *proportio* between God and the creature, no traversable distance between the infinite perfection of God and the degree to which a creature may have a certain perfection (*Inst.* 3.8.13 [1:215]). Cf. Mastricht, *TPT* 2.15.12 (96-97). In this way, God's attributes are "properties," belonging peculiarly to him alone. At the same time, as Turretin observes, they are not properties in an ordinary sense since properties in creatures are something following on essence (ἐπουσιῶδες) while in God they are his essence (*Inst.* 3.5.2 [205]).

[25]In this connection, Thomas and others call God an "analogical" cause and not a "univocal" cause since his effects cannot share in parity and fullness all that he is (see Thomas, *De hebdomadibus* 2 [271]; *De potentia* 7.7 corp. [203]; *ST* Ia.4.2 corp. [51-52]; 4.3 corp. [54]; 13.5 ad 1 [147]; Ia.25.2 ad 2 [292]; Johann Alsted, *Theologia naturalis* [Antonius Hummius, 1615], 1.16 [158-59]; 17 [174]; cf. Voetius, *Selectarum disputationum theologicarum* 1.13 [233]).

[26]Cf. Thomas, *ST* Ia.15.1-3 (199, 201-2, 204); Alsted, *Theologia naturalis* 1.16 (145-47, 153-58). In the classical metaphysical tradition, an exemplar cause is distinct from a formal cause in that the former is extrinsic to the creature while the latter is intrinsic to the creature.

[27]So Thomas, *De ente et essentia* 5 (378); *In librum Beati Dionysii De divinis nominibus expositio*, ed. Ceslai Pera (Turin-Rome: Marietti, 1950), 5.2.661 (245-46); *ST* Ia.7.1 ad 3 (72); 8.1 ad 1 and 3 (82); Turretin, *Inst.* 3.8.15-16 (1:216); Mastricht, *TPT* 2.9.6 (118). It is precisely in being infinite, then, that God is distinct from us, so he need not have a restricted form of being in order to be distinct. It can be said that all distinctness is founded on negation or one thing lacking what another has, which is at least on the surface akin to some statements in Spinoza (*Ethica*, in *Opera*, vol. 2, *Tractatus de intellectus emendatione/Ethica*, ed. Carl Gebhardt, electronic ed.

ordinarily signified by creaturely words. This stands against our tendency to overestimate the depth of our knowledge of God or the descriptive prowess of academic theology. On the other hand, God does genuinely communicate what he has. Creatures have in a partial and relative way what he is wholly and absolutely.[28] The scriptural teaching on God's communicative purposes thus gives us hope that our words may be applied to God with intellectual and spiritual benefit. Even as Scripture chastens our descriptive work, it presents an ontological basis upon which the veracity of human speech about God may be grounded. More than that, the Holy Spirit himself speaking in Scripture uses ordinary words (*wisdom, holiness, love, faithfulness*) to communicate knowledge of God. He implicitly authorizes us to use such words in prayer, in preaching, and in dogmatic theology.

The transcendence of God and the communicative work of God must both be respected in developing an account of how our language may be applied to God *in se*. An analogical view of theological speech attempts to honor divine transcendence and divine communication by maintaining that the sense in which our language applies to God is neither exactly the same as nor entirely different from the way in which it applies to creatures. However, the concept of analogy has a long history and has not been free from criticism. In order to offer a responsible commendation of an analogical view of theological description, it is crucial that we take into account its historical development and, afterward, some key objections raised against it.

ANALOGY IN MEDIEVAL AND EARLY MODERN THOUGHT

Understanding analogy. Given his influence on this topic, it is fitting to note Aristotle's view of analogy before proceeding to the works of Christian

---

[Charlottesville, VA: InteLex, 2008], 1, def. 5 and 6 [45, 46]; prop. 8 [49-51]; prop. 14-15 [56-60]). However, that applies not to the Creator-creature distinction but only within the horizon of created being, for God is distinct and incommunicable by his positive, absolute plenitude (cf. Bavinck, *RD* 2:159-60, 177).

[28]The limited, partial mode in which creatures share what God has is not grounded in God's having finite parts in himself but rather in what it means for anything to be distinct from God in the first place. In order for anything to be distinct from God, it must be finite. The creature will therefore not share all that God is. Instead, the creature will share what God has insofar as this is communicable according the creature's limited constitution and according to the divine decree to actualize such communication in distinct ways for distinct kinds of created effects.

writers.[29] The Stagirite famously illustrates his understanding of analogy by using the example of health, observing different ways in which something might be called "healthy." One thing might be called "healthy" by preserving health, another by producing it, another by signaling it, another by in fact having it. Similarly, something may be called a "being" (τὸ ὄν) in different ways: for example, by being a substance (οὐσία), by being an "affection" or disposition of a substance, by being a quality of a substance, or by being a generation or production of a substance. That subject which is healthy or has health is what is principally called "healthy," and those other things we call healthy are deemed such by reference to that principally healthy thing. Likewise, substance is principally called τὸ ὄν, and other things are called "beings" by way of an analogy or certain correspondence and similarity to substance. While substance exists per se and in its own right, a quality, for example, exists in that it inheres in act in a substance. "Being" is thus predicated in different modes according to a πρὸς ἕν analogy (an analogy "toward one" or by reference and likeness to a principal thing, i.e., substance). This form of analogy is often called an "analogy of attribution." In Aristotle's metaphysics, the πρὸς ἕν analogy serves as a way to affirm the diversity of being while also securing the unity of being as a subject of scientific study. Because of the relationship of the various categories of being to a primal category (substance), being in its different modes can be studied in a single science.[30] Another form of analogy also appears in Aristotle's thought, where there is a correspondence between features of two things, in the sense that a feature of one is to it as a similar feature of another is to the other: a is to b as c is to d. A quality proper to one thing is analogous to a similar quality that is proper to another in that it is (proportionally) in its own substance as the other quality is (proportionally) in its substance.[31] This is often called an "analogy of proper proportion" (or "proportionality").

---

[29]While the particular phrase *analogia entis* does not appear in earlier Christian writers with the frequency and connotations it now has in contemporary discussion, they certainly do explore the analogical nature of "being" and other terms (cf. Thomas Joseph White, "Introduction: The *Analogia Entis* Controversy and Its Contemporary Significance," in White, *Analogy of Being*, 1-2).

[30]Aristotle, *Aristotelis Metaphysica*, ed. W. Jaeger, Oxford Classic Texts (Oxford: Clarendon, 1957), 4.1, 1003a-1005a (59-64).

[31]E.g., Aristotle, *Metaphysica* 12.1071a (248-49).

Various Christian authors have built on Aristotle's reflections on analogy. Boethius, for example, distinguishes between equivocal and univocal predication in commenting on Aristotle's *Categories*. Two things are called "equivocal," he writes, when they have in common only a name by which they are denominated or described, not the *ratio* or content of the name. In contrast, two things are called "univocal" when they have in common not only a name but also the same *ratio* or content of the name.[32] Yet, within Boethius's discussion of equivocity he identifies situations in which the *ratio* of a particular name given to two things is not entirely dissimilar in its multiple applications. For example, some things are called "equivocals" "according to similitude," like a painting of a man and a true man. Others are called "equivocals" "according to proportion," like unity is a "principle" with respect to number and a point is a "principle" with respect to a line. Some equivocals are both "descended" from one primal thing, like a "medicinal tool" and a "medicinal" or healthy coloration derive their names from "medicine" or the act of healing itself. Other equivocals are "referred to one," like "riding" may be called "salutary" and "food" also may be called "salutary."[33]

In the thirteenth century Thomas continues the Christian development of Aristotle's reflections, discussing analogy both with respect to the relationships that exist among creatures and with respect to the relationship between creatures and God.[34] Because of his influence in medieval and

---

[32]Boethius, *In Categorias Aristotelis*, in *Opera omnia*, vol. 2, PL 64 (Paris, 1847), 1 (163, 167).

[33]Boethius, *In Categorias Aristotelis* 1 (166). I take it the difference in these last two sets of "equivocals" is that the latter that are merely "referred to one" have no ontological relationship to one another.

[34]A number of studies of Thomas on analogy have appeared in recent times, often seeking to correct some misunderstandings associated with Cajetan's reading of Thomas. See, e.g., Hampus Lyttkens, *The Analogy Between God and the World: An Investigation of Its Background and Interpretation of Its Use by Thomas of Aquino* (Uppsala: Lundequistska, 1953); Gerald B. Phelan, *St. Thomas and Analogy* (Milwaukee: Marquette University Press, 1941); George P. Klubertanz, *St. Thomas Aquinas on Analogy: A Textual Analysis and Systematic Synthesis* (Chicago: Loyola University Press, 1960); Battista Mondin, *The Principle of Analogy in Protestant and Catholic Theology* (The Hague: Martinus Nijhoff, 1963), esp. parts 2-4; E. J. Ashworth, "Analogy and Equivocation in Thirteenth-Century Logic: Aquinas in Context," *Mediaeval Studies* 54 (1992): 94-135; Montagnes, *Doctrine of the Analogy of Being*; Ralph M. McInerny, *Aquinas and Analogy* (Washington, DC: Catholic University of America Press, 1996); Wippel, *Metaphysical Thought of Thomas Aquinas*, 65-93, 543-75. Some emphasize that Thomas's writing on analogy is focused on the semantic or logical level of inquiry (e.g., McInerny; see also Laurence Paul Hemming, "*Analogia non Entis sed Entitatis*: The Ontological Consequences of the Doctrine of Analogy," *IJST* 6 [2004]: 118-29), while others argue that it is directly bound up with certain ontological commitments (e.g., Wippel, *Metaphysical Thought of Thomas Aquinas*; cf. Lawrence Dewan,

contemporary theology and in the present study, I will devote more space to his view than the others in this section. Thomas conveys his understanding of analogy across a range of works in his corpus. In *De principiis naturae*, he discusses the ways in which various things may stand in unity with one another. Beyond the stricter kinds of unity (in number, in species, in genus) there is unity or "agreement" (*convenientia*) by analogy.[35] A predicate, he writes, may apply to something univocally, equivocally, or analogically. In univocal predication, not only a common name but also a common *ratio* or definition of a name applies to two different things. In such a case, the predicate indicates a genus under which two things are equally located. In equivocal predication, only a common name (not the *ratio* or definition of it) applies to two different things. In analogical predication, there is a commonality of both the name and, in a qualified way (*non ex toto*), the diverse *rationes* of the name too. The commonality of the *rationes* consists in that they are all "referred to one thing" (*attribuuntur uni alicui eidem*) from which the feature named (e.g., health) is in some sense derived. That one thing to which a plurality of analogates are referred for their unity may be a particular end, a particular agent, or a particular subject. Of special importance here is the case in which the basis for analogical unity is a subject. For Thomas, *ens* is analogically predicated of quantity, quality, and other accidental instances of being because they have substance (*ens* in its primary mode) as their subject. "Being," Thomas reasons, is not a genus encompassing both substance and accidents because it applies to substance in a primary way (*per prius*) and to accidents in a derivative way (*per posterius*). Among beings there is a relative ordering and hierarchy, while a genus applies to its sundry species (e.g., animal to man and donkey) equally and without this relative hierarchy. Due to the relationship between substance and accidents, being is therefore not predicated univocally across the

---

"St. Thomas and Analogy: The Logician and the Metaphysician," in *Form and Being: Studies in Thomistic Metaphysics* [Washington, DC: Catholic University of America Press, 2006], 81-95; Alan Philip Darley, "Predication or Participation? What Is the Nature of Aquinas' Doctrine of Analogy?," *Heythrop Journal* 57 [2016]: 312-24. For a mediating approach, see Gregory P. Rocca, *Speaking the Incomprehensible God: Thomas Aquinas on the Interplay Between Positive and Negative Theology* (Washington, DC: Catholic University of America Press, 2004), 127-34. I follow the second approach here, with an appreciative nod toward Rocca's way of explaining the relationship between the logical and ontological dynamics of analogy.

[35] Here *convenientia*, *analogia*, *proportio*, and *comparatio* all appear to be roughly synonymous.

categories of being.[36] Thomas also adds that the principles of different beings agree "according to proportion": the matter of a substance, for example, relates to its substance like the matter of a quantity relates to its quantity.[37]

In a number of works, Thomas presents his view of analogy in relation to the question of theological language and the Creator-creature relationship. In the commentary on the *Sentences*, he writes that the unity of Creator and creature is "by a community not of univocation but of analogy." Analogical "community," though, is twofold: either by posterior things participating in a prior thing or by one thing receiving its existence and *ratio* from another. God does not participate with creatures in something prior to both himself and creatures, so in the unity of Creator and creature just the latter sort of analogy applies: "The creature does not have existence except as it descends from the first being, nor is it called a being except insofar as it imitates the first being."[38] Later in this commentary, Thomas remarks that univocity assumes a "community according to the *ratio* of nature" with diversity according to (individual) existence, which community cannot apply in the case of God and creatures because God's nature is identical with his own existence. Accordingly, "being" is not predicated univocally of God and

---

[36]It may be worth pausing to note that this means Thomas does not accept the metaphysical framework of Parmenides, whose monism was built on the principle that beyond being there is only nonbeing. As Thomas unfolds the reasoning of Parmenides, he observes that nonbeing is nothing (*nihil*) and thus cannot produce diversity in being. Therefore, for Parmenides, since there is nothing to diversify being, all being must remain one. Thomas, however, takes it to be a fact that there are diverse beings and diverse categories of beings (substance and the various categories of accidents) in which beings have various modes of existing. He therefore denies that being is a genus that would have to be diversified by factors external to it (see Thomas Aquinas, *In duodecim libros Metaphysicorum Aristotelis*, ed. M.-R. Cathala and R. M. Spiazzi [Turin-Rome: Marietti, 1950], 1.9.138-39 [41-42]; cf. Wippel, *Metaphysical Thought of Thomas Aquinas*, 66-73, 87-89). In Thomas's view, then, being applies to the many, and its unity consists not in that it is a genus equally applicable to all things but rather in that, on the level of created being (or the "predicamental" level), it always stands in some correspondence or πρὸς ἕν analogy to substance (*In Metaphysicorum* 4.1.535-44 [151-52]). To elaborate, in medieval philosophy and theology, to identify being as a genus applicable under the same *ratio* to the many would inevitably raise questions about (1) how being could be diversified (for a genus is differentiated by factors extrinsic to it) and (2) how it could remain a transcendental concept predicable equally and under the same *ratio* across the categories of things that in fact have diverse modes of existing. As noted below, when Scotus defends the univocity of being, he will argue that his view does not require being to be a genus and does not stipulate that all beings have the same mode of existing in reality.

[37]Thomas Aquinas, *De principiis naturae*, in *Opera omnia*, vol. 43, Leonine ed. (Rome: Editori di San Tommaso, 1976), 6 (46-47).

[38]Thomas, *Sententiarum*, prol., q. 1, a. 2 ad 2 (10).

creatures. A predicate like "being" or "knowledge" is predicated analogically of God and creatures insofar as creatures imperfectly imitate God and are thus "like God" (even as God is, strictly speaking, not "like" creatures).[39] In the same work, Thomas provides another ramification of analogy under three types: (1) analogy according to mental "intention" only (*secundum intentionem tantum, et non secundum esse*), where something is thought to belong to multiple things (with reference to a first) even though in reality it is properly in the first only; (2) analogy according to being only (*secundum esse et non secundum intentionem*), where something belongs to multiple things in reality in an analogical manner but is thought by the mind to apply to them univocally; and (3) analogy according to both intention and being (*secundum intentionem et secundum esse*), where something applies in an analogical manner to multiple things both in the intention of the mind and in reality. For Thomas, the third type of analogy is in view when being is predicated of substance and accidents and when various things (truth and goodness, for example) are predicated of God and creatures. Truth and goodness are in God and then in creatures with greater and lesser degrees of perfection.[40] Significantly, Thomas is clearly deploying the notion of analogy here in a way that underscores that a given perfection is not merely caused by God but also truly present in God himself.[41]

In *De veritate*, Thomas presents an alternative account of analogy. Once again he denies that something (in this case, knowledge) can be attributed to God and creatures univocally. However much creatures might imitate God, nothing can belong to creatures according to the same *ratio* with which it belongs to God, for all that is in God is identical with his own *esse*. Yet pure equivocity is ruled out because some similarity between God and creatures is presupposed in God's knowing creatures by knowing himself and in our ability to learn about God by studying created beings. To explain how this analogical "community" does not undermine the Creator-creature distinction or the "infinite distance" between God and creatures, Thomas explains how analogy or *proportio* can have different meanings. On the one hand, "agreement according to proportion" can apply when two things have

---

[39]Thomas, *Sententiarum* 1.35.1.4 sol. and ad 6 (819-21).
[40]Thomas, *Sententiarum* 1.19.5.2 ad 1 (492).
[41]Cf. Wippel, *Metaphysical Thought of Thomas Aquinas*, 549-50.

a proportion toward one another in that they have a "determined distance" or some mutual "habitude" between them. Thomas calls this an "agreement of proportion" (*convenientia proportionis*). For example, the number two has such a distance or habitude to the number one, in that two is its double. On the other hand, there may be an agreement not of two things proportionate to one another but of two proportions to one another. Thomas calls this an "agreement of proportionality" (*convenientia proportionalitatis*), and it echoes Aristotle's identification of an analogy in which *a* is to *b* as *c* is to *d*. Here Thomas gives an example: sight is to the eye as understanding is to the mind. Because creatures have no habitude or relation to God in which his perfection is determined by them, only this second form of analogy—an analogy of "proportionality"—can apply in the case of God and creatures. God's knowledge is to God as the creature's knowledge is to the creature. This "similitude of proportionality" does not compromise the "infinite distance" between God and the creature or entail a mutual habitude between them. Creatures are like God, but, in accord with Isaiah 40:18 ("To whom will you compare me?"), God is not like creatures.[42]

In later works, Thomas does not persist in limiting the Creator-creature analogy to that of "proportionality." He returns to the "analogy of attribution" in which the perfections of creatures are referred back to God.[43] To conserve space, this can be presented in a composite sketch of relevant portions of the *Summa contra Gentiles*, *De potentia*, and *Summa theologiae*. Thomas stresses that nothing belongs to God and creatures univocally, for created effects are

---

[42]Thomas Aquinas, *Opera omnia*, vol. 22/1.2, *Quaestiones disputatae de veritate*, Leonine ed. (Rome: ad Sanctae Sabinae 1970), 2.11 corp. and ad 1, 2, 4 (78-80).

[43]In light of Thomas's *De veritate*, Cajetan famously linked the analogy of proportionality to the analogy *secundum esse* described in Thomas's *Sentences* commentary and argued that the analogy of proportionality uniquely upholds that a given perfection is truly found in God himself (see his *De nominum analogia. De conceptu entis*, ed. P. N. Zammit [Rome, 1952], 3.23-30 [23-30]). On this point, his reading of Thomas is criticized by various authors (e.g., Montagnes, *Doctrine of the Analogy of Being*, 120-40; McInerny, *Aquinas and Analogy*, 3-29; Wippel, *Metaphysical Thought of Thomas Aquinas*, 90n87, 553). However, for a more recent effort to explain Cajetan's own constructive aims in *De nominum analogia*, see Joshua P. Hochschild, *The Semantics of Analogy: Rereading Cajetan's "De Nominum Analogia"* (Notre Dame, IN: University of Notre Dame Press, 2010). In my view, it is important to recognize that Thomas's treatment of analogy in *De veritate* is not his last word on the matter and that the analogy of attribution too can uphold presence of God's perfections in God himself. At the same time, I believe that one helpful point made in the *De veritate* treatment is that God and creatures have no *proportio* or determinate distance between them. While they do have an ontological relationship, it is not a mutually constitutive one.

not formally "adequate" to the divine power by which they are wrought. God is an analogical agent who produces his likeness in his effects, but in only a limited fashion. For God's perfections are really identical with his own essence, while the creature's perfections (wisdom, goodness, power, and so on) are qualities added to essence. God has his perfections in an unlimited or "universal" way, while creatures have their various perfections by participation in God's perfection and thus in a limited or "partial" way. God's perfections "preexist" in him in a simple and preeminent manner, while creatures' perfections exist in them in a divided manner. Moreover, the attributes used to reference God's perfections do not circumscribe their referent (*res significata*), while the attributes used to reference creatures' perfections do to some degree comprehend their referents. In addition, what is predicated univocally of two things is simpler than and prior to both of them, but, according to Thomas, nothing is ontologically or conceptually simpler than or prior to God. Univocity also assumes a parity in the modes of existing of two things, but God is his own *esse*, and creatures exist only by participation in *esse*.[44] *Ens* (a term derived from the verb *esse*) therefore cannot be predicated univocally of God and creatures, for it is predicated of God in an absolute manner (essentially and *secundum prius*) and of creatures in a derivative manner (by participation and *secundum posterius*).[45] To put it differently, *ens*

---

[44]On the senses in which creatures participate in *esse*, see Wippel, *Metaphysical Thought of Thomas Aquinas*, 120-21.

[45]Furthermore, for Thomas, since *esse* within the order of created being is the concrete actualization of essence it is not included in genus or species but rather lies on the side of that which individuates things (see, e.g., *Quaestiones de quolibet* 2.2.2 [4] [216-18]; *ST* Ia.3.5 corp. [44]). Thus the meaning of the commonality of *ens* and *esse* within the horizon of created being might be summarized as follows. First, *ens* or *esse* commonly applies to various categories of things (delineated in the ten Aristotelian *praedicamenta*) by an analogical correspondence in which things in the nine accidental *praedicamenta* depend on substances. Given the evidently diverse modes of existing of substances, quantities, qualities, and so on, *ens* is not restricted to one genus and is not itself a genus equally and univocally applicable to all the categories of being. Second, *ens* or *esse* commonly applies to distinct individuals in that all individual things exist, but it is not a genus or species that accounts for the common determinations of a group of individuals. Rather, it can be said to apply similarly to individuals across categories or within a category, genus, or species by an analogy of proportionality (e.g., the *esse* of Peter is to Peter as the *esse* of John is to John) (cf. Montagnes, *Doctrine of the Analogy of Being*, 87-88; Wippel, *Metaphysical Thought of Thomas Aquinas*, 93, 545-46; Thomas Joseph White, "'Through Him All Things Were Made' (John 1:3): The Analogy of the Word Incarnate According to St. Thomas Aquinas and Its Ontological Presuppositions," in White, *Analogy of Being*, 265-66nn47-48). Outside the framework of created being altogether is God, who does not merely "have" *esse* in a generic or specific determination but rather is his own unlimited act of being.

cannot be abstracted from God and the creature to function as a conceptual genus under which the two fall, for in its application to creatures it always "carries with it an awareness of it as ordered to . . . and as dependent upon the primary analogate" (i.e., God).[46] Pure equivocity, however, also is ruled out. For, among other things, it would conflict with the fact that knowledge of creatures leads to knowledge of God (so Rom 1:20). Thomas therefore reiterates his commitment to analogy and distinguishes between two kinds of analogy of attribution. The first is an analogy of many to one (*multa ad unum*), in which the analogates both participate in something prior, which cannot occur when God is one of the analogates. The second is an analogy of one to another (*unum ad alterum*), which applies to creatures and God as creatures are entirely dependent on God for all that they possess.[47] In these texts, it is evident that Thomas's deployment of the analogy of attribution (in its *unum ad alterum* form) (1) precludes any common factor in which God and creatures alike might participate, (2) assumes that the referring of created perfections back to God entails the presence of each perfection in a "preeminent" or "superexcellent" manner in God's own being, and (3) is built, at the predicative level, on the ontological relationship of creatures to God, a relationship explicated in terms of causality and participation.

Univocity and its early Reformed discontents. A little later in the medieval period Scotus registered concerns about the analogical view of theological description.[48] It needs to be recognized that he did not articulate his view of univocity in direct response to Thomas's view of analogy. Scotus's more immediate dialogue partner was Henry of Ghent, who developed the notion of analogy in a way different from Thomas.[49] In particular, while

---

[46]Wippel, *Metaphysical Thought of Thomas Aquinas*, 571.

[47]Thomas Aquinas, *SCG* 1.32-34 (97-98, 102, 103-4); *De potentia* 7.7, 202-5; *ST* Ia.13.5, 146-47.

[48]Below I will explain why I do not accept Scotus's doctrine of univocity, but I also do not subscribe to a reading of Scotus that is often associated with the movement of Radical Orthodoxy. In that view, Scotus anticipates the separation of creatures from God in modern secularist ideology by undermining creatures' ontological dependence on God (see, e.g., John Milbank, *The Word Made Strange: Theology, Language, Culture* [Oxford: Blackwell, 1997], 9, 41-49). While Milbank (*Theology and Social Theory: Beyond Secular Reason*, 2nd ed. [Oxford: Blackwell, 2006], xxv-vi) and Catherine Pickstock ("Duns Scotus: His Historical and Contemporary Significance," *MT* 21 [2005]: 569-70n2), for example, do point out that Scotus is held by many to be a transitional figure in the history of Christian thought, I do not intend to argue that he is straightforwardly responsible for problematic developments in modern philosophy.

[49]In Denys Turner's words, "What Thomas defends is not what Scotus rejects" (*Faith, Reason and the Existence of God* [Cambridge: Cambridge University Press, 2004], 139).

Henry affirmed the πρὸς ἕν analogy, or analogy of attribution between the creature and God, he also held that one might conceive of *ens* in a certain indeterminate sense that appears equally applicable to both God and creatures. While not existent outside the mind as a common factor under which God and creatures would both really be situated, this "confused" notion of *ens*, lacking the peculiar modes of existing proper to God and creatures, appears inclusive of both.[50] In his critique of Henry, Scotus pushes the unity of the concept of being further and argues that it is in fact a univocal concept. To be sure, Scotus does not abandon the doctrine of analogy entirely, but he believes that analogical description of God is rightly anchored in univocal description.[51] In his view, such univocal description is marked by a conceptual unity in which both affirming and negating the concept in a particular case would entail a contradiction. Further, this conceptual unity should enable the term at hand to function as a middle term in a syllogism.[52]

When he considers the manner in which God is "naturally knowable" by us in our present state, Scotus reasons that natural knowledge of God requires a doctrine of univocity. For when we discover a certain perfection in creatures (e.g., wisdom), we can observe the formal *ratio* of that perfection "in itself" (*in se et secundum se*) and remove from it any imperfection it has in creatures. After this, we can attribute it to God in the most perfect manner. This procedure assumes that we glean a univocal concept of the perfection from creatures and then utilize this in understanding and describing God.

---

[50]On Henry's view as a backdrop to Scotus's arguments, see Stephen Dumont, "Henry of Ghent and Duns Scotus," in *Routledge History of Philosophy*, vol. 3, *Medieval Philosophy*, ed. John Marenbon (New York: Routledge, 1998), esp. 296-307. Note also Turner, *Faith, Reason and the Existence of God*, 136-39, where he observes that Henry thought an attribute predicated of creatures and God involved two distinct concepts (rather than one concept applicable to creatures and God in distinct ways) and states that this incited the Scotist concern that analogy without grounding in univocity will lead to an infinite regress in trying to determine how the concepts might be alike. Dumont's work has been especially helpful to me in framing Scotus's understanding of univocity. In addition to the aforementioned essay, see Dumont's "The Univocity of the Concept of Being in the Fourteenth Century: John Duns Scotus and William of Alnwick," *Mediaeval Studies* 49 (1987): 1-31; Dumont, "Transcendental Being: Scotus and Scotists," *Topoi* 11 (1992): 135-48; Dumont, "Scotus's Doctrine of Univocity and the Medieval Tradition of Metaphysics," in *Was ist Philosophie im Mittelalter?*, ed. Jan A. Aertsen and Andreas Speer (Berlin: de Gruyter, 1998), 193-212. See also Richard Cross, *Duns Scotus* (Oxford: Oxford University Press, 1999), 33-39; Daniel P. Horan, *Postmodernity and Univocity: A Critical Account of Radical Orthodoxy and John Duns Scotus* (Minneapolis: Fortress, 2014), 157-88.

[51]See, e.g., Scotus, *Ordinatio* 1.8.1.3, nn. 83-84 (4:191-93).

[52]Scotus, *Ordinatio*, 1.3.1.1, n. 26 (3:18).

If no common formal *ratio* of the perfection may be abstracted from the perfection as it is in creatures—a formal *ratio* that is equally applicable to God (though it must be framed in the highest manner in God's case)—then one could no more conclude from the observation of creatures that God is wise than one could conclude that God is a stone.[53] Scotus presents several other arguments for univocity. He argues that *ens* must be a univocal concept applicable to God and creatures by isolating it from its characteristic modes in God and creatures. It is possible, Scotus reasons, to be certain that God or the first principle is a being while also doubtful about whether he is finite or infinite, created or uncreated. *Ens* is therefore a distinct concept in its own right, distinct from the concepts of "finite being" and "infinite being." Being in and of itself (*ex se*) is not automatically comprehended under the concept of finite or infinite being. It is thus a univocal concept, equally applicable to God or the creature.[54] It should be emphasized, though, that Scotus does not posit a common factor in reality by which God and creatures are constituted. In other words, Scotus does not envision an ontological participation in something prior to both God and creatures. Indeed, God and creatures "agree in no reality," he writes. It is possible to have a common concept "without agreement in reality," he contends.[55] In other words, Scotus's account of univocity is evidently concerned with epistemology and semantics, not an overarching ontological structure in which God fits alongside creatures.

Scotus also argues that while *ens* is a univocal concept, it is not a genus that would problematically need to be differentiated somehow by nonbeing. He draws a distinction between (1) a genus that is contracted to and perfected in a species by a certain differentiating factor external to the genus and (2) a concept that is contracted to a particular being by an intrinsic mode of that being. *Ens* is one such concept that is distinguished in God and creatures not by a distinguishing factor added to *ens* but rather by a mode

---

[53]Scotus, *Ordinatio* 1.3.1.1, nn. 39-40 (3:26-27); 1.8.1.3, nn. 70-79 (4:184-89).

[54]Scotus, *Ordinatio* 1.3.1.1, nn. 27-29 (3:18-19); cf. 1.8.1.3, n. 81 (4:190).

[55]Scotus, *Ordinatio* 1.8.1.3, nn. 82 and 142 (4:190, 224). It should be noted, though, that Scotus still holds that the common concept of *ens* remains a "real" concept in that it signifies something extramental (God's being). What enables it to be both a "common" as well as a "real" concept, without undermining God's simplicity by purporting to describe a being of God distinct from his proper being, is that it indicates God's being in an imperfect manner (see Dumont, "Transcendental Being," 139).

or grade of being really identical with the concrete *ens* in view. In God's case that mode is infinity, and in the creature's case it is finitude.[56]

The differences between Thomas, Henry of Ghent, and Scotus on the subject of analogy sparked ongoing debates throughout the Middle Ages.[57] Though different from both Thomas and Scotus on a range of theological issues, William of Ockham in the early fourteenth century aligns with Scotus on the topic of univocity but adds some of his own emphases. Ockham remarks that Scotus's position is essentially correct even as he identifies what he takes to be certain weaknesses in the Subtle Doctor's arguments.[58] Building on Scotus's work, Ockham maintains that "one simple common concept" like *ens* is predicable of both God and creatures, and he does this out of a concern to emphasize the limits of our knowledge of God. According to Ockham, we cannot know God *in se* in our current state—we know God intuitively and in himself only when we enjoy the beatific vision— nor can we know God by any "simple concept proper to him." Instead, we know God by a "complex proper concept" composed of "simple and common concepts."[59] Ockham then argues that we can possess a simple common concept applicable to God and creatures that can be predicated of God "quidditatively" or with respect to what he is (*in quid*).[60] We must have such a quidditative concept of him because any concept that we predicate of him "denominatively" or in a merely descriptive way presupposes that we have some underlying knowledge of the one whom we are describing. For Ockham, then, since we do have a simple common concept that applies

---

[56]Scotus, *Ordinatio* 1.3.1.1, nn. 158-66 (3:95-103); 1.8.1.3, nn. 136-50 (4:221-27). On this, see Dumont, "Univocity of the Concept of Being," 10-14; Dumont, "Scotus's Doctrine of Univocity," 209-11. Dumont writes that in God this intrinsic mode of being is only modally (not formally) distinct from God's essence ("Transcendental Being," 138-39), while Horan emphasizes that it is formally distinct from God's essence (*Postmodernity and Univocity*, 180-84).

[57]One account of this given shortly after the beginning of the Reformation can be found in Juan de Rada, *Controversiae theologicae inter S. Thomam et Scotum* (Venice, 1599), 21 (424-43).

[58]William of Ockham, *Opera theologica*, vols. 1-4, *Scriptum in librum primum Sententiarum (Ordinatio)*, ed. Gedeon Gál et al. (St. Bonaventure: ex Typographia Collegii S. Bonaventurae, 1967-2000), 1.2.9 (2:298-306).

[59]A simple concept is one that is not joined to or modified by another (like "being" rather than "infinite being"). A complex concept is thus one that is joined to and modified by another. A common concept is one applicable to more than one thing, while a proper concept is distinctly applicable to just one thing.

[60]More specifically, we can possess a simple common concept that is predicable of God *in quid* in the "first mode" (i.e., as a predicate that is included in the definition of the subject). The various "modes" of quidditative or *per se* predication are found in Aristotle's *Posterior Analytics*.

quidditatively to God (as well as creatures), we also have a univocal word (*vox*) corresponding to that concept that is applicable to both God and creatures.[61] Nevertheless, he writes, there is a strict sense in which nothing is univocally predicable of God and creatures since "nothing is in the creature, whether essential or accidental, that has a perfect similitude with anything that really is in God." "Saints and authorities" reject univocity in this sense, Ockham comments.[62] Moreover, a univocal is a universal, and universals do not in fact exist outside the mind as something really present in or distinct from individual things themselves (or things in those individuals), which means that a univocal term does not correspond to any common feature with "real unity" in the those things to which it is applied. To be sure, this does not mean that the univocal concept or word is "fictitious": a univocal can still correspond to many real particulars. Nevertheless, the univocal itself is not really intrinsic to the particular or included in the essence of the particular (*illa vox non est aliquid de essentia Dei vel creaturae*), which entails that it is not simpler than the particular itself as though it should be ontologically prior to God (or the creature).[63]

The position of Francisco Suárez also interests us here because it was worked out with reference back to medieval debates between Thomists and Scotists and arrived on the intellectual scene as Protestant theology proper was becoming more elaborate.[64] Suárez affirms key tenets of those who uphold an analogy of being between God and the creature but then also shows great sympathy to the doctrine of univocity. He recognizes the

---

[61]Ockham believes that univocity applies properly to words and only "improperly" or in an extended sense to concepts.

[62]Ockham, *Ordinatio* 1.2.9.3 (2:312-17).

[63]Ockham, *Ordinatio* 1.2.9.2 (2:312); ad dubia 3, 4, 7 (2:331-32, 335-36). For an extended treatment of Ockham's view of universals, see Marilyn McCord Adams, *William Ockham* (Notre Dame, IN: University of Notre Dame, 1987), 1:3-141. It seems, then, that Ockham affirms that a univocal term concerns God "quidditatively" in that it can function in our speech about God to state what God is, but he also denies that a univocal term concerns God's essence (a term traditionally used synonymously with quiddity) in that it is not something really present in God himself.

[64]On locating Suárez within the Thomistic tradition, see, e.g., E. J. Ashworth, "Suárez on the Analogy of Being: Some Historical Background," *Vivarium* 33 (1995): 50-75. For representations of his philosophical tendencies as lying somewhere between Thomism and Scotism, see, e.g., Daniel Heider, "Is Suárez's Concept of Being Analogical or Univocal?," *American Catholic Philosophical Quarterly* 81 (2007): 21-41; Victor Salas, "Between Thomism and Scotism: Francisco Suárez on the Analogy of Being," in *A Companion to Francisco Suárez*, ed. Victor M. Salas and Robert L. Fastiggi (Leiden: Brill, 2014), 336-62.

two kinds of analogy discussed above, noting that they are sometimes distinguished as the analogy of proportionality versus the analogy of proportion, sometimes as the analogy of proportion versus the analogy of attribution. For Suárez, the analogy of proportionality ("proportion" in the second expression of the distinction) does not apply with respect to *ens* in its application to God and creatures, for the creature is called *ens* "by reason of its own *esse* absolutely," whereas the analogy of proportionality, in his understanding of it, would require that the secondary analogate (the creature) be called *ens* just by virtue of having some similarity to the divine *esse.*[65] The creature has actuality and is "something" (*aliquid*) in itself, not merely by a relation or comparison to God.[66] In Suárez's assessment, the analogy of attribution does have a significant role to play in the application of *ens* to God and creatures—not in its *multa ad unum* form but in its *unum ad alterum* form, and not in its extrinsic form but in its intrinsic form where the content of the term in question (*ens*) is intrinsic to the secondary analogate (the creature) as well as the primary analogate (God). *Ens* is predicated of the creature as it depends on God and is a being by finite participation and imitation of the existence of God. *Ens* is predicated of God as a being *per essentiam,* one who exists by virtue of what he is, not by causation or participation in an outside source of existence.[67]

Suárez argues, though, that the intrinsic analogy of attribution does not preclude a common, univocal concept of *ens.* The fact that an effect (here, created existence) is not "adequate" to its divine cause shows only that a created being cannot have a "specific" and "ultimate" similitude to its divine cause, not that it cannot be similar with respect to some more common or general *ratio* or predicate. Suárez takes into account the Thomistic arguments (1) that the creature is inadequate to God not just as a particular kind of being (*tale ens*) but also simply as a being and (2) that the being of the creature is dependent on God and can possess only the measure of

---

[65]It appears that in Suárez's judgment, on this approach, the creature would still be called *ens* by virtue of something that belongs to it (i.e., its own *esse*), but by that *esse* taken as relative to the divine *esse* rather than that creaturely *esse* taken absolutely. This estimation of the analogy of proportionality appears to be opposite that of Cajetan.

[66]Francisco Suárez, *Opera omnia,* vol. 26, *Disputationes metaphysicae* (Paris: Vivès, 1861), 2.28.3.3-4, 11 (13-14, 17).

[67]Suárez, *Disputationes metaphysicae* 2.28.3.5, 12, 14-17 (14, 16-19).

perfection included in its limited genus, while the being of God is *a se* and essentially includes all perfection. For Suárez, however, these arguments fail to show that *ens* cannot be "one common objective concept" or "one common formal concept." For, according to Suárez, in those arguments the creature is being conceived as "finite and limited being," not under the "most abstract" and "most confused" (or "indistinct") concept of being as simply "that which is" or that which "exists outside nothing." Ontologically (*in re*), *ens* always applies to the creature with an "essential subordination" to God, but there is still a "precise" and abstract concept of being—being in potency, being as only potentially including those things that might fall under it (*inferiora*)—whose intelligible content is in itself common and univocal, neither finite nor infinite. To be sure, the abstract common concept of being itself stipulates that when it is applied to particulars it will apply to them unequally (to God as independent and to creatures as dependent on him), making the common concept of *ens* somewhat different from typical univocal terms (and different from what one finds in Scotus). Yet the similarity to other univocal terms remains in that the abstract concept has a common *ratio* (intelligible content) in itself that can subsequently be applied to God or the creature.[68] While Thomas did not posit an abstract concept of being that might include or "descend" into concepts of the being of God and the creature and into substance and accidents as *inferiora*, Scotus posited such a concept and argued that it is indifferent and equally applicable to the complex concepts into which it might descend (its *inferiora*). Suárez, however, posits an abstract common concept of *ens* (in contrast to Thomas), but he contends that this concept has a singular *ratio* only in a "confused" or "indistinct" version of it and still potentially (if not actually) includes the ordering of the diverse modes of existing and *rationes* of certain kinds of beings, making it unequally applicable to its *inferiora* (against Scotus).[69]

---

[68]Suárez, *Disputationes metaphysicae* 2.28.3.6-9, 14-21 (14-16, 17-21). Suárez comments that some Thomists held that there is a common concept of being, though they resisted the conclusion that it is a univocal concept since they thought the common concept had no reference to *inferiora* (things that fall under it). Suárez's contention, by contrast, is that the abstract concept of *ens* is potentially ordered to *inferiora* (2.28.3.9, 18 [15-16, 19-20]).

[69]Compare Salas, "Between Thomism and Scotism," 350-62; Salas, "Francisco Suárez, the Analogy of Being, and Its Tensions," in *Suárez's Metaphysics in Its Historical and Systematic Context*, ed. Lukáš Novák (Berlin: de Gruyter, 2014), 97-102. Salas argues that Suárez's focus on being as "aptitudinal" (apt to exist, rather than actually existing) facilitates his contention that there is a

In the sixteenth and seventeenth centuries Reformed Protestants as-
sessed the arguments of various medieval and Roman Catholic writers on
the matters of analogy and univocity, including Thomas, Scotus, Cajetan,
Suárez, and others. The early Reformed certainly drew on the resources of
medieval philosophy and theology in an eclectic manner, but on this particular topic they essentially stood in continuity with Thomas's approach
and criticized Scotus's doctrine of univocity.[70] Girolamo Zanchi, for example,
writes that a univocal term is one that is the same in both name and *ratio*
or definition when applied to multiple things. An analogical term is one that
is the same in name and yet somewhat (but not entirely) diverse in *ratio* or
definition when applied to multiple things. That to which an analogous
term applies in a secondary or derivative sense has some "proportion" or
"agreement" with some primary analogate so that it too receives the name
ascribed to the primary analogate. According to Zanchi, predicates like
"goodness" that are applied to God and to creatures are analogous, for in
God goodness is "most perfect" and identical to the divine essence itself,
while in creatures it is imperfect and an accident.[71] If such a predicate were
purely equivocal (the same in name alone when applied to God and creatures), this would presuppose a lack of order between God and the creature.
However, "between God and things created by God there is a most beautiful
order," in which God is both the efficient and the final cause of the creature:
"from him and through him and to him are all things" (Rom 11:36). It is by
this order that created things make known something of God's eternal
power and deity (Rom 1:20). Like Thomas and Suárez, Zanchi is quick to
clarify that this analogy between God and the creature is not an analogy of

---

confused concept of being that can be considered without reference to any particular modes of
existing. Further, Salas reasons, Suárez's belief that the distinction between *ens* itself and the
diverse modes of existing of particular beings is a rational distinction (rather than a real modal
distinction akin to that of Scotus) enables him to state that the confused concept of being must
potentially include the diverse modal ordering of beings.

[70]There has been discussion recently about whether some of the Reformed orthodox favored a
Scotistic doctrine of univocity, but I am in agreement with the position of Richard Muller that
the Reformed embraced an essentially Thomistic doctrine of analogy (see his "Not Scotist:
Understandings of Being, Univocity, and Analogy in Early-Modern Reformed Thought," *Reformation & Renaissance Review* 14 [2012]: 127-50).

[71]Though Zanchi (unlike Suárez) does not explicitly distinguish here between an external and an
internal sort of proportion or agreement that a secondary analogate might have with a primary
analogate, he certainly assumes the attributes in view to be intrinsic to creatures, calling them
accidents and perfections that are *in creaturis*.

"many to one"—for "nothing is prior to God"—but rather an analogy of "one to another."[72]

In treating the features of a system of logic, Bartholomäus Keckermann discusses the notion of "similitude," observing that it can be "simple" (when one term is compared to another) or "complex" (when two proportionate terms are compared to another set of two proportionate terms). He identifies the former as the analogy of proportion but seems to assume that it must take the *multa ad unum* form and then identifies the latter as the analogy of proportionality. After this Keckermann comments that "God and creatures are said to differ in more than genus" but "agree" in analogous names insofar as the natures of creatures are "images" of God.[73] In his systematic theology, Keckermann roots this analogous "agreement" between God and creatures in God's causal activity: creatures as such have a "likeness" and "similitude" of God because "every effect is similar in something to its own cause."[74] Focusing on the particular question of "being" in his metaphysics, Keckermann denies that *ens* ("that which is" or "that which has essence") might be applied to God in an ordinary manner. God does not merely "have" or instantiate some essence under which he is delimited but rather is his own essence; he is *super ens* and "supersubstantial."[75] Elaborating on YHWH's question in Isaiah 40:18, 25—"To whom will you compare me?"—Keckermann writes, "You must not think about me as a substance or accident or some species of being but as the one who is above every being or above every substance and accident."[76]

In Johann Alsted's metaphysics he explicitly identifies equivocal, univocal, and analogical uses of the name "being." *Ens* is not strictly speaking a genus that is conferred on its species "equally." It is only an "analogical" genus or can have only an analogical unity in its various applications to substance

---

[72]Girolamo Zanchi, *De natura Dei, seu de divinis attributis* (Neostadii Palatinorum, 1598), 1.10 (28-30).

[73]Bartholomäus Keckermann, *Systema logicae*, in *Operum omnium quae extant* (Geneva, 1614), 1.2.4 (1:673-74); 2.5 (1:679).

[74]Bartholomäus Keckermann, *Systema s.s. theologiae*, in *Opera omnium*, 1.5 (2:80, separate pagination).

[75]Suárez would identify this construal of the being of God as "Platonic" and, in the logic of his own metaphysics, deny that it was necessary to uphold the Creator-creature distinction (*Disputationes metaphysicae* 2.28.3.13 [17]).

[76]Bartholomäus Keckermann, *Scientiae metaphysicae brevissima synopsis et compendium*, in *Operum omnium*, 1.2 (1:2015).

and accidents, to God and creatures. Alsted characterizes this as a πρὸς ἕν (toward one) or ἀφ᾽ ἑνὸς (from one) analogy in that accidents depend on substance to exist and creatures depend on God to exist. Within this analogy or "order," "being" is predicated principally of God since he exists by his own essence and secondarily of creatures since they exist by participation in God's existence.[77] In his work on natural theology Alsted sketches a method for speaking of God that initially might appear to diverge from an analogical approach: begin with the term *ens* (conceived as a genus), and then modify *ens* with a "term of difference," either *summum* (highest) or some more particular qualifier that highlights God's absolute perfection. However, right after this Alsted clarifies that in God *ens* and essence are one and the same. God's existence is not a distinct "contraction" of a broader divine essence but just is his "most singular essence." According to Alsted, then, Scotus errs in claiming that *ens* is a univocal predicate. It is predicated of God first (*secundum prius*)—and must be predicated of him since he does exist in an eminent manner—and of creatures in a derivative manner (*secundum posterius*).[78] Later in the same work Alsted states that a univocal view of the perfections predicated of God and creatures would require a "proportion" between them, by which he means a "parity" or "mutual" similarity. However, "between the finite and the infinite there is no proportion."[79] These perfections are in creatures in a limited manner because creatures participate in God in a limited way, while the perfections are in God "supereminently."[80]

Toward the end of the period of Reformed orthodoxy, Peter van Mastricht illustrates well key features of a broadly Reformed approach to the question of analogy. He mentions the distinction between God's incommunicable and communicable attributes and comments that there is no "trace" (*vestigium*) of the former in creatures. In light of texts like Genesis 1:26-27,

---

[77]Johann Alsted, *Metaphysica* (Herbornae Nassoviorum, 1613), 1.1 (32-33). On *ens* as an "analogical genus," cf. Johannes Maccovius, *Metaphysica*, ed. Adrianus Heereboord, 3rd ed. (Leiden, 1658), 1.1 (2-3). Alsted, Maccovius, and others who call *ens* an "analogical" genus mean that there is an analogical agreement between *ens* in its application to substance and accidents and to God and creatures, not that *ens* is a univocal concept or that God and creatures equally participate in some ontological principle.

[78]Alsted, *Theologica Naturalis* 1.3 (31-32).

[79]Alsted clarifies that if the notion of *proportio* is used at all of God and creatures, it is not a *proportio* συμμετρίας but a *proportio* ἀναλογίας.

[80]Alsted, *Theologia naturalis* 1.17 (174-75).

2 Corinthians 3:18, and 2 Peter 1:4, the attributes described as "communicable" do have a *vestigium* in creatures. The communicable attributes, he adds, are not univocally or "equally" (*ex aequo*) predicated of God and creatures, for "between the infinite and the finite there is no proportion in any way." Nor are they equivocal, for knowledge of the creature does help to facilitate knowledge of the Creator. The communicable attributes, then, are analogically predicated of God and creatures. The thing signified by a given attribute is "principally" and "originally" in God and "participatively" and "with a degree of diminution" in creatures. Mastricht clarifies that a given attribute is not applied to God merely "causally" as if he only caused the thing signified to be in creatures but did not have it in himself. Instead, it is "truly," "essentially," "eminently" in God himself.[81] Indeed, Mastricht points out in expounding the traditional "threefold way" (*via triplex*) of obtaining knowledge of God that if God is the cause of the various perfections in creatures, the perfections must belong eminently to God, for "no one can bestow on another what he neither formally nor eminently has."[82] We could no doubt consider other writers in a historical examination of analogy and univocity, but with this sampling of medieval and early modern authors in hand, it is time now to offer some constructive remarks on the material en route to dealing with more recent treatments of analogy and univocity.

Preliminary assessment. I have already made clear at the beginning of this chapter my interest in appropriating a doctrine of analogy for the work of Christian *theologia*. What should be learned and taken into account, then, from the advocates of analogy and the advocates of univocity covered here? I will offer some preliminary comments here, and then my subsequent reflection on more recent analyses of analogy and univocity will occasion further refinement of our understanding of what can be drawn from the earlier authors in a contemporary retrieval of analogy.

First, it is crucial to note that the analogy of attribution (not just the analogy of proportionality) does allow for the terms or "names" predicated of primary and secondary analogates to be truly present in both. The theological use of this kind of analogy by Thomas, Zanchi, and others

---

[81]Mastricht, *TPT* 2.5.7-8 (94-95); cf. 5.12 (96-97). Mastricht also denies that being in particular is a "univocal genus" (2.3.10 [79]).
[82]Mastricht, *TPT* 2.2.19 (70).

emphasizes that the divine perfections are not predicated of God merely because God causes them to exist in creatures but because they are truly present in God himself. Indeed, as Mastricht puts it, the perfections are "principally" and "originally" in God himself. This is something that must be remembered in view of the recent criticisms about the sufficiency of analogy that will be discussed below.

Second, the analogy of attribution applies in the case of God and creatures only its in *unum ad alterum* form, not its *multa ad unum* form. As Thomas, Zanchi, Suárez, and others stress, there is nothing prior to God in which he must participate in order to be what he is. It is vital to bear this in mind in a contemporary theological landscape where, as we saw in the previous chapter, Barth and others have worried that medieval and early Protestant theologians located God under a generic concept "being" and straightforwardly used this concept to ascertain what God must be like. In fact, the notion of an analogy of being comes into play precisely because *ens* is not a generic concept equally applicable to substance and accidents or to God and creatures. In their different ways, Keckermann's statement that God is *supra ens* and Alsted's construal of being as a *genus analogicum* are intended to make this point.

Third, while I will argue below that the analogy of attribution can be incorporated into the practice of *theologia* without undermining God's transcendence, it is important to clarify that there is no "proportion" between God and creatures. This I take to be a worthwhile emphasis in Thomas's treatment of analogy in *De veritate* and in early Reformed authors like Alsted and Mastricht. There is no quantifiable distance or number of degrees, no mutually constitutive relation between a given perfection as it is in God and that perfection as it is in the creature. We creatures receive our being and qualities from God. We are constituted by our relation to God, and thus we are compared to him, but he, the infinite font of all being and goodness, is not compared to us.

Fourth, a close reading of Scotus (and Suárez too) shows that he ought not to be vilified as claiming that God and creatures must participate in something ontologically prior to both. Univocity by itself arguably does not entail an eradication of the Creator-creature distinction. Scotus's account of univocity is focused on semantic and epistemological concerns, not so much the ontological relationship between God and creatures. Indeed, the example of Ockham illustrates that holding to a doctrine of univocity does not even automatically signal that one wishes to stress the knowability of God. For Ockham, univocity helps to make the point that we have no "simple" concept that is proper to God himself. In other words, one can use a doctrine of univocity, with its separation of the conceptual from the ontological, to minimize human knowledge of God *in se* in a way that is not possible if one is working with a doctrine of analogy.[83]

Fifth, the decidedly semantic nature of Scotus's doctrine of univocity appears to bring him closer to Thomas's view than one might have initially thought. However, an important difference remains in that Scotus and Ockham (not quite Suárez) believe we can arrive at an entirely abstract concept of being that is in itself equally applicable to both God and creatures. Thomas does not posit such a concept. For Thomas, the content of the concept of *ens* always includes either that the being in view is caused and finite or that the being in view is uncaused and divine.[84] I think Thomas's approach is correct here since our concept of "being" never truly occupies a middle ground in which its content is stripped of all reference to causation and finitude (or

---

[83] Along with others, Wolf Krötke picks up on this and comments, "The consequence [of the turn toward univocity] is nevertheless not a greater precision of univocal speech." Indeed, "the negation of the speakability of God holds the field more firmly than in the doctrine of analogy" (*Gottes Klarheiten: Eine Neuinterpretation der Lehre von Gottes Eigenschaften* [Tübingen: Mohr Siebeck, 2001], 29).

[84] Thomas does acknowledge that one can distinguish between a perfection itself (being, goodness, life, and so on) and the mode in which it is in the subject (God or the creature) (*ST* Ia.13.3 ad 1 [143]; 13.9 ad 3 [159]). However, he does not posit (as Scotus does) that one can isolate the aspect of its *ratio* that applies in the case of God or creatures in such a way that it is altogether abstracted from the particular divine or creaturely mode of existing and thus independent of those modes of existing in their hierarchical relation and able to function as a univocal concept. For similar but slightly different discussion on this point, see Montagnes, *Doctrine of the Analogy of Being*, 83-85. The point can also be reinforced by the observation that analogy (or the analogy of being in particular) in Thomas's thought follows on judgments about what is true of God and creatures (not just the mental act of "simple apprehension") and so will always have reference to things' actual modes of existing (so Rocca, *Speaking the Incomprehensible God*, 151-73, 351-52). Montagnes speaks of Thomas distinguishing between the *ratio* and the *modus* of a perfection. However, I prefer to talk about different *aspects* of the *ratio* of a perfection, one of which (it might be said) concerns the *modus* in which the perfection is particularized in a subject. For this coheres with the notion that the *ratio* itself is a focal point of analogical unity and diversity and thus should in some sense include or reference that *modus* that distinguishes the analogates, *per prius* or *per posterius* (cf. Rocca, *Speaking the Incomprehensible God*, 146-53; see also Dominic D'Ettore, "*Una ratio* versus *Diversae rationes*: Three Interpretations of *Summa theologiae* I, Q. 13, AA. 1-6," *Nova et Vetera* 17 [2019]: 39-55).

infinity). It is always (even if sometimes implicitly) determined as caused or uncaused, finite or infinite. To pick up some of the language that Suárez uses, in saying this we are not unwittingly shifting the conversation away from "being" as such to certain kinds of beings (*talia entia*). Instead, we are observing that talk of "being" from the outset includes at least a nascent recognition that any being that might come under discussion is a being by participation or, uniquely, a being by essence. In this connection, it is intriguing that Suárez himself remarks that *ens* is unlike typical univocal terms like *animal* in that its own *ratio* ("that which is") already stipulates that it cannot be predicated of things equally. It is predicated of some things existing dependently and to one who is *a se*.[85] A related point is that the sense of "being," and other names predicated of God and creatures, is never detached from the structure of reality. Significantly, if theological speech is always shaped by how God himself actually is, this can help us to avoid eliding the Creator-creature distinction and exaggerating the depth of our knowledge of God. It can also help us to avoid thinking we are trapped, as it were, in our conceptual landscape without an ability to signify and describe God himself.[86]

Finally, it is perhaps worth indicating how a Thomistic approach to the question of analogy and univocity can resist the Scotist claim that our speech about God must have a "univocal core" in order to ground our natural knowledge of God and ultimately the way in which supernatural theology

---

[85]In later medieval debates about analogy, some Thomists, like John Capreolus, distinguished between an "objective" concept of being (the object represented) and a "formal" concept of being (the mental act of conceiving or representing the object). In this line of reasoning, the "objective" concept of being is unified by an analogy of attribution while the "formal" concept may have one *ratio* that applies more perfectly to one analogate and less perfectly to another (on which, see Ashworth, "Suárez on the Analogy of Being," 70-75; Domenic D'Ettore, "The Fifteenth-Century Thomist Dispute Over Participation in an Analogous Concept: John Capreolus, Dominic of Flanders, and Paul Soncinas," *Mediaeval Studies* 76 [2014]: 248-57). For a broader history of developments in the fourteenth- to sixteenth-century literature, see Jennifer Ashworth, "Philosophy of Language: Words, Concepts, Things, and Non-Things," in *The Routledge Companion to Sixteenth-Century Philosophy*, ed. Henrik Lagerlund and Benjamin J. Hill (New York: Routledge, 2017), 363-69; Dominic D'Ettore, *Analogy After Aquinas: Logical Problems, Thomistic Answers*, Thomistic Ressourcement 11 (Washington, DC: Catholic University of America Press, 2019). I would suggest that if the "objective-formal" distinction is utilized, the *ratio* of the formal concept is not entirely separate from concrete beings' ordered modes of existing (and is certainly not detached from those modes when the concept is applied to concrete beings) and therefore would not decline or apply to them univocally.

[86]To be fair, Scotus himself would agree that once "being" and other names are applied to God they should be predicated of him in a manner reflective of God's unique being.

draws on our natural awareness of God in its description of him.[87] Thomas's approach helps us circumvent the loss of divine transcendence, on the one hand, and the loss of a natural awareness of God that provides traction for supernatural theology, on the other. Though created effects do not possess a univocal commonality with their divine cause, it is possible to move from a knowledge of those effects to a knowledge of God. Though a created effect cannot enable a perfect knowledge of its divine cause, it can yield at least some (however incomplete) knowledge of its cause.[88] Indeed, apprehending a perfection (e.g., *esse*, wisdom) in creatures and then applying it to God in an analogical manner does not entail rejecting all the known content of the attribute when it is applied to God. If it did entail this, then Scotus's claim that one might as well conclude that God was a stone would have some force. It entails simply recognizing that certain aspects of the *ratio* or content of the attribute (esp. its real distinction from essence and its caused, finite mode) do not apply in the case of God. Though more could be said about the debates between followers of Thomas and followers of Scotus, we should now take into account some more recent assessments of analogy and univocity.

Concerns About Analogy
and Divine Otherness in Recent Theology

Barth and Pannenberg. Some of the modern concerns about analogy center on whether it upholds the otherness and sovereignty of God. Many authors could be considered here, but Barth and Pannenberg are especially incisive on this topic and will receive the bulk of the attention here.[89] Early in his *Church Dogmatics* Barth forcefully rejected the notion of an *analogia entis*

---

[87]John Milbank accepts the Scotist framing of the issue and claims that in rejecting univocity Thomas foregoes the possibility of our reasoning from created things to truth about God (see his "Intensities," *MT* 15 [1999]: 454-56).

[88]Thomas, *ST* Ia.2.2 ad 3 (30). See also the distinction between a *propter quid* demonstration and a *quia* demonstration in the excursus on Thomas's demonstration of God's existence in chap. 2.

[89]If space permitted, it would be fitting to examine Eberhard Jüngel's treatment of analogy as well (see his *God as the Mystery of the World: On the Foundation of the Theology of the Crucified One in the Dispute Between Theism and Atheism*, trans. Darrell L. Guder [Grand Rapids: Eerdmans, 1983], 261-98). Though influenced by Barth in many ways, Jüngel's emphases also seem somewhat different. He worries that a Creator-creature analogy that does not have the incarnation as the focal point of a correspondence between God and humanity will leave us with an unknown God who is made out to be either just like us ("dogmatic anthropomorphism") or utterly distant from us ("symbolic anthropomorphism") and cannot in either case be concretely related to or distinguished from us. For Jüngel, it is in the incarnation that God decisively establishes

(in particular, Erich Przywara's articulation of it), calling it an "invention of the anti-Christ" and a decisive reason not to become Roman Catholic.[90] Barth rejects Przywara's conception of the *analogia entis* because of his insistence on a fundamental discontinuity between God and the world and his attendant commitment to theology as a discipline informed and governed not by general human experience of the fallen created order but by God's free revelatory activity in the person of Jesus Christ.[91] For Barth, there is no place for a general ontology that presumes to set the conditions for Christian description of God. All true talk about God can arise only on the basis of and in response to the Lord's free and gracious decision to address us in his Word. At this point Roman Catholicism, according to Barth, goes wrong in assimilating Christ the divine Word to the being of the church so that "grace becomes nature" and "the personal act of divine address becomes a constantly available relationship" within which an *analogia entis*, a "presence of a divine likeness of the creature even within the fallen world," can form the basis of our speech about God's being.[92] Roman Catholicism errs here because, in Barth's view, given the extent of human sin as apprehended by the Reformers, there can no longer be a "direct discernment of the original relation of God to man" that may then be subsequently "confirmed by the Gospel." All such knowledge of our relation to God is restored to us only in the special revelation of the gospel.[93] The "cosmos . . . stands in contradiction to God." Even when God does address us through creaturely means he communicates only indirectly to us because of our creaturely nature and our sinfulness and remains veiled in a manner that precludes the epistemic directness of an *analogia entis* between God and creatures.[94]

---

and expresses his relationship to and distinctness from the world and so enables human speech about himself.

[90] Barth, *CD* I/1, xiii. For Przywara's account, see his *Analogia Entis: Metaphysics, Original Structure and Universal Rhythm*, trans. John R. Betz and David Bentley Hart (Grand Rapids: Eerdmans, 2014). For more on Przywara and his relationship to Barth, see Keith L. Johnson, *Karl Barth and the* Analogia Entis (London: T&T Clark, 2010); John R. Betz, "After Barth: A New Introduction to Erich Przywara's *Analogia Entis*," in White, *Analogy of Being*, 35-87.

[91] My sense of the overarching structure of Barth's view of analogy is indebted especially to Johnson, *Karl Barth and the* Analogia Entis.

[92] Barth, *CD* I/1, 36-38, 40-44.

[93] Barth, *CD* I/1, 130; cf. IV/1, 177.

[94] Barth, *CD* I/1, 166-69. Later on Barth does take into account the Roman Catholic theologian Gottlieb Söhngen's approach to the analogy of being, in which the *analogia entis* is drawn into the sphere of and grafted onto an *analogia fidei* where the *analogia entis* is based on the believer's

A little later in the *Church Dogmatics*, Barth discusses his reservations about an analogy of being in connection with the concept of the *imago Dei*. He contends that after the fall there is "no conformity of man to God," "no point of contact between God and man" that might preserve in us an aptness to receive God's Word. In other words, human beings as creatures—creatures who are now fallen—have in their "humanity and personality" completely lost the *imago Dei*. The *imago Dei* is "not just, as it is said, destroyed apart from a few relics; it is totally annihilated." There is thus no *analogia entis*, no being that is common to God and humanity in its natural and fallen state. The only similarity possible is one actualized by God in the event of revelation, in which God enables human persons to receive his revelation by faith. In that event there is a correspondence between the human decision to receive God's revelation and God's decision to bring human persons into fellowship with himself. There emerges on the human side a correspondence to God parsed not in terms of deification but in terms of a "union with what is believed," which takes place, as justification by grace does, in the human person's apprehension of Christ by faith.[95] Barth does not reject the notion of an analogical "fellowship" or "agreement" between our words and the God to whom they refer. What Barth rejects is the claim that our words or the created beings to which they typically refer have their own "immanent" and "static" capacity to correspond to the being of God apart from the grace of revelation wherein God sovereignly decides to enable human words to express divine truth.[96]

In Barth's assessment of fellow Protestant theologian Johann Quenstedt on the topic of analogy, he seizes the opportunity to speak more about the relationship between the *analogia entis* and justification by grace. He takes Quenstedt to be representative of the Protestant orthodox and of Thomas and other medieval lights who affirm a doctrine of analogy. In Barth's judgment, Quenstedt rightly affirms an analogy of attribution between God

---

participating in Christ and becoming a child of God by faith (*CD* II/1, 79-84). Barth does not believe this to be an accurate representation of official Roman Catholic teaching, but the fact that he is very amenable to Söhngen's *analogia fidei* and Christ-centered *analogia entis* shows that he is willing to acknowledge a carefully defined ontological agreement of the creature with God.

[95]Barth, *CD* I/1, 236-41.

[96]Barth, *CD* II/1, 224-36.

and the creature by virtue of which our words (*essence, spirit, goodness, justice,* and so on) can be truthfully applied to God as well as creatures. However, Barth believes Quenstedt has failed to take up the analogy of attribution into a properly theological and, indeed, Protestant view of God's relationship to creatures. For Quenstedt asserts that the created analogate possesses its likeness to God not only by an extrinsic relation or habitude to God but by properly possessing that likeness in its own right in an intrinsic analogy of attribution. Barth regards this as inconsistent with Quenstedt's own Lutheran affirmation of justification by grace through faith and would like to have seen Quenstedt apply the logic of justification to "the problem of the knowledge of God." According to a Protestant doctrine of justification by grace, "what converts the creature into an analogue of God does not lie in itself and its nature." Instead, "what converts the creature into an analogue of God," what brings about humanity's fellowship with God, is the creature's reception of the grace of God that comes to us from without in the person of Christ. At the epistemological level, what enables us to know and speak of God is not mere observation of the created order but rather faith's apprehension of God in Christ. For Barth, Quenstedt is focused on determining how there might be some agreement or fellowship between God and creatures with respect to "being in general," while Barth seeks to understand such a fellowship with respect to "the particular being of grace" given only in God's revelation. In Quenstedt's framework, creatures as beings already are "relatively" what God himself is "absolutely." We have a "given and constant" similarity to God and have no need of revelation or faith to possess or discover a correspondence between ourselves and God. Barth therefore asks, "In this [intrinsic analogy of attribution] where is the freedom of the gracious God which Quenstedt knows so well when he speaks of [justification]?" The implication of Quenstedt's understanding of analogy, then, is that there is a "being in which God and man—the former absolutely, the latter relatively—participate," a being that is "superior to God" and determines what God and creatures are, what the relationship between them is, and what establishes the veracity of our speech about them. It is only by a "lucky inconsistency" that Quenstedt and the Protestant orthodox retain the Reformers' awareness of human sin and God's grace. It would be far more consistent with Protestant sensibilities to see Christology as the "life-centre" of theology proper. Ultimately, Barth says, the doctrine of analogy in Quenstedt and the Protestant orthodox fails to align with the teaching of Scripture, for in Scripture "it is not a being common to God and man which finally and properly establishes and upholds the fellowship between them, but God's grace."[97]

It appears that Barth's underlying reason for viewing the agreement between God and creatures in conjunction with the doctrine of justification is that, in his understanding of it, the being of creatures is itself rooted in the grace of God, which is to be understood through the lens of the incarnation and justification. John 1:3 is significant here: all things were made through Christ.[98] On the one hand, creation is the "external basis" for the covenant of grace in which God establishes fellowship between humanity and himself through Christ, in the sense that the existence of created being is presupposed in the actualization of human fellowship with God. On the other hand, however, the covenant of grace is the "internal basis" and presupposition of the existence of created being, for in God's purposes the covenant of grace takes priority and creation is "the theatre of the history of the covenant of grace" and "the way to the covenant." Accordingly, Christ is the goal of creation and also "the beginning just because he is the goal" (see Eph 1:10; Col 1:15-16). The following is particularly noteworthy in connection with the question of analogy for Barth: "That the covenant is the goal of creation is not something which is added later to the reality of the creature. . . . It already characterises creation itself and as such."[99] To be sure, Barth affirms with Genesis 1:31 that created being is good, but he hastens to add that it is such only because in actualizing it God has "justified" it in taking it up into his purpose of "instituting and fulfilling the covenant between the divine Creator and man." Creation thus shares in the perfection of God "as the arena, instrument and object of His living action" in Christ, which can be known by us only as we apprehend in faith what God does in Christ.[100] In

---

[97]Barth, *CD* II/1, 237-43. Cf. Bruce L. McCormack, *Orthodox and Modern: Studies in the Theology of Karl Barth* (Grand Rapids: Baker Academic, 2008), 177-79.

[98]See Barth, *CD* II/2, 91-93; III/1, 29-31. In the latter section, Barth appeals to various writers of the tradition who in some way see creation as a work of God's goodness and grace (e.g., Augustine, Anselm, Thomas, Polanus).

[99]Barth, *CD* III/1, 43-46, 94-97, 229-32. Cf. IV/1, 9-10.

[100]Barth, *CD* III/1, 366-88. Cf. IV/3.1, 96, 114-23, 137-39, 163-64.

addition, given the fall, "any tenable distinction between man as created by God and the sinful determination of his being is possible only if his sinful nature . . . is minimised." The only possible way now to see the true nature of humanity—and human persons are still God's handiwork—lies in seeing humanity as God's covenant partner through his revelation in Christ, the true and "proper" man.[101]

The positive content of the ontological agreement between humanity and God thus lies in human persons being in and like Christ and bearing witness to God's revelation in Christ: "To be a man is to be with Jesus, to be like Him. To be a man is to be in the sphere where the first and merciful will of God toward His creatures, His will to save and keep them from the power of nothingness, is revealed in action." Barth comments that "man *in abstracto*" (i.e., apart from "the divine will to pity, help and save") is defenseless against "the threat of surrounding non-being" but is secured by God in and only in the elect man Jesus Christ. Again, "Man *is* the being which is addressed in this way by God. . . . He does not first have a kind of nature in which he is then addressed by God. . . . He is from the very outset, as we may now say, 'in the Word of God.'"[102] In this schema, salvation is the "fulfilment of being," for created being "in itself" does not have "a part in the being of God." Put quite strikingly, "Created being as such needs salvation [*Das geschaffene Sein als solches bedarf des Heils*], but does not have it: it can only look forward to it."[103] True human being, then, has a correspondence to God as human beings "give themselves to God" just as he has "given Himself for man." It is in gratitude and active obedience to the divine Word that human beings are aligned with God.[104] In other words, human beings, in living in loving fellowship and mutuality with one another, image Christ being for us as man, and Christ as man for us images the intra-divine love between the Father and Christ the Son. Barth calls the similarity in these relationships an

---

[101]Barth, *CD* III/2, 28-32, 40-46. Cf. III/2, 124-25, 134-37. On the broader questions about Barth in relation to supralapsarianism and infralapsarianism, see Shao Kai Tseng, *Karl Barth's Infralapsarian Theology: Origins and Development, 1920–1953*, New Explorations in Theology (Downers Grove, IL: IVP Academic, 2016), including the foreword by George Hunsinger, in which he maintains (contra Tseng) that Barth was a supralapsarian.

[102]Barth, *CD* III/2, 145-51, cf. IV/1, 92-93; IV/2, 19.

[103]Barth, *CD* IV/1, 8; Barth, *Die Kirchliche Dogmatik* (Zollikon-Zürich: Evangelischer Verlag, 1953), IV/1, 7.

[104]Barth, *CD* III/2, 182, 207; IV/1, 41-42.

analogia relationis.[105] Indeed, in some of the latest material in the *Church Dogmatics*, Barth is prepared to say that Christians exist "in analogy and correspondence" to what Christ is as they are children of God made such by the original divine Son.[106]

Pannenberg's concerns about the doctrine of analogy are informed by Barth's, and his contribution to the discussion of analogy can be presented more briefly. In an essay originally written in 1959, he states that by patristic "reflection upon the similarity between cause and effect, the otherness of God was reduced and robbed of its radicality." For Pannenberg, reflecting on the similarity of an effect to its cause is appropriate only when the cause "operates because of a necessity of its essence." In pagan thought the "world-ground is exhaustively occupied in discharging the world from itself," so "one can presuppose a similarity between the effects and that imperceptible ground which they only approximately represent." However, if the cause in question (in Christian theology, God the Creator) brings about its effects contingently, then seeking such similarity is no longer legitimate. Thus "a causally grounded, analogical connection of the operation of God with his essence can be maintained only on the presupposition of the Greek under-standing of God as the necessarily operative ground of the world."[107] However,

> if God operates contingently, acts freely, and if the properties of his effects are different from his essence, then the properties of the divine operation, be-cause of its contingency, permit no reflection upon a similarity of the effects with the essence of God, and thus do not allow any statement that would transfer a creaturely perfection to God in a superlative sense.[108]

Yet, Pannenberg writes, "this is not to say that God's contingent action had nothing to do with his essence. But the connection is of a different sort than in the case of a cause that acts out of necessity." Here Pannenberg suggests

---

[105]Barth, *CD* III/2, 219-22, 267-69; cf. IV/1, 191-92; IV/2, 528-33; IV/3.2, 597-607. On this aspect of Barth's account, see Bruce L. McCormack, "Karl Barth's Version of an 'Analogy of Being,'" in White, *Analogy of Being*, 122-23, 135-44. This theme is also central in the recent constructive proposal of Archie J. Spencer, *The Analogy of Faith: The Quest for God's Speakability*, Strategic Initiatives in Evangelical Theology (Downers Grove, IL: IVP Academic, 2015), chap. 5.

[106]Barth, *CD* IV/3.2, 532-33.

[107]Wolfhart Pannenberg, "The Appropriation of the Philosophical Concept of God as a Dogmatic Problem of Early Christian Theology," in *Basic Questions in Theology: Collected Essays*, trans. George H. Kelm (Minneapolis: Fortress, 1971), 2:171.

[108]Pannenberg, "Appropriation of the Philosophical Concept of God," 2:171.

that, with a necessary effect, there is an "indeterminate, underlying cause *expressing* its essence by imparting itself," whereas, with a contingent effect, there is "the agent *producing* properties for himself." The "world-ground" "imparts itself out of necessity" and "appears in its effects only in a fragmentary way—to the extent that despite the participation of its effects in its being, it itself remains 'at a distance' behind them." That is, "the universal world-ground cannot be one with its individual effects, but appears in a fragmented way in their multiplicity." However, in choosing to act, a free agent brings about freely chosen effects and in so doing "is himself present in his effects." Therefore, the "contingently operative biblical God is present in his effects not by means of the participation of these effects in their origin, but in a 'personal mode,' i.e., by the choice of his acts he decides about the properties to which he binds himself precisely by this choice." In other words, he "chooses 'this' specific act in its particularity and makes it his own, so that now it really is a property of his eternal essence. It is *in that way* that the contingently acting God of the Bible demonstrates his essence in his act."[109]

In a later reflection on the doctrine of analogy, written as an afterword to an earlier historical study of the topic, Pannenberg indicates that he remains sympathetic to the cautions of Barth and Hermann Cremer against inferring from the "givenness of the world" the truth about a divine cause (*eine göttliche Ursache*). For, Pannenberg judges, the testimony of the Bible compels us "to speak of the attributes of God only on the basis of his action." Significantly, this not only upholds God's transcendence of the world but also affirms that he is actively present in it. It is by his action that God "appropriates" his attributes as attributes of his own essence. To be sure, Pannenberg writes, creation itself is the beginning of God's historical action, but learning from creation about God himself is less a matter of perceiving a similarity of creatures to their divine source than a matter of discerning what the free bringing forth of creatures expresses about God's goodness, power, and wisdom. At the same time, the doctrine of analogy does rightly

---

[109]Pannenberg, "Appropriation of the Philosophical Concept of God," 172. Compare Colin Gunton, "The End of Causality? The Reformers and their Predecessors," in *The Doctrine of Creation: Essays in Dogmatics, History and Philosophy*, ed. Colin E. Gunton (Edinburgh: T&T Clark, 1997), 63-82.

remind us that all our statements about God and even God's action itself must be purged of their anthropomorphic tendencies. For this reason, theological statements must constantly stand under the correction of the biblical teaching on how God has revealed his attributes, especially in the incarnation of his Son.[110]

Response to Barth and Pannenberg. Barth and Pannenberg present significant challenges to those who wish to employ a doctrine of analogy in the work of Christian description of God *in se*. Here I will offer three points in response to their concerns. First, while Barth's criticism of the *analogia entis* contains salutary reminders about the place of God's grace in conforming us to the image of his Son and about our dependence on supernatural revelation, his understanding of the relationship between nature and grace is problematic and yields a lopsided Creator-creature analogy that is rooted in redemptive grace alone. In particular, I do not think that Barth's system of thought allows us sufficiently to understand creation or nature as a biblical category in its own right and as the stage on which the fall and redemption (contingently) take place. To be sure, he does distinguish between creation as such and the covenant of grace and does affirm the goodness of created being. But then he also comments that for humanity as such, humanity without reference to God's will *to save* (not merely God's will to give humanity an original righteousness or God's will to sustain and instruct humanity in the Garden), "the fall and original sin are an ontological necessity" due to the "threat of surrounding non-being."[111] Or, even more poignantly, "Created being as such needs salvation."[112] It seems that in the logic of Barth's framework creation as such is not good without the help of salvific grace. It seems that created humanity as such does not image God and then only contingently fall into sin. Creation as such is brought into being and upheld at all only by *saving* grace.[113] However, the scriptural narrative of

[110]Wolfhart Pannenberg, "Nachwort 2006," in *Analogie und Offenbarung: Eine kritische Untersuchung zur Geschichte des Analogiebegriffs in der Lehre von der Gotteserkenntnis* (Göttingen: Vandenhoeck & Ruprecht, 2007), 214-15.

[111]Barth, *CD* III/2, 146.

[112]Barth, *CD* IV/1, 8.

[113]Barth does state that given God's will to save humanity and secure our fellowship with him, it is inexplicable that human beings would reject their Creator. Indeed, according to Barth, sin is in this sense an "ontological impossibility" (*CD* III/2, 146-47). However, insofar as the divine will to save presupposes sin from which humanity must be saved, the claim that this salvific

creation, sin, and redemption, together with the emphasis that God's gracious work has a restorative character (e.g., Acts 3:21; Rom 12:2; Eph 4:24; Col 3:10), requires us to confess an original goodness of created being as such, a fall into sin that is not ingredient in human nature as such, and a redemptive recovery of something (i.e., human nature rightly ordered to God) that once existed and was good in its own right. In short, if Barth worried that in Roman Catholicism "grace becomes nature," I would be concerned that in his account nature becomes grace—redemptive grace— over against the inner logic of the biblical economy.[114]

There is a broad sense in which all that God does is gracious, a broad sense in which creation itself can be considered a work of grace since God owes nothing to creatures prior to their origin but nevertheless richly blesses them in the constitution and provisions of their natural life.[115] While Barth

---

will is fundamental to the being of creation would still imply that sin and the fall are intrinsic to the very being of creation. It is similar with Barth's statement that in the fall humanity "forfeits" God's "predetermined salvation" (IV/1, 10). If it is a forfeiting of not simply fellowship with God but rather *salvation*, this implies that creation by its very nature is fallen, for otherwise there would be no need of salvation.

[114]Keith Johnson has insightfully stressed that in the development of his theology Barth did eventually recognize the need to affirm some positive relationship between created (and fallen) humanity and God even before the incarnation took place. Barth aimed to establish this relationship without foregoing his Christ-centered notion of analogy and the knowledge of God by claiming that "the created order itself, and thus created human being as such, is a function of God's decision to reconcile sinful humans in and through Jesus Christ." This move is consummated in Barth's configuration of the doctrine of election where "Jesus Christ is both the subject and object of election and thus the beginning and end of creation" ("Natural Revelation in Creation and Covenant," in *Thomas Aquinas and Karl Barth: An Unofficial Catholic-Protestant Dialogue*, ed. Bruce L. McCormack and Thomas Joseph White [Grand Rapids: Eerdmans, 2013], 145). In this way, according to Johnson, Barth does have a framework for affirming a Creator-creature analogy and a "natural revelation." However, I do not think this alleviates the problems with Barth's approach. There still appears to be in Barth's theology an assumption that the fall is a necessary unfolding or necessary feature of creation itself. If creation is established by reconciling grace, what about creation as such entails its enmity with God, an enmity that must be presupposed in the very notion of reconciliation? Also, I doubt that a "natural revelation" whose content is the saving work of Christ and whose content can be apprehended only within the sphere of the covenant of grace is meaningfully called "natural" in keeping with the way Paul describes the knowledge of God possessed (and distorted) by the human race in Rom 1:18-23. In addition, if one disagrees with Barth's understanding of the role of Christ's humanity in election and believes that the immutability of God in the incarnation and the divine power of Christ's saving work can be set forth in a different manner (see "The *Logos Asarkos* and *Extra Calvinisticum*" [in chap. 3] and "*Theologia* and God's Freedom for Us" [in chap. 4]), then his account loses much of its force.

[115]See Thomas, *ST* Ia.21.4 corp. and ad 4 (261-62). Among the early Reformed, see, e.g., Franciscus Junius, *De vera theologia* (Leiden, 1594), 10 (65); Polanus, *Syntagma* 5.2 (256); Turretin,

recognizes a distinction between grace taken in such a broad sense and grace taken in a salvific or redemptive sense,[116] he clearly emphasizes that nature is characterized from the outset by *salvific* or reconciling grace. But if this does disrupt the logic of the economy and call into question the restorative dimension of grace, then Barth's view of the nature-grace relation, whatever the merits of some of its constituent features, need not govern our approach to the doctrine of analogy.[117] If Barth's view of nature and grace is problematic, then so too is his construction of a parallel between the Creator-creature analogy and the doctrine of justification by grace and his concomitant assertion that there can be only an extrinsic analogy of attribution between God and creatures. For created being participates in and displays the goodness and perfection of God even by virtue of its being created by God, not just by virtue of God's saving grace.[118]

To say this is not to slip into a "Pelagian" approach to the matter of human fellowship with God. Created being that participates in and exhibits God's perfection is not something won by human merit. It is a gift. Nor does a likeness of created being to God entail that, after the fall, natural knowledge of God by itself empowers us to obtain right fellowship with God. Creatures know something of God but persistently suppress it (so Rom 1:18-23) and need the renewing effects of the word and Spirit of God to experience right fellowship with him (Rom 12:2; 1 Cor 2:6-16). Moreover, affirming that the creature enjoys a certain likeness to God simply by virtue of being created by God does not entail that after the fall human beings can be justified in the Pauline sense by something residing within us. Human beings are still made in the image of God, and yet the image is so marred by sin that we lack an inhering quality of righteousness or total fulfillment of God's law by which we might be acquitted and accepted by the divine judge.[119] Our only

---

Inst. 5.11.16 (1:521). Yet see also the comments of Mastricht, *TPT* 2.17.14 (180), regarding the care with which God's works of nature and God's works of grace should be distinguished.

[116]Barth, *CD* IV/1, 8-9.

[117]Of course, God's redemptive grace is more than restorative: it brings us not just back to the state of integrity but onward to the state of glory. Nevertheless, while this grace is more than restorative, it is not less.

[118]Moreover, it seems to me that Barth's use of the concept of justification in his account of creation and analogy threatens to detach it from its customary forensic usage in Scripture and Protestant dogmatics.

[119]A Roman Catholic author like White also can affirm this, even if disagreements between Rome and Protestantism on the doctrine of justification remain: "Our wounded natural capacity for

hope lies in receiving by faith the righteousness of Christ, which undoes the work of the first Adam (Rom 5:12-21). One can affirm a similitude of human beings to God by virtue of creation, even one that endures after the fall, and still embrace a robustly Protestant view of the *imago Dei* and Adam's fall. In such a view something belonging to the integrity of human nature itself (i.e., our original righteousness before God) is lost in the fall so that there is a corruption of human nature itself, not just a loss of a supernatural gift apart from which human nature and natural human knowing would perhaps retain their wholeness.[120] In this connection, Barth's exposition of nature, grace, and analogy is not a necessary outworking of Protestant soteriological commitments. On this point he is not so much being Protestant as he is being, well, Barthian.[121]

The end and therefore the original impetus of human existence certainly is union and communion with the triune God, but affirming this does not require us to say that the constitution of human nature is such that communion could be actualized only by *redemptive* grace. Furthermore, if one affirms that created human nature was good in its own right and did not necessarily include in its constitution an ordering toward saving grace, this does not entail that the work of the Son in establishing our fellowship with God is left as an afterthought on God's part. Even creation and our creaturely relation to God are brought about and upheld through the Son. Indeed, even if one believes that our fellowship with God would have been perfected by an incarnation of the Son even apart from the fall, such an approach does not entail that human beings require salvation in order to have an analogical likeness and fellowship with God (on all of this, see the section "Christ the Source and Telos of Theological Knowledge, in

---

God . . . can *in no way* procure for us the gift of justification or salvation" (*Wisdom in the Face of Modernity: A Study in Thomistic Natural Theology*, 2nd ed., Faith and Reason: Studies in Catholic Theology and Philosophy [Ave Maria, FL: Sapientia, 2016], 283n103).

[120]On this aspect of Reformed theological anthropology, see, e.g., Turretin, *Inst.* 5.9-11 (1:509-21).

[121]My sense of how being Protestant should shape one's view of the Creator-creature analogy is thus different from that of Johnson in *Karl Barth and the* Analogia Entis, or Spencer in *Analogy of Faith*. David Bentley Hart has quipped, *pace* Barth, that the *rejection* of the analogy of being is "the invention of antichrist" and perhaps "the most compelling reason for not becoming Protestant" (*The Beauty of the Infinite: The Aesthetics of Christian Truth* [Grand Rapids: Eerdmans, 2003], 242). I am insisting here that affirming a Creator-creature analogy established by God's act of creation can and should be a point of common ground for Protestants, Roman Catholics, and Eastern Orthodox believers.

chap. 3).[122] Furthermore, if we say that created human nature as such is good and images God even without reference to saving grace, and that the fall and redemption are not ingredient in human nature as such or requisite for a Creator-creature analogy, we are not positing two separate moments in the divine decree. To remain aligned with the logic of the economy, we can maintain that there is within the decree a logical priority of created human existence to the fall and to God's saving work without suggesting that there is a disunity or chronological development within the decree. In other words, God's original and eternal plan for the human race does include the fall (a fall permitted rather than authored by God) and redemption, but this simply does not mean that created human nature as such needed redemption in order to enjoy fellowship with God. In sum, Barth's view of analogy understates the goodness of created being as such and the similarity to God that creatures have even by virtue of their simply being created by God.

Second, while Barth is understandably concerned about human beings having license to take up whatever features of created being they like and then attribute these to God (perhaps for self-serving ends), affirming an ontological likeness of creatures to God does not by itself justify such a practice. At this point it is important to distinguish between different ways in which an *analogia entis* and an analogous attribution of creaturely names to God might function in Christian theology. In this study, I have no interest in suggesting that there is an *analogia entis* in the sense of a unity of divine and created being by common participation in a being superior to both. That would be an analogy of attribution of the *multa ad unum* sort rightly denied by Thomas, Zanchi, and others. That Barth assumes in his critique of Quenstedt that an intrinsic analogy of attribution must entail the *multa ad unum* schema reveals a serious misunderstanding of the historical usage of analogy. The *unum ad alterum* analogy of attribution that is invoked by Thomas and various early Protestant authors—and that I would commend in Christian *theologia* today—underscores the fact that creatures derive their being and perfections from the God who is entirely *a se*. It underscores the

---

[122]For examples of this sort of approach, see Edwin Chr. van Driel, *Incarnation Anyway: Arguments for a Supralapsarian Christology* (Oxford: Oxford University Press, 2008); Joel R. Beeke and Mark Jones, *A Puritan Theology: Doctrine for Life* (Grand Rapids: Reformation Heritage, 2012), chap. 9.

fact that God participates in nothing beyond himself, nothing that we might purport to know first and then claim as a basis on which we can attribute to God's being whatever we like.

The analogy of attribution is also not meant to function here as a principle of dogmatic theology. It is not what generates dogmatic reasoning, what supplies its content, or what norms its claims about God. To deploy an older Protestant saying, the "external principle of knowing" (*principium cognoscendi externum*) in dogmatic theology is God's revelation in Holy Scripture. The "proximate" and "immediate" efficient cause of the Christian knowledge of God developed in dogmatics is the word of God. For "the first principle into which all theological dogmas are resolved is *Dominus dixit*."[123] Thus, in keeping with the earlier chapter on the place of natural theology in Christian *theologia*, the theologian does not begin his or her work by taking initiative to survey whatever potential creaturely analogues might seem helpful for description of God. Instead, bound from the beginning to the word of God, the theologian reads Scripture and learns from Scripture the names and attributes that God would have us apply to himself. But precisely in Scripture we also learn that God's works reflect his perfection, which helps us to understand why he authorizes us to use ordinary words in our speech about him. And we are invited to recall our experience of creaturely wisdom or justice, for example, in understanding the meaning of God's wisdom or justice, even as Scripture leads us to recognize the significant dissimilarity between (fallen) creatures and God. There is thus a positive role for an intrinsic analogy of attribution not as a principle of dogmatics but as a resource to explicate how creaturely names are not arbitrarily applied to God and how they convey true knowledge of God. In addition, when the Christian believer is donning the "spectacles" of Scripture,[124] he or she can look out on the natural world and, with the guidance of Scripture, perceive aright the many ways in which it discloses the majesty of its Creator. Indeed, it is by virtue of this ontological resemblance and the consequent analogical predication found in Scripture and Christian proclamation that someone outside the body of Christ and its patterns of speaking can first

---

[123]Polanus, *Syntagma* 1.14 (16).

[124]For the metaphor, see John Calvin, *Institutes of the Christian Religion*, ed. John T. McNeill, trans. Ford Lewis Battles, LCC 20-21 (Louisville: Westminster John Knox, 1960), 1.6.1 (1:70).

apprehend the gospel's verbal disclosure of God's triune identity and respond in faith.[125]

Third, though Pannenberg rightly distinguishes between (1) an impersonal "world-ground" that would supposedly produce created being by a natural necessity and (2) the personal and free Creator revealed in Holy Scripture, the implications he draws from the distinction do not necessarily follow from it. In particular, the fact that God creates the world not from a "necessity of nature" but with what the scholastics call a "liberty of indifference" does not mean that the world will not bear a likeness to God by virtue of being created by him.[126] It is with and not in spite of that "liberty of indifference" that God grants to creatures a participation in his life and wisdom and love and power. To what else would creaturely perfections ultimately bear a resemblance, to what other exemplar would they owe their character if not the being of the one Creator of all things? We certainly cannot say that God beheld some other coeternal source of perfection and goodness and chose it to be the archetype for created natures and activities. He alone is *a se* and eternal and does not give his glory to another. It seems to me we have to say that in freely choosing to give life to the world and to fill it with creatures possessing a plurality of perfections, God by a "hypothetical necessity"—a necessity following on a free decision—would have his own being as the exemplar cause in order to accomplish that end. God alone is the font of all being, and there simply was no other exemplar cause.[127]

---

[125]On the apprehension of the gospel presupposing some (analogical) apprehension of God by nature and some prior grasp of the meaning of terms used in supernatural revelation, compare the argument of Thomas Joseph White, "Through Him All Things Were Made," 246-79, esp. 272n57). In the order of discovery in the natural acquisition of knowledge of God, the analogy of being features earlier than Scripture (with sundry infralapsarian distortions of this knowledge), but Scripture is superior to it as principle and norm of the dogmatic theology authorized to reform natural theology.

[126]A "necessity of nature" is a propensity intrinsic to the nature of something on account of which it seeks some end, while a "liberty of indifference" is a freedom to do or not to do something without detriment to the being or completeness of the acting subject.

[127]Cf. Polanus, *Syntagma* 2.9 (143), where he calls God the "exemplar and cause of all perfection, of nature and grace." The absence of a preexisting material cause does not rule out the analogy of created effects to God, as suggested by Stephen Holmes ("The Attributes of God," in *The Oxford Handbook of Systematic Theology*, ed. John Webster, Kathryn Tanner, and Iain Torrance [Oxford: Oxford University Press, 2007], 58), where he states that the doctrine of *creatio ex nihilo* precludes the *via causalitatis*. Even given the absence of preexisting matter, if God did not create haphazardly, that implies an exemplar cause according to which created natures are formed.

Yet the analogy of created effects to their divine cause does not mean that God is present to his creatures in a restricted way. It is true that God's created effects never fully represent all that God himself is, but this is not an obstacle to God's presence with creatures. There is no need to drive a wedge between causality and participation, on the one hand, and personal, free action and presence, on the other. God causes things to be and to set forth his glory and does so freely. Because he is *a se* and transcends the created order, he can be immediately present to his creatures. Further, when Pannenberg suggests that, in acting in certain ways to perform his works, God is choosing to "bring about properties" that he then includes in his essence, it is not clear what it would mean for God to "bring about" a property and then render that a constituent feature of his essence. Such a move is actually counterproductive to illuminating God's presence with his creatures, for it seems to imply that the God who meets us in the economy is different from God as he eternally and originally is.

Whatever helpful cautions we might glean from Barth and Pannenberg, we need not let their concerns prevent us from appropriating the *unum ad alterum* analogy of attribution in the work of Christian *theologia*. Affirming and using that analogy does not automatically lead to neglecting the transcendence and otherness of God or our dependence on God's revelation for our knowledge of God. However, on the other end of the spectrum are some recent writers who contend that the doctrine of analogy is in fact insufficient. That is, it does not go far enough to secure or illumine human knowledge of God himself. I will address these concerns next.

CONCERNS ABOUT THE SUFFICIENCY OF ANALOGY

Survey of recent authors. Some have argued that an analogical view of theological predication undermines genuine knowledge of God in himself. Such authors often commend a Scotist doctrine of univocity. One significant critic of the view that all speech about God is analogical is the Christian philosopher William Alston, who analyzes what Thomas in particular says about analogy.[128] Alston focuses on those terms (like *knowledge,*

---

[128]For a broader collection of Alston's essays on human description of God, see William P. Alston, *Divine Nature and Human Language: Essays in Philosophical Theology* (Ithaca, NY: Cornell University Press, 1989).

goodness, and so on) whose content, according to Thomas, entails nothing inherently creaturely and can therefore apply "properly" or literally to God. Alston calls these "pure perfection terms" and comments that given Thomas's view of divine simplicity, the fact that we apply these terms "not in one fell conceptual swoop but only as divided up conceptually into different aspects . . . implies a fundamental inadequacy in our talk about God." For, as Alston reads him, Thomas holds that God's simplicity entails that there can be "no distinction at all between any divine parts or aspects of any sort whatever." Thus, "Whatever you say truly of God, it is the same 'thing' that makes it true." For Alston, this means that the structure of our statements about God, in which subject and predicate are distinct from one another, always contradicts God's simplicity. Those statements therefore cannot correspond to God's being. "And," Alston remarks, "if truth goes, the game is up with theology." To be sure, Alston recognizes (against Cajetan's take on analogy) that even in the analogy of attribution in Thomas's theology the various perfections attributed to God are taken to be intrinsic to God himself, not just caused by God to exist in creatures. However, Alston still argues that Thomas's approach does not sufficiently facilitate human knowledge of God himself. Alston is especially critical of Thomas's tendency to assert that a given perfection found in creatures is present in God in a more "eminent" way without specifying what the divine analogue or more "eminent" way actually is: "We simply indicate that it is a higher form of a creaturely perfection but without being able to say just what the higher form is."[129] Precision of expression is not always required to ascertain whether a statement is true, but, Alston writes, Thomas gives us no way to determine which features of a creaturely attribute (e.g., knowledge) apply to God and which do not:

> He has disavowed any attempt to be specific about what knowing or willing come to in the divine case, except that they constitute a "higher mode" of the sort of thing we have in human knowing and willing. But if we can't spell out the ways in which the higher version is like and unlike the lower analogue,

---

[129]William P. Alston, "Aquinas on Theological Predication: A Look Backward and Look Forward," in *Reasoned Faith: Essays in Philosophical Theology in Honor of Norman Kretzmann*, ed. Eleonore Stump (Ithaca, NY: Cornell University Press, 1993), 147, 149, 167-69; Alston, "Religious Language," in *The Oxford Handbook of Philosophy of Religion*, ed. William J. Wainwright (Oxford: Oxford University Press, 2005), 236, 239-40.

how can we even address the question of whether principles that hold of the lower form also hold of the higher form?[130]

Put differently, within the logic of Thomas's view, we can affirm that there is a likeness between divine and human knowledge, but "we cannot make fully explicit what this likeness amounts to" and so must wonder "how we can suppose that we are saying anything reasonably determinate about God."[131] In Alston's judgment, then, it is better to analyze our concepts carefully and come to "specify a very abstract structure that can plausibly be claimed to be equally found in God and creatures . . . though the mode of realization of this abstract structure is, no doubt, enormously different."[132] By isolating this "abstract univocal core," we can apply the "abstract component" univocally ("in just the same sense") to God and creatures in order to "specify the relevant analogy" between God and creatures. We can then also acknowledge that certain "concrete" developments of a given term are exclusively fitting for either God or creatures.[133]

Similarly, David Clark states that "the main conclusion of contemporary theology is that theological analogy, as Aquinas articulated that concept, does not help us understand God." Like Alston, Clark believes the analogy of attribution is insufficient if it allows us to conclude only that a given perfection is in God "in an unknown degree and in an unknown way." Building on Alston's account of univocity, Clark suggests that it is possible to possess a concept whose meaning is identical in the case of God and creatures but whose ontological realization in God and creatures is entirely distinct. Action, for example, might be predicated of God and creatures alike in the sense of "bringing about a change in the world." The "univocal core" might remain even as it is applied in God's case without inclusion of "finite or physical features."[134]

Another writer who builds on Alston's work is Nicholas Wolterstorff. According to Wolterstorff, though, while Alston is right to hold that "pure perfection terms" are predicated literally of God as well as creatures, Alston

---

[130] Alston, "Aquinas on Theological Predication," 172-73.
[131] Alston, "Religious Language," 240-41.
[132] Alston, "Aquinas on Theological Predication," 177.
[133] Alston, "Religious Language," 242.
[134] David K. Clark, *To Know and Love God: Method for Theology* (Wheaton, IL: Crossway, 2003), 392-97.

has misunderstood Thomas's view and unnecessarily rendered Thomas an opponent on the issue of analogy and univocity. On Wolterstorff's reading of him, Thomas actually upholds the univocity of such "pure perfection terms" in his description of God and creatures. Wolterstorff argues that in Thomas's account of analogy both God and creatures have the "same perfection" (e.g., wisdom) that applies to both in a literal manner, which entails that the perfection designated by a predicate like "wisdom" is univocal in the case of God and creatures. The "thing signified" (*res significata*) is "identical" and the name for it has "exactly the same sense" in its application to God and its application to creatures. The thing predicated of God and creatures (the "predicate term") is itself univocal. The analogical dimension of Thomas's account is to be located, then, not in the names themselves (e.g., wisdom, goodness) but in the manner in which we predicate the names of God and creatures. For, in Thomas's view, we predicate them of God as a simple being and of ourselves as complex beings.[135] "The 'is' in 'God is wise' necessarily has a different force, a different *ratio*, from the 'is' in 'Socrates is wise.'" Thus "the analogy is to be located, not in the sense (meaning) of the predicate term itself but in the copula." The diversity in the *ratio* of our speech about God and our speech about creatures—the diversity that is constitutive of analogical predication—"pertains to the predicating, not to what's predicated, to the copula, not to the predicate term." Wolterstorff believes that English translations of the *Summa theologiae* tend to obscure this point and emphasizes that in Ia.13.5 Thomas says that "no name applies to God according to the same *ratio* according to which *it is said* of a creature," not that the name itself possesses a diverse *ratio*. Thomas "says that the term is not *said of* (*dicitur*) God and creatures according to the same *ratio*," not that "the word is not used in the same sense."[136]

---

[135]Wolterstorff infelicitously speaks of God's "participating" in his perfections in a manner different than we do ours.

[136]Nicholas Wolterstorff, "Alston on Aquinas on Theological Predication," in *Inquiring About God: Selected Essays*, ed. Terence Cuneo (Cambridge: Cambridge University Press, 2010), 1:121-30. Bruce Marshall also has argued recently that Thomas incorporates a doctrine of univocity in his view of theological description ("Christ the End of Analogy," in White, *Analogy of Being*, 303-13). Marshall makes this claim with reference to Thomas's Christology where Thomas says that the human nature and actions of God the Son apply to him *vere et proprie*. However, leaving aside the christological intricacies for the moment, I would point out that since Marshall's argument concerns the humanity of Christ it does not bear on the questions in this chapter about the sense in which the *divine* attributes or names are predicated of God.

Other authors' engagement of the doctrine of analogy has focused less on refuting (or reinterpreting) Thomas and more on drawing from Scotus's thought. While emphasizing that there is no "extramental reality that is a common component of both God and creatures," Thomas Williams argues that "there are concepts under whose extension both God and creatures fall" in order to uphold the intelligibility of our speech about God.[137] He comments that if we offer a statement about God (e.g., "God is wise") but allow for the predicate to be purely equivocal, we will be obligated then to identify the sense in which God is wise. But this new term or expression that we introduce also "will be drawn from the repertoire of expressions we use in order to talk about creatures. And so we must ask again: does this expression have the same sense when predicated of God as when predicated of creatures? If it does, we have arrived at univocal predication." It is only univocal predication that will "terminate the regress" and prevent us from falling into "an infinite stutter." In Williams's mind, analogy does not help here because in order for analogy to uphold the intelligibility of our speech about God, it would require us to explain either (1) the sense in which a predicate applies to God or (2) the relation between the sense in which it applies to God and the sense in which it applies to creatures. But to do (1) we return to the regress of "substitute expressions" that must terminate in univocity, and to do (2) we take up a "composite expression" that makes clear the sense of the predicate in its application to God and adds some "relational expression," which also must be reducible to a univocal expression in order to be rendered intelligible. In short, "we come in the end always either to univocity or unintelligibility."[138]

Having discussed Scotus's view of univocity from a primarily historical and descriptive perspective in previous works,[139] Richard Cross also considers the fecundity of this view in contemporary theology and addresses some objections against it. He argues that it is not a matter of "ontotheology," of "idolatrously placing something real higher than God—namely, Being." For, as Cross puts it, "concepts are not things in the real world." Stressing that Scotus's position on univocity is decidedly semantic, Cross

---

[137]Thomas Williams, "The Doctrine of Univocity Is True and Salutary," *MT* 21 (2005): 577-78.
[138]Williams, "Doctrine of Univocity," 578-79.
[139]See Cross, *Duns Scotus*, 33-39; Cross, *Duns Scotus on God* (Aldershot: Ashgate, 2005), 249-59.

comments that it is "neutral on the question of the degree of real, ontological likeness between God and creatures."[140] More recently, Daniel Horan has drawn out some implications of Scotus's view and presented a significant challenge to those who wish to affirm that all speech about God is analogical. There must be a univocal basis for analogical speech, Horan contends, since univocity is the "condition of the possibility for any theology": "All language about God and, therefore, any natural or revealed statements relating to the divine essence necessarily presupposes the univocal predication of some concept. Analogy, Scotus asserts, is simply equivocation without an a priori univocally predicable concept."[141] For Horan, this leaves us with a thorough-going apophaticism:

> Without a concept that is abstractable from creation in this world, one is not able to garner terms or concepts of God apart from revelation. Additionally, such a denial presents the problem of exclusive apophaticism and theologically discursive docetism. Apart from revelation, we have no ability to know or say anything about God. Revealed knowledge of God then becomes something that appears without a correlative relationship to reality as such. Univocity, on the other hand, provides both the condition of the possibility for kataphatic theology, while additionally grounding revealed truth in conceptual reality.[142]

Response. How might we respond to these criticisms of analogy and arguments for univocity? Does the view that all our speech about God is analogical end up undermining the claim that we truly know God himself? I will offer five points in response to these critiques.

First, Wolterstorff is mistaken in his assertion that Thomas embraces a doctrine of univocity with respect to the divine perfections and is mistaken in suggesting that univocity is an entailment of literality. The case for univocity certainly does not rest on the claim that Thomas advocated it, but for the sake of clarity it should be noted that Thomas does view the *ratio* of the perfection or name itself (e.g., wisdom) as a locus of analogical diversity and unity. Wolterstorff's argument turns on his observation that in *Summa theologiae* Ia.13.5 Thomas says that "no name agrees with God according to that

---

[140]Richard Cross, "Idolatry and Religious Language," *Faith and Philosophy* 25 (2008): 191-92.
[141]Horan, *Postmodernity and Univocity*, 185.
[142]Horan, *Postmodernity and Univocity*, 186.

ratio according to which *it is said* of the creature."[143] From this Wolterstorff infers that it is not the *ratio* or sense of the name per se but rather its being "said" or predicated of God or the creature in which the analogical diversity and unity is to be located. Because Thomas uses the example of wisdom here, Wolterstorff comments, "Aquinas does not say that the term 'wise' has a different meaning when applied to God and to creatures."[144] However, in this article, Thomas states that the *ratio* (the content or definition of the term) is changed by the ontological status of the subject (*genus variatum mutat rationem*). Thomas joins the *ratio* or sense of the term to the ontological landscape by stating that the *ratio* of a name in the creature's case is shaped by creatures having their perfections "dividedly and multiply." Likewise, in God's case the sense of the term is shaped by God having his perfections in a simple manner. The sense of a given name applied to God or the creature is already informed by the structure of the *res significata*. The fact that the name with its *ratio* is then "said" of God or the creature does not indicate that the act of predication itself is what generates the analogical diversity and unity but rather just reflects that the purpose of the name is to be used in our speech about God or the creature—it is meant to be "said." It seems to me that Wolterstorff's rather forced reading of Thomas is meant to promote a separation of the sense of a name from the way in which it is realized in the subject, but Thomas's account resists such separation.

At the same time, the denial of univocity does not signal a denial of all literality in our speech about God. Analogy characterizes the (diverse but still similar) sense in which our words apply to God, while the question of whether a name is metaphorical or literal in its application to God concerns whether the content of the name (not just the way in which it is predicated) is intrinsically creaturely, whether the name signifies something that properly belongs to creatures only. For Thomas, all our names for God are analogical, but they may be either metaphorical or literal. They are always predicated of God in a sense diverse from but similar to the sense in which they are predicated of creatures. Then, if the content of a given name (e.g., "rock") is intrinsically creaturely, the analogical similitude on God's part lies in God's effects (e.g., protection) rather than God's being itself. In

---

[143]*Sed nullum nomen convenit Deo secundum illam rationem, secundum quam dicitur de creatura.*
[144]Wolterstorff, "Alston on Aquinas on Theological Predication," 129.

that case the name applies metaphorically to God. If the content of another name (e.g., "wisdom") is not intrinsically creaturely, the analogical similitude on God's part lies immediately in God himself, and the name applies literally to God. Analogy deals with the *ratio* or sense of a name whereas literality deals with whether the analogical content of the name on God's side lies in God's effects or in God himself.[145] The affirmation of analogy and denial of univocity therefore does not commit us to holding that all our speech about God is metaphorical.

Second, against authors like Alston and Clark, it is incorrect to suggest that Thomas fails to specify what it means that God's perfections are in him in a "more eminent" way. In the *Summa theologiae* Thomas succinctly states that a name like "wisdom" is predicated of God in a distinct way in that (1) it does not signify a quality belonging to God but rather God's essence itself and (2) it does not circumscribe the fullness of God's wisdom but rather "leaves the thing signified not fully grasped [*incomprehensa*]."[146] God's simplicity and infinity are mysterious to us and transcend full human description, but that does not mean the claim that a given perfection is (1) really identical to God's essence and (2) infinite in God's case is unintelligible or so vague as to leave us without any understanding of the manner in which the perfection is found in God. Indeed, it is one of the tasks of the doctrine of the divine attributes to avoid giving the impression that our speech about God expresses or even could express all that God is, directing the human mind and heart to what is true of God while precisely in doing so alerting us to the fact that we creatures do not know the fullness of that truth. To my mind, fulfillment of that task is aptly helped along by Thomas's statements about the way in which the perfections are in God "more eminently" (i.e., in the unity and infinity of his essence), together with his willingness to recognize that the material content of the perfections exceeds our comprehension.[147]

---

[145]See Thomas, *ST* Ia.13.3 (143); 19.11 corp. (249).

[146]Thomas, *ST* Ia.13.5, corp. (146).

[147]Another way of responding to Alston and Clark is to emphasize that in Thomas's thought one begins with a knowledge of some created effect and the fact that it displays God's perfection in some way or is referred back to one who possesses the attribute discerned in the effect in an absolute and full manner (in an analogy of attribution). One never discards that knowledge when seeking greater understanding of how the attribute discerned in the effect applies to God. Alston and Clark's critique might be more effective if it were aimed at an approach that utilizes

Third, in a Thomistic view of analogy, our speech about God is not falsified by God's simplicity like Alston infers. A statement like "God is wise" would be falsified by God's simplicity if it implicitly included or were explicitly accompanied by the claim that the subject and the predicate in the sentence refer to two really distinct things. But our ascription of a perfection to God does not and need not include such a claim. If we arrive at the theological conviction that God's attributes are really identical to God's essence, we can make a statement like "God is wise" while bearing in mind that God's relationship to his wisdom is different from a human being's relationship to his or her wisdom: the subject (God) is wise in that he has wisdom as an aspect of his own essence. That our predication of various perfections of God remains true and viable even within the sphere of the doctrine of divine simplicity is confirmed by Thomas in his commentary on the *Sentences*, for example. There he stresses that the *ratio* or intelligible content of a given attribute is present not just in the human mind or even in God's outward works but in God himself.[148]

Fourth, in Thomas's view the *ratio* or sense in which an attribute is applicable to God or creatures is itself informed by the way in which the material content of the attribute is present in God or creatures. In other words, the sense is not to be separated from the way in which the thing signified is actual in the subject. If, as authors like Clark and Cross suggest, this commitment is set aside and the sense of the predicate is separated from the ontological structure of the subject, it seems to me that the door is open to either overstating or understating our knowledge of God. That is, when the sense of our theological speech is separated from its ontological basis in God, its descriptive depth is no longer directly delimited by the reality of God himself but must rather be addressed and clarified in a second step in the descriptive process.[149] Of course anyone who does wish to separate the sense

---

only the four-term analogy of proper proportionality and agonizes over our lack of comprehension of one or more of the terms (especially God's essence) (see also the comments on Kant and the analogy of proportionality in Archie J. Spencer, "Causality and the *Analogia entis*: Karl Barth's Rejection of Analogy of Being Reconsidered," *Nova et Vetera* 6 [2008]: 346-47), but that is not the approach found in Thomas.

[148]Thomas, *Sententiarum* 1.2.1.3 (63-72).

[149]It is still true that we will have used various predicates in describing God before refining our understanding of the sense of those predicates, if indeed the sense of the predicate is informed by the being of the subject. Put differently, we use our language in discursive reasoning and

of the predicate and the subject's ontological structure would presumably clarify that when attributing a purportedly univocal predicate to God one would simply add that the way in which that predicate is true of God is different from the way in which it is true of creatures. My response would be not that a two-stage practice of this sort will automatically yield problems in theology proper (though it certainly allows for problems) but rather that it is not necessary. For what advocates of univocity are pursuing—the intelligibility of the divine names, the alleviation of an "infinite stutter" in Williams's words—is already to be found in a doctrine of analogy. This is because in a doctrine of analogy the aspect of the *ratio* that a divine name (e.g., wisdom) has in common with the name in its application to creatures is not eliminated simply because that aspect is always joined to other intelligible content that the divine name has.[150] In other words, what we know of true wisdom in created beings is not altogether put aside if the sense or content itself of the divine attribute of wisdom includes that God's knowledge or act of knowing is really identical with his essence and is infinitely greater than our knowledge. That the formal content of the perfection itself in God's

then allow the substance of the results of such reasoning recursively to shape our understanding of the language itself (compare Rocca, *Speaking the Incomprehensible God*, 341-49).

[150]In appropriating Thomas here, I read him differently from Marshall in "Christ the End of Analogy," 292-303. Marshall contends that because the *modus significandi* of any name is intrinsically creaturely, we cannot know the *ratio* of any divine name. For Marshall, there still is some unknown *ratio* of the divine name that must be related to the name in its creaturely application, but we will not grasp this *ratio* until the beatific vision. However, as I understand Thomas, the creaturely nature of the *modus significandi* consists in that the structure of our predication reflects that a creature's attributes are qualities distinct from essence and are more or less comprehensible to us (so *De potentia* 7.5 corp. and ad 2 [199]). Cf. Rocca, *Speaking the Incomprehensible God*, 341-52, where he distinguishes (1) the *res significata* of a divine name, (2) the *ratio* or meaning of the name, and (3) the *modus significandi* of the name; and E. J. Ashworth, "Aquinas on Analogy," in *Debates in Medieval Philosophy: Essential Readings and Contemporary Responses*, ed. Jeffrey Hause (New York: Routledge, 2014), 240-41. In God's case, the content of a divine name is really identical with his essence and exceeds our comprehension (so *ST* Ia.13.5 corp. [146]). But this does not entail that the *ratio* of a divine name is entirely unknowable in this life. We know something of the *ratio* or intelligible content of the divine name from our knowledge of the *ratio* of the corresponding creaturely name. And we know that the *ratio* of the divine name includes that the thing signified is essential and infinite in God (in *ST* Ia.13.5 the analogical *ratio* is clearly informed by ontological considerations). What we do not know is the *ratio* of the divine essence as such and in its entirety or the infinite depth of any of God's essential perfections. In other words, we know the *ratio* of a divine name but in an imperfect manner and in a way that does not presume we have knowledge of God's essence as such or a definitive comprehension of God's perfections. I take this to be a brief but accurate distillation of claims Thomas makes in *Sententiarum* 1.2.1.2-3 (61-72); *De Trin.* 6.3 (166-68); *ST* Ia.13.2 corp. and ad 1 and 3 (141-42); 13.7 corp. (146-47).

case (e.g., wisdom) is multidimensional does not entail that one of those dimensions (the one most accessible to us) is lost under another that is more mysterious to us (i.e., that the act of knowing is really identical to God's essence and has no limit).[151] Thus the aim of an account of univocity—circumventing an infinite descriptive regress in which the content of God's attributes is never truly understood—is secured by a doctrine of analogy without ever implying (as the doctrine of univocity at least initially does) that the content of a perfection applies equally to God and creatures, and without inviting accounts of the divine perfections in which the mere

---

[151] I would therefore reject the notion that in an analogical approach we are doomed to seek after the meaning of one divine name by endlessly appealing to other descriptions of God that can never themselves be understood except by eventual recourse to univocity (on this problem, see, e.g., David B. Burrell, *Analogy and Philosophical Language* [New Haven, CT: Yale University Press, 1973], 132-33; Kai Nielsen, "Analogical Talk About God: A Negative Critique," *The Thomist* 40 [1976]: 32-60; W. Norris Clarke, "Analogy and the Meaningfulness of Language about God: A Reply to Kai Nielsen," *The Thomist* [1976]: 61-95). I think there are two points to be made here. First, when we encounter, for example, God's wisdom, love, or causal action, we do not bracket all prior understanding of wisdom, love, and causation and hope to understand these terms only by deferring to others. Instead, we retain our prior awareness of the meaning of such terms. With an awareness that there is some commonality between the sense in which these apply to the creature and the sense in which they apply to God, we inquire about how the sense will also be in some way distinct in God's case given the ontological distinction between Creator and creature. In some cases, we may have to acknowledge that even some terms we use to express God's distinction from the world (and that we use to qualify the sense in which terms like *wisdom* or *love* apply to God) are themselves subject to further analogical refinement. For example, if we recognize that God's wisdom is infinite, we have to clarify that God's infinity is not a quantitative or continual infinity or an openness to ongoing addition. It is, rather, a negative infinity, an infinity that in its plenitude does not permit addition (e.g., Polanus, *Syntagma* 2.10 [144-45]). Though infinity is used analogically here, such elaboration on it is not itself restricted to analogical use of all words. The term applied to God remains analogical even if our explanation of it does not employ only analogical locutions. Second, it is possible to take a formally negative attribute like independence or infinity to be what Burrell calls a "formal feature" of God that simply serves as an apophatic qualifier rather than an attribute in the vein of wisdom or love ("Distinguishing God from the World," in *Language, Meaning and God: Essays in Honor of Herbert McCabe OP*, ed. Brian Davies [repr., Eugene, OR: Wipf and Stock, 2010], 75-91). Alternatively, one might deploy the language of "incommunicable attributes" and point out that infinity is not at all communicated to creatures and therefore has no analogue in creatures, placing it, strictly speaking, outside the discussion of analogy and univocity. To the extent that an incommunicable attribute like independence or infinity does still have intelligible content, it can still be qualified as noted above. In addition, if an incommunicable attribute like eternity has both a negative aspect (there is no succession in God's life) and a positive aspect (God has absolute duration and full possession of life) (e.g., Polanus, *Syntagma* 2.11 [145]), the sense of terms like *duration* or *life* will be open to further clarification. Ultimately, the more familiar aspect of the *ratio* of a divine name like wisdom that builds from our experience of created things provides a ground and entry into the conceptual refinement that might otherwise appear to be a fideistic game. In short, the *modus operandi* of a doctrine of analogy is not skepticism but faith's apprehensive knowledge seeking discursive understanding.

grammatical structure of our speech about God becomes a basis on which material conclusions about God's being are drawn.[152]

Fifth and finally, in an analogical account of theological language a divine attribute still shares an aspect of its *ratio* with the corresponding creaturely attribute. It therefore does not yield the nominalist, "docetic" apophaticism that Horan would understandably reject. In an analogical account, God gives us words in his revelation to use in our speech about him and in so doing is communicating truth about himself, confirming this by reiterating in texts like Genesis 1:26-27 or Ephesians 4:24 that the created beings and actions that our words customarily describe do bear an ontological resemblance to God and his actions by virtue of which these words, when applied to God, are expressive of reality. Thus the divine names or attributes are not arbitrarily assigned to God as they would be in a strictly nominalist view, nor do they only *seem* to correspond to reality as they would in a "docetic" framework. With the abiding similarity in the *ratio* of divine and creaturely names in an analogical account, there is, then, a strong impetus for the necessary kataphatic element in theology proper. Furthermore, even if the *analogia entis* by itself is not a proper cognitive principle of Christian theology, the analogical view advocated here does not rule out the practice of natural theology altogether. In keeping with the discussion of natural theology in chapter two, while the effects of sin compel us to conclude that the influence of Scripture is needed for a rightly ordered apprehension of natural revelation, creation does still have an ontological likeness to God that points us to God and affords some preparation for the "school of grace."

CONCLUSION

In this chapter we have explored the doctrine of analogy in relation to the practice of Christian *theologia*. I began with Scripture's teaching on God's transcendence and his will to communicate something of his goodness and perfection to creatures. Taken together, divine transcendence and divine

---

[152]For an example of this problem, see J. P. Moreland and William Lane Craig, *Philosophical Foundations for a Christian Worldview* (Downers Grove, IL: IVP Academic, 2003), 524-26, where the authors assume that since omnipotence and goodness are two distinct "properties" they therefore cannot be one in God. Graham Oppy identifies the problem when he notes that "the surface syntactic form" of our statements is wrongly taken to establish the structure of God's being ("The Devilish Complexities of Divine Simplicity," *Philo* 6 [2003]: 17).

communication compel us to be cautious in theological description while also hopeful that the creature's participation in God may enable a truthful use of creaturely language in theology proper. This led into a historical exploration of the doctrine of analogy. There I contended that the analogy of attribution in particular, which is expounded by Thomas and taken up by the Protestant orthodox, should have a place in theology proper today. This analogy is an agreement or similitude between two analogates, one of which (the creature) has something in a limited way and in dependence on another (God) who possesses it (e.g., being, wisdom, goodness, power) in an absolute, essential, and independent manner. In its "one to another" form—rather than its "many to one" form—the analogy of attribution stipulates that creatures are referred to the triune God as the ultimate source of their natures and perfections, instead of both creatures and God being referred (*per impossibile*) to some other source above God.[153]

After this, I took into account significant concerns from Barth and Pannenberg about positing an analogy of being between God and creatures. In response to Barth, I argued that creatures are analogous to God in God's creative work as well as his redemptive work, and that this fits with an authentically Protestant view of sin and grace. In response to Pannenberg, I argued that the contingency of creation does not eliminate the likeness of created effects to their divine cause, for there would have been no exemplar other than God the Creator that created perfections could image. I then examined some recent concerns about whether the doctrine of analogy adequately secures our knowledge of God himself. In response, I drew attention to the fact that a Thomistic doctrine of analogy does specify the sense in which a perfection is in God in a more "eminent" manner. I also pointed out that the aspect of the *ratio* of a divine perfection that is similar to the *ratio* of a creaturely perfection is still upheld in an analogical view in which other aspects of that *ratio* preclude a doctrine of univocity. Thus, providing responses to those who think a doctrine of analogy might be either too presumptuous or too cautious has afforded an opportunity to clarify the underlying logic for implementing the analogy of attribution in particular in contemporary discourse about God *in se*.

---

[153]In emphasizing the importance of the analogy of attribution, I do not intend to negate the value of the analogy of proportionality. I take it, though, that the analogy of attribution provides the context in which the analogy of proportionality should be understood.

Conclusion

T
HIS STUDY HAS ATTEMPTED TO SET forth a rationale for the
pursuit of *theologia* in the strict sense of the word: knowledge of God
in himself without primary reference to the economy. The argument has
worked from the material content of Scripture toward theological conclusions on the knowledge of God that are informed by the insights of various
writers throughout the history of the church. It has also attempted to clarify
certain matters related to the actual practice of reasoning and speaking about
God in himself (e.g., how Scripture and the incarnation relate to one another
as sources of theological understanding, how metaphysical terms may be
predicated of God). The first chapter offered a scriptural case for the pursuit
of knowledge of God in himself, discussing the object and "genus" of theological knowledge, the limitations and development of that knowledge, and
the considerations necessary to avoid the danger of despairing before what
Luther and others have called a *Deus absconditus*. The second chapter
explored the contribution of the natural knowledge of God. After working
through pertinent scriptural texts on the natural knowledge of God, I took
into account various insights from the Christian tradition and also addressed
some key objections in order to clarify the role of natural knowledge in
theology proper. Such knowledge provides traction for the reception of
supernatural revelation, but its insufficiency and suppression by sinners underscores the need for it to be corrected and augmented by the gospel. Chapter
three then treated the supernatural revelation that culminates in the incarnation of Jesus Christ. That chapter sought to qualify the epistemological role

of Christology in the light of Scripture and yet also honor what the person and work of Christ positively contribute to our knowledge of God *in se*. There I noted that, among other things, the biblical account of the incarnation actually corroborates God's transcendence of the economy and the need for Christian *theologia*.

Chapter four then addressed the question of metaphysics in relation to theology proper. There I untangled and distinguished metaphysics and discourse about God *in se* and argued that metaphysical concepts may be utilized in the doctrine of God without undermining the Creator-creature distinction. Moreover, this chapter considered how a strong understanding of God's aseity can alleviate other worries about so-called metaphysical accounts of God (i.e., that God could not condescend to us in the economy and that God's essence and economic action would be at odds with one another). Finally, chapter five addressed the problem of how our creaturely words can be used to express the truth about God, without either denying God's transcendence or our knowledge of him in that transcendence. This involved attending to Scripture's teaching on God's transcendence and communicative action, drawing insights from traditional discussion of analogy and univocity and providing further clarity in my commendation of analogy in response to the objections of authors like Karl Barth, Wolfhart Pannenberg, and William Alston.

Having made a case for the study of God in himself, I would like to close with four notes or hopes regarding future work in the doctrine of God. First, it seems right to acknowledge that this volume has been mostly a tilling of the ground for further study of God in his aseity and transcendence of the economy. Other recent authors have already been tilling and cultivating, and my hope is that this book may stimulate such work all the more. There is much to be done in providing the church and academy with faithful and spiritually robust teaching on God's prevenient fullness from which he generously acts toward us creatures.

Second, in the doctrine of God there is no need to set Christology (or, more broadly, supernatural revelation) and contemplation of God *in se* against each other. God's revelation in the incarnation does not restrict us to description of God's economic works, and the description of God *in se* is a matter of following God's revelation of himself rather than looking away from it in the pejorative sense of the term *metaphysics*. On a related note, there is no need for Protestants to feel beholden to the legacy of Barthian theology proper (however that may be interpreted). Barth can be an insightful and thought-provoking dialogue partner without being allowed to dictate the conditions under which theology proper must be done today. Protestants can and should be catholic and avail themselves of the work of Athanasius, Augustine, Boethius, John of Damascus, Peter Lombard, Thomas Aquinas, and many other pre-Reformation theologians.

Third, though the study of God in himself should be done with an alertness to the danger of idle curiosity, it should not be paralyzed by a fear of "speculation." As we have seen, God himself has chosen to grant us knowledge of things that do not pertain immediately to the economy or to human responsibilities within it. And such knowledge is indirectly and ultimately practical anyway, inciting wonder and worship, fostering humility, and, insofar as God's goodness and perfection may be participated in and imaged by us, engendering creaturely representations of God by those who have been transformed by his Spirit.

Finally, that *theologia* is not immediately practical and certainly not oriented to questions of technique and efficiency is in fact one of its salutary aspects. Contemporary preoccupation (even in the church and in academic programs preparatory for church ministry) with "mission statements," "measurable outcomes," and the like needs to be relativized by the joy of knowing the triune God. It needs to be relativized by a strong sense of the fact that the greatest thing a minister of the gospel or a professor of theology can do for others is to communicate faithfully about the rich wisdom and goodness and holiness and love of the triune God—and their free and gracious exercise in the economy.

Bibliography

Adams, Marilyn McCord. *William Ockham*. 2 vols. Notre Dame, IN: University of Notre Dame Press, 1987.

Aertsen, Jan A., et al., eds. *Nach der Verurteilung von 1277: Philosophie und Theologie an der Universität von Paris im letzten Viertel des 13. Jahrhunderts. Studie und Texte/After the Condemnation of 1277: Philosophy and Theology at the University of Paris in the Last Quarter of the Thirteenth Century. Studies and Texts.* Miscellanea Mediaevalia 28. Berlin: de Gruyter, 2001.

Agostini, Igor. "The Knowledge of God's *Quid Sit* in Dominican Theology: From Saint Thomas to Ferrariensis." *American Catholic Philosophical Quarterly* 93 (2019): 191-210.

Allen, Michael. *Grounded in Heaven: Recentering Christian Hope and Life on God.* Grand Rapids: Eerdmans, 2018.

Alsted, Johann. *Metaphysica.* Herbornae Nassoviorum, 1613.

———. *Theologia naturalis.* Frankfurt, 1615.

Alston, William. "Aquinas on Theological Predication: A Look Backward and Look Forward." In *Reasoned Faith: Essays in Philosophical Theology in Honor of Norman Kretzmann*, edited by Eleonore Stump, 145-78. Ithaca, NY: Cornell University Press, 1993.

———. *Divine Nature and Human Language: Essays in Philosophical Theology.* Ithaca, NY: Cornell University Press, 1989.

———. "Religious Language." In *The Oxford Handbook of Philosophy of Religion*, edited by William J. Wainwright, 220-43. Oxford: Oxford University Press, 2005.

Althaus, Paul. *The Theology of Martin Luther.* Translated by Robert C. Schultz. Philadelphia: Fortress, 1966.

Ames, William. *Bellarminus enervatus.* Vol. 4. Amsterdam, 1628.

———. *Medulla theologica*. 2nd ed. Amsterdam, 1634.

Aristotle. *Aristotelis Metaphysica*. Edited by Werner Jaeger. Oxford: Clarendon, 1957.

Ashworth, E. J. "Analogy and Equivocation in Thirteenth-Century Logic: Aquinas in Context." *Mediaeval Studies* 54 (1992): 94-135.

———. "Aquinas on Analogy." In *Debates in Medieval Philosophy: Essential Readings and Contemporary Responses*, edited by Jeffrey Hause, 232-42. New York: Routledge, 2014.

———. "Philosophy of Language: Words, Concepts, Things, and Non-things." In *The Routledge Companion to Sixteenth-Century Philosophy*, edited by Henrik Lagerlund and Benjamin J. Hill, 350-72. New York: Routledge, 2017.

———. "Suárez on the Analogy of Being: Some Historical Background." *Vivarium* 33 (1995): 50-75.

Athanasius. *Contra Gentes*. In *Contra Gentes and De incarnatione*. Edited and translated by Robert W. Thomson. Oxford: Clarendon, 1971.

———. *Athanasius Werke*. Vol. I/1.2, *Orationes I-II contra Arianos*. Edited by Karin Metzler and Kyriakos Savvidis. Berlin: de Gruyter, 1998.

———. *Athanasius Werke*. Vol. I/1.3, *Oratio III contra Arianos*. Edited by Karin Metzler and Kyriakos Savvidis. Berlin: de Gruyter, 2000.

Athanasopoulos, Constantinos, and Christoph Schneider, eds. *Divine Essence and Energies: Ecumenical Reflections on the Presence of God in Eastern Orthodoxy*. Cambridge: James Clarke, 2013.

Augustine. *Confessionum libri XIII*. Edited by Lucas Verheijen. CCSL 27. Turnhout: Brepols, 1981.

———. *De civitate Dei*. Edited by Bernard Dombart and Alphonse Kalb. 2 vols. CCSL 47-48. Turnhout: Brepols, 1955.

———. *De magistro*. Edited by K. D. Daur. CCSL 29. Turnhout: Brepols, 1970.

———. *De Trinitate, libri XV*. Edited by W. J. Mountain. 2 vols. CCSL 50-50A. Turnhout: Brepols, 1968.

———. *In Evangelium Ioannis, tractatus CXXIV*. CCSL 36. Turnhout: Brepols, 1954.

Aus der Au, Christina. "Das Extra Calvinisticum—mehr als ein reformiertes Extra?" *Theologische Zeitschrift* 64 (2008): 358-69.

Barr, James. *Biblical Faith and Natural Theology*. Oxford: Clarendon, 1993.

Barth, Karl. *Church Dogmatics*. Edited by Geoffrey W. Bromiley and Thomas F. Torrance. Translated by Geoffrey W. Bromiley et al. London: T&T Clark, 2009.

———. *Die Kirchliche Dogmatik*. Vol. IV.1. Zollikon-Zürich: Evangelischer Verlag, 1953.

———. "No!" In *Natural Theology: Comprising "Nature and Grace" by Professor Dr. Emil Brunner and the Reply "No!" by Dr. Karl Barth*. Translated by Peter Fraenkel. Reprint, Eugene, OR: Wipf and Stock, 2002.

———. *The Epistle to the Romans*. 6th ed. Translated by Edwyn C. Hoskyns. Oxford: Oxford University Press, 1968.

———. *The Way of Theology in Karl Barth: Essays and Comments*. Edited by H. Martin Rumscheidt. Reprint, Allison Park, PA: Pickwick, 1986.

Basil of Caesarea. *Contre Eunome*. Translated and edited by B. Sesboüé, G. M. de Durand, and L. Doutreleau. 2 vols. Sources Chrétiennes 299, 305. Paris: Éditions du Cerf, 1982–1983.

Bauckham, Richard. *Gospel of Glory: Major Themes in Johannine Theology*. Grand Rapids: Baker Academic, 2015.

———. *Jesus and the God of Israel: God Crucified and Other Studies in the New Testament's Christology of Divine Identity*. Grand Rapids: Eerdmans, 2008.

———. *The Testimony of the Beloved Disciple: Narrative, History, and Theology in the Gospel of John*. Grand Rapids: Baker Academic, 2007.

———. *The Theology of the Book of Revelation*. New Testament Theology. Cambridge: Cambridge University Press, 1993.

Bavinck, Herman. *Reformed Dogmatics*. 4 vols. Edited by John Bolt. Translated by John Vriend. Grand Rapids: Baker Academic, 2003–2008.

Beale, G. K. *A New Testament Biblical Theology: The Unfolding of the Old Testament in the New*. Grand Rapids: Baker Academic, 2011.

Betz, John R. "After Heidegger and Marion: The Task of Christian Metaphysics Today." *MT* 34 (2018): 565-97.

Blackwell, Ben C., John K. Goodrich, and Jason Maston, eds. *Paul and the Apocalyptic Imagination*. Minneapolis: Fortress, 2016.

Boethius. *Opera Omnia*. Vol. 2, *In Categorias Aristotelis*. PL 64. Paris, 1847.

———. *The Theological Tractates. The Consolation of Philosophy*. Translated by H. F. Steward, E. K. Rand, and S. J. Tester. LCL 74. Cambridge, MA: Harvard University Press, 1973.

Boyer, Steven D., and Christopher A. Hall. *The Mystery of God: Theology for Knowing the Unknowable*. Grand Rapids: Baker Academic, 2012.

Brakel, Wilhelmus à. *The Christian's Reasonable Service*. Edited by Joel Beeke. Translated by Bartel Elshout. 4 vols. Grand Rapids: Reformation Heritage, 1992.

Brock, Cory, and Nathaniel Gray Sutanto. "Herman Bavinck's Reformed Eclecticism: On Catholicity, Consciousness and Theological Epistemology." *SJT* 70 (2017): 310-32.

Burrell, David B. *Analogy and Philosophical Language*. New Haven, CT: Yale University Press, 1973.

———. "Distinguishing God from the World." In *Language, Meaning and God: Essays in Honor of Herbert McCabe OP*, edited by Brian Davies, 75-91. Reprint, Eugene, OR: Wipf and Stock, 2010.

Butner, D. Glenn, Jr. "Communion with God: An Energetic Defense of Gregory Palamas." *MT* 32 (2016): 20-44.

———. *The Son Who Learned Obedience: A Theological Case Against the Eternal Submission of the Son*. Eugene, OR: Wipf and Stock, 2018.

Cajetan, Tomasso de Vio. *De nominum analogia. De conceptu entis*. Edited by P. N. Zammit. Rome, 1952.

Calvin, John. *Institutes of the Christian Religion*. Edited by John T. McNeill. Translated by Ford Lewis Battles. 2 vols. LCC 20-21. Philadelphia: Westminster, 1960.

———. *Ioannis Calvini opera quae supersunt omnia*. Vol. 2, *Institutio Christianae religionis* (1559). Edited by Guilielmus Baum et al. Brunswick: Schwetschke, 1864.

Caputo, John D. *Heidegger and Aquinas: An Essay on Overcoming Metaphysics*. New York: Fordham University Press, 1982.

Charnock, Stephen. *The Works of Stephen Charnock*. Vol. 4, *A Discourse of the Knowledge of God*. Edinburgh: Banner of Truth, 1985.

———. *The Existence and Attributes of God*. 2 vols. in 1. Grand Rapids: Baker, 1996.

Chrysostom, John. *Homiliae CXXXVIII in Johannem*. PG 59. Paris, 1862.

Clark, David K. *To Know and Love God: Method for Theology*. Wheaton, IL: Crossway, 2003.

Clarke, W. Norris. "Analogy and the Meaningfulness of Language About God: A Reply to Kai Nielsen." *The Thomist* (1976): 61-95.

Coccejus, Johannes. *Summa doctrinae de foedere et testamento Dei*. 5th ed. Amsterdam, 1683.

Cremer, Hermann. *Die christliche Lehre von den Eigenschaften Gottes*. 2nd ed. Gütersloh: Bertelsmann, 1917.

Cross, Richard. *Duns Scotus*. Great Medieval Thinkers. Oxford: Oxford University Press, 1999.

———. *Duns Scotus on God*. Aldershot: Ashgate, 2005.

———. "Idolatry and Religious Language." *Faith and Philosophy* 25 (2008): 190-96.

Darge, Rolf. "Suárez on the Subject of Metaphysics." In *A Companion to Francisco Suárez*, edited by Victor M. Salas and Robert L. Fastiggi, 91-123. Leiden: Brill, 2014.

Darley, Alan Philip. "Predication or Participation? What Is the Nature of Aquinas' Doctrine of Analogy?" *Heythrop Journal* 57 (2016): 312-24.

Dauphinais, Michael, and Matthew Levering, eds. *Reading John with St. Thomas Aquinas: Theological Exegesis and Speculative Theology.* Washington, DC: Catholic University of America Press, 2010.

De Haan, Daniel. "The Doctrine of the Analogy of Being in Avicenna's *Metaphysics of the Healing.*" *Review of Metaphysics* 69 (2015): 261-86.

D'Ettore, Dominic. *Analogy After Aquinas: Logical Problems, Thomistic Answers.* Thomistic Ressourcement 11. Washington, DC: Catholic University of America Press, 2019.

———. "The Fifteenth-Century Thomist Dispute Over Participation in an Analogous Concept: John Capreolus, Dominic of Flanders, and Paul Soncinas." *Mediaeval Studies* 76 (2014): 248-57.

———. "*Una ratio* versus *Diversae rationes*: Three Interpretations of *Summa theologiae* I, Q. 13, AA. 1-6." *Nova et Vetera* 17 (2019): 39-55.

Dewan, Lawrence. "St. Thomas and Analogy: The Logician and the Metaphysician." In *Form and Being: Studies in Thomistic Metaphysics*, 81-95. Studies in Philosophy and the History of Philosophy 45. Washington, DC: Catholic University of America Press, 2006.

———. "St. Thomas and the Principle of Causality." In *Form and Being: Studies in Thomistic Metaphysics*, 61-80. Studies in Philosophy and the History of Philosophy 45. Washington, DC: Catholic University of America Press, 2006.

———. "The Existence of God: Can It Be Demonstrated?" *Nova et Vetera* 10 (2012): 731-56.

Diller, Kevin. *Theology's Epistemological Dilemma: How Karl Barth and Alvin Plantinga Provide a Unified Response.* Strategic Initiatives in Evangelical Theology. Downers Grove, IL: IVP Academic, 2014.

Dorner, Isaak A. *Divine Immutability: A Critical Reconsideration.* Translated by Robert R. Williams and Claude Welch. Minneapolis: Fortress, 1994.

———. *System of Christian Doctrine.* Translated by Alfred Cave and J. S. Banks. 4 vols. Edinburgh: T&T Clark, 1880.

Driel, Edwin Chr. van. *Incarnation Anyway: Arguments for a Supralapsarian Christology.* Oxford: Oxford University Press, 2008.

———. "'Too Lowly to Reach God Without a Mediator': John Calvin's Supralapsarian Eschatological Narrative." *MT* 33 (2017): 275-92.

Duby, Steven J. "Atonement, Impassibility and the *Communicatio Operationum.*" *IJST* 17 (2015): 284-95.

———. "Divine Action and the Meaning of Eternity." *JRT* 11 (2017): 362-75.

———. "Divine Immutability, Divine Action and the God-World Relation." *IJST* 19 (2017): 144-62.

———. *Divine Simplicity: A Dogmatic Account.* London: Bloomsbury, 2016.

———. "Election, Actuality and Divine Freedom: Thomas Aquinas, Bruce McCormack and Reformed Orthodoxy in Dialogue." *MT* 32 (2016): 325-40.

———. "'For I Am God, Not a Man': Divine Repentance and the Creator-Creature Distinction." *JTI* 12 (2018): 149-69.

———. "Trinity and Economy in Thomas Aquinas." *Southern Baptist Journal of Theology* 21 (2017): 29-51.

Dumont, Stephen. "Henry of Ghent and Duns Scotus." In *The Routledge History of Philosophy.* Vol. 3, *Medieval Philosophy*, edited by John Marenbon, 205-27. New York: Routledge, 1998.

———. "Scotus's Doctrine of Univocity and the Medieval Tradition of Metaphysics." In *Was ist Philosophie im Mittelalter?*, edited by Jan A. Aertsen and Andreas Speer, 193-212. Berlin: de Gruyter, 1998.

———. "The Univocity of the Concept of Being in the Fourteenth Century: John Duns Scotus and William of Alnwick." *Mediaeval Studies* 49 (1987): 1-31.

———. "Transcendental Being: Scotus and Scotists." *Topoi* 11 (1992): 135-48.

Dunn, James D. G. *The Theology of Paul the Apostle.* Grand Rapids: Eerdmans, 1998.

Duns Scotus, John. *A Treatise on God as First Principle: A Latin Text and English Translation of "De Primo Principio."* Edited and translated by Allan B. Wolter. Chicago: Franciscan Herald Press, 1966.

———. *Opera omnia.* Vol. 16, *Lectura in librum primum Sententiarum.* Edited by P. Carolo Balić. Vatican: Typis Polyglottis Vaticanis, 1960.

———. *Opera omnia.* Vols. 1-4, *Ordinatio.* Edited by P. Carolo Balić. Vatican: Typis Polyglottis Vaticanis, 1950–1956.

———. *Opera philosophica.* Vols. 3-4, *Quaestiones super libros Metaphysicorum Aristotelis.* Edited by R. Andrews et al. St. Bonaventure: St. Bonaventure University, 1997.

———. *The Examined Report of the Paris Lecture: Reportatio I-A.* Translated by Allan B. Wolter and Oleg V. Bychkov. St. Bonaventure: St. Bonaventure University, 2004.

Edwards, Mark. *Aristotle and Early Christian Thought.* London: Routledge, 2019.

Emery, Gilles. "Essentialism or Personalism in the Treatise on God in Saint Thomas Aquinas?" *The Thomist* 64 (2000): 521-63.

———. "The Personal Mode of Trinitarian Action in Saint Thomas Aquinas." *The Thomist* 69 (2005): 31-77.

———. *The Trinitarian Theology of St Thomas Aquinas.* Translated by Francesca Aran Murphy. Oxford: Oxford University Press, 2007.

———. "*Theologia* and *Dispensatio*: The Centrality of the Divine Missions in St. Thomas's Trinitarian Theology." *The Thomist* 74 (2010): 515-61.

———. *Trinity, Church, and the Human Person: Thomistic Essays.* Faith and Reason: Studies in Catholic Theology and Philosophy. Ave Maria, FL: Sapientia, 2007.

Feingold, Lawrence. *The Natural Desire to See God According to St. Thomas Aquinas and His Interpreters.* Faith and Reason: Studies in Catholic Theology and Philosophy. 2nd ed. Ave Maria, FL: Sapientia, 2004.

Feldmeier, Reinhard, and Hermann Spieckermann. *God of the Living: A Biblical Theology.* Translated by Mark E. Biddle. Waco, TX: Baylor University Press, 2011.

Feser, Edward. *Five Proofs of the Existence of God.* San Francisco: Ignatius, 2017.

Freddoso, Alfred J. "Ockham on Faith and Reason." In *The Cambridge Companion to Ockham*, edited by Paul Vincent Spade, 326-49. Cambridge: Cambridge University Press, 1999.

Fretheim, Terence C. *What Kind of God? The Collected Essays of Terence E. Fretheim.* Edited by Michael J. Chan and Brent A. Strawn. Winona Lake, IN: Eisenbrauns, 2015.

Franks, Christopher A. "The Simplicity of the Living God: Aquinas, Barth, and Some Philosophers." *MT* 21 (2005): 275-300.

Gaine, Simon Francis. *Did the Savior See the Father? Christ, Salvation and the Vision of God.* London: Bloomsbury, 2015.

Gavrilyuk, Paul L. *The Suffering of the Impassible God: The Dialectics of Patristic Thought.* Oxford Early Christian Studies. Oxford: Oxford University Press, 2004.

Gerrish, B. A. "'To the Unknown God': Luther and Calvin on the Hiddenness of God." *Journal of Religion* 53 (1973): 263-92.

Gibson, David. *Reading the Decree: Exegesis, Christology and Election in Calvin and Barth.* London: Bloomsbury, 2009.

Gillespie, Michael Allen. *The Theological Origins of Modernity.* Chicago: University of Chicago Press, 2008.

Gilson, Etienne. *Being and Some Philosophers.* 2nd ed. Toronto: Pontifical Institute of Mediaeval Studies, 1952.

Gioia, Luigi. *The Theological Epistemology of Augustine's "De Trinitate."* Oxford: Oxford University Press, 2008.

Goodwin, Thomas. *The Works of Thomas Goodwin*. Vol. 1, *An Exposition of the First Chapter of the Epistle to the Ephesians*. Reprint, Grand Rapids: Reformation Heritage, 2006.

Gordley, Matthew E. *New Testament Christological Hymns: Exploring Texts, Contexts and Significance*. Downers Grove, IL: IVP Academic, 2018.

Gordon, James R. *The Holy One in Our Midst: An Essay on the Flesh of Christ*. Minneapolis: Fortress, 2016.

Gordon, Liran Shia, and Avital Wohlman. "A Constructive Thomistic Response to Heidegger's Destructive Criticism: On Existence, Essence and the Possibility of Truth as Adequation." *Heythrop Journal* 60 (2019): forthcoming.

Green, Adam, and Eleonore Stump, eds. *Hidden Divinity and Religious Belief*. Cambridge: Cambridge University Press, 2016.

Gregory of Nyssa. *Ad Ablabium, Quod non sint tres dei*. In *Gregorii Nysseni opera*, vol. 3/1, *Opera dogmatica minora*, edited by Fridericus Mueller, 35-57. Leiden: Brill, 1958.

Grier, Michelle. *Kant's Doctrine of Transcendental Illusion*. Cambridge: Cambridge University Press, 2001.

Gunton, Colin E. *Act and Being: Towards a Theology of the Divine Attributes*. Grand Rapids: Eerdmans, 2002.

———. "The End of Causality? The Reformers and Their Predecessors." In *The Doctrine of Creation: Essays in Dogmatics, History and Philosophy*, edited by Colin E. Gunton, 63-82. London: T&T Clark, 1997.

Habets, Myk. "Putting the 'Extra' Back into Calvinism." *SJT* 62 (2009): 441-56.

Hafemann, Scott J. "'Divine Nature' in 2 Pet 1,4 Within Its Eschatological Context." *Biblica* 94 (2013): 80-99.

Hall, Alexander W. "Natural Theology in the Middle Ages." In *The Oxford Handbook of Natural Theology*, edited by Russell Re Manning, 57-72. Oxford: Oxford University Press, 2013.

———. *Thomas Aquinas and John Duns Scotus: Natural Theology in the High Middle Ages*. London: Continuum, 2000.

Hart, David Bentley. "No Shadow of Turning: On Divine Impassibility." *Pro Ecclesia* 16 (2002): 184-206.

———. *The Beauty of the Infinite: The Aesthetics of Christian Truth*. Grand Rapids: Eerdmans, 2003.

Hauerwas, Stanley. *With the Grain of the Universe: The Church's Witness and Natural Theology*. Grand Rapids: Baker Academic, 2001.

Healy, Nicholas M. "Karl Barth, German-Language Theology, and the Catholic Tradition." In *Trinity and Election in Contemporary Theology*, edited by Michael T. Dempsey, 229-43. Grand Rapids: Eerdmans, 2011.

———. "Natural Theology and the Christian Contribution to Metaphysics: On Thomas Joseph White's *Wisdom in the Face of Modernity.*" *Nova et Vetera* 10 (2012): 539-62.

Hector, Kevin W. *Theology Without Metaphysics: God, Language and the Spirit of Recognition*. Cambridge: Cambridge University Press, 2011.

Heidegger, Martin. *Basic Writings*. Edited by David Farrell Krell. New York: HarperCollins, 1977.

———. *Being and Time*. Translated by John Macquarrie and Edward Robinson. Oxford: Blackwell, 1962.

———. *The End of Philosophy*. Translated by Joan Stambaugh. Chicago: University of Chicago Press, 2003.

———. *Identity and Difference*. Translated by Joan Stambaugh. New York: Harper & Row, 1969.

———. *Introduction to Metaphysics*. Edited and translated by Gregory Fried and Richard Polt. 2nd ed. New Haven, CT: Yale University Press, 2000.

———. *Nietzsche*. Vol. 3, *The Will to Power as Knowledge and as Metaphysics*; vol. 4, *Nihilism*. 2 vols. in 1. Edited by David Farrell Krell. Translated by Frank A. Capuzzi and David Farrell Krell. San Francisco: HarperSanFrancisco, 1991.

———. *Pathmarks*. Edited by William McNeill. Cambridge: Cambridge University Press, 1998.

———. *The Principle of Reason*. Translated by Reginald Lilly. Bloomington: Indiana University Press, 1991.

———. *The Question Concerning Technology and Other Essays*. Translated by William Lovitt. New York: Harper & Row, 1977.

Heider, Daniel. "Is Suárez's Concept of Being Analogical or Univocal?" *American Catholic Philosophical Quarterly* 81 (2007): 21-41.

Hemming, Laurence Paul. "*Analogia non Entis sed Entitatis*: The Ontological Consequences of the Doctrine of Analogy." *IJST* 6 (2004): 118-29.

Hilary of Poitiers. *La Trinité*. Edited by I. J. Doignon, G. M. de Durand, M. Figura, C. Morel, G. Pelland. 3 vols. Sources Chrétiennes 443, 448, 462. Paris: Éditions du Cerf, 1999–2001.

Hill, Daniel J. *Divinity and Maximal Greatness*. New York: Routledge, 2005.

Hill, Wesley. *Paul and the Trinity: Persons, Relations, and the Pauline Letters*. Grand Rapids: Eerdmans, 2015.

Hinlicky, Paul R. *Divine Simplicity: Christ the Crisis of Metaphysics.* Grand Rapids: Baker Academic, 2016.

Hochschild, Joshua P. *The Semantics of Analogy: Rereading Cajetan's De Nominum Analogia.* Notre Dame, IN: University of Notre Dame Press, 2010.

Holmes, Christopher R. J. "The Aseity of God as a Material Evangelical Concern." *JRT* 8 (2014): 61-78.

———. *The Lord Is Good: Seeking the God of the Psalter.* Studies in Christian Doctrine and Scripture. Downers Grove, IL: IVP Academic, 2018.

Holmes, Stephen R. "The Attributes of God." In *The Oxford Handbook of Systematic Theology*, edited by John Webster, Kathryn Tanner, and Iain Torrance, 54-71. Oxford: Oxford University Press, 2007.

Horan, Daniel P. *Postmodernity and Univocity: A Critical Account of Radical Orthodoxy and John Duns Scotus.* Minneapolis: Fortress, 2014.

Horton, Michael S. *The Christian Faith: A Systematic Theology for Pilgrims on the Way.* Grand Rapids: Zondervan, 2011.

Hume, David. *A Treatise of Human Nature: A Critical Edition.* Vol. 1, *Texts.* Edited by David Fate Norton and Mary J. Norton. Oxford: Oxford University Press, 2007.

———. *Dialogues Concerning Natural Religion.* Edited by Dorothy Coleman. Cambridge: Cambridge University Press, 2007.

Hunsinger, George. "Election and the Trinity: Twenty-Five Theses on the Theology of Karl Barth." *MT* 24 (2008): 179-97.

———. *Evangelical, Catholic, and Reformed: Doctrinal Essays on Barth and Related Themes.* Grand Rapids: Eerdmans, 2015.

———. *How to Read Karl Barth: The Shape of His Theology.* Oxford: Clarendon, 1993.

———. *Reading Barth with Charity: A Hermeneutical Proposal.* Grand Rapids: Baker Academic, 2015.

Hütter, Reinhard. "Attending to the Wisdom of God—from Effect to Cause, from Creation to God: A *Relecture* of the Analogy of Being According to Thomas Aquinas." In *The Analogy of Being: Invention of the Antichrist or the Wisdom of God?*, edited by Thomas Joseph White, 209-45. Grand Rapids: Eerdmans, 2011.

Jenkins, John. *Knowledge and Faith in Thomas Aquinas.* Cambridge: Cambridge University Press, 1997.

Jenson, Robert W. "Once More the Logos Asarkos." *IJST* 13 (2011): 130-33.

———. *Systematic Theology.* 2 vols. Oxford: Oxford University Press, 1997.

John of Damascus. *Die Schriften des Johannes von Damaskos.* Vol. 1, *Dialectica.* Edited by Bonifatius Kotter. Berlin: de Gruyter, 1969.

―――. *Die Schriften des Johannes von Damaskos.* Vol. 2, *Expositio fidei.* Edited by Bonifatius Kotter. Berlin: de Gruyter, 1973.

Johnson, Keith L. *Karl Barth and the* Analogia Entis. London: Bloomsbury, 2011.

―――. "Natural Revelation in Creation and Covenant." In *Thomas Aquinas and Karl Barth: An Unofficial Catholic-Protestant Dialogue,* edited by Bruce L. McCormack and Thomas Joseph White, 129-56. Grand Rapids: Eerdmans, 2013.

Jones, Paul Dafydd. *The Humanity of Christ: Christology in Karl Barth's "Church Dogmatics."* London: T&T Clark, 2008.

Jüngel, Eberhard. *God as the Mystery of the World.* Translated by Darrell Guder. Grand Rapids: Eerdmans, 1983.

Junius, Franciscus. *De vera theologia.* Leiden, 1594.

Kant, Immanuel. *Critique of Pure Reason.* Edited and translated by Paul Guyer and Allen W. Wood. Cambridge: Cambridge University Press, 1998.

―――. *Prolegomena to Any Future Metaphysics.* Edited and translated by Gary Hatfield. Rev. ed. Cambridge Texts in the History of Philosophy. Cambridge: Cambridge University Press, 2004.

Karger, Elizabeth. "Ockham's Misunderstood Theory of Intuitive and Abstractive Cognition." In *The Cambridge Companion to Ockham,* edited by Paul Vincent Spade, 204-26. Cambridge: Cambridge University Press, 1999.

Kärkäinnen, Veli-Matti. *A Constructive Christian Theology for the Pluralistic World.* Vol. 2, *Trinity and Revelation.* Grand Rapids: Eerdmans, 2014.

Keating, James F., and Thomas Joseph White, eds. *Divine Impassibility and the Mystery of Human Suffering.* Grand Rapids: Eerdmans, 2009.

Keckermann, Bartholomäus. *Brevis et simplex consideratio controversiae hoc tempore a nonnullis motae, de pugna philosophiae et theologiae.* In *Praecognitorum philosophicorum, libri duo,* 2 (181-200). Hanau, 1612.

―――. *Scientiae metaphysicae brevissima synopsis et compendium.* In *Operum omnium quae extant,* 1:2013-40. Geneva, 1614.

―――. *Systema logicae.* In *Operum omnium quae extant,* 1:541-832. Geneva, 1614.

―――. *Systema s.s. theologiae.* In *Operum omnium quae extant,* 2:65-232 Geneva, 1614.

King, Peter. "Scotus on Metaphysics." In *The Cambridge Companion to Duns Scotus,* edited by Thomas Williams, 15-68. Cambridge: Cambridge University Press, 2002.

Klubertanz, George P. *St. Thomas Aquinas on Analogy: A Textual Analysis and Systematic Synthesis*. Chicago: Loyola University Press, 1960.

Kooi, Cornelis van der. "The Identity of Israel's God: The Potential of the So-Called Extra Calvinisticum." In *Tradition and Innovation in Biblical Interpretation*, edited by W. Th. van Peursen and J. W. Dyk, 209-22. Leiden: Brill, 2011.

Krötke, Wolf. *Gottes Klarheiten: Eine Neuinterpretation der Lehre von Gottes Eigenschaften*. Tübingen: Mohr Siebeck, 2001.

Leff, Gordon. *William of Ockham: The Metamorphosis of Scholastic Discourse*. Manchester: Manchester University Press, 1975.

Levering, Matthew. "Christ, the Trinity, and Predestination: McCormack and Aquinas." In *Trinity and Election in Contemporary Theology*, edited by Michael T. Dempsey, 244-73. Grand Rapids: Eerdmans, 2011.

———. "God and Greek Philosophy in Contemporary Biblical Scholarship." *JTI* 4 (2010): 169-85.

———. *Scripture and Metaphysics: Aquinas and the Renewal of Trinitarian Theology*. Challenges in Contemporary Theology. Oxford: Blackwell, 2004.

Lindholm, Stefan. "Would Christ Have Become Incarnate Had Adam Not Fallen? Jerome Zanchi (1516–1590) on Christ as Mediator." *JRT* 9 (2015): 19-36.

Lisska, Anthony. *Aquinas's Theory of Perception: An Analytic Reconstruction*. Oxford: Oxford University Press, 2016.

Loewenich, Walther von. *Luther's Theology of the Cross*. Translated by Herbert J. A. Bouman. Minneapolis: Augsburg, 1976.

Lombard, Peter. *Sententiae in IV libris distinctae*. 2 vols. 3rd ed. Spicilegium Bonaventurianum 4B-5. Rome: Collegii S. Bonaventurae ad Claras Aquas, 1971–1981.

Long, Steven A. *Natura Pura: On the Recovery of Nature in the Doctrine of Grace*. New York: Fordham University Press, 2010.

Longeway, John Lee. Introduction to William of Ockham, *Demonstration and Scientific Knowledge in William of Ockham: A Translation of "Summa Logicae III-II: De Syllogismo Demonstrativo," and Selections from the Prologue to the "Ordinatio,"* 1-140. Notre Dame, IN: University of Notre Dame Press, 2007.

Lubac, Henri de. *The Mystery of the Supernatural*. Translated by Rosemary Sheed. Milestones in Catholic Theology. New York: Herder and Herder, 1998.

Luther, Martin. *De servo arbitrio*. In *D. Martin Luthers Werke: Kritische Gesamtausgabe*, 18:551-787. Weimar: Böhlaus, 1908.

———. *Disputatio Heidelbergae habita*. In *D. Martin Luthers Werke: Kritische Gesamtausgabe*, 1:350-74. Weimar: Böhlau, 1883.

———. *D. Martin Luthers Werke: Kritische Gesamtausgabe*. Vol. 42, *Genesisvorlesung (cap. 1-17)*. Weimar: Böhlau, 1911.

———. *D. Martin Luthers Werke: Kritische Gesamtausgabe*. Vol. 40/1, *In Epistolam S. Pauli ad Galatas Commentarius*. Weimar: Böhlau, 1911.

Lyttkens, Hampus. *The Analogy Between God and the World: An Investigation of Its Background and Interpretation of Its Use by Thomas of Aquino*. Uppsala: Lundequistska, 1953.

Macaskill, Grant. "History, Providence and the Apocalyptic Paul." *SJT* 70 (2017): 409-26.

———. "Name Christology, Divine Aseity, and the I Am Sayings in the Fourth Gospel." *JTI* 12 (2018): 217-41.

Maccovius, Johannes. *Loci communes theologici*. Edited by Nicolaus Arnoldus. 2nd ed. Amsterdam, 1658.

———. *Metaphysica*. Edited by Adrianus Heereboord. 3rd ed. Leiden, 1658.

MacDonald, Neil B. *Metaphysics and the God of Israel: Systematic Theology of the Old and New Testaments*. Grand Rapids: Baker Academic, 2006.

Markus, R. A. "Augustine: Reason and Illumination." In *The Cambridge History of Later Greek and Early Medieval Philosophy*, edited by A. H. Armstrong, 362-73. Cambridge: Cambridge University Press, 1967.

Markschies, Christoph. "Does It Make Sense to Speak about a 'Hellenization of Christianity in Antiquity'?" *Church History and Religious Culture* 92 (2012): 5-34.

Marrone, Stephen P. *The Light of Thy Countenance: Science and the Knowledge of God in the Thirteenth Century*. 2 vols. Leiden: Brill, 2001.

Marshall, Bruce D. "Aquinas as Postliberal Theologian." *The Thomist* 53 (1989): 353-402.

———. "Christ the End of Analogy." In *The Analogy of Being: Invention of the Antichrist or the Wisdom of God?*, edited by Thomas Joseph White, 280-313. Grand Rapids: Eerdmans, 2011.

———. "*Quod Scit Una Uetula*: Aquinas on the Nature of Theology." In *The Theology of Thomas Aquinas*, edited by Rik Van Nieuwenhove and Joseph Wawrykow, 1-35. Notre Dame, IN: University of Notre Dame Press, 2005.

———. "The Trinity." In *The Blackwell Companion to Modern Theology*, edited by Gareth Jones, 183-203. Oxford: Blackwell, 2004.

———. "The Unity of the Triune God: Reviving an Ancient Question." *The Thomist* 72 (2010): 1-32.

Mastricht, Petrus van. *Idea theologiae moralis.* Utrecht, 1724.

———. *Novitatum Cartesianarum gangraena.* Amsterdam, 1677.

———. *Theoretico-practica theologia.* 2nd ed. Utrecht, 1724.

Mathews, Gareth B. "Knowledge and Illumination." In *The Cambridge Companion to Augustine*, edited by Eleonore Stump and Norman Kretzmann, 171-85. 1st ed. Cambridge: Cambridge University Press, 2001.

Maurer, Armand. *The Philosophy of William of Ockham: In the Light of Its Principles.* Toronto: Pontifical Institute of Mediaeval Studies, 1999.

McCormack, Bruce L. "The Actuality of God: Karl Barth in Conversation with Open Theism." In *Engaging the Doctrine of God: Contemporary Protestant Perspectives*, edited by In Bruce L. McCormack, 185-242. Grand Rapids: Baker Academic, 2008.

———. "Atonement and Human Suffering." In *Locating Atonement: Explorations in Constructive Dogmatics*, edited by Oliver D. Crisp and Fred Sanders, 189-208. Grand Rapids: Zondervan, 2015.

———. "Divine Impassibility or Simply Divine Constancy? Implications of Karl Barth's Later Christology for Debates over Impassibility." In *Divine Impassibility and the Mystery of Human Suffering*, edited by James F. Keating and Thomas Joseph White, 150-86. Grand Rapids: Eerdmans, 2009.

———. "Election and the Trinity: Theses in Response to George Hunsinger." *SJT* 63 (2010): 203-24.

———. "Grace and Being." In *The Cambridge Companion to Karl Barth*, edited by John Webster, 93-101. Cambridge: Cambridge University Press, 2000.

———. "Karl Barth's Christology as a Resource for a Reformed Version of Kenoticism." *IJST* 8 (2006): 243-51.

———. *Karl Barth's Critically Realist Dialectical Theology: Its Genesis and Development 1909–1936.* Oxford: Clarendon, 1995.

———. "Karl Barth's Version of an 'Analogy of Being.'" In *The Analogy of Being: Invention of the Antichrist or the Wisdom of God?*, edited by Thomas Joseph White, 88-144. Grand Rapids: Eerdmans, 2011.

———. "The Lord and Giver of Life: A 'Barthian' Defense of the Filioque." In *Rethinking Trinitarian Theology: Disputed Questions and Contemporary Issues in Trinitarian Theology*, edited by Robert J. Wozniak and Giulio Maspero, 230-53. London: T&T Clark, 2012.

———. "The Only Mediator: The Person and Work of Christ in Evangelical Perspective." In *Renewing the Evangelical Mission*, edited by Richard Lints, 250-69. Grand Rapids: Eerdmans, 2013.

———. *Orthodox and Modern: Studies in the Theology of Karl Barth.* Grand Rapids: Baker Academic, 2008.

———. "Processions and Missions: A Point of Convergence Between Thomas Aquinas and Karl Barth." In *Thomas Aquinas and Karl Barth: An Unofficial Catholic-Protestant Dialogue*, edited by Bruce L. McCormack and Thomas Joseph White, 230-53. Grand Rapids: Eerdmans, 2013.

———. "Seek God Where He May Be Found: A Response to Edwin Chr. van Driel." *SJT* 60 (2007): 62-79.

———. "Why Should Theology Be Christocentric? Christology and Metaphysics in Paul Tillich and Karl Barth." *Wesley Theological Journal* 45 (2010): 42-80.

———. "'With Loud Cries and Tears': The Humanity of the Son in the Epistle to the Hebrews." In *The Epistle to the Hebrews and Christian Theology*, edited by Richard Bauckham, Daniel R. Driver, Trevor A. Hart, and Nathan Mac-Donald, 37-68. Grand Rapids: Eerdmans, 2009.

McCormack, Bruce L., and Thomas Joseph White, eds. *Thomas Aquinas and Karl Barth: An Unofficial Catholic-Protestant Dialogue.* Grand Rapids: Eerdmans, 2013.

McFarland, Ian A. "Spirit and Incarnation: Toward a Pneumatic Chalcedonianism." *IJST* 16 (2014): 143-58.

McGinnis, Andrew M. *The Son of God Beyond the Flesh: A Historical and Theological Study of the* Extra Calvinisticum. London: Bloomsbury, 2014.

McGrath, Alister E. *Re-imagining Nature: The Promise of a Christian Natural Theology.* Oxford: Wiley-Blackwell, 2017.

———. *The Open Secret: A New Vision for Natural Theology.* Oxford: Blackwell, 2008.

McInerny, Ralph. "Analogy and Foundationalism in Thomas Aquinas." In *Rationality, Religious Belief, and Moral Commitment*, edited by Robert Audi and William J. Wainwright, 271-88. Ithaca, NY: Cornell University Press, 1986.

———. *Aquinas and Analogy.* Washington, DC: Catholic University of America Press, 1996.

———. *Praeambula Fidei: Thomism and the God of the Philosophers.* Washington, DC: Catholic University of America Press, 2006.

Middleton, J. Richard. *The Liberating Image: The* Imago Dei *in Genesis 1.* Grand Rapids: Brazos, 2005.

Milbank, John. "Intensities." *MT* 15 (1999): 445-97.

———. *Theology and Social Theory: Beyond Secular Reason.* 2nd ed. Oxford: Blackwell, 2006.

————. *The Word Made Strange: Theology, Language, Culture*. Oxford: Blackwell, 1997.

Molnar, Paul D. "Can Jesus' Divinity Be Recognized as 'Definitive, Authentic and Essential' if It Is Grounded in Election? Just How Far Did the Later Barth Historicize Christology?" *Neue Zeitschrift für systematische Theologie und Religionsphilosophie* 52 (2010): 40-81.

————. "Can the Electing God Be God Without Us? Some Implications of Bruce McCormack's Understanding of Barth's Doctrine of Election for the Doctrine of the Trinity." *Neue Zeitschrift für Theologie und Religionsphilosophie* 49 (2007): 199-222.

————. "The Obedience of the Son in the Theology of Karl Barth and Thomas F. Torrance." *SJT* 67 (2014): 50-69.

Moltmann, Jürgen. *God in Creation: A New Theology of Creation and the Spirit of God*. Translated by Margaret Kohl. Minneapolis: Fortress Pres, 1993.

————. *The Crucified God: The Cross as the Foundation and Criticism of Theology*. Translated by R. A. Wilson and John Bowden. Minneapolis: Fortress, 1993.

Mondin, Battista. *The Principle of Analogy in Protestant and Catholic Theology*. The Hague: Martinus Nijhoff, 1963.

Montagnes, Bernard. *The Doctrine of the Analogy of Being According to Thomas Aquinas*. Translated by E. M. Macierowski. Milwaukee: Marquette University Press, 2004.

Moreland, Anna Bonta. *Known by Nature: Thomas Aquinas on Natural Knowledge of God*. New York: Crossroad, 2010.

Muller, Richard A. *Christ and the Decree: Christology and Predestination in Reformed Theology from Calvin to Perkins*. Grand Rapids: Baker Academic, 2008.

————. *Dictionary of Latin and Greek Theological Terms: Drawn Principally from Protestant Scholastic Theology*. Grand Rapids: Baker, 1985.

————. "The Dogmatic Function of St. Thomas' Proofs: A Protestant Appreciation." *Fides et Historia* 24 (1992): 15-29.

————. "Not Scotist: Understandings of Being, Univocity, and Analogy in Early-Modern Reformed Thought." *Reformation & Renaissance Review* 14 (2012): 127-50.

————. *Post-Reformation Reformed Dogmatics: The Rise and Development of Reformed Orthodoxy ca. 1520 to 1725*. Vol. 3, *Divine Essence and Attributes*. Grand Rapids: Baker Academic, 2003.

———. *Post-Reformation Reformed Dogmatics: The Rise and Development of Reformed Orthodoxy ca. 1520 to 1725.* Vol. 4, *The Triunity of God.* Grand Rapids: Baker Academic, 2003.

Nagasawa, Yujin. *Maximal God: A New Defence of Perfect Being Theism.* Oxford: Oxford University Press, 2017.

Nash, Ronald H. *The Light of the Mind: St. Augustine's Theory of Knowledge.* Lexington: University of Kentucky Press, 1969.

Nielsen, Kai. "Analogical Talk About God: A Negative Critique." *The Thomist* 40 (1976): 32- 60.

Nonnenmacher, Burkhard. "Natürliche Theologie und Offenbarung." *Neue Zeitschrift für Systematische Theologie und Religionsphilosophie* 59 (2017): 311-30.

Oakes, Kenneth. *Karl Barth on Theology and Philosophy.* Oxford: Oxford University Press, 2012.

———. "Theology, Economy and Christology in John Webster's *God Without Measure* and Some Earlier Works." *IJST* 19 (2017): 491-504.

Ockham, William. *Opera theologica.* Vols. 1-4, *Scriptum in librum primum Sententiarum (Ordinatio).* Edited by Gedeon Gál et al. St. Bonaventure: ex Typographia Collegii S. Bonaventurae, 1967–2000.

———. *Opera theologica.* Vol. 9, *Quodlibeta septem.* Edited by Joseph C. Wey. St. Bonaventure: St. Bonaventure University, 1980.

O'Connor, Timothy. "Scotus on the Existence of a First Efficient Cause." *International Journal for Philosophy of Religion* 33 (1993): 17-32.

Oord, Thomas Jay. *The Uncontrolling Love of God: An Open and Relational Account of Providence.* Downers Grove, IL: IVP Academic, 2015.

Owen, John. *A Brief Declaration and Vindication of the Doctrine of the Trinity.* In *The Works of John Owen*, vol. 2, *Communion with God*, edited by William H. Goold, 366-440. Edinburgh: Banner of Truth, 1965.

———. *Christologia.* In *The Works of John Owen*, vol. 1, *The Glory of Christ*, edited by William H. Goold, 1-273. Edinburgh: Banner of Truth, 1965.

———. *A Dissertation on Divine Justice.* In *The Works of John Owen*, vol. 10, *The Death of Christ*, edited by William H. Goold, 482-624. Edinburgh: Banner of Truth, 1967.

———. "God the Saints' Rock." In *The Works of John Owen*, vol. 9, *Sermons to the Church*, edited by William H. Goold, 237-55. Edinburgh: Banner of Truth, 1965.

———. *Meditations and Discourses on the Glory of Christ.* In *The Works of John Owen*, vol. 1, *The Glory of Christ*, edited by William H. Goold, 274-417. Edinburgh: Banner of Truth, 1965.

———. *Of the Mortification of Sin in Believers*. In *The Works of John Owen*, vol. 6, *Temptation and Sin*, edited by William H. Goold, 1-87. Edinburgh: Banner of Truth, 1967.

———. *Posthumous Sermons*. In *The Works of John Owen*, vol. 9, *Sermons to the Church*, edited by William H. Goold, 518-622. Edinburgh: Banner of Truth, 1965.

———. *The Works of John Owen*. Vol. 12, *The Mystery of the Gospel Vindicated*. Edited by William H. Goold. Edinburgh: Banner of Truth, 1966.

———. *The Works of John Owen*. Vol. 17, *Theologoumena pantodapa*. Edited by William H. Goold. Edinburgh: T&T Clark, 1862.

———. *The Works of John Owen*. Vol. 20, *An Exposition of the Epistle to the Hebrews, with Preliminary Exercitations*. Vol. 3. Edited by William H. Goold. Edinburgh: T&T Clark, 1862.

Owens, Joseph. "Aristotle and Aquinas." In *The Cambridge Companion to Aquinas*, edited by Norman Kretzmann and Eleonore Stump, 38-59. Cambridge: Cambridge University Press, 1993.

———. *The Doctrine of Being in the Aristotelian Metaphysics: A Study in the Greek Background of Mediaeval Thought*. Toronto: Pontifical Institute of Mediaeval Studies, 1951.

———. "Up to What Point Is God Included in the Metaphysics of Duns Scotus?" *Mediaeval Studies* 10 (1948): 163-77.

Palamas, Gregory. *Défense des saints hésychastes: Introduction, text critique, traduction et notes*. Translated by Jean Meyendorff. Louvain: Spicilegium Sacrum Lovansiense, 1959.

Pannacio, Claude. *Ockham on Concepts*. Aldershot: Ashgate, 2004.

Pannenberg, Wolfhart. "The Appropriation of the Philosophical Concept of God as a Dogmatic Problem of Early Christian Theology." In *Basic Questions in Theology: Collected Essays*, 2:119-83. Translated by George H. Kehm. Philadelphia: Fortress, 1971.

———. "Nachwort 2006." In *Analogie und Offenbarung: Eine kritische Untersuchung zur Geschichte des Analogiebegriffs in der Lehre von der Gotteserkenntnis*, 212-15. Göttingen: Vandenhoeck & Ruprecht, 2007.

———. *Systematic Theology*. Translated by Geoffrey W. Bromiley. 3 vols. Grand Rapids: Eerdmans, 1991–1993.

Pattison, George. *God and Being: An Enquiry*. Oxford: Oxford University Press, 2011.

Paulsen, Steven D. "Luther on the Hidden God." *Word and World* 19 (1999): 363-71.

Pasnau, Robert. *Thomas Aquinas on Human Nature: A Philosophical Study of Summa Theologiae Ia 75-89*. Cambridge: Cambridge University Press, 2002.

Pelletier, Jenny E. *William Ockham on Metaphysics: The Science of Being and God*. Leiden: Brill, 2013.

Phelan, Gerald B. *St. Thomas and Analogy*. Milwaukee: Marquette University Press, 1941.

Pickstock, Catherine. "Duns Scotus: His Historical and Contemporary Significance." *MT* 21 (2005): 543-74.

Plantinga, Alvin. "Reason and Belief in God." In *Faith and Rationality: Reason and Belief in God*, edited by Alvin Plantinga and Nicholas Wolterstorff, 16-93. Notre Dame, IN: University of Notre Dame Press, 1983.

Plested, Marcus. *Orthodox Readings of Aquinas*. Oxford: Oxford University Press, 2012.

Polkinghorne, John C. "Kenotic Creation and Divine Action." In *The Work of Love: Creation as Kenosis*, edited by John C. Polkinghorne, 90-106. Grand Rapids: Eerdmans, 2001.

Pruss, Alexander R. *The Principle of Sufficient Reason: A Reassessment*. Cambridge: Cambridge University Press, 2006.

Przywara, Erich. *Analogia Entis: Metaphysics; Original Structure and Universal Rhythm*. Translated by John R. Betz and David Bentley Hart. Grand Rapids: Eerdmans, 2014.

Rahner, Karl. *The Trinity*. Translated by Joseph Donceel. London: Burnes and Oates, 1970.

Rada, Juan de. *Controversiae theologicae inter S. Thomam et Scotum*. Venice, 1599.

Rea, Michael C. *The Hiddenness of God*. Oxford: Oxford University Press, 2018.

Rist, John M. "Augustine, Aristotelianism, and Aquinas: Three Varieties of Philosophical Adaptation." In *Aquinas the Augustinian*, edited by Michael Dauphinais, Barry David, and Matthew Levering, 79-99. Washington, DC: Catholic University of America Press, 2012.

Ritschl, Albrecht. *Theology and Metaphysics*. In *Three Essays*, 149-218. Translated by Philip Hefner. Philadelphia: Fortress, 1972.

Rocca, Gregory P. *Speaking the Incomprehensible God: Thomas Aquinas on the Interplay of Positive and Negative Theology*. Washington, DC: Catholic University of America Press, 2004.

Rogers, Katherin A. *Perfect Being Theology*. Edinburgh: Edinburgh University Press, 2000.

Rooney, James Dominic. "Being as Iconic: Aquinas on 'He Who Is' as the Name of God." *IJST* 19 (2017): 163-74.

Rowe, C. Kavin. "God, Greek Philosophy, and the Bible: A Response to Matthew Levering." *JTI* 5 (2011): 69-80.

———. *One True Life: The Stoics and Early Christians as Rival Traditions.* New Haven, CT: Yale University Press, 2016.

———. *World Upside Down: Reading Acts in the Graeco-Roman Age.* Oxford: Oxford University Press, 2009.

Salas, Victor. "Between Thomism and Scotism: Francisco Suárez on the Analogy of Being." In *A Companion to Francisco Suárez*, edited by Victor M. Salas and Robert L. Fastiggi, 336-62. Leiden: Brill, 2014.

———. "Francisco Suárez, the Analogy of Being, and Its Tensions." In *Suárez's Metaphysics in Its Historical and Systematic Context*, edited by Lukáš Novák, 97-102. Berlin: de Gruyter, 2014.

Sanders, Fred. *The Triune God.* New Studies in Dogmatics. Grand Rapids: Zondervan, 2016.

Schleiermacher, Friedrich. *The Christian Faith: A New Translation and Critical Edition.* Translated by Terrence N. Tice, Catherine L. Kelsey, and Edwina Lawler. Edited by Catherine L. Kelsey and Terrence N. Tice. 2 vols. Louisville: Westminster John Knox, 2016.

Schnabel, Eckhard J. *Paul the Missionary: Realities, Strategies and Methods.* Downers Grove, IL: IVP Academic, 2010.

Schumacher, Lydia. *Divine Illumination: The History and Future of Augustine's Theory of Knowledge.* Oxford: Wiley-Blackwell, 2011.

Sokolowski, Robert. *God of Faith and Reason: Foundations of Christian Theology.* Washington, DC: Catholic University of America Press, 1995.

———. "The Science of Being as Being in Aristotle, Aquinas, and Wippel." In *The Science of Being as Being: Metaphysical Investigations*, edited by Gregory T. Doolan, 9-35. Washington, DC: Catholic University of America Press, 2011.

Sonderegger, Katherine. *Systematic Theology.* Vol. 1, *The Doctrine of God.* Minneapolis: Fortress, 2015.

Soskice, Janet Martin. "Athens and Jerusalem, Alexandria and Edessa: Is There a Metaphysics of Scripture?" *IJST* 8 (2006): 149-62.

Spencer, Archie J. "Causality and the *Analogia entis*: Karl Barth's Rejection of Analogy of Being Reconsidered." *Nova et Vetera* 6 (2008): 329-76.

———. *The Analogy of Faith: The Quest for God's Speakability.* Strategic Initiatives in Evangelical Theology. Downers Grove, IL: IVP Academic, 2015.

Spinoza, Baruch. *Ethica.* In *Opera.* Vol. 2, *Tractatus de intellectus emendatione/ Ethica.* Edited by Carl Gebhardt. Electronic ed. Charlottesville, VA: InteLex, 2008.

Strange, Daniel. *Their Rock Is Not Like Our Rock: A Theology of Religions.* Grand Rapids: Zondervan, 2014.

Stump, Eleonore. *The God of the Bible and the God of the Philosophers.* Marquette: Marquette University Press, 2016.

———. "The Nature of a Simple God." *Proceedings of the ACPA* 87 (2014): 33-42.

Suárez, Francisco. *Opera omnia.* Vols. 25-26, *Disputationes metaphysicae.* Paris: Vivès, 1861.

Sudduth, Michael. *The Reformed Objection to Natural Theology.* Farnham, UK: Ashgate, 2009.

Sumner, Darren O. *Karl Barth and the Incarnation: Christology and the Humility of God.* London: Bloomsbury, 2014.

———. "Obedience and Subordination in Karl Barth's Trinitarian Theology." In *Advancing Trinitarian Theology: Explorations in Constructive Dogmatics,* edited by Oliver D. Crisp and Fred Sanders, 130-46. Grand Rapids: Zondervan, 2014.

———. "The Twofold Life of the Word: Karl Barth's Critical Reception of the *Extra Calvinisticum.*" *IJST* 15 (2012): 42-57.

Sutanto, Nathaniel. "Herman Bavinck and Thomas Reid on Perception and Knowing God." *Harvard Theological Review* 111 (2018): 115-34.

Swain, Scott R. *God of the Gospel: Robert Jenson's Trinitarian Theology.* Strategic Initiatives in Evangelical Theology. Downers Grove, IL: IVP Academic, 2013.

Thomas Aquinas. *Compendium theologiae.* In *Opera omnia,* 42:5-210. Leonine ed. Rome: Editori Di San Tomasso, 1979.

———. *De ente et essentia.* In *Opera omnia,* 43:367-81. Leonine ed. Rome: Editori Di San Tommaso, 1976.

———. *De potentia.* In *Quaestiones disputatae,* 2:1-276. 10th ed. Edited by P. Bazzi et al. Turin-Rome: Marietti, 1965.

———. *De principiis naturae.* In *Opera omnia,* 43:1-47. Leonine ed. Rome: Editori di San Tommaso, 1976.

———. *De substantiis separatis.* In *Opera omnia,* 40/D-E: D41-80. Leonine ed. Rome: ad Sanctae Sabinae, 1968.

———. *Expositio libri De hebdomadibus.* In *Opera omnia,* 50:231-97. Leonine ed. Rome: Commissio Leonina; Paris: Éditions du Cerf, 1992.

———. *Opera omnia.* Vol. 2, *Commentaria in octo libros Physicorum Aristotelis.* Leonine ed. Rome: ex Typographia Polyglotta, 1884.

──. *Super Boetium De Trinitate*. In *Opera omnia*, 50:1-230. Leonine ed. Rome: Commissio Leonina; Paris: Éditions du Cerf, 1992.

──. *In Duodecim libros Metaphysicorum Aristotelis expositio*. Edited by M.-R. Cathala and R. M. Spiazzi. Turin-Rome: Marietti, 1950.

──. *In libros Peri Hermeneias expositio*. In *Opera omnia*, 1:1-128. Leonine ed. Rome: ex Typographia Polyglotta, 1882.

──. *In libros Posteriorum Analyticorum expositio*. In *Opera omnia*, 1:129-403. Leonine ed. Rome: ex Typographia Polyglotta, 1882.

──. *De divinis nominibus*. Edited by Ceslai Pera. Turin-Rome: Marietti, 1950.

──. *Opera omnia*. Vols. 4-12, *Summa theologiae*. Leonine ed. Rome: ex Typographia Polyglotta, 1888–1906.

──. *Opera omnia*. Vols. 13-15, *Summa contra Gentiles*. Leonine ed. Rome: Typis Riccardi Garroni, 1918–1930.

──. *Opera omnia*. Vol. 22 in 6 books, *Quaestiones disputatae de veritate*. Leonine ed. Rome: ad Sanctae Sabinae, 1970–1976.

──. *Opera omnia*. Vol. 25/2, *Quaestiones de quolibet*. Leonine ed. Rome: Commissio Leonina; Paris: Éditions du Cerf, 1996.

──. *Opera omnia*. Vol. 45/1, *De anima*. Leonine ed. Rome: Commissio Leonina; Paris: J. Vrin, 1984.

──. *Opera omnia*. Vol. 47/2, *Sententia libri Ethicorum*. Leonine ed. Rome: ad Sanctae Sabinae, 1969.

──. *Super epistolas S. Pauli lectura*. Vol. 1, *Super epistolam ad Romanos lectura*. 8th ed. Edited by P. Raphaelis Cai. Turin-Rome: Marietti, 1953.

──. *Super Evangelium S. Ioannis lectura*. 5th ed. Edited by P. Raphael Cai. Turin-Rome: Marietti, 1952.

──. *Scriptum super libros Sententiarum*. Vol. 1. Edited by R. P. Mandonnet. Paris, 1929.

──. *Scriptum super Sententiis*. Vol. 3. Edited by Maria Fabianus Moos. Paris, 1933.

Thompson, Marianne Meye. *The God of the Gospel of John*. Grand Rapids: Eerdmans, 2001.

──. "'Light' (φῶς): The Philosophical Content of the Term and the Gospel of John." In *The Prologue of the Gospel of John: Its Literary, Theological, and Philosophical Contexts; Papers Read at the Colloquium Ioanneum 2013*, edited by Jan G. van der Watt, R. Alan Culpepper, and Udo Schnelle, 273-83. Tübingen: Mohr Siebeck, 2016.

Thomson, Iain. "Ontotheology? Understanding Heidegger's *Destruktion* of Metaphysics." *International Journal of Philosophical Studies* 8 (2000): 297-327.

Tollefsen, Torstein Theodor. *Activity and Participation in Late Antique and Early Christian Thought.* Oxford: Oxford University Press, 2012.

Tonner, Philip. *Heidegger, Metaphysics and the Univocity of Being.* London: Continuum, 2010.

Torrance, T. F. *The Christian Doctrine of God: One Being, Three Persons.* Edinburgh: T&T Clark, 1996.

Trueman, Carl. *Grace Alone: Salvation as a Gift of God.* Grand Rapids: Zondervan, 2017.

Tseng, Shao Kai. *Karl Barth's Infralapsarian Theology: Origins and Development, 1920–1953.* New Explorations in Theology. Downers Grove, IL: IVP Academic, 2016.

Turner, Denys. *Faith, Reason and the Existence of God.* Cambridge: Cambridge University Press, 2004.

Turretin, Francis. *Institutio theologiae elencticae.* 3 vols. 2nd ed. Geneva, 1688.

Van Til, Cornelius. *The Defense of the Faith.* Edited by K. Scott Oliphint. 4th ed. Phillipsburg, NJ: P&R, 2008.

Vanhoozer, Kevin J. *Remythologizing Theology: Divine Action, Passion, and Authorship.* Cambridge Studies in Christian Doctrine. Cambridge: Cambridge University Press, 2010.

Voetius, Gisbertus. *Selectarum disputationum theologicarum, Pars Prima.* Utrecht, 1648.

Velde, Rudi te. *Aquinas on God: The "Divine Science" of the "Summa Theologiae."* Reprint, New York: Routledge, 2016.

———. *Participation and Substantiality in Thomas Aquinas.* Leiden: Brill, 1995.

Walton, John H. *Ancient Near Eastern Thought and the Old Testament: Introducing the Conceptual World of the Hebrew Bible.* Grand Rapids: Baker Academic, 2006.

Webster, John. *God Without Measure: Working Papers in Christian Theology.* Vol. 1, *God and the Works of God.* London: Bloomsbury, 2015.

———. "*Non ex aequo*: God's Relation to Creatures." In *Within the Love of God: Essays on the Doctrine of God in Honour of Paul S. Fiddes,* edited by Anthony Clarke and Andre Moore, 95-104. Oxford: Oxford University Press, 2014.

———. "Trinity and Creation." *IJST* 12 (2010): 4-19.

———. "What Makes Theology Theological?" *Journal of Analytic Theology* 3 (2015): 17-28.

Weinandy, Thomas G. *Does God Suffer?* Notre Dame, IN: University of Notre Dame Press, 2000.

Westerholm, Martin. "Kant's Critique and Contemporary Theological Inquiry." *MT* 31 (2015): 403-27.

———. *The Ordering of the Christian Mind: Karl Barth and Theological Rationality.* Oxford: Oxford University Press, 2015.

Westphal, Merold. "Aquinas and Onto-theology." *American Catholic Philosophical Quarterly* 80 (2006): 173-91.

———. "The Importance of Overcoming Metaphysics for the Life of Faith." *MT* 23 (2007): 253-78.

———. *Transcendence and Self-Transcendence: On God and the Soul.* Bloomington: Indiana University Press, 2004.

Whitaker, William. *Disputations on Holy Scripture.* Reprint, Orlando: Soli Deo Gloria, 2005.

White, Thomas Joseph. "How Barth Got Aquinas Wrong: A Reply to Archie J. Spencer on Causality and Christocentrism." *Nova et Vetera* 7 (2009): 241-70.

———. "Introduction: Thomas Aquinas and Karl Barth—An Unofficial Catholic-Protestant Dialogue." In *Thomas Aquinas and Karl Barth: An Unofficial Catholic-Protestant Dialogue*, edited by Bruce L. McCormack and Thomas Joseph White, 1-39. Grand Rapids: Eerdmans, 2013.

———, ed. *The Analogy of Being: Invention of the Antichrist or the Wisdom of God?* Grand Rapids: Eerdmans, 2011.

———. "The Voluntary Action of the Earthly Christ and the Necessity of the Beatific Vision." *The Thomist* 69 (2005): 497-53.

———. "'Through Him All Things Were Made' (John 1:3): The Analogy of the Word Incarnate According to St. Thomas Aquinas and Its Ontological Presuppositions." In *The Analogy of Being: Invention of the Antichrist or the Wisdom of God?*, edited by Thomas Joseph White, 246-79. Grand Rapids: Eerdmans, 2011.

———. *Wisdom in the Face of Modernity: A Study in Thomistic Natural Theology.* Faith and Reason: Studies in Catholic Theology and Philosophy. 2nd ed. Ave Maria, FL: Sapientia, 2016.

Williams, Rowan. *On Christian Theology.* Challenges in Contemporary Theology. Oxford: Blackwell, 2000.

Williams, Thomas. "The Doctrine of Univocity is True and Salutary." *MT* 21 (2005): 575-85.

Willis, E. David. *Calvin's Catholic Christology: The Function of the So-Called Extra Calvinisticum in Calvin's Theology.* Leiden: Brill, 1966.

Wippel, John. "Essence and Existence." In *The Cambridge History of Later Medieval Philosophy: From the Rediscovery of Aristotle to the Disintegration of Scholasticism 1100–1600*, edited by Norman Kretzmann, Anthony Kenny, and Jan Pinborg, 385-410. Cambridge: Cambridge University Press, 1982.

———. "Norman Kretzmann on Aquinas' Attribution of Will and of Freedom to Create to God." *Religious Studies* 39 (2003): 287-98.

———. *The Metaphysical Thought of Thomas Aquinas: From Finite Being to Uncreated Being*. Washington, DC: Catholic University of America Press, 2000.

———. "The Parisian Condemnations of 1270 and 1277." In *A Companion to Philosophy in the Middle Ages*, edited by Jorge J. E. Garcia and Timothy B. Noone, 65-73. Oxford: Blackwell, 2002.

———. "Thomas Aquinas and the Condemnation of 1277." *The Modern Schoolman* 72 (1995): 233-71.

Witsius, Herman. *De oeconomia foederum Dei cum hominibus*. Leeuwarden, 1685.

Wolfe, Judith. *Heidegger and Theology*. London: Bloomsbury, 2014.

Wolter, Allan B. *The Philosophical Theology of John Duns Scotus*. Edited by Marilyn McCord Adams. Ithaca, NY: Cornell University Press, 1990.

Wolters, Al. "'Partners of the Deity': A Covenantal Reading of 2 Peter 1:4." *Calvin Theological Journal* 25 (1990): 28-44.

Wolterstorff, Nicholas. "Can Belief in God Be Rational if It Has No Foundations?" In *Faith and Rationality: Reason and Belief in God*, edited by Alvin Plantinga and Nicholas Wolterstorff, 135-86. Notre Dame, IN: University of Notre Dame Press, 1983.

———. *Inquiring About God: Selected Essays*. Vol. 1. Edited by Terence Cuneo. Cambridge: Cambridge University Press, 2010.

Wood, Rega. "Scotus's Argument for the Existence of God." *Franciscan Studies* 47 (1987): 257-77.

Zanchi, Girolamo. *De Incarnatione Filii Dei*. Heidelberg, 1593.

———. *De natura Dei, seu de divinis attributis, libri V*. Neostadii Palatinorum, 1598.

Ziegler, Philip G. *Militant Grace: The Apocalyptic Turn and the Future of Christian Theology*. Grand Rapids: Baker Academic, 2018.

Zimmermann, Albert. *Ontologie oder Metaphysik? Die Diskussion über den Gegenstand der Metaphysik im 13. und 14. Jahrhundert*. Leiden: Brill, 1965.

Author Index

Subject Index

Scripture Index